THE

UNITED STATES;

POWER AND PROGRESS.

BY

GUILLAUME TELL POUSSIN,
LATE MINISTER OF THE REPUBLIC OF FRANCE TO THE UNITED STATES.

FIRST AMERICAN, FROM THE THIRD PARIS EDITION.

TRANSLATED FROM THE FRENCH,

BY

EDMUND L. DU BARRY, M. D.,
SURGEON U. S. NAVY.

PHILADELPHIA:
LIPPINCOTT, GRAMBO AND CO.,
SUCCESSORS TO GRIGG, ELLIOT AND CO.
1851.

Entered according to the Act of Congress, in the year 1850, by
LIPPINCOTT, GRAMBO & CO.,
in the Clerk's Office of the District Court for the Eastern District of Pennsylvania.

PHILADELPHIA:
T. K. AND P. G. COLLINS,
PRINTERS.

TRANSLATOR'S PREFACE.

The history of the American colonies—the circumstances which led to their federal organization—the patience and energy with which they worked out their national independence, and developed the vast political association now denominated the United States—the industry and ability with which the people of these States sought to realize the stupendous agricultural, commercial, and industrial resources of their immense Continent, with its fertile territory, its magnificent rivers, its inland seas, and its varied climates—their subsequent gigantic strides towards the highest pinnacle of national greatness; in fine, the character of the American people themselves, connected together by a vast chain of internal communication, enjoying in the highest degree all the elements of material prosperity, and united by common hopes, common sentiments, common interests, and common historical associations—may well claim the attention of the gravest historian, of the most enlightened statesman, and of every one interested in the progress of civilization.

To develop the consecutive steps of this progress is the object of the present work. A resident in the United States for many years, the author has enjoyed ample opportunities of observing the practical workings of democracy. A member of the Board of Topographical Engineers appointed by the American Government to examine the physical resources of our territory for national defence, and to trace the lines required to form a complete base of operations, in time of war, on the assailable portions of our frontier, his descriptions of the internal improvements of the United States may be considered the result of direct experience. With feelings warmly interested in our national welfare, his work has been, in the truest sense of the term, a labor of love. As such, we commend it to the American reader.

The translator deemed it unnecessary to swell the present volume with the agricultural, commercial, and manufacturing statistics contained in the original work, taken from tables published in the year 1840; for these statistics, though of great advantage to the French reader at the period of their publication, can scarcely be considered valuable at the present time to the American reader, who can at any moment avail himself of far more ample and satisfactory materials. Besides, we may say, without using metaphorical language, that the lapse of ten years, in our rapidly growing country, renders the statistics of the prior decennial period almost antiquated.

In conclusion, the translator need only say that he has endeavored to perform his task with the utmost fidelity. The manner in which it has been accomplished he leaves to the judgment of the impartial reader.

CONTENTS.

CHAPTER IV.

1608—1620.

COLONIZATION OF THE FRENCH, ENGLISH, AND DUTCH.

CHAPTER V.

1620—1639.

COLONIZATION OF NEW ENGLAND.

CHAPTER VI.

1620—1653.

COLONIZATION OF THE FRENCH, ENGLISH, AND DUTCH.

CHAPTER VII.

1630—1700.

NEW ENGLAND COLONIES.

CHAPTER VIII.

1623—1700.

ENGLISH AND DUTCH COLONIES—NEW AMSTERDAM, NEW YORK, NEW JERSEY.

CHAPTER XI.

1671—1700.

FRENCH COLONY—NEW FRANCE.

CHAPTER XII.

1700—1750.

FRENCH COLONIES—NEW FRANCE.

CHAPTER XIII.

1750—1763.

FRENCH COLONY—NEW FRANCE.

CHAPTER XVI.

1783—1800.

THE AMERICAN UNION.

CHAPTER XVII.

1678—1717.

FRENCH COLONIES—LOUISIANA.

CHAPTER XVIII.

1717—1731.

FRENCH COLONIES—LOUISIANA.

CHAPTER XIX.

1732—1769.

FRENCH COLONIES—LOUISIANA.

CHAPTER XX.

1512—1821.

SPANISH COLONIES—LOUISIANA, FLORIDA.

CHAPTER III.

NATIONAL DEFENCE.

CHAPTER IV.

NATIONAL DEFENCE.

CHAPTER V.

NATIONAL DEFENCE.

CHAPTER VI.

NATIONAL DEFENCE.

CHAPTER VII.

NATIONAL DEFENCE.

CHAPTER VIII.

NATIONAL DEFENCE.

CHAPTER IX.

NATIONAL DEFENCE.

CHAPTER X.

NATIONAL DEFENCE.

CHAPTER XVI.

RELIGION IN THE UNITED STATES.

CHAPTER XVII.

EDUCATION IN THE UNITED STATES.

CHAPTER XVIII.

AGRICULTURE.

CHAPTER XIX.

COMMERCE.

CHAPTER XX.

MANUFACTURES.

CHAPTER XXI.

CHAPTER XXII.

INTRODUCTION.

The progress of science applied to arts and manufactures has wrought a thorough change in the condition of every country. Everywhere we witness the manifestation of new ideas and new tendencies, whose influence, felt in all ranks of life, affects our habits, transforms our manners, changes our tastes, and even insinuates itself into all the details of private life.

In view of this state of things, how can we explain the divergence so obstinately maintained between a government and its people? Does the former wish ever to forget that it is only a moderator and guide of mankind? Do not the latter, in provoking an expansion of the social forces, advance with too much precipitation towards the accomplishment of a revolution hereafter necessary?

Nevertheless, obstinate resistance will always be more dangerous than too hasty progression. In going too fast, we run the risk of losing our way. But ideas are imperishable. When a torrent is swelling before us, it is folly to attempt to check its progress by decayed dikes. We should rather seek to open for it a wide passage, and thus to transform its transitory overflow into a fertile inundation.

Nations can no longer remain strangers one to another. A new and powerful element of civilization has appeared to place them in permanent contact. Steam overcomes distances with the same facility that ideas traverse lines of frontier, and fly over the walls of a rampart. In a few days we pass from one continent to another; and when every sea shall be regularly furrowed, and Europe shall be covered with railroads, intercourse of people with people will become far more frequent than at present, because a voyage will then, by its cost and duration, be no longer beyond the reach of those who are not blessed with fortune. Every class of society will profit by these increased facilities; and then will the overflowing tide of population in one country be discharged into another where the means of existence are to be found in greater abundance.

Everything, therefore, tends to impel the various people of the earth in one direction; and the epoch of national isolation is passed, never to return.

Independent nations no longer recognize prohibitive systems. For the future, these systems will sanction only the conflict between individual interests and general interests.

Experience has demonstrated that one of the effects of this prohibitive policy is to make us overlook and violate the simplest laws of political economy; for it has led to the encouragement of ephemeral manufactures in defiance of the natural conditions of their existence, and, by the abusive employment of the artificial elements of power, has given to these manufactures so great a development that all due relation between consumption and supply is utterly destroyed.

As a result of this prohibition, populations are confined at home. Thus deprived, on their own soil, of the means of seeking a foreign market for their products, the amount of their exports is exceedingly limited. In fine, the prosperity of all is compromised in the highest degree; and it is here especially that distress and poverty are in reality the offspring of abundance.

Such is the inevitable effect of all such exclusive laws—laws which, in the end, are favorable only to the wealthiest, the ablest, and the most fortunate of mankind.

This state of misery, a direct result of the prohibitive system, evidently impels society towards other destinies, and the people, perhaps excited by an antagonism augmenting from day to day in intensity, will be drawn into a tremendous struggle as decisive as it will be terrible; for it will be a struggle for existence itself, and not for the maintenance of a principle of honor, or for the satisfaction of national ambition.

Such are the apprehensions which now occupy the mind, in view of the phenomena now exhibited by the social organization of every people. The future we have delineated is undoubtedly frightful; for it menaces that general peace for the maintenance of which so many noble interests have already been sacrificed. But, to be serious, this peril is not unavoidable, especially if rulers, becoming more enlightened relative to their real interest, shall seek to identify themselves with the great movement which the diffusion of knowledge has created among every people!

To keep pace with these ideas and new necessities would be an act of wisdom, and tend to preserve society in a normal state. The people should be taught to harmonize their interests, even when they appear to be conflicting, rather than to persevere in restrictive measures, which can only hasten the day of the struggle between nations and their rulers.

But the question of international relations is so intimately allied with that of democracy that it will sooner or later be naturally settled by the triumph of this great cause of the people, which is every day gaining additional adherents.

When, in the course of human progress, the people shall govern themselves, national distinctions will lose their wonted influence; for the people will then consider themselves as members of the great human family, which ought to be united by the closest bonds through the desire, common to each individual, of personal liberty and physical welfare. They will learn that, if Providence has bestowed on each portion of the globe peculiar resources, the common interest of mankind requires that these advantages should become productive through reciprocal exchanges; and that these exchanges will be better understood, and will be the more briskly effected, in proportion as they are encouraged by a liberal policy.

In the present state of affairs, nations exhaust themselves in efforts which benefit only a few individuals. The masses are becoming impoverished. Everywhere commerce is suffering. Nowhere is it based on the principles of an enlarged reciprocity. A nation which holds the empire of the seas may thereby acquire preponderance, and impose its will upon other nations. Thus, while a plethora engorges all the channels of industrial life, the British nation, to escape its terrible effects, condemns other nations to consume only its own products. But if this monopoly, which it wishes to exercise by force, and at any cost, has become the supreme condition of its existence, the temerity of pretending to impose it on all mankind is no less culpable than unexampled.

But, on the other side of the Atlantic, a nation is now rising, which, though of the same race, and moved by the same ambition, is in every respect better adapted to become one of the greatest powers among the commercial nations of the world. Day by day it is advancing farther and farther into the lists, and already menaces with disastrous competition the former queen of the seas, its only rival. But yesterday the American nation was a people of consumers; to-day it reveals its power and its just pretensions to lavish on the other nations of the world its immense natural wealth, and the marvelous products of its industry. Why should it not covet the rich inheritance of Great Britain, of which it will one day be able to dispossess it?

To consummate these ambitious views, it pursues a course entirely the opposite of that which has so well served the interests of England. The ascending movement of the one has been occasioned by the energy of its compact aristocracy. The supremacy of the ocean will be obtained by the other through the force of democratic principles. On the banner of the one is inscribed the motto, *Dieu et mon droit;* on that of the other will be inscribed the *freedom of the seas*, thus recognizing that grand and salutary principle, that *the flag of a vessel protects its merchandise.* This sacred principle will powerfully contribute to the reconstruction of the sooial edifice.

In its defence, the American nation will rely not only on its navy, but on its ambition and its commercial interests. Its strength lies in the sovereignty of the people. To this, in fact, it owes its origin and its unexampled prosperity. Founded, principally, on the love of liberty, on patriotism, on the attachment of the citizen to the constitution of his choice, the Union presents the imposing spectacle of a compact nation provided with all the elements of strength and durability. Its citizens, happy under the empire of their institutions, would only lose by modifying them; and they will not risk the experiment—for they would thus compromise the future, of which their present prosperity is the most solid guarantee.*

A faithful picture of the social condition of the Americans will always be a vast subject for study. The great lessons it contains seem to me to derive increased value from the state of affairs at the present time, when the people of every nation are directing

* The present financial and commercial crisis (January, 1843) is due to circumstances of a purely transient nature, and are not calculated to influence the deductions of the philosopher or statistician.

their efforts towards the consummation of the same object, and are constantly seeking to realize the principle of political equality.

American democracy is certainly destined to sustain, at some period, a struggle in which other maritime nations will be involved. Thence will arise specific interests and new conditions, which it will be difficult to appreciate, but worthy of the reflections of those who are interested in the progress of civilization. I cherish the hope that my work, by the positive nature of its elements, will furnish a solid basis for the deductions of the statesman.

I do not seek to disguise the difficulty of such a task. In this industrial history of the American people, I have felt the necessity of sustaining my efforts by associating with my recollections the sentiment of a pious duty; and I have seized with eagerness the present opportunity of giving an accurate knowledge of those works, at present so renowned, conceived and executed by our countrymen.*

I have divided my work into two parts. In the first, I have traced the origin, the institutions, and especially the political tendencies of the Americans. In the second, I have shown their military resources, and have exhibited the development of their agriculture, commerce, and manufactures.

In this work, the reader will find positive information mixed with a multitude of personal observations, relative to a people with whom I have lived, whose progress I have followed, and in whose welfare I feel interested as deeply as though I had been born among them. I have exercised my utmost care to avoid entering into speculations; and in view of so vast and so prolific a subject, this was a matter of no small difficulty.

I have thought it would be difficult for the reader to appreciate the national character of the Americans without exhibiting their early history. The political or industrial character of a nation depends as much on its origin as on the circumstances in which Providence has placed it. In my opinion, therefore, it seemed indispensable to reproduce the principal traits in the character of the early American settlers.

In going back to the period when their early establishments

* The American nation has expended more than two hundred million dollars in works designed for national defence.

were formed, I have been led to examine the important question involved in the influence of the various systems of colonization pursued by Europeans on their arrival in the New World. My researches were directed to the discovery of the earliest settlements in America, of which history has preserved authentic traces. A thoroughly French sentiment has keenly animated me in this department of my labor—a labor in which I have sought to exhibit the part my country acted in those struggles which took place on the waters and on the soil of the New World, and the dignity and courage with which she sustained the honor of the French name.

In my undertaking, I have been aided by the works of all the authors cotemporaneous with the various periods alluded to in my history. With these works, our libraries at Paris are richly supplied.

I have also consulted the archives of the navy and of the colonies, the portfolios, manuscripts, and charts of which have been kindly placed at my disposal by the honorable head of that department.

I have consulted with profit various American periodicals,* which afforded me the means of comparing excellent statistical documents with those furnished me either by the kindness of the minister of the United States at Paris, or by my old friend Robert Walsh, one of the most distinguished of American publicists.

To all who have been so kind as to take an interest in my labors, I return my very sincere thanks.

* "North American Review"—"Hunt's Merchant's Magazine."

AMERICAN POWER.

PART I.

ORIGIN—INSTITUTIONS—POLITICAL SENTIMENTS OF THE UNITED STATES.

HISTORICAL INVESTIGATIONS OF THE DISCOVERIES, PRIMARY ESTABLISHMENTS, AND OF THE VARIOUS SYSTEMS OF COLONIZATION PURSUED IN AMERICA.

CHAPTER I.

1000—1529.

DISCOVERIES AND FIRST SETTLEMENTS OF THE SCANDINAVIANS, SPANISH, FRENCH, AND ENGLISH.

Scandinavian colony—Christopher Columbus—The Normans, Rochellese, and Dieppese—Americus Vespucius—Gaspard Cortereal—Peter de Guy—John Davis of Harfleur—Thomas Aubert of Dieppe—John Ponce de Léon—Baron de Léry—Vasquez de Ayllon—Verazani—Pamphilius de Narvaez.

THE name of Christopher Columbus must for ever be identified with the discovery of America. The rights of this illustrious navigator to the glory attached to one of the most remarkable events in the history of the world are as sacred as they are well-founded. In truth, there is nothing fabulous, equivocal, or doubtful in the recital of these facts, which reveal a boldness of thought, a power of genius, a pertinacity and perseverance in this celebrated navigator almost superhuman. To solve the great question of the formation of the globe, which then agitated all minds, it required no less than the combination, in a single man, of these great qualities, impelled by an extreme religious faith: Christopher Columbus possessed them all!

Honor, then, in our name, and in that of all future generations, to the memory of Columbus, the immortal benefactor of humanity!

If, as a powerful genius, he has claims upon our veneration, he has still more upon our gratitude, for having, by his discovery, and the moral influence which it was to exercise upon the destinies of the world, advanced the emancipation of society!

My object being to record, in chronological order, all the facts relating to the discovery and colonization of North America, it shall of course be my task to point out the documents,* recently published by the able writers of the North, relative to that period of the Middle Ages which has for so long a time remained unknown. These documents, for which we are indebted to an author as distinguished as he is erudite, prove, if not quite positively, at least very plausibly, that America was discovered in the tenth or eleventh century by Scandinavian navigators, and that at that period a continuous intercourse was kept up between the eastern coast of America and Scandinavia.

It is, however, but justice to state, that the passage of these colonies, upon this portion of the New World, has left such faint traces, that they would scarcely be found again or verified; and the proofs presented in support of the visit of these Scandinavian navigators to the shores of Massachusetts and Rhode Island appear at least very vague.

Some English writers have also maintained that Madoc, a Welsh prince, was driven upon the coast of Florida about the year 1171, and there established a colony; but this has never been proved.

Christopher Columbus had long meditated upon the shape of the earth, and had frequently consulted the writings of Marco Polo and of John Mandeville, who, in the thirteenth century, had visited Asia far beyond the limit given to it by Ptolemy, and had arrived at the conclusion that, by sailing in a westerly direction, he must, after a short run, reach the eastern extremity of the Continent of Asia, which he called *India.* He experienced the greatest difficulties in securing the adoption of his views and of his project. Fortunately, he found means, by the vigor of his mind and the enthusiasm of his convictions, to overcome the opposition against which he had to contend. He had conceived the idea of delivering the Holy Sepulchre from the hands of the Infidels; and

* Memoirs of the Discovery of America in the Tenth Century, by Charles Christian Rafn, or Antiquitates Americanæ, sive Scriptores Septentrionales rerum ante Columbianarum in Americâ.

to effect this pious object he intended to devote the riches he expected eventually to receive from his discoveries. This idea sustained him to the end of his life.

After having settled the plan of his expedition, traced beforehand the course he was to pursue, and made the calculations upon which he based his theory, he at length put to sea on Friday, the 5th of August, 1492,* with three small vessels, the *Santa Maria*, commanded by himself; the *Pinta*, by Martin Alonzo Pinzon; the *Nina*, by Vincent Vañez Pinzon. Only one of these vessels, of about one hundred tons burden, had a deck. The other two were mere coasting vessels. The expedition numbered one hundred and twenty persons. Columbus reached the Canaries, and then steered a direct westerly course, without deviating from the line he had traced for himself; and, after a hazardous voyage of seventy days, the cry of "Land!" was heard, on the 12th of October following, from the vessel which he commanded in person. Columbus landed on one of the Bahama Islands, called by the Indians *Guenahaud;* by himself *San Salvador*, which name it still retains; and by the English *Cat Island.*

Columbus, following his all-engrossing thoughts, imagined himself on one of the islands bordering the Continent of Asia; hence, he called the natives *Indians*—a designation applied to all the aborigines of the New Continent.

Thus, as if by a miracle, was Columbus's theory of the conformation of the globe happily solved—a theory due to his superior genius, which alone, by comprehending the necessary calculations, was able to develop it as a *truth.* And from that time the communication, that was to exert so great an influence upon man, between the Old and New World, and reduced in our day to an ordinary voyage of ten days, thanks to the discovery of those great geniuses, Watt and Fulton, has been for ever established.

An immense result, incalculable in its consequences, which Christopher Columbus himself was far from foreseeing! For, in the settled opinion which he had adopted as to the extent of Asia, he looked upon his discoveries as the continuation *of the long chain of the Indies*, and had no idea that he had discovered a NEW WORLD. It was, then, by a great error in geography that Columbus was led to his magnificent discoveries.

* Washington Irving's Life of Columbus.

His opinion was supported by all scientific men, and all the most celebrated navigators of those days; and, for a long time, influenced all subsequent expeditions.

From San Salvador, Columbus examined the Lucayas Islands. On the 28th of October, he discovered the Island of Cuba, and on the 6th of December Hayti, whence, on the 4th of January, 1493, he sailed on his return to Spain.

The news of Columbus's discovery produced a wonderful effect upon every mind. All the rival powers of Europe were seized with a species of delirium, which goaded them to new adventures. Each was desirous of enlarging the area of his estates, of spreading abroad the Christian faith, and especially of enriching his treasury. Expeditions were everywhere preparing.

England, always ready to take possession of new territories in order to extend its influence, entered with zeal into these projects of discovery. Columbus had applied to Henry the Seventh, but had not met with a favorable reception. The communication of his plans, however, had attracted the attention of some of the scientific men of that country to a conception so bold, and had induced a desire in their minds also to undertake some voyages of discovery. But England, at that period, was far from being celebrated for its navigation, and for the knowledge of its mariners. It had remained more than a century behind all other nations, who had exhibited, on the contrary, great activity and great zeal for commerce and maritime enterprises.

English vessels and mariners had not yet ventured far from their own shores. Under these circumstances, they were compelled to have recourse to the navigators of foreign nations to accomplish their designs. Hence it was, that Sebastian Cabot, a Venetian adventurer, who resided in Bristol, obtained, in 1496, from Henry the Seventh, for himself and his three sons, the privilege of sailing under the English flag, in all directions, for the purpose of discovering lands unknown, or uninhabited by any Christian nation, and taking possession of them in the name of the King of England. This permission was granted on the 5th of March, 1496, two years after the return of Columbus; but Cabot did not sail until two years afterwards. He sailed from Bristol on the 4th of May, 1497, with his son, Sebastian, on board of a government vessel, having also under his orders a small flotilla, equipped by the merchants of Bristol.

Cabot had adopted the views of Columbus as to the conformation of the globe. He undertook his voyage, expecting to find a north-west passage to India; and, to his great regret,* discovered land on the 28th of July, 1497, but did not go on shore at any point. He sailed in sight of the Island of Newfoundland, which he named *Prima Vista;* his crew here caught a great quantity of fish; among the rest, seals, salmon, soles, and *boccalaos* (a species of codfish) or *cabelien.* He called this country Labrador, which afterwards received the name of *Cabelien.* He sailed as far north as fifty-six degrees, and then took a south-westerly course, in the vicinity of Florida, in about thirty-six degrees, in the hope of finding the long wished-for passage; but, despairing of success, he determined to return to England, where, to his great mortification, his voyage met with so little encouragement, that he formed the resolution of offering his services to the Catholic sovereigns, Ferdinand and Isabella.†

But little is known concerning this voyage; the accounts of it are vague and incomplete.

If we can place any reliance on the accounts of L'Escarbot,‡ who himself visited the coast of North America in 1606, the eastern coast of this Continent must have already been known long before by the Normans and Basques, who were in the habit of going to Newfoundland, to the Gulf of St. Lawrence, to the coast of Labrador, and to the north of the Island of Newfoundland for the purpose of fishing. He says, in fact, "that persons from Dieppe, Malouins, and Rochelle, and other French navigators, the most of them, at least, had for many centuries frequented the Grand Banks and the coast of Newfoundland." He also asserts that the names known, and the language spoken, upon that portion of the Continent, were half Basque; a proof, according to him, that the Basques must have for a long time visited this coast.

Some English and Danish navigators attempted, about this

* Hakluyt, vol. iii. p. 7.

† S. Cabot—"Sailing," he says, "along the coast, in order, if possible, to find an opening which would penetrate it, I saw that the land still extended as far as the fifty-sixth degree of latitude; and, perceiving that here the coast inclined towards the east, and despairing of finding a passage, I retraced my course, and sailed along this coast, steering towards the Equator. I reached that part of the Continent now known as Florida, when, my provisions getting short, I determined to return to England."

‡ L'Escarbot, 207–209.

period, to find a north-west passage to India, and by this means discovered some of the points on the eastern coast of North America, but without any other results.

Besides, in these times of papal supremacy, since the last discoveries of Columbus in the name of the Spanish crown, the rights of Spain were considered to extend to all the lands and seas arising from them, because Pope Alexander the Sixth had, in his famous bull of the 2d of May, 1493, conceded the right of property to Ferdinand and Isabella, under the single condition of their introducing and disseminating the Catholic faith; after the same manner that Pope Nicholas the Fifth had, by his bull of 1454, granted to the Kings of Portugal entire sovereignty over all the lands discovered by the Portuguese to the east of the Atlantic. The King of England, after the fruitless voyage of Cabot, entirely renounced sending new expeditions of discovery to the coast of America.

Americus Vespucius, by an inexplicable usurpation, but of which many examples are to be found, gave his name to the discovery of Columbus, without having in the least contributed to it. This navigator, a great man, nevertheless, appears to have made important voyages to Brazil in 1501, and wrote some memoirs, which remained a long time in manuscript, and upon the reputation of which he obtained the glory of the discovery of the two Americas. As far back as 1498 and 1499, Christopher Columbus* and Pinzon had discovered this country, and taken possession of it in the name of the Spanish crown; and, in 1500, Don Pedro Alvarez Cabral in the name of the crown of Portugal.

Juan Vaz Costa Cortereal, a gentleman of the household of the Infant Don Fernando, accompanied by D'Alvaro Marteus Hornera, undertook, in 1463 and 1464, a voyage, and examined the northern seas, by order of Alphonso the Fifth, King of Portugal. He discovered the land of *Boccalaos* (a region for codfish), since known as Newfoundland.

Gaspard Cortereal, his son, attempted to discover a north-west passage to India. In 1500, he visited the coast of Newfoundland, which he explored and described with care. One of these islands, near Cape Breton, bore his name, and was thus noted for a long time on the charts published in 1559. He discovered the Gulf and River St. Lawrence.

* Washington Irving.

Under the reign of Louis the Twelfth, the French also endeavored to discover a north-west passage to India—the object of all the voyages and naval expeditions of that period. They discovered Canada, frequented the Island of Newfoundland in 1504, and were the first to commence the cod fishery, of which other nations afterwards shared the profits and advantages. Peter de Guy, a nobleman of Montz, in one of his voyages, undertaken in 1506, touched at Cadia or Acadia, since known as Nova Scotia, explored its coasts, and took possession of it in the name of the King of France. During the same year, Davis, of Harfleur, published a chart of the coast and vicinity of Newfoundland. Upon that chart all that was found south of the River St. Lawrence was called *New France;* the northern portion is marked as *terra incognita* and lands of France. The following names are to be seen on the chart: Angoulême, a name given by Angoumoisin; Flora, Paradise, Port-Real, Port of Refuge, Cape Breton, and an island named Cape Breton.

A certain Thomas Aubert, or Hubert, a pilot of Dieppe, and engaged in the cod fisheries near the Banks of Newfoundland, landed in Canada in 1508, and brought with him to France a native, who excited a great deal of curiosity.

Since the first voyage of Columbus, many of his companions separately engaged in voyages of adventure, and sought treasures with insatiable avidity—riches which the wily Indian promised his unwelcome visitor, in order to get rid of him.

Ponce de Léon, a man of great ambition, who had accompanied Columbus in his second voyage, in 1495, received with avidity and credulity one of those fabulous tales of the natives as to the existence of vast treasures, and especially of a certain spring, in one of the Bermuda Islands, to which they gave the name of *Bimini*, whose waters had the power of rejuvenating. He possessed a large fortune. He equipped three vessels at his own expense; and, on the 5th of March, 1512, he sailed from Porto Rico, of which he was governor,* and on Saturday, the 27th of March, he hove in sight of Florida, in latitude thirty degrees and eight minutes. In consequence of the weather, he was unable to land until the 2d of April. He gave the land the name of Florida, as much on account of the brilliant aspect pre-

* Herrera.

sented by the quantity of flowers which covered the country, as in honor of Palm Sunday, *Pascua florida*, when he had first perceived them. Its name, in the Indian dialect, is *Cautio*.

He visited the anchorages on that coast, landed at different points, had several engagements with the natives, doubled the outhern point of Florida, and explored the Tortugas Islands. He finally became wearied of his fruitless searches for gold-mines, and, above all, of the promised fountain, and determined to return to Porto Rico, leaving behind him, to finish his adventurous cruise, Juan Perez de Ortubia, who, by the by, was not more fortunate than himself.

The only result of the romantic expedition of Ponce de Léon was that this chief grew somewhat older, and became impoverished; though he added the important discovery of Florida to the list of those already made by the Spaniards.

In 1517, Cortez discovered Mexico, and penetrated, in 1535, as far as California.

The sole object of all the voyages undertaken, up to this time, by the navigators and adventurers of all nations, was either the discovery of a north-west passage or of some great treasure. No voyage had been undertaken for the purpose of forming colonies in the New World. That of Baron Léry de Saint Just, in 1518, under Francis the First, was the first undertaken with the avowed object of forming a colony. L'Escarbot, in speaking of this bold navigator, thus expresses himself: "His courage impelled him to great actions, and his great desire was to establish there a French colony." He landed cattle upon Sable Island to supply the colony; while Salem* states that they were only transported to the New World by the English, one hundred years later. Unfortunately, this island was so unfavorable to the establishment of a permanent colony, that the emigrants whom Baron Léry had left there were compelled to abandon it for want of water.

In 1520, the Spaniards, under Luc Vasquez de Ayllon, again visited Florida. This officer was at that time engaged in the slave trade, which he deemed essential to the success of the new possessions in the Antilles. He sailed from Hispaniola, examined the coast of Florida, and landed at the mouth of a river, that he named the Jordan (*Chicora*), which emptied into the sea near the

* Vol. iii. p. 136.

point of St. Helena, and called by him Guadalpa. He made several excursions into the interior, with the hope of discovering the gold mines of which the Indians had spoken to him, but was not more fortunate than his predecessors. He, however, carried off several Indians, whom he brought as prisoners to St. Domingo, where they were sold as slaves, and sent to work in the mines.

In 1521, Ponce de Léon made a second voyage to Florida, with two vessels equipped at his own expense. He was driven off with loss by the Indians, and, being himself wounded, died shortly after in the Island of Cuba.

A second expedition was in the same year undertaken by Vasquez de Ayllon; but he was not more fortunate than his predecessor.

Francis the First again bent his mind upon establishing colonies in the New World. John Verazani, a Florentine, to whom he confided an expedition, made three successive voyages in the years 1523, 1524, and 1525, to the coast of America, and he named that part of the continent *New France*. He particularly explored that part of it contiguous to Spanish Florida, from the thirty-second to the forty-seventh degree of north latitude, and planted settlements at its most southern extremity. He died during his third voyage, at a time when he expected to make these establishments permanent.

The Spanish navigator, Pamphilius de Narvaez, in the name of his sovereign, Charles the Fifth, made, in 1527, a voyage to Florida. He landed near the Bay of Tanepe. Like his predecessor, he came to find gold, but found nothing but sand and misery.

After having penetrated far into the country, he lost nearly all his men, a portion of whom returned to the coast, probably at Pensacola, which Narvaez had named Santa Cruz, and perished in trying to reach Cuba in small boats. Another portion, not less intrepid, made the attempt to reach Mexico by land, and out of this number only four succeeded, after having endured indescribable fatigues and privations. They must have crossed the Mississippi, the Red River, Texas, and those immense marshes which form a border to the Gulf of Mexico. These four individuals were Alvaro, Nuñez de Cabeza, Vaca Dorantes, and a negro named Estavanaco. They crossed the interior of Florida as far as the port of Culiecan, in California, whence they were sent to Mendoza, Viceroy of Mexico.

Under Henry the Eighth, Robert Thome, of Bristol, in 1527, undertook a voyage of discovery to the north, but was unsuccessful.

The English, in 1529, according to Hakluyt,* sent two vessels to the eastern coast of North America, and explored Newfoundland, Labrador, and Cape Breton, and the shores of a country which they named Arembec. But these were also failures.

Hence it is proved, most incontestably, that the French sailed along the coast of North America at a very remote period, and greatly anterior to that when the English visited it.

From Cabot's last voyage, undertaken in the name of Henry the Seventh, to the year 1529, the English sent no vessels to the coast of North America. Nevertheless, they have never ceased, since that period, to found, upon the discoveries of that navigator, their rights of sovereignty in America.

Upon the same principle, and certainly with more reason, could the French claim possession of the coast and territories of Africa. As far back as the fourteenth century, and long before any other nation of Europe had known them, they had not only discovered them, but had traded with them, and had even made settlements there.†

* Hakluyt, vol. iii. p. 129.

† *Chronological History of the New World.* The opinion to which we allude here, that the Normans of Dieppe had first discovered Guinea, where, in 1365, they had made some settlements, has just been refuted by M. Santarem, in a conscientious and able work, recently published under the title of *Researches into the Priority of the Discovery of Countries situated upon the West Coast of Africa beyond Cape Bojador, and upon the Progress of Geographical Science subsequent to the Voyages of the Portuguese in the Fifteenth Century.* This distinguished man insists that he has proved that the priority of this discovery belongs to Portuguese navigators, and rests his arguments upon considerations, facts, and motives, which, upon this point, appear to us to be conclusive.

CHAPTER II.

1530—1568.

DISCOVERIES AND FIRST SETTLEMENTS OF THE FRENCH AND SPANIARDS.

James Cartier—River St. Lawrence—Montreal—Fernando de Soto—Florida—Mississippi—Luis Moscoso de Alvaredo—Pensacola—Mobile—Francis de la Roche, de Roberval, first governor of the French possessions in America—James Cartier founds Royal Isle—Tristan de Luna visits Florida—Schisms of the Anglican Church, of Calvin—Religious discussions—Reformers, Brownists, Puritans, Independents, Congregationalists—John Ribaut and René de Laudonnière, in Carolina, discover Port Royal Bay; make the first settlements there; give French names to the rivers—Destruction of this colony by Pedro Ménendez—Settlement of St. Augustine—Dominic de Gourges revenges himself upon the Spaniards.

If the fanaticism and religious zeal of the fifteenth century led to the discovery of the New World, the religious struggles which marked the sixteenth and seventeenth centuries have greatly contributed to people it with a race of choice men, equally distinguished for their profound faith and their love of liberty.

The commencement of the sixteenth century was marked by the heresy of Luther, by the reforms of John Calvin, and the foundation of the Society of Jesus by Ignatius Loyola. The object and tendency of this society were to oppose the progress of reform, at the head of which was Calvin. Loyola's followers planted their standard upon all points of the globe: in India, Thibet, Cochin China, China, Ethiopia, Abyssinia, California, in the plains of Paraguay, and in the glaciers and snows of Canada.

From 1525 to 1534, the French made but fruitless efforts to colonize America. In this latter year, James Cartier, from St. Malo, made a first voyage of discovery towards the Island of Newfoundland, and, on the day of the Feast of St. Lawrence, entered the gulf and waters of a great river, to which he gave the name of St. Lawrence.* To the natives, inhabiting the inferior

* Charlevoix.

part of this river, it was known as the *Ouitabua*, a Huron name; and to the Iroquois, who inhabited the superior part, as the *Cadaraqui*. Cartier, having determined to winter in these waters, built a fort on the banks of the river, took regular possession of the country in the name of Francis the First, made treaties with the Indians, and visited the principal establishment of the Hurons, situated on the Island of *Ochelaga*, which he named Montreal, in consequence of the splendid view from it, and of the appearance of richness which was unfolded to the beholder from the top of the hill which commands the centre of that island.

No spectacle could more readily produce upon the mind of Cartier a favorable impression than the nature and resources of the country, which were developed beneath his eyes, in an immense horizon, bisected by the majestic river whose waters mingle with the ocean a hundred miles off to the north.

After having thus become intimately acquainted with the principal entrance to this new country, visited the great lakes, and made treaties with the peaceful inhabitants of these shores, he left a garrison at the post which he had established below Quebec, and returned to France, where, by an unpardonable inconsistency, the object of this important undertaking appears, for a time at least, to have been forgotten.

According to Hakluyt,* a number of individuals from London equipped, in 1536, another armament, with the avowed intention of attempting again to make discoveries in North America; which proves, beyond a doubt, that this coast was then but little known to English navigators. This expedition, for want of provisions, was reduced to the last extremity, and, after having abandoned itself to excesses, which can find an excuse only in the imperious and fatal law of necessity, fell in with a French vessel, bound on a fishing expedition to the great banks of Newfoundland, took forcible possession of it, pillaged it, and made use of it to return to England. Hore, from London, accompanied by one hundred and twenty persons belonging to the first class of society, was at the head of one of these enterprises.

One of the most important voyages made, up to this time, by the Spaniards in Florida, was that undertaken, in 1539, by

* Hakluyt, vol. iii. p. 112.

Fernando de Soto. The preparations for this expedition were considerable, both in men and money. He carried with him nine hundred infantry and three hundred cavalry. Soto had been the companion of Pizarro. He was consumed with a desire to distinguish himself, and especially to acquire new riches. He neglected nothing for the completion of all his preparations, that he might realize the great expectations he entertained concerning the discovery of the immense riches which that country was supposed to contain. He landed in Florida, at the Sancto Spiritu Bay in the Gulf of Mexico, advanced boldly into the interior with all his warriors, both cavalry and infantry, took a westerly direction, and penetrated to the territory of the Cherokees, seeking the gold-mines which, three centuries after, were worked to great advantage. He spent nearly four years with his troops, in Florida and Louisiana, in search of riches which he was not destined to discover. He also explored the White River and the Washita, and finally died, on the borders of the Mississippi, on the 21st of May, 1542.

Luis Moscoso de Alvaredo then took command of his troop, reduced, from fights, fatigues, and mortality, to less than one-half of its original number. They built a boat on the shores of the river, descended it, and reached Panuco, in New Mexico, after running for fifteen days along the coast.

It was during the adventurous expedition of De Soto, that the Spaniards discovered Pensacola, called by the natives *Anchen*, or *Anchusé*; and Mobile, named *Movilla*, from the name of the tribe living there at the time.

In 1540, the French became more active in colonizing their American possessions, and attached more importance to their establishments. During this year, Francis the First appointed Francis de la Roche lieutenant-general of his new territories in Canada, Hochelaga, Saguenay, and other places, and authorized him to settle the lands and countries above designated, build forts, and take families there.

From 1541 to 1542, James Cartier, appointed captain-general of five discovery ships, arrived at Cape Breton (Royal Island), fortified himself, and formed a first settlement there. He then pushed his exploration, up the St. Lawrence, to a distance of two hundred miles beyond its mouth, where he founded a French colony, which, at a later period, received the protection of the

Marquis of Roberval, under Charles the Ninth. But the severity of the climate checked the success of these first establishments; and France again forgot the importance it should have attached to the colonization of America.

In 1549, the Spaniards attempted a new expedition to Florida, under the direction of Peter Assumada, Julius Samare, and five Dominican monks, who marched in front with great crosses, supposing by that means to make an impression upon the Indians. Nevertheless, this did not protect them from being assassinated and burnt by the natives. Don Tristan de Luna, who was attached to this expedition, again visited Pensacola, and named it the Bay of St. Mary.

But differences in religious opinion soon began to disturb French society. Under the cloak of religion, horrible cruelties had been committed by the troops of the king upon Huguenot cities. In England, Henry the Eighth had constituted himself head of the Anglican Church, and thus occasioned a schism. But Thomas Cranmer, Archbishop of Canterbury, entirely changed the religion of the kingdom, and established heresy in its place. Calvinism in France found a powerful protector in Margaret de Valois, Queen of Navarre, which caused this sect to increase with rapid strides; while in England, again, Queen Mary, daughter of Catharine of Aragon, and elder sister of Edward, whom she succeeded to the throne in 1553, re-established the Catholic religion. This circumstance led, in 1554, to the persecution of the Protestants, who sought refuge upon the Continent. A great number retired to Geneva, where, under the ministry of Calvin, they formed a community.

Upon the accession of Elizabeth, who succeeded her sister Mary in 1558, Protestantism assumed the ascendency. The Huguenot refugees then returned to England, in consequence of the deep-rooted prejudices which they entertained against the church that had persecuted them. But they did not find in Elizabeth that protection which they had imagined she would extend to them, and, as for the rest, were unsuccessful in changing the forms of the church.

The spirit of reform continued to gain proselytes, who were, nevertheless, obliged quietly to submit to the stronger power—the union of church and state.

Among the reformers of this period, who were desirous of introducing modifications in the doctrines and discipline of the church, a great number selected a Mr. Brown as their chief, who reduced to systematic form all the changes which his co-religionists particularly insisted upon, and thus gave birth to the sect since known as *Brownists*, commonly called Puritans. From this sect of reformers sprang that known as *Independents* or *Congregationalists*.

Brown strove to prove the corrupt state of the Anglican Church; that its ministers were illegally appointed; that its ordinances, rules, and precepts were not in conformity with the Holy Scriptures, and consequently without force. He insisted that every community of Christians had a right to assemble and worship God according to its own doctrines, that it constituted, in fact, a communion, or church, with powers to regulate its own affairs, for which they were answerable to God alone; in short, that, in matters of faith and religion, churches ought to be governed by the majority. These doctrines of the new reformers were, in fact, so completely democratic, that they excited the hatred of the civil and ecclesiastical authorities of England.

But what is most remarkable is that the chief of this church reform was gained over to the orthodox party. Brown entered into the communion of the church. Notwithstanding the desertion of their chief, the reformers steadfastly maintained their doctrines, and saw their numbers sensibly increase, and exercise, in the end, a powerful influence.

Thus, alongside of the Established Church, much more powerful from its political influence than from its action upon the hearts of men, we have daily seen, since that period, new churches arise, which, created from pure conviction and examination, have combated the dogmas of Anglicanism, and reproached the church for her inconsistencies. Beside those temples erected at public expense, were daily seen new chapels raised by voluntary subscriptions. Beside priests living by their devotion to, or upon the property of, the church, other priests preached a new faith, and the good will of their adherents soon assured their prosperity. Hence, even by the effect of the Protestant principle, the Anglican religion was losing ground.

Such was the origin of those numerous emigrations, which we shall see hereafter reap the inheritance of liberty that the genius of Columbus had conquered for future generations, by bequeathing to them a New World to fertilize.

The year 1559 was marked by the beginning of religious troubles in France. Henry the Second issued, at Ecouen, his terrible edict of June, which punished with death all Lutherans. Under Francis the Second, the religious quarrels assumed a still graver aspect, and, finally, served as a pretext, in 1560, for the famous conjuration of Amboise.

Towards the commencement of the reign of Charles the Ninth, these troubles became in a degree quieted. A sort of tranquillity, the precursor of much greater troubles, appeared to reign for a short period, consequent upon the intervention of Admiral Coligny. The Huguenots became less uneasy. By a royal edict they were permitted the free exercise of their religion—the first which had been issued in their favor.

Admiral Coligny had long desired to establish a place of refuge for the Huguenots. He applied himself assiduously to the realization of his project, by seeking to found a Protestant empire in America. To effect this object, he organized an expedition of discovery, under John Ribaut of Dieppe, and René de Laudonnière. This expedition, in 1552, arrived upon the coast of Florida—the same that had been explored by Verazani in 1523—and landed a little to the north of the Spanish possessions, at the mouth of the River St. John, which he named May River, having discovered it on the first day of that month. The French navigators extended their researches along the whole coast, as far as Cape Virginia, by sailing towards the north-east, and exploring the entrance of a deep bay, which they called Port Royal; and, after having assured themselves of the advantages which this part of the country presented for the establishment of a colony, they took possession of it in the name of their sovereign, in honor of whom they gave it the name of Carolina, which it still bears.

An establishment was at length formed at the mouth of the St. John, under the name of Fort St. Charles, and placed under the command of René de Laudonnière.

Florida was at that period well known by the Spaniards, who had there made numerous excursions, as we have just seen. They had even established several posts upon points of the coast in the gulf where their expeditions had landed.

Thus, the excellent harbor of St. Joseph, where the water is twenty-two feet in depth over the bar—and which is now settled so advantageously by the Americans, that they export from it nearly one hundred and ten thousand bales of cotton annually—was highly valued by the Spaniards, even at that remote period, because of its good anchorage.

In fact, the Spaniards, having been the first to discover Florida, and to traverse its territory, as well as the Valley of the Mississippi, were in the habit of considering this possession as a dependency of New Mexico, which they had previously discovered and settled themselves.

As for the English, they had not yet a single settlement upon the American Continent. Their vessels, however, sometimes visited these shores for the purpose of trading with the natives. They had thus occasion, in 1563, to carry relief to the French settlers in Carolina; and, desirous of making this country known to their sovereign, Queen Elizabeth, they took on board some of these settlers, in proof of the advantageous relations they might obtain over it.

In 1564, John Ribaut built a second fort in Carolina, and named it Fort Charles; and René de Laudonnière, in his second voyage, erected another fort at the mouth of the river *Hitanachi*, also called *Saint Esprit*, the command of which he gave to Captain Albert. It would seem that this was the foundation of the present city of Charleston, situated at the mouths of Cooper and Ashley Rivers; whence it follows that this post, situated on one of the best anchorages on that portion of the southern coast of North America, was occupied one hundred years before the English had founded a single establishment upon the continent!

John Ribaut returned to France. He again visited the Carolina colony in 1565, and relieved De Laudonnière in his command.

The emigrants, who settled in Carolina, were, for the most part, Calvinists. They imparted to the rivers that watered these fertile countries French names, which, reminding them of France, thus seemed, while they increased their attachment to the land of their adoption, to mentally carry them back to that of their birth. They thus merged in the one feeling their regrets for having been compelled to fly in consequence of their religious opinions, and their gratitude to the soil which enabled them to live free.

The colony of Carolina extends from the River St. John, whose promontory was called French Cape, to the thirty-third degree of latitude; and the rivers emptying into the sea along that coast were, beginning at French Cape, the Dauphin, the Seine, the Somme, the Loire, the Charente, and the Gironde.

Unfortunately for this colony, and for the permanence of its settlements, France again found itself torn by civil dissensions, and divided by absurd quarrels about theology. The settlers of Carolina were forgotten, and they were left to resist alone the jealousy of the English and the Spaniards. The former saw with pain the settlement of the French upon the American Continent—the object of their desires and cupidity; while the second, their neighbors and rivals, under a religious pretext, fell suddenly upon the weak settlements of the French, and, in the name of faith, committed upon these isolated and defenceless inhabitants the most cruel excesses.

This expedition of freebooters took place on the 20th of September, 1565, under the orders of one Don Pedro Menendez de Avilez. He landed on the coast of Florida on the 8th of September, the day of the Feast of St. Augustine, whose name he gave to the fort which he founded with great solemnity, proclaiming Philip the Second sovereign of North America! The city of St. Augustine must, therefore, be forty years older than any other city founded by Europeans in the United States.

Thus was the French colony of Carolina, in its infant state, destroyed, by an attack as cowardly as it was detestable for its barbarity. It was founded at a period, when, in consequence of discoveries and settlements to the north and south, made anterior to those of the English, France might have claimed and extended its sovereignty over the whole of the new continent.

This cowardly attack remained unnoticed, on the part of the ministers of Charles the Ninth. But a humble citizen, Captain Dominic de Gourgues, of Mont-de-Marsan (Landes), took upon himself to revenge his fellow-countrymen, by inflicting upon the Spaniards the same acts of cruelty.

This devoted warrior, moved by a remarkable feeling of patriotism and intrepidity, obtained loans, and sold his property, to equip three vessels, manned with one hundred and fifty soldiers and eighty seamen, with provisions for one year. The expedition sailed from Bordeaux on the 2d of August, 1567.

De Gourgues was completely successful in his attack upon the forts occupied by the Spaniards. The garrisons were all put to the sword, and the small number that were taken alive were hung to the same trees on which, three years before, they had hung the French.

De Gourgues, not having a sufficient force to garrison the forts, and establish himself in a country where the Spaniards might easily bring troops much more numerous than his own, employed the Indians to destroy the entrenchments, and then, on the 8th of May, 1568, sailed for France.

From that period till the end of the century, very little was thought about America. Our unfortunate country was convulsed by the wars of religion during the reigns of Charles the Ninth and Henry the Third; and in 1572, the horrible outrage of a king upon the people of his capital was enacted—an outrage likely to be more than once repeated before the slow but durable education of the people will be consummated.

CHAPTER III.

1570—1608.

DISCOVERIES AND COLONIZATION OF THE FRENCH AND ENGLISH.

Elizabeth, Queen of England, engaged in creating a navy—Martin Frobisher—Letters patent granted to Humphrey Gilbert for the discovery of unknown lands; he perishes on his voyage—New letters granted to Sir Henry Gilbert; his fruitless voyage—John Davis—New letters granted to Sir Walter Raleigh—Discovery of Virginia—Sir Richard Greenville at the Island of Roanoke; he leaves settlers there; they perish—Hariot; introduction of tobacco into Europe; abandonment of the colonization of Virginia—Chaton and Noel in the Gulf of St. Lawrence—Ravillon commences a sealing voyage—Marquis de la Roche appointed Lieutenant-General of the French Possessions in America; he leaves settlers on Sable Island—Mr. Chauvin founds Tadoussac—Captain Grosnold—Captain Champlain—Commandant de Chatte—Martin Pring visits the coast of Maine—Messieurs de Montz, Champlain, de Pautrincourt, and Pontgravé—Establishment of Port Royal (Annapolis)—Establishments upon the St. Croix River—Captain Champlain on the coast of New England—George Weymouth—Second voyage of Sieur de Pautrincourt; he is accompanied by L'Escarbot—James the First, King of England, concedes to his subjects all that part of America bearing the name of Southern and Northern Virginia—A company from Plymouth seeks to settle in Northern Virginia—Second expedition under the orders of Raleigh Gilbert; it visits the shores of the Kennebec—Captain Newport and the celebrated author, John Smith, settle Southern Virginia, and found establishments upon James River, which flows into Chesapeake Bay—Firm administration of this new colony—Conclusion.

England did not, for more than sixty years after the fruitless efforts of Cabot, recall her attention to America; and the honor of having there founded, in a measure, the first establishments, was reserved for Queen Elizabeth—famous for her activity, her skill, and especially for her spirit of enterprise.

The kingdom was quiet during nearly the whole of her happy reign. Commerce took a great start, and prospered. Navigation was studied as a science; perfected, and rendered more practical as an art. The mechanic arts acquired a remarkable degree of improvement. In short, it was resolved to create a navy and sailors, and eventually voyages of discovery were greatly multiplied.

One of the first was undertaken in 1576, by one Martin Frobisher, with the object of discovering a north-west passage to the East Indies. This voyage produced no result.

The same adventurer made a second voyage in 1577, as much with the view of discovering a passage to India, as in the hope of finding gold mines. The avarice and cupidity of those times were such that hundreds of volunteers presented themselves, and offered to accompany him in his adventurous researches. Nor was this second voyage more fortunate than the first. He encountered icebergs, islands of sand, and saw nothing but iron-bound coasts, upon which he encountered great danger, without realizing any useful result. He undertook a third voyage in 1578.

In 1578, Queen Elizabeth granted letters patent to Sir Humphrey Gilbert, under the protection of the Earl of Warwick, for the discovery of unknown lands. These letters stated that Sir Humphrey Gilbert* was authorized to discover, and take possession of, lands unknown, or inhabited by savage nations, but unoccupied by Christian nations; that he had plenary rights and powers over the country that he should take possession of. Besides, it was stated that subjects of Great Britain might settle in the colonies established by Sir Humphrey Gilbert, who was to enjoy the rights of property over all the lands, on condition of paying to the crown of England a rent of one-fifth of the proceeds of all the gold or silver mines he might discover, and of rendering homage to the supremacy of his sovereign. Under these titles and clauses, Sir Humphrey and his heirs were to enjoy the right of establishing and governing these colonies according to their good pleasure.

Sir Humphrey, however, was unable to commence the enterprise which he had so much at heart, until five years after these letters patent had been granted him. Having at length succeeded in forming a pretty considerable expedition, he sailed for the coast of America, for the purpose of planting a colony to the north of Florida. He landed upon the Island of Newfoundland, where, according to Hakluyt,† the natives presented him with samples of minerals, which he postponed testing, in the fear of exciting

* Hakluyt, vol. iii. pp. 143, 165.

† Ibid., p. 165.

the attention of the French, already settled on those shores, and by that means exposing to them the resources they possessed.

Sir Humphrey Gilbert was not fortunate in his attempts to establish himself in America. He perished in a gale off Cape Breton, and the remainder of his expedition returned to England. Hence, Sir Humphrey's expedition, while it gained nothing for England, confirmed the existence of the French settlements in those harbors.

Sir Adrien Gilbert, younger brother of Sir Humphrey, also provided with royal letters patent to seek a north-west passage to China and the Moluccas, and to establish himself on unknown lands, in 1583 sailed in the same direction taken by his brother, but with the same unsuccessful result. He had five vessels, of different sizes, and two hundred and sixty men.

In 1585, John Davis, with a view to the improvement of English commerce, made a voyage to the coast of America, in order to discover a north-west passage, and by that means shorten the route to India. He sailed with three small vessels. The first land he saw was an island near the southern extremity of Greenland, to which he gave the name of *Desolation.* He then crossed the strait which bears his name, sailed as far north as the sixty-sixth degree of latitude, and at the approach of winter returned to England.

The following year he again sailed with a much more considerable force, visited the coast at the sixtieth degree of latitude, and then sailed to the sixty-seventh degree of north latitude, and discovered an excellent harbor, at which he anchored. He also discovered Cumberland Straits. The season being far advanced, he again returned to England.

Sir Walter Raleigh had not accompanied his parent, Sir Humphrey. He was not discouraged by his death; but, on the contrary, exhibited a still greater desire to form settlements in America. He begged, and obtained new letters patent from the queen, the terms of which were more liberal than those previously accorded. These granted, for example, the right of British citizenship to all who would join Sir Walter Raleigh in the foundation of his colony; and all other emigrants or travelers were prohibited from settling within two hundred miles of his colony, for the period of six years.

These letters patent were issued in 1584.* During this year, he sent two vessels, under the command of Captains Philip Amades and Arthur Barlow, whom he instructed to examine the coasts and the country, and to satisfy themselves as to the facilities presented for the establishment of colonies.

These captains made several discoveries to the south. They landed at Roanoke Island, in the thirty-sixth degree of north latitude, and so glowing and marvelous were their descriptions of the country, that it was named *Virginia*, in honor of the virgin queen Elizabeth.

Sir Richard Greenville, one of the first associates of Sir Walter Raleigh, sailed, in 1585, with seven vessels. He anchored at Roanoke Island, where he left eight hundred settlers, who devoted more time to the discovery of mines than to the providing of means for their future support. They were soon reduced to such a state of misery, that Sir Francis Drake, who touched at that point in 1586, returning from a cruise on the coast of Carthagena, was forced to take them back to Europe. They arrived in England in 1587.

A very short time after the departure of the colonists, Sir Walter Raleigh himself arrived at his colony, but found it deserted. Sir Richard Greenville made another voyage to Virginia, left fifty emigrants, and founded a settlement at the northern point of Roanoke Island. Upon this spot Sir Walter Raleigh intended to found a city that should bear his name; but this has since been given, in honor of the founder of Virginia, to the capital of the State of North Carolina, within the limits of which Roanoke Island is situated.

This island is almost a desert, being a sandy soil, unfit for agriculture. While there, in 1818, a few vestiges of the first establishments of Sir Richard Greenville and his companions still remained; but as for inhabitants, there were only a few hardy seamen, whose sole means of existence was to watch, night and day, for vessels that might be driven upon that coast—an occurrence which, owing to the frequent and heavy gales off Cape Hatteras, often takes place. But what I saw in their cabins, and in their smacks, led me strongly to suspect that these men were the original cause of these wrecks; in short, that they were *wreckers*.

* Hakluyt, vol. iii. p. 296.

Towards the close of 1587, Sir Walter Raleigh sent one hundred and seventeen emigrants to his Roanoke colony, there to make settlements; but they found, upon the whole island, nothing but *the bones of one European.* What became of the unfortunate companions of Sir Richard Greenville has never been known.

Among the first adventurers who visited the establishment of Roanoke was Thomas Harriot, a mathematician, who had particularly applied himself to collect information upon the character of the soil, the climate, the natural productions, the fish, and the animals of Virginia, and especially the habits, manners, and numbers of its natives. He published his interesting results. His work made such a favorable impression upon the minds of the English, that it contributed greatly to increase the taste and desire of emigrating to America, which already existed to a great degree.

The native Americans extensively cultivated the potatoe, corn, and tobacco,* of which they made considerable use. Sir Walter Raleigh brought some of the tobacco to Europe, which caused a marked change in the manners of the fashionable youths of that period, as its use spread rapidly among them.

The enterprising spirit of Sir Walter was not checked by the failure of his first attempts. In 1588, he sent out another expedition, under the command of Captain John White.† It would appear that this expedition had not been provided with the requisite means to form their establishment; and, by a resolution of the new colonists, Captain White was obliged to return to Europe to demand assistance. Unfortunately, this demand reached England at a time when the fleet of Philip the Second, surnamed the *Invincible,* being at sea, created considerable uneasiness. Raleigh was then too much engrossed with the affairs of England to be able to devote any time to the new colony; and the colonists were from that time abandoned to their miserable fate.

Thus ended the last attempts to form settlements in Virginia during the reign of Elizabeth. Raleigh, led away by other projects, in which his feelings were more involved, transferred all his rights to the colonization of America to Thomas Smith and a

* This plant derives its name from Tabasco, in Mexico, where the Spaniards first observed its use.

† Smith's History of Virginia.

company of merchants, who made no immediate efforts to continue the establishment in Virginia.

In 1590, two English vessels landed at the Roanoke colony; but their commandants were informed that the inhabitants had abandoned it and retired to another point, called by the natives Crooton. Surprised, while on this coast, without shelter for their vessels, by one of those gales so frequent off Cape Hatteras, they made no further search, and returned to England without having obtained the slightest information as to the fate of their unfortunate fellow-countrymen. This colony was not, for many years, thought of in England.

In 1588, France, under the reign of Henry the Third, who had inherited the troubles and misfortunes heaped upon the kingdom by his predecessor, granted the exclusive trade of the Gulf of St. Lawrence to Chaton and Noel, nephews of James Cartier; but this grant was soon revoked.

In 1591, Ravillon repaired to the Gulf of St. Lawrence, in order to explore the seal-fisheries which abounded in those latitudes.

At last, Henry the Fourth revived those projects of colonization which had so often been abandoned, and, in 1598, the year in which the edict of Nantes had been issued in favor of the Protestants, he appointed the Marquis de la Roche his lieutenant-general for Canada, Hochelaga, Labrador, Rosembegue, Newfoundland, the River of the Great Bay and adjacent territory; authorized him to equip vessels, raise troops, and carry with him all persons necessary to the establishment of a colony; to build forts and cities, to concede lands, fiefs, other lordships under different titles; and to make such laws for the government of those countries as would be necessary for them.

The Marquis de la Roche anchored off Sable Island, where he landed some of his crew, and sailed towards the main land; but, in returning to Sable Island, he encountered a heavy gale, which compelled him to make sail direct for France.

Those whom he had left remained on Sable Island five years, during which time they lived upon the cattle that had been left there eighty years before by Baron Léry.

The Sieur Chauvin, a gentleman of the chamber of Henry the Fourth, who, after the death of the Marquis de la Roche, had obtained the same terms, in 1601 made another fruitless attempt to form an establishment at Tadoussac, on the left shore of the River St. Lawrence, ninety leagues above its mouth. This was the first post at which the French began the fur trade with the natives.

In 1602, an English captain, Bartholomew Grosnold,* equipped a vessel at his own expense, and sailed towards North America, hoping to make some discoveries. He examined the landing places as far north as latitude forty-three degrees; landed at Cape Cod, which he thus named from the quantity of cod fish in its vicinity; entered Buzzard's Bay, and visited several islands, the largest of which he named Martha's Vineyard, because of the number of its vines; treated and traded with the Indians; and returned to England with a large cargo of sassafras—a plant then considered a specific in certain diseases: but he derived no permanent advantage from his voyage.

On the death of the Sieur Chauvin, Commander Chatte, Governor of Dieppe, obtained letters from Henry the Fourth to form a settlement in Canada. He engaged the services of the Sieur Champlain. This celebrated navigator made a voyage to America, which, in consequence of the extensive explorations he made in that country, was highly successful. Champlain was a native of Saintonge, and a captain in the French service. He constantly served in Canada, from 1603 to 1629, and had consequently been twenty-six years in making important discoveries in the interior, and upon the coast, from the Gulf of St. Lawrence to New York, whose immense importance he had clearly recognized, by reason of the direct communication which the Hudson River opened with the Lakes, the head waters of the St. Lawrence, and the sea. He took a large share in the colonization of Canada, and displayed great activity and remarkable sagacity in his intercourse with the natives. Champlain may justly be considered the founder of Canada, as well as one of its most able and interesting historians.

Commander Chatte having died this year, the Sieur Montz, another gentleman of the king's chamber, succeeded him in his undertaking. He had accompanied Sieur Chauvin as an amateur, in his last voyage to Canada, and had found the climate of Tadoussac uncomfortably severe; he consequently formed the

* Smith, p. 105.

determination of removing his settlements more to the south, on some points of the continent blessed with a kindlier temperature. He associated himself in this enterprise with the Sieur de Pautrincourt, and accompanied him on a voyage.

The letters patent granted to the Sieur de Montz were dated November 8, 1608, and were directed to him as lieutenant-general of the king in Acadia.

In this year, upon the recommendation of Hakluyt, the city of Bristol, at its own expense, sent a vessel to North America, under the orders of Captain Martin Pring. This navigator touched at the same places, on the coast of Maine and Massachusetts, which Captain Grosnold had visited before him; but he formed no establishments.*

In 1604, the Sieur de Montz organized an expedition for America, composed of two vessels, in one of which he embarked with Champlain and De Pautrincourt. The other was intrusted to the Sieur de Pontgravé, a merchant of St. Malo, and was particularly intended for the fur trade with the natives along the coast called the *Etchemins*, which they were to visit, towards Camseau and the Island of Cape Breton.

The vessel upon which De Montz had embarked made land upon the coast of Acadia, at Port Rossignal; keeping in sight of the coast, he made for another point, which he named *Port au Mouton*. He afterwards reached Cape Sable, and made sail towards St. Mary's Bay, where he anchored. After remaining there several days, he weighed anchor, and explored a large bay, which he called *French Bay*, known by the English as the *Bay of Fundy*, whence there is a channel leading to a port which received the name of *Port Royal*, because of the excellent anchorage it afforded. The Sieur de Pautrincourt found this place so much to his taste, that he requested its cession to him, that he might settle there with his family. He obtained this grant under the title of Acadia, under which denomination was comprised all the country from the fortieth to the forty-sixth degree of north latitude.

He left Port Royal to reconnoitre the mines, of which the natives had spoken, and reached the River St. John on the 24th of June. Departing thence, he kept nigh the coast until he

* Smith.

arrived at the mouth of a river, where he formed a settlement upon a small island, which he named St. Croix. The river itself subsequently received this name. It is now the boundary line between the United States and the British Possessions in America. When, in 1820, I visited this part of the frontier of the United States, I found upon the island the visible remains of the ancient French fortifications. The situation of the post of St. Croix having been found unhealthy, and but slightly advantageous, it was determined, in 1605, to remove the establishment to Port Royal, now Annapolis, in the Province of Nova Scotia.

Thus, in the course of this year, Captain Champlain explored and visited the whole extent of the coast since known as New England, and took possession of it in the name of France, for he planted a cross with the arms of Henry the Fourth on the land of the Quinibiquis; on that where Boston was afterwards founded by the English; and at Cape Blanc, now Cape Cod. He even visited the Bay of New York, whence he returned to Port Royal, then the chief of all the French establishments in America.

In 1605, George Weymouth made a voyage of discovery to the coast of New England, which he carefully examined, to ascertain the facilities it offered for the planting of settlements. This voyage, however, did not yield any important result. All that was done was to ascertain that these places were already known by French names.*

The Sieur de Pautrincourt, in 1606, made a second voyage, accompanied by L'Escarbot, author of some excellent memoirs upon the discoveries and settlements of the French in America, who remained at Port Royal. He then devoted all his energies to the erection of new buildings; for this purpose, he again visited the entire coast, and compelled his settlers to cultivate wheat, and even to plant vines. During this year, Captain Champlain returned to France.

While the French were engaged with zeal, activity, and intelligence in the colonization of their American colonies, James the First, King of Great Britain, disposed of these countries, by a royal charter, in favor of his subjects, as though they belonged to the British crown, or were entirely unknown and uninhabited.

* Smith, pp. 18, 20.

In fact, in consideration of the reports furnished by Captain Grosnold, who was in command of a preceding expedition, two new companies were formed in England to colonize America, and obtained, from King James the First, letters patent in their favor.

These letters patent were dated the 10th of April, 1606; they divided, by an imaginary line, that part of the continent of America, situated between the thirty-fourth and forty-fifth degrees of north latitude, into two almost equal parts: one was called the *Northern Colony*, and the other the *Southern Colony*, of *Virginia.*

The name *Virginia*, it may be remembered, had been given, with incredible presumption, by English navigators to all that portion of the continent comprised between Acadia and Florida, by virtue of Raleigh's discovery, in 1584, of a single isolated point to the south of Cape Hatteras.

James the First granted the Southern Colony to Sir Thomas Gates & Company, of London—meaning that portion comprised between the thirty-fourth and forty-first degrees of north latitude, extending fifty miles along the coast north and south from the point of their first settlement: it was to extend only one hundred miles in the interior. This colony retained the name of Virginia, which it still bears, but with modifications as to its internal boundary.

The Northern Colony of Virginia, better known as the *Plymouth Colony*, which it took in consideration of its founders, who belonged to a port of that name in England, was to extend along the coast from the thirty-eighth to the forty-fifth degrees of north latitude, and extend indefinitely into the interior as far as the shores of the Pacific Ocean. These grants, however, rested upon the supposition that the territory was not already occupied by the subjects of other nations. And the only conditions imposed by royal generosity were that the grantees should acknowledge the sovereignty of the crown of England, and pay a tax of one-fifth of all the gold or silver mines, and one-fifteenth of all the other minerals they should discover.

It would appear that, as far back as 1606, the Plymouth Colony made the first attempt to insure their right to this grant; but the vessel sent out under the command of H. Chalton was taken by the Spaniards near the Antilles. At this period, the Spaniards would not acknowledge the right of any nation to navigate those seas, as this interfered, according to their ideas, with the rights to their American possessions acquired by the discovery of Christopher Columbus.

A second expedition was sent out under the orders of Captain Raleigh Gilbert, and under the protection of George and Popham. It anchored in Kennebec River, and founded, with forty-five colonists, a settlement to which the name of St. George was given. But the emigrants found the climate so severe, that they abandoned this post, in 1608, for the vessel sent out to carry them assistance.

Thus ended, for that time, the attempts made by the English to colonize the eastern portion of the Continent of America. Smith says that the country was thought too cold, barren, and mountainous for a settlement, and that it had the appearance of a field sown with rocks.

This appears to me to be quite a perfect description of this portion of America, whose rugged character, repulsive aspect, and iron-bound coast must have made the most unfavorable impression upon the minds of those who had just arrived from Europe.

The London Company, towards the end of the year 1606, sent an expedition to Virginia, under the orders of Captain Newport, accompanied by John Smith, the celebrated author of the "History of Virginia." This expedition had a very long passage. It sailed from London on the 9th of December, and did not arrive in the Chesapeake Bay till the 26th of April, 1607.*

Towards the end of May, this colony made a settlement on James River, which received this name in honor of King James. In June, Newport returned to England. One of the first laws instituted in this colony compelled all colonists to perform labor, and to clear their lands, under the penalty of being deprived of any share of the provisions. The company to which these two Virginia colonies had been conceded received a charter, conferring upon them the right to trade, to use a common seal, and consequently to act both as commercial and political bodies. A special clause specified the administrative form to be adopted for the government of the colonies. Thus, the superior administration was confided to a council residing in England, and appointed by

* Stith, pp. 41, 44. Smith, p. 150.

the crown; and the colony was to be governed by laws emanating from this council. A council residing in the colony, but also appointed by the crown, was charged with a secondary jurisdiction. The right of remaining an English citizen was granted to all the colonists, and all necessary articles were admitted free of duty into the colony; and they were permitted to trade freely with all nations. The duties imposed upon the introduction of manufactured articles, or upon foreign productions, were, for the period of twenty-one years, to be applied to the payment or reduction of the expenses of the colony. In fine, the Protestant religion, as that of the crown, was to be predominant.

Such was, from the commencement, the administrative and governmental organization of the oldest English colonies in America, in conformity to the letter of the royal charter granted and accepted at that time, and which, in our day, would certainly not have been so readily admitted by emigrants from the same country; for it was dictated in direct violation of the inalienable and sacred rights of liberty which belong to every individual.

From what we have stated in the three preceding chapters, we deduce the evident proof of the priority of the French over the English in attempts to establish colonies in America: for Baron Léry, on the part of France, sought to found a colony at a period so remote as 1518; while Humphrey Gilbert, on the part of England, did not attempt, until 1583, sixty-five years later, to create a settlement in Virginia.

It is also proved that the French anticipated England fifty years in the foundation of their first colony; since that of James Cartier took place in 1535, while that of Sir Walter Raleigh was so late as 1585. The first permanent settlement was formed by the French, in 1604, upon the coast of Etchemins, afterwards removed to Port Royal; while that of the English in Virginia dates from 1607, and this was on a very small scale.

In fine, as a geographical fact, based upon the discoveries made, and the establishments founded by Europeans in America, it is proved by what has already been asserted, and equally verified by the charts of that period,* that, upon the Continent of America, the English had taken possession of only that portion known as *Virginia;* that *New Belgium* was to be found a

* Naval Depot of Charts.

little to the north of this point; and that all the eastern portion, including the River St. Lawrence, was known as *New France*. But there is no question as to *New England*.

CHAPTER IV.

1608—1620.

COLONIZATION OF THE FRENCH, ENGLISH, AND DUTCH.

Quebec founded by Champlain; he examines Lake Ontario, Sorrel River, Lake Champlain, the Mohawk, and Hudson.—Colony of *New Holland*, or New Belgium—Discovery of Captain Hudson; first settlement upon Manhattan Island—The Sieur de Pautrincourt—Attack on the French settlements of Port Royal by the inhabitants of Virginia, under the orders of Captain Argall—This officer visits New Holland with the intention of opposing the rights of the Dutch—Fort Orange founded by the Dutch—Champlain penetrates into the interior of Canada; attacks the Iroquois—Caron, the missionary, on Lake Huron.—Colony of *Virginia;* spirit of its administration—Jamestown founded by Captain Smith; he returns to England—Lord Delaware, his successor—Martial law in force until the arrival of Governor Yeardley—First colonial assembly—The colony receives a constitution and an independent administration from the proprietors—First African slaves introduced into Virginia.

The chronological order followed in this historical summary leads us naturally to the foundation of Quebec* by Champlain in 1608, from which period dates the permanency of the Canada colony, and the definitive and permanent acknowledgment of French influence and power in the New World; which, by a more judicious course of conduct, it might have been possible to preserve until this day, and to have transmitted unshaken to posterity.

Champlain† continued to employ all his intelligence and rare activity in acquiring an exact knowledge of the immense territory whose conquest he was to insure to his native country. He penetrated deep into the interior, and, in the midst of toilsome and adventurous journeys, made surveys and plans of the country over which he traveled, and everywhere collected valuable informa-

* Charlevoix, vol. i. p. 120.
† Naval Official Manuscripts.

tion upon the resources and riches of these unknown countries. He everywhere tried to conciliate the good will of the numerous natives; visited their establishments; traded with some, made treaties of peace and alliance with others; and imparted to all an exalted idea of the power of their new visitors.

In 1609, Champlain, led away by his indefatigable and adventurous spirit, joined a party of Hurons and Algonquins, who were going to war against the Iroquois, or Five Nations, then living near the sources of the Hudson and Mohawk Rivers. He by this means made an examination of the River Sorrel, and entered Lake Iroquois—to which he gave his own name—and that of St. Sacrament, now known as *Lake George.*

Champlain was the first to visit by sea the whole coast from Acadia to New York Bay,* which he entered. He also examined the country which has since received from the English the name of *New England.* He even raised the arms of France upon the soil of *Cape Blanc,* since known as Cape Cod, and by the Dutch as *Stactemhook.* France could then, in all justice, have claimed a title to the possession of that country, as her sailors had been the first to explore it.

COLONY OF NEW HOLLAND, OR NEW BELGIUM.

At the beginning of the seventeenth century, Holland was in the first rank as a maritime and commercial nation. Her merchant marine was very extensive, numbering ten thousand sail and eighty-four thousand seamen. Her flag was seen flying in every sea. The advantages which the colonization of America might offer in a commercial point of view had not escaped the speculating genius of her merchants. Hence did the Holland Company accept the services of an English captain, Henry Hudson, a celebrated navigator, who had already, in search of a passage to India, made two voyages to the coast of America, and given, on his return, an interesting account of his discoveries.

The Dutch East India Company intrusted an expedition to Hudson; and, accompanied by his son, he sailed from Amsterdam in April, 1608, with a crew half Dutch and half English.

* Official Manuscripts.

He at first sailed along the coast of Norway as far as Cape North. He afterwards visited the White Sea, the coast of Nova Zembla, and the entrance into the Straits of Waigatz; but the presence of icebergs having closed the passage, he made other attempts towards the west. He reached the coast of Greenland; thence he proceeded to Newfoundland, explored Acadia, arrived at Penobscot Bay, doubled Cape Cod, and, steering to the south-west, found the entrance into the Chesapeake. This was the extreme southern point of his navigation. Hudson then coasted along the shores, but did not land; he visited the entrance of the Delaware, and took possession, in the name of Holland, of the neighboring shore of Cape May. In continuing his course along the shores, he reached the latitude of Sandy Hook, whence he penetrated into Manhattan Bay, and into the great river that has since borne his name.

He ascended this river to the site of the present city of Albany, a distance of one hundred and sixty English miles; then, selecting various points where useful establishments might be formed, he returned to Europe to render an account of the results of his expedition to the company in Amsterdam.

In 1610, Hudson again put to sea in the employment of an English company, and sailed with the fixed idea of finding a north-west passage to India. He entered the immense bay which now bears his name, and so impressed was he with its vastness, that he thought for an instant he had succeeded in the object of his hopes. Desirous of a confirmation of his wishes, he had the courage to pass a winter in this latitude, that he might, on the return of spring, lose no time in prosecuting his researches. Spring having set in, he renewed his course; but he perished, the victim of his daring courage, and of the cowardly and criminal desertion of his crew.

In the course of this year, the Dutch, by virtue of the rights resulting to them from Hudson's voyage, founded their first establishment, which extended from the entrance of the Delaware Bay to the mouth of the Mohawk on the Hudson. This territory received the name of *New Belgium.* Fort Amsterdam (since New York) was erected on Manhattan Island, at the mouth of the Hudson.

Sir Thomas Bulton, wishing to follow up Hudson's work, sailed in 1612 with two vessels; one under his own command, the other under that of Captain Ingram. With a fair wind, he sailed directly towards the sea Hudson had discovered. He ascended two hundred leagues to the south-west, and wintered at Port Nelson, where he lost half of his crew. In the spring, he returned to England.

Bulton had scarcely returned, when Hall and Baffin sailed, with the intention of sharing the glory of the discovery.

Hall was assassinated by a savage, and Baffin hastened to return; but with the resolution of shortly undertaking another voyage. His desire was realized in 1615.

The colonization of Acadia by the French appeared already to excite the jealous cupidity of the English established in Virginia. They even began to show their dissatisfaction openly when the Sieur de Pautrincourt—whose courageous and persevering zeal enabled him to contend against all difficulties—arrived at Port Royal with timely assistance to consolidate the colony he had founded, and caused a great number of Indians in the vicinity of his colony to be baptized, in the hope that, through the extension of religion, the influence of France might be augmented.

In the mean while, a certain Captain Argall was sent by the Virginia colony to trade with the natives on the coast to the north, and to ascertain whether any other nation would dare to attempt an establishment on that portion of the continent which King James the First claimed as belonging to his crown, and to which, by merely applying his signature at the bottom of the royal charter, he had extended the rights of jurisdiction and disposal. This violent, avaricious, and blood-thirsty captain put into Penobscot Bay, where he was informed by the Indians that the French had formed the establishment of St. Sauveur, under the auspices of the Sieur de Guercheville; and, falling suddenly upon the poor, inoffensive, and unprotected colonists, he carried them off, and burned and pillaged their post. By this means, the greater number of them perished. Thus commenced the first act of violence and usurpation of the Anglo-Saxons on the French colonies, in the present State of Maine.

Argall returned to the Virginia colony, boasted of his shameful depredations, and returned the same year to attack the colony of Port Royal and St. Croix. Finding this also without the means of resistance, he treated it with the same degree of inhumanity he had exhibited towards that of St. Sauveur, and thus gave a mortal blow to the establishments of the Sieur de Montz.

The living wreck of the French colony of Acadia, which had escaped from Argall's horrible pillage, was taken on board of the Sieur de Pautrincourt's vessels, which, in the mean time, had arrived to supply the colony with provisions.

M. de Pautrincourt applied to Louis the Thirteenth for redress from England for these strange and brutal attacks in time of profound peace. This indefatigable and courageous founder of Acadia died a short time afterwards, and the violence committed by the English was left unpunished!

Argall, returning from the horrible destruction of the French establishments, landed, in 1613, in the Bay of New York, and, for the first time, saw the Dutch establishments founded on the point of *Manhattan Island.* Having a more numerous disposable force than these poor inhabitants, he easily compelled them to acknowledge the supremacy of the crown of England. He then returned to Virginia.

The Dutch, however, even after Argall's visit, continued to extend their establishments. They built Fort Nassau, on the Delaware; explored the Connecticut River, on the banks of which they built Fort Bonne Esperance (Good Hope); and founded, at the head of navigation, on the Hudson River, the post of Orange, now Albany, which presented better facilities for the fur trade with the Indians—the principal object of their cupidity.

It was through this post, by means of exchanges with the Dutch, that the Iroquois were furnished with firearms, with which they waged such cruel and desperate wars against the French, recently established upon the St. Lawrence, and in its vicinity.

Nevertheless, Champlain perseveringly continued, during all this time, an active and intelligent *reconnaissance* of Canada; he even made a map of it. He penetrated far into the interior of the country towards Lake Superior, and carried the war into the midst of the Iroquois and Mohawks, and thrice invaded their country. These Indians were very warlike, and incomparably brave; but he attacked them in their intrenchments, in the heart of their villages, and succeeded twice in defeating them. They had never before heard the report of, or seen, an arquebuse; for they had not then had any intercourse with Europeans. Their weapons consisted of stone-axes, and arrows tipped with gun-flints or silex, which they made very sharp.

The Iroquois became so intimidated by the noise of firearms, that, notwithstanding their rare courage, they were eventually constrained to sue for peace, and even to trust to the generosity of Champlain for the settlement of the terms.

Nevertheless, this state of war continued without intermission until the year 1621, at which period the first peace was concluded with the Iroquois, whose territory was added to the dominions of New France.

VIRGINIA COLONY.

We have shown, in the preceding chapter, in chronological order, the origin of the Virginia colony. We shall now take up the most prominent facts which occurred during the first period of its organization. They will exhibit, what might already have been predicted, the spirit of independence, which, at a later period, was to bring these American colonies to so elevated a social position among civilized nations.

The charter, under which the colony of Virginia had been constituted, had been revised, as clearly as we can ascertain, more with the object of retaining the colonists in a state of dependence upon the mother country than of leaving them free to administer their own concerns, according to circumstances and the wants created by their novel situation. Thus, influenced by this spirit, the authorities in London were careful to exclude from the administrative council one of the most capable men among the emigrants, Captain Smith, whose rare energy and talents rendered him so popular among his new fellow-citizens. Nevertheless, this want of favor only served to increase his popularity in Virginia.

Now, as at this difficult period the new colonists had been several times on the eve of abandoning their settlement, in consequence chiefly of Indian aggressions, they were compelled to apply to this able chief for the means of repelling the constant attacks of the natives, and of extricating themselves from their critical position.

It was under these circumstances that Captain Smith, in 1608, ordered the building of a small town, which, in honor of King James the First, was named *Jamestown.* In its construction, he watched over, and zealously shared, the labors of the colonists; and the town thus became a place of shelter and refuge against the Indians, and afforded the means of repulsing their assaults.

Moreover, the proprietors and founders of the colony, powerful and rich, displayed great energy, zeal, and perseverance in sending to it assistance. By this means the colony not only so far succeeded in overcoming its first difficulties as to maintain itself, but eventually became prosperous.

To prevent the colonists from devoting themselves exclusively to hunting and trading with the Indians, a remarkable ordinance was promulgated—that each colonist should labor for the permanent establishment of the colony, to entitle him to a share of the assistance and provisions arriving from Europe.

Captain Smith returned to England in 1609.* The colony then numbered two hundred inhabitants and sixty houses. After his departure, it relapsed into its wonted state of internal discord, and would have sunk a second time, but for the timely arrival of Lord Delaware and his companions in 1610, who gave it a fresh impulse.

Lord Delaware succeeded Captain Smith, and restored order in the colony; but his residence was brief. Sickness and the climate of the country compelled him to return to England. He was followed by Sir Thomas Dale, who placed the colony under *martial law.* In 1611, Sir Thomas Gates arrived at Jamestown with additional colonists and abundant succor, which contributed in giving so vigorous an impulse to the colony, that, notwithstanding the violent and brutal authority of Captain Argall as lieutenant governor, its prosperity and consolidation gradually augmented.

Meantime, the English nation was rapidly regaining the ground she had lost during the civil wars which marked the sixteenth century. She directed all her energies to the acquisition of civil rights, and liberty of conscience and action; and every new emigration of colonists to America felt the stimulus of this state of feeling. All the emigrants arrived with a determination to claim the *right of self-government.* In 1619, Governor Yeardley

* Smith.

superseded Argall.* He saw the necessity, in consequence of this spirit of freedom, of convoking an assembly, where each plantation should have a right to be represented by a delegate, and of thus granting to it the rights and prerogatives of a legislature. Eleven communities sent representatives to this convention, the first act of which was *the repeal of martial law*, which had remained in force until that time.

Thus, the administration of Yeardley commenced under happy auspices. The first popular assembly held in America was organized under him; a remarkable governmental fact—as interesting as it is important to notice, because it fixes the starting-point of the democratic era in America.

This assembly caused a new charter to be granted to the Colonization Company of Virginia. The London Company issued its memorable ordinance† on the 24th of July, 1621, which contained the following provisions:—

The governor of the colony, representing the king, and the permanent council, answering as a Chamber of Peers, were to be appointed by the London Company. A popular assembly, composed of delegates appointed directly by the colonists, and, as it were, representing the House of Commons, was to hold its sessions annually. Such, at least, was the analogy which the authors of that charter preserved between this new colonial legislation and that of the mother country.

The fact is that all which these new legislative provisions presented as truly democratic was owing, not to the identity of the forms adopted with those of the constitution of Great Britain, but rather to the degree in which they diverged from that standard.

After all, the legislative administration of Virginia differed but little from that of England. It was even a faithful copy of it, with a few rare exceptions.

Moreover, by a feeling of self-reliance, very commendable for those times, it was provided that, after the installation of the new government, no order from the crown should be binding upon the colony, unless it had been approved by the General Assembly.

As for the courts of justice, they were to conform themselves to English laws. Thus were introduced into the New World, as

* Stith, pp. 157–161. † Ibid., p. 181.

rights acquired and acknowledged, the representative system and the trial by jury.

From that period the colonists ceased to be under the control of the will of a commercial company, and by this means conquered, for themselves and their descendants in perpetuity, *the title and prerogatives of free citizens.*

Husbandry then advanced with such rapid strides that European workmen could not be obtained in sufficient number for the wants of the colony. In the year 1620, a Dutch vessel of war landed twenty negroes at Jamestown, to be put up for sale. They were the first Africans carried into Virginia—and this contagious example was extensively imitated!

CHAPTER V.

1620—1639.

COLONIZATION OF NEW ENGLAND.

The eastern coast of America receives the name of *New England*—The English make several voyages to it for the purpose of trading with the natives—*Plymouth Colony;* its establishment; its early governmental and administrative organization —James the First grants new letters patent to a company under the title of *Grand Council of Plymouth for Colonizing New England,* whose object was to prevent the *Puritans* from settling in New England—Captain John Mason, member of the Council of Plymouth, receives the domain of *Mariana,* in New Hampshire—First establishments of Portsmouth; its advantages for the fisheries—Royal concession of Acadia, under the name of Nova Scotia, by King James, to Sir William Alexander—Designation of what was then meant by *Acadia*—Grant of Charles the First to Sir Fernando Gorges—Geographical division of the Continent of North America.

THE Virginia Company had sent Captain Smith upon the eastern coast of America, for the purpose of trading with the natives. This able navigator took advantage of this mission to make a detailed *reconnaissance* of its bays, harbors, and rivers. He collected much information upon the nature of the country, the fertility of its soil, and its resources—of which he carried back to England so favorable a description that young Prince Charles, son of James the First, afterwards Charles the First, gave it the name of *New England.*

The origin of this name, which still obtains at this day, dates from that period. But that portion of the coast especially examined by Captain Smith, to which the name was given, appeared so unimportant, absorbed, as it was, by the immensity of country known under the name of *Canada*, comprising the whole northern extent of the continent, that he entreated the Prince of Wales, in handing him the map, to order that the French names, which then alone designated the various points upon that coast, should be replaced by English ones.

However favorable may have been the reports of Captain Smith, their only result was, for some time, to encourage new expeditions for the purpose of trading with the natives.

The country appeared so forbidding, the climate so severe and inhospitable, and the success of the establishments so contingent, as to afford little chance that emigrants could be induced to colonize it.

It was fortunate for humanity and for future generations, that there already existed, in a certain class of society in Europe, a spirit that was willing to brave all difficulty, all privation, and all danger; a spirit, in short, that did not fear to land and to settle on these iron-bound coasts, however repulsive and dangerous they might be even to brave adventurers who dared to seek there a refuge against the tyranny of conscience to which they were subjected. That spirit had its source in holy inspiration, which thus induced men to exile themselves, that they might obey the dictates of their conscience, and pray to God according to their sincere belief!

PLYMOUTH COLONY.

The division of factions had powerfully shaken society in Europe, and especially in England, since 1614. A great number of Puritans, in their flight from the religious despotism to which they could not submit, had been compelled at first to remove to Holland. They settled at Leyden, under the orders of John Robinson. But they made, in that country, no proselytes to their doctrines; the Dutch were much too phlegmatic, and much too quiet, for their restless and turbulent spirit. They then cast their eyes towards the New World, which presented a prospect far more accordant with their principles and ideas.

They applied to the Virginia Colonization Society for a grant of land within their limits, and obtained it; but King James, without wishing to discourage them in their undertaking, would, nevertheless, give no guaranty that they should be entirely sheltered from persecution.

On the 6th of September, 1620, they sailed with the expectation of arriving in the Hudson River; but their captain, probably from design, steered to the north of Cape Cod, consequently beyond the limits of the Virginia society.

On their debarkation, they appointed John Carver governor of their colony for one year, and immediately organized an administrative government. They afterwards commenced to explore the whole coast in their vicinity, in order to insure to themselves the most favorable locality for the foundation of an establishment. On the 17th of December, 1620, they selected a position in a bay to which they gave the name of Plymouth, in compliment to the city where their society had received the last marks of hospitality in Europe.

The first step taken by these bold and resolute emigrants was marked, as I have just stated, by a very remarkable act of independence and sound judgment. They had given themselves a governor of their choice, and adopted administrative forms in accordance with the dominant principle of their ideas of religion and liberty, without in any wise troubling themselves about the spirit and conditions of the royal letters in virtue of which they had just established themselves under the protection of the crown of England.*

The official declaration made by these emigrants, in constituting themselves a body politic, on the first day of their landing, cannot be read without interest.

"In the name of God, amen: We, the undersigned, loyal subjects of our sovereign lord, *and feared*, James, by the grace of God King of Great Britain, France, and Ireland, Defender of the Faith, having, for the honor of our king and country, undertaken a voyage, with the intention of founding and establishing a colony in the northern part of Virginia, do create and form, by

* Salmon's Modern History, vol. i. p. 533.

these presents, solemnly and mutually, before God, and each of us here present, a civil and political society, to direct, preserve, constitute, and organize such just and equitable laws, ordinances, acts, institutions, and employments, as from time to time shall be judged most advantageous and most favorable to the happiness of the colony, to which we promise obedience and submission."

It was under this compact that the government of Plymouth colony, then composed of one hundred and three persons, was organized; but fatigue and disease reduced the colonists in the space of one year to less than one-half of their original number. The executive power was placed in the hands of a governor and a superior council, annually elected by a meeting of the free members of the colony. Every freeman, for slavery had most unfortunately already stained the American soil, belonging to the established church, had a right to vote upon all subjects of general interest. Their jurisprudence was, for the most part, borrowed from the sacred books of Moses.

In consequence of this provision, the general council was charged with regulating the public business, and deciding all suits, by the simple light of reason, without the aid of any code.

In accordance with the criminal jurisprudence of the Jews, false testimony, sacrilege, blasphemy, and adultery were punished with death.

Those who were detected lying, drunk, or dancing, were publicly whipped, and exposed astraddle upon a rail to the laughter of the multitude. Pleasure, as well as vice and crime, was interdicted. In short, a transgression of the sanctity of the Sabbath was punished by a heavy fine.

This form of government continued until the year 1634, at which period the colony was incorporated with that of Massachusetts.

Hence, though the Plymouth colony was founded upon a grant derived from the Plymouth Company organized in 1606, it was not established under its auspices. The fact is, that company did not make any serious efforts to fulfil the conditions of the letters patent it received; consequently, King James the First granted, by new letters patent, more extensive powers and privileges in favor of the Duke of Lenox, the Marquis of Buckingham—who, being the favorite of the Prince of Wales, then exercised the greatest influence upon the mind of the king—and other associates. This new company assumed the title of *Grand Council of Plymouth for Colonizing New England.*

The object of the King of England, in conferring these new powers upon men so distinguished and influential was to prevent the colonization of New England by *Puritan* emigrants, in whose loyalty he had not full confidence. Notwithstanding all the advantages secured by this second royal grant, the latter company did not succeed any better than the former. The king was therefore compelled, as a last resort, to abandon his resolution relative to the *Puritans.* In fact, this was in some respects the only class of men sufficiently fanaticized by a dominant idea of religious liberty to persevere, under a climate so severe, in the colonization of lands so unfruitful and so unpropitious.

In 1621, Captain John Mason, then engaged in the Newfoundland fisheries, was one of the Council of Plymouth. He asked for and obtained the grant called *Mariana,* extending from *Cape Ann* to the sources of the *Merrimack River.* At a later period, he obtained an extension of this domain as far into the interior as the shores of the River St. Lawrence, and to the Great Lakes. This new domain took the name of *Lacuna,* and principally constituted the territory since known as *New Hampshire.*

A grant which, at best, was made in direct violation of the rights of property acquired by the French, by their establishments on the River St. Lawrence; but these were already very little respected by the Anglo-Saxon race, who had but recently established themselves in the vicinity of the French possessions.

A great number of fishermen placed themselves under the orders of John Mason, upon the borders of the Piscataqua, and established fisheries and salt ponds upon the place where Portsmouth now stands, the capital and principal sea-port of *New Hampshire.*

The advantages of this locality for fishing were so great that upwards of one thousand inhabitants were soon collected upon one of the sand islands at the entrance of the harbor of Portsmouth; while at the present time, on the same spot, there are scarcely one hundred.

But the spirit of independence of the Puritans of New England was already so manifest in all the acts of these new inhabitants, that one of the most celebrated men of that period, William Laud, Archbishop of Canterbury, observed with extreme jealousy the concessions granted to the Puritans by the crown; and sought, by secret agents, to obtain correct information as to the dispositions of the colonists. Hence, as far back as 1635, a certain Burdett, from Piscataqua—according to Hutchinson, who gives an account of all the acts and doings of the inhabitants of New England—insinuated that the loyal intentions of the colonists, who did not seek so much to adopt *new domestic administrative forms*, as to put in *action the principles of sovereignty*, ought to be mistrusted; that, besides, the colonists, from principle, considered it *perjury and treason, in their general court, to make an appeal to the king or his government.*

The encroachments of the English upon the property of the French became more and more threatening; 1613 had seen the settlements of Acadia, St. Sauveur, and Penobscot devastated by an English freebooter from the colony of Virginia. Since that period, the Anglican missionaries had penetrated into the midst of the native inhabitants of that coast, and established meeting-houses and stores among them; and by that means all New England had been settled in violation of the incontestable rights of discovery and prior colonization by the French. At a still later period, by the intervention of the same agents, the new English colonies, from the coast of New England, insolently extended their jurisdiction as far as the borders of the River St. Lawrence—a river eminently French by all the titles that can be created by discovery, colonization, battles, victories, and finally by treaties with the natives. In 1620, King James the First tried to put his royal seal upon all these encroachments, by conceding to Sir William Alexander the peninsula of Acadia, under the new name of *Nova Scotia*. The object of these letters patent, as indicated by the title they bore, was "the settlement of *vacant lands, or lands inhabited by infidels.*" Now, since 1604, all this country had been occupied, inhabited, and cultivated by the French, as we have already seen. This prince, then, could not have had the least right to make these royal dispositions.

Anterior to the treaty of Utrecht, the English had never been established in that country, though it had been the scene, it is true, at various times, of transient invasions on their part: but subsequent treaties have in all instances combated these pretensions, and, by settling the disputes to which they might have given rise, clearly exposed them. The English, therefore, have never been able to establish any rights to these possessions, except those of invasion, either violently or furtively conducted.

It must be remarked that, at that time, Acadia included all the territory from east to west comprised between French Bay or *Cape Fourchu*, and *Canseau* or *Campseau*, which is a large peninsula. Hence, it was erroneous to give the name of Acadia to other parts of the continent of America. It is a geographical error, with no importance, at this period, except in its relation to history; and the error, moreover, has been sufficiently corrected by the coincidence of two authors, strangers to each other, the Sieur Denis, a Frenchman, and Sir William Temple, an Englishman, who have agreed upon this point in their works published in 1672. We may then regard this an established fact.

In 1639, King Charles granted to Sir Fernando Gorges, by royal charter, containing important privileges, the right of property over an immense domain situated upon the present territory of the State of Maine. As to the powers and immunities arising from the title as proprietor of this domain, they were assimilated to those of the Count Palatine of Durham. The majority of the proprietors, composing a species of landed aristocracy, were to enjoy specific rights, and to order and promulgate all laws judged good and useful, and not contrary to the laws of England.

However, the advantages attached to this royal grant do not appear to have determined many emigrants to settle upon that domain at an early period; for, a long time afterwards, the government of the Massachusetts colony extended its jurisdiction over that province.

In accordance with the historical and geographical authorities of that day, the distinct divisions acknowledged upon the continent of America are embraced in the following classification:—

L' Oues-Grone-Lande belonged to the Danes.

L' Esto-Lande, or land of Labrador, also called *New Britain*, or country of the Esquimaux, to the English.

Canada, or New France, to the French. Under this name was comprised all the territory, north and south, watered by the River St. Lawrence; with the Island of Newfoundland and Acadia, which formed, for the purposes of administration, two distinct parts, but known, nevertheless, under the generic name of *New France*.

New England belonged to the English, and comprised all the extent of coast between the Kennebeck or Quinebequi River and a line drawn from *Cape Cod* to the shores of the Hudson, near a point where Albany is now situated.

New Holland, or New Belgium, belonged to the Dutch. It comprehended all the coast from *Cape Cod* to the *Delaware* inclusive, and extended to the line of the Iroquois, where commenced the domination of France in Canada. Thus, this colony covered all the territory of Connecticut, Rhode Island, New York, and New Jersey.

Virginia belonged to the English. Under this name was particularly designated the country comprised between the *Chesapeake* and *Albemarle River,* including Maryland, Virginia, and the Carolinas.

Finally, at the extreme south were found *French* and *Spanish Florida.**

CHAPTER VI.

1620—1653.

COLONIZATION OF THE FRENCH, ENGLISH, AND DUTCH.

Canada colony; its population somewhat increases under Louis the Thirteenth—The Sieur d'Aunay de Charnisé and M. de la Tour; jealousy between these two chiefs—French posts in Canada—New Amsterdam founded—Establishment on *Long Island*—Northern Colony of Virginia, or *Grand Council of Plymouth;* its governmental and administrative organization—Salem founded—Fiscal exaction of Laud, which drives numerous emigrants to New England—The Colony of New Plymouth assumes its own authority to remove the seat of the company from the mother country to America—John Winthrop elected governor—Dorchester, Charleston, and Boston founded—The Dutch extend their establishments—Gustavus Adolphus forms the project of creating a colony in America—Canada colony—The colony created by Richelieu does not fulfil its engagements—The colony of New France succeeds it—Hostilities between France and England, during which the establishments in Canada fall into the hands of the English—Evil system of French colonization.

In the years 1620, 1621, and 1622, during the reign of Louis the Thirteenth, emigrations very rapidly increased the number of

* Depot of Naval Charts.

the inhabitants of Canada and Acadia; and the religious troubles which broke out under this reign contributed in a great measure to produce this result. The Sieurs d'Aunay de Charnisé and De la Tour were at the head of a very considerable party of emigrants. They attempted to found an establishment at *Hève;* but they afterwards removed to Port Royal, where they formed a union with M. de Pautrincourt's colonists. M. de la Tour afterwards detached himself, and founded an establishment upon the River St. John. But the rivalry which existed between these two chiefs was soon shared by their respective colonists. They made war against each other; and thus, by this absurd discord, destroyed all the fruits of their enterprise—the object of which had been to found permanent establishments, which ought to have been the only end of their common zeal. In these impious struggles, M. de la Tour was worsted, and then tranquillity seemed to be restored in the two settlements.

M. de Charnisé dying a few years afterwards, M. de la Tour returned to Port Royal, married the widow of his rival, and thus concentrated in his own hands a large share of the interests of the colony.

The French settlements in America were at this time of but little importance. The principal ones were Port Royal, Tadoussac, and Quebec. These wretched posts were simply surrounded by a miserable palisade, their only defence against the Indians, or against the aggressions of freebooters, who then exercised a sort of right to pillage wherever they could attack with a superior force. Nevertheless, national vanity called these miserable hovels forts. The castle of Quebec alone had a stone foundation; the basis of the others was earth. Scarcely fifty families could be found in the largest of these posts.

Upon the whole line occupied by the French, small isolated stations or farms were to be found at great distances apart, where the fur trade was carried on with the natives; but they were so bare of any means of defence, even against the Indians, that they rather added to the weakness of the French colony than to its strength.

Moreover, an extreme want of energy seemed to characterize the creation and existence of these French establishments. This was the result of the system adopted by an exclusive colonization company created by Richelieu in 1626. This company had nothing but their own interests in view; and their only object was to enrich themselves by the fur trade. Could it be otherwise, when, instead of that energy which freedom of action, free commerce, and the formation of such an establishment as they desired would infallibly have given to the colonists, the great object sought was to smother the advancement of the colony by creating a monopoly for the advantage of the few? And has France ever acted differently when the proposition has been made to her to found a colony in a foreign land?

Under the happy influence of the commercial genius of the Dutch, the colony of New Amsterdam augmented from year to year. The post of Orange had acquired importance because of the facilities it offered for carrying on the fur trade with the Indians. Active intercourse had been established, and valuable exports made under the Dutch flag. In fine, notwithstanding the hostile visit and the representations of Argall in 1613, the persevering Dutch, in 1623, permanently founded their new city of Amsterdam, the site of the present city of New York. From that period, new rural habitations, small, but gay and comfortable, presented at the point of Manhattan Island the appearance of a handsome village, protected by a *blockhouse* built upon the *Battery*, now the most beautiful promenade of the great American city. On Long Island, there were also some small farms, tenanted by the pioneers of Dutch civilization from the neighboring shore.

In short, New Amsterdam had already fixed the attention of European speculators, in consequence of the value and importance of its exports, which placed her in regular communication with the mother country.

The industrious activity of the Anglo-Saxons also gave a remarkable impetus to the colony of *Southern Virginia.* The colony of *Northern Virginia* alone, notwithstanding the influence of her patron, the Duke of Buckingham, the most powerful subject of that time, had, since 1620, made but little progress. At length, the Puritans, under the management of a certain Mr. White, obtained, in 1627, from the Virginia Company, by a cession of its rights, permission to establish themselves on this territory.

But the Puritans, in their feeling of mistrust as to the legality of such a retrocession, thought it most prudent to make direct application to King Charles the First, who, in 1628, granted them new letters patent, with the privilege of making and adopting the necessary laws and regulations for the government of their society.

By this new charter, the colonies had the right of selling land, and of governing themselves according to their own laws. Their government was to consist of a governor, a deputy governor, and an administrative council of ten members, to be appointed the first time by the crown, and afterwards by the free members of the company.

The executive power was vested in the governor and the administrative council; the legislative power was retained by the titular proprietors, or free members of the company. They were empowered to pass such laws as they might judge necessary for the welfare of the colony; provided, always, that these did not clash with those of the mother country.

The company had obtained very large grants of property on the single condition of paying to the crown one-fifth of all the gold or silver that might be found on the plantations; for, at that period, it was still the prevailing opinion that the country contained mines of the precious metals, and this stimulated the spirit of enterprise which carried so many emigrants towards the New World.

In the transaction of ordinary affairs, the governor and deputy governor, assisted by seven members of the council, composed a species of court, which held a session one day in each month. A general assembly of all the members of the company took place four times a year. The object of these quarterly assemblies was the admission of those who were qualified to all the prerogatives of *free members* of the company; that is to say, to vote upon public business; to nominate public officers; and to make the laws and regulations necessary for the administration of the colony.

The governor, deputy governor, and members of the council were elected by the General Assembly, which sat in the spring.

Let us here remark that each member of the society, being entitled to a vote in the choice of a governor and members of the council, and in the making of all the laws, enjoyed this privilege by virtue of the common law of England. Hence, the charter of this company contained the fundamental principle of those public liberties which brought forward and assured the supremacy of democracy in the New World.

But we must also observe that all the inhabitants of the colony did not indiscriminately enjoy the right of voting. Universal suffrage was then by no means admitted. To be entitled to a vote, it was necessary to fulfil certain requirements imposed by the colonists, always arbitrary, it is true, and often absurd and unjust; but these requirements formed a part of the social compact under which they had united themselves, as a body politic and commercial, to re-establish the territory conceded by their royal charter.

The new association of Puritans, under the title of *Grand Council of Plymouth*, sent to America, in 1629, an expedition composed of five vessels, carrying more than three hundred adventurous emigrants. They arrived on the New England coast, near Cape Ann, on the 20th of July, and touched at a port, which they named Salem*—in allusion probably to the Holy Scriptures, or perhaps in allusion to that repose they came to seek.

The emigrants, immediately after their arrival, constituted themselves into a religious and political association. They adopted the disciplinary forms of the *Independents*, or *Congregationalists*, and formally declared their opposition to the forms and doctrines of the *Episcopalians*, or of the Established Church. This manifestation gave, from the commencement, a particular impress to the civil institutions of these colonies.

At the same period, the arbitrary and intolerant principles and the fiscal extortions of the ambitious Laud, Archbishop of Canterbury, in England, forced a great number of non-conformists to seek an asylum in New England. Among these emigrants were several titled and rich persons, who voluntarily exiled themselves with their families and their fortunes. Through their intervention and influence, an important modification was introduced into the administrative constitution of the colony. The charter of Charles the First placed the administrative and superior seat of the company at London; it was transferred to America, and the superior administration was established in New England.

This measure was a bold conception; its execution was still more important, inasmuch as it must necessarily exercise the greatest influence upon the future interests of the colony.

The removal of the seat of administrative and executive power took place in 1630. At this period, fifteen hundred emigrants

* Salmon, vol. iii. p. 537.

arrived in New England. John Winthrop, one of the latter, was elected governor, and Thomas Dudley was one of a superior council composed of eighteen members.

At this period, two new establishments were founded, one at Dorchester, and the other at Charlestown, on Charles River; but the inhabitants of Charlestown, having observed that the opposite side of the river afforded a more favorable position for the establishment of a city, drove away, without any other right than their own will, a minister of the Anglican Church, who had there constructed for himself a small retreat, and laid the foundation of Boston, destined to become the capital of the colony.

Thus, through usurpation of property, was the capital of New England built—by emigrants, too, who had arrived with exalted religious ideas, flying, they said, from the violence and persecution they had suffered in their own country!

Singular disposition of man, who justifies in his own eyes acts which he reproves in others, as though whatever the object, the iniquity of the action be not the same!

The Puritan character, and its ruling spirit, were soon revealed in all their force from the very day the emigrants set foot on American soil. In the promulgation of the regulations which were to govern the colony, two, among others, attract our particular notice. The one fixed the *price of wheat;* the other declared that the Indians should be deprived of all the lands they did not cultivate; and the colonists were forbidden, under pain of a heavy penalty, to sell them spirituous liquors or ammunitions of war.

While the English were thus founding their first establishments in New England, the Dutch—who on their part claimed possession of the coast as far as Cape Cod, in virtue of discoveries made in their name by Captain Hudson—were actively extending their own on the shores of the Connecticut River. They had already, by following the course of this river, gone far into the interior, and had founded a post on its banks, the present site of Hartford. From this point they extended their commercial relations with the Indians on the shores of the St. Lawrence, and thus created a diversion alarmingly injurious to the French interests in Canada.

Founded on the same rights of discovery, they also planted settlements on the shores of the Delaware, where they had purchased from the natives a certain extent of territory. This colony, however, existed but a short time; it was destroyed by the Indians.

It was about this time also, 1626 or 1628, that Gustavus Adolphus, the most enlightened of the Scandinavian kings, conceived the idea of establishing a colony in America, which should be the refuge and the asylum of the persecuted of all denominations. He founded a colonization society, in the formation of which people of all nations were invited to take part. This company was to enjoy very extensive privileges.

The French establishments in Canada made but slow progress. Quebec contained scarcely fifty inhabitants, most of whom were Franciscan priests; but the zeal of these missionaries for the conversion of the infidels was great; and Caron, Viel, and Sagard, who had already penetrated into Upper Canada, lived and established missions among the nations inhabiting the vicinity of the shores of the Niagara (*Unghira*).

The company created by Richelieu, not fulfilling its engagements, was by a royal edict, in 1628, supplanted by a company of a hundred associates, among whom were Richelieu himself, Champlain, Rossilly, and many other rich and well-educated persons. This company took the name of the *Company of New France*. Its powers were immense. It could create, found, and form establishments throughout Canada; fortify, and govern them at pleasure; and make war or peace. The whale and cod fisheries were free for all Frenchmen; but the company had the *perpetual monopoly of the fur trade with the Indians*.

Titles of nobility were granted to twelve of the principal members of the society. The company had the privilege of trading free of duty; and the advantages conceded by the crown extended so far as to permit the free entry of all manufactured articles into Canada—a remarkable advantage at a period when national industry was depressed by numberless restrictions.

The company, during the first few years, was to send from two to three hundred laborers to Canada, and thirteen thousand colonists within the space of twenty-five years.

Unfortunately, its vessels, in their first voyage, were taken by the English, then at war with France. This war resulted from the open intervention which the Duke of Buckingham had induced Charles the First to make in favor of the Protestants, who had taken refuge in La Rochelle, the last foothold of Calvinism in France.

In consequence of these hostilities, caused by the jealousy existing between the two ministers of France and England, nearly all our possessions in America became the easy prey of the English, who were more numerous and better supplied with provisions than the French; for the posts in Canada, adorned with the title of forts, were nothing but miserable huts, without means of defence, and in want of everything.

Quebec, thanks to the heroic energy of its generous and brave chief, Captain Champlain, although deprived of defences, resisted longer than any of the others; until finally the garrison, reduced by famine, was, in April, 1629, compelled to surrender. Though it was then the most important post of the colony, it numbered only one hundred inhabitants. We may judge, by its weakness, of the abandoned state in which it had been left by the French, at a time they should have displayed unanimity and perseverance in their means of defence and colonization.

Louis the Thirteenth, however, having concluded a treaty with England before the fall of Quebec, Canada and Acadia were, in 1632, restored to France by the treaty of St. Germain-en-Laye, and the colony was enabled to resume its operations of colonization, which had been interrupted. This period of suspension was, nevertheless, a great check to the progress of affairs in Canada; and either from this cause, or from the incapacity of its chiefs, the company was under the necessity of applying for an extension of its prerogatives, which was easily obtained.

The fact is that the system adopted by Richelieu, in colonizing our possessions in America, was clogged from its origin by a radical defect. Its sole object was to favor the fur trade. Consequently, influenced by no other interest than that of individual aggrandizement, in subjection to the action of a monopoly which appropriated everything to itself, the government founded no establishments with the object of fertilizing the country, of developing its agricultural riches, or of felling its admirable timber, or even of increasing its population: it only sought to take military possession of the country, so as to secure the most favorable points for trade with the natives.

Richelieu had directed all the resources in his power towards the accomplishment of this commercial system; hence the church, through its missionaries, and the army by the sword, were his two most powerful auxiliaries, and the only means employed to obtain occupation of the country: the first, by the intervention of the faith to which the zeal of the missionaries sought daily to attach the red man; the other, by inducing respect for the power of French arms through frequent combats, in which the valor and the courage so natural to the French nation had a vast field for display.

Numerous, but weak posts were then spread over a vast extent, always well chosen, but without certain means of communication; because the five tribes of Iroquois, inhabiting the borders of Lake Ontario, the head waters of the St. Lawrence, the western part of New York and Lake Erie, intercepted the communication of the St. Lawrence with the upper lakes. Besides, the Indians, having clearly perceived the weakness of the system pursued by our government, made frequent successful irruptions on the establishments of the French pioneers.

Champlain was a brave and skillful man, but too much led by the religious fanaticism of the times. For him, the salvation of a soul was worth an empire. Hence, all his efforts, and all his intelligence were directed towards the conversion of the natives. He unreservedly confided to the Jesuits the task of preaching the true faith to the infidels, and of organizing the frontier possessions of the French in America. His dominant thought was to establish a durable alliance with the Indians. To insure it he advanced his missions into the territory of the Mohawks and Hurons. In fact, the object of the French colony, at that period, was more particularly to favor the interests of the church than those of colonization.

In 1635, a seminary for instruction was established in Quebec, the first institution of the kind created in America. During the same year, a charity hospital was founded; also an Ursuline convent for the education of girls.

In 1640, Montreal was made the seat of a commercial station for the fur trade with the natives. At this period, the English had not yet approached the River St. Lawrence; but the Dutch, in possession of the shores at the mouth of the Hudson River, had established relations with the Five Nations, among whom it was then thought necessary to establish a mission post.

In 1641, Charles Raymbault established the St. Mary mission, and thus opened a communication with the Sioux of the Mississippi. During the same year, the Ursulines obtained the titles of their establishment on the Three Rivers (*Trois Rivières*).

In the following year, the missionaries crossed from Montreal to Fort Orange, at the head of navigation of the Hudson River, in the direction of the course of Champlain canal, and there met the Dutch traders. In 1646, Gabriel Drouillet, the missionary, accompanied by a single Indian, crossed from Quebec, on the shores of the St. Lawrence, to the banks of the Kennebec River, where a French settlement had been formed; and thus traced through the forests of Maine the first path of a communication which, two centuries later, was to be effected by steam over a rail-road. Finally, in 1648, the brave De la Mothe-Cadillac, accompanied by some zealous missionaries, reached Lake Superior; he explored all that immense inland sea, and predicted the future greatness of these fertile regions.

That part of the peninsula, between Lake Huron and Lake Michigan, which they especially visited, was then inhabited by the Huron Indians, a great number of whom were at that early period converted to Christianity by the Jesuit missionaries, who erected a chapel at the Falls of the St. Mary, and another on the Island of St. Joseph.

The Hurons were almost entirely destroyed by the Iroquois, their implacable enemies.

Finally, some Canadian hunters advanced as far as Green Bay, where they passed the winter.

Notwithstanding the able efforts of the Jesuits, the colonization of New France on the borders of the Lakes, and particularly in the western part of New York, experienced great resistance on the part of the five tribes of Iroquois, in consequence of which the trade with the natives suffered exceedingly; whilst the inhabitants of Boston and Salem, as stirring, active, and industrious as the inhabitants of Canada were the reverse, deprived the Canadians of their fisheries, from which they also excluded the English.

In 1655, the colony of Acadia lost its active and intrepid chief, M. de la Tour. He was succeeded by M. de Rochelle, one of his creditors, who abandoned these establishments to his two sons. At that time, when the colony was, as it were, without a chief, when a profound peace reigned, the inhabitants of Boston, who had always coveted this property, resolved to seize it. Appearing before Port Royal with a considerable force, they succeeded in their attempt. Upon the representations of the French government, England disavowed the conduct of the Bostonians, and restored Port Royal. This circumstance led to the definite settlement between the two nations of the boundary of Acadia.

Up to that period, France had the ascendency over the other European nations in the colonization of North America. If she had then been able to settle the western part of New York, and to insure to herself the outlet of the Hudson on the Atlantic, she might have been complete mistress of the whole country. Unfortunately, the English had the supremacy on the coast, an advantage which they delayed not in confirming by depriving the Dutch of their colony, and thus rendering themselves masters of the important avenue, presented by the Hudson, from the shores of the Atlantic to the inland lakes.

CHAPTER VII.

1630—1700.

NEW ENGLAND COLONIES.

Massachusetts Bay colony; its rapid growth—The inhabitants publish a bill of rights—Political organization—Confederation of the New England colonies—New charter of William and Mary—The colony subjected to a provincial government—Extent of the new province—*Connecticut and New Haven colony;* its government, founded on religious dogmas, a perfect democracy—*Rhode Island colony*—Foundation of Providence and Newport—The emigrations from England become more numerous—Cromwell about to embark for America; is prevented by a royal edict—The government of Rhode Island likewise founded in a spirit of pure democracy—The spirit of religious tolerance which distinguishes the inhabitants of this colony.

MASSACHUSETTS BAY COLONY.

THE Massachusetts Bay colony, although founded since that of Virginia, may, nevertheless, be considered as the stock from which have grown all the English colonies in America. It is, in fact, from the period of its foundation that we may date the rapid and uniform progress of those establishments by which England insured, in the seventeenth century, its permanent dominion in the New World, from Maine to Florida.

This circumstance makes it, as it were, almost impossible to give simultaneously an account of the foundation and the early administrative measures of these colonies, however it might be abridged; therefore I have preferred, for the sake of perspicuity, and the interest of the object I propose to myself, to present a rapid exposition of the most important facts concerning each colony, from its origin to the period of its regular administrative progress.

It was principally during the reign of Charles the First that the Massachusetts Bay colony so rapidly increased. Emigrants arrived in such great numbers that, in 1634, the free members of the colony judged it proper to proclaim a bill of civil and religious rights, which they regarded as an inalienable endowment. They decreed, moreover, that the *General Court*—an assemblage of all citizens having a right to vote, of the governor, deputy governor, and members of the superior council—should have the exclusive power to pass laws, impose taxes, select candidates for public duties, and sell lands; that for the future each community, instead of voting in mass, should be represented at this court by two deputies, but that each free member of the colony should have the right to vote directly for public officers.

Hence, from this period, the colony can no longer be considered as a company whose powers were defined, and the forms of government regulated, by a granted charter, but as a society having acquired or assumed a certain political liberty, and adopted of its own free will a constitution and form of government, copied, it is true, from those of England, but still essentially differing from them on many points.

The first emigrants had brought with them an intolerable religious despotism; but they had also been instigated by a feeling of liberty, which was to survive their generation. Their emigration to the New World was in itself a declaration of their rights. They came, guided by a conscientious feeling, to worship God agreeably to their convictions; they admitted, in fact, the freedom of political institutions, and equally enjoyed all civil rights. This political liberty gradually brought with it a corresponding degree of religious freedom.

The Massachusetts colony became so flourishing, that, to facilitate its administration, it was necessary to divide it into four counties—Essex, Middlesex, Suffolk, and Norfolk.

But the civil war that broke out in England towards the end of the reign of Charles the First soon checked its progress. England was afterwards stricken with a foreign war; and the common danger to which the New England colonies were exposed made them feel the necessity, in 1637, of uniting themselves into a confederated body.

The colony continued the administration of its affairs under this form of government until the year 1684, when Charles the Second completely modified the original charter granted by his predecessor; and from that time until 1691 the colony was in a state of continual misunderstanding with the metropolis. Under the reign of William and Mary, it received a new charter, which, under the title of *Province of Massachusetts Bay in New England*, introduced a provincial administration.

The new charter reserved to the crown the appointment of a governor and council. The governor, with the consent of the council, appointed the judges, the attorney-general, the associates, justices of the peace, the officers of the council and of the courts of justice. The other civil officers were elected by the council and General Assembly. The proprietors elected their representatives, who, having the right to select their presiding officer, formed the superior chamber.

The *General Court*, with the same organization granted by the first charter, composed a court of equity and appeal, and was also a legislative body.

The colony, under this new title, comprised, at that time, the territory of the old colony of Massachusetts Bay, that of the colony of New Plymouth, of the province of Maine, of Acadia or Nova Scotia, and of all the country between Nova Scotia and Maine. New Hampshire became a royal colony, attached to the government of Massachusetts.

CONNECTICUT AND NEW HAVEN COLONY.

The Connecticut and New Haven colonies, now forming the State of Connecticut, had, in 1630, been granted by the *Council of Plymouth* to the Earl of Warwick. Charles the First confirmed this grant, which, in 1631, was transferred to Lords Say, Brook, Scale, and others.

In 1632, these new proprietors sent adventurers to reconnoitre the coast and interior of the country. Their expedition penetrated as far as Windsor; but the first establishments were founded by David Gardner, in 1635, at Saybrook, where about one hundred colonists were collected together.

Several other companies, detached from the Massachusetts colony, established themselves at Hartford, Windsor, Wethersfield, and other places; but remained under the jurisdiction of the old colony, of which they became, as it were, the outposts.

These several companies of emigrants adopted a form of government similar to that of Massachusetts, with the exception that two of the principal inhabitants of each burgh, or community, were sent to the General Assembly to represent them, according to the English usage.

In 1638, the inhabitants of these new establishments, perceiving that they were not all comprised within the jurisdiction of Massachusetts, determined to unite under one administration, bearing the title of *Connecticut colony.* For this purpose, all those who were entitled to a vote met at Hartford, and adopted a constitution similar to the charter of the Massachusetts colony, with the exception that the General Court was convoked twice a year, and not but once, like that of the latter.

The executive power of this colony was constituted on the same basis and principles as those of the Massachusetts colony. Justice was to be administered according to the established laws; in default of which, according to the *word of God.* The governor was to be annually elected, and ineligible the second year.

The New Haven colony was founded, in 1638, by a small company of emigrants, who had arrived at Boston the previous year, under the control of the Rev. M. Davenport. Their religious opinions led them to isolate themselves, so as to secure a more tranquil observance of their peculiar principles. These emigrants, adopting the opinion that the Indians were the sole legitimate proprietors of the soil on which they had just settled, purchased territory near New Haven, directly from the natives, where they founded their first establishment.

Their form of government was based on the principles of their church, which with them held the first and most exalted rank. No one was permitted to vote who was not a member of the church, of which membership he was compelled to furnish proofs by a certificate which his own particular minister could alone give. Thus were the evangelical ministers both masters and administrators of this colony.

In imitation of the primitive Christians, the colonists of New Haven adopted the principle of common property, the agrarian law, and equal distribution.

An obligation was imposed on all civil or military employees to profess the Christian faith. Moreover, every citizen was alike an elector and eligible to office. The members were appointed in proportion to numerical population; and magistrates as well as legislators were annually re-elected by a plurality of votes. Trial by jury was also introduced.

All the colonists, but more especially the public officers, were compelled to attend divine service; and whoever failed in his religious duties was liable to severe punishment.

The New Haven colony, like that of Connecticut, was administered by an assembly, whose members were elected by the people; but none except those who were members of the established church had a right to a seat!

The Connecticut and New Haven colonies continued this system of administration until the accession of Charles the Second, when, fearing their constitution was not firmly enough established by these precedents, the colonists implored its sanction by the crown, giving as a reason why they had not before solicited the royal favor, "that they had preferred dispensing with a royal charter to receiving one from an illegitimate prince!"

In 1662, Charles the Second granted a new charter to the Connecticut colony, by which both the Connecticut and New Haven colonies were constituted under a single administration, similar to that of Massachusetts Bay. But the New Haven colonists refused to accede to the new dispositions of this charter until the year 1665, when they were finally and definitively united under one and the same administration.

In 1665, the government of Great Britain, wishing to deprive the colony of certain privileges already conceded, demanded a return of the charter which had been granted to it in 1662. The colonists refused to return it; and notwithstanding all the crafty efforts made to obtain this original paper, it was effectually concealed from the servile agents of British power in the hollow of an old oak.* This passive but brave resistance of the people of Connecticut to the encroachments of the crown of England had a fortunate result. The colony, in 1688, officially recovered the free exercise of the franchises granted by its first charter, which it was enabled to preserve entire until the year 1817, when the constitution of the present State of Connecticut was revised.

In 1698, an important modification was introduced into the administrative organization of the colony: two legislative bodies were created, and an executive power organized. Such were, from the commencement, the governmental form and institutions of the Connecticut colony. These remained in their integrity until the year 1817. This colony presented, consequently, during the whole period of its existence, the imposing spectacle of the most perfect democracy which has ever been organized. Founded on the principle of free labor, and favoring equality, the people were truly the source of all power. But that people were Puritans!

This colony persevered more strictly in its principles, and was less troubled with discussions concerning faith and religious dogmas than any other in New England; and we can easily, at this day, trace the influence which religious principles have exercised on the political and social features of this State. The fact is that religious ideas were rooted in the mind and heart of the inhabitants, as the earliest impressions of infancy are fixed in the heart and mind of man; stamping a seal on his mature age, and teaching him to set aside bigotry, and to retain those profound feelings of right which alone can direct the soul, and preserve it from the contagion of social vices. Such has been the happy influence of Puritanism in Connecticut, whence it has spread over a great portion of the Union, exerting its

* This oak is still standing, and recognized by all as the Charter Oak.

powerful influence on the ruling spirit and enlightened religious feelings which at the present time characterize the American nation.

RHODE ISLAND COLONY.

The emigrants of the Massachusetts Bay colony had brought with them the seeds of religious discord, which very soon became manifest after their arrival. Their religious fanaticism soon carried them to much greater excesses of severity, and even of persecution against their co-religionists and associates, than those to which they had been subjected on their native soil.

A certain Roger Williams, of Salem, having, in 1635, published a profession of faith different, in its dogmas and discipline, from that of the founders of Boston, was tried at the bar of the General Court, and condemned to exile. Roger Williams, having collected his proselytes, emigrated with them to the southward of Massachusetts Bay colony, and settled near the head of Narraganset Bay.

The founders of Salem and Boston considered themselves the legitimate proprietors of the Indian territory on which they had settled, in virtue of the royal charter granted by Charles the First. Roger Williams, on the contrary, looked on the Indians as the sole legitimate proprietors, having the right to cede or sell the lands on which he desired to settle. His first care, then, was to visit the country he had selected for the establishment of his colony, to create a kindly feeling on the part of the natives, and treat with them for the cession of a certain portion of territory in the vicinity of Narraganset Bay. It was after having fulfilled all these conditions, that Providence was thus founded by him in 1636.

Hence, neither violence nor cupidity had any part in the origin of Rhode Island, unlike that of the Massachusetts Bay colony.

Some time after this, a new dissenter, named Hutchinson, was also banished, with his followers, from the Massachusetts colony. He joined the colony of Providence. From this union sprang the *Colony of Rhode Island;* the land had been purchased, in 1638, from the Indians. Newport was founded in 1639; but, fearing lest their title to this property, thus directly obtained from the Indians, would not suffice to resist the encroachments of their powerful neighbors of the Massachusetts colony, the people of Rhode Island determined to send Roger Williams to England to obtain from the crown a confirmation of their right. In 1643, through the Earl of Warwick, he obtained the grant which they solicited, and in 1644 it received the sanction of the two Houses. Charles the First had, in the meanwhile, been driven from his capital.

An historical fact, worthy of being here recorded, is that, about the year 1640, emigrations from England had become so considerable, that the king became alarmed, and issued a royal decree forbidding any one to go to America, without first having obtained a special permission from the authorities. Whilst this edict was in full force, in the midst of intestine wars which had armed one-half of England against the other, the principal malcontent chiefs who had engaged in the rebellion against Charles the First, among whom was Cromwell, were on the eve of emigrating to America. It would seem that the latter had already embarked on board of a vessel anchored in the Thames, when he was stopped by the royal authority.* A strange example of that providential intervention which not unfrequently prompts man to act indirectly against himself!

In 1647, the colonists organized their first assembly. To effect this organization, they had placed the legislative power in the hands of six commissioners, appointed directly by the constituted districts. This assembly sat also as a *superior court.*

The executive power was confided to a president, assisted by four councillors, selected from the free colonists who were entitled to a vote. This council also performed the functions of a court of justice.

Each district was also governed by a council, composed of six members elected by the people, thus forming a municipal council; so that the district and colony were administered on the same principle.

Rhode Island had, therefore, like Connecticut, a democratic organization; and these two colonies presented the singular spectacle of two democracies under the protection of a monarchical government, of which they acknowledged themselves to be dependencies!

* The royal injunction extended to Lords Say and Brook, the Earl of Warwick, Hampden, Pym, and many others.

This form of government endured until 1663, when Charles the Second granted to the colonists a new charter, under the title of *Rhode Island Colony and Providence Plantations*—which were thus definitively united, and administered on the same principles as those which governed the colonies of Massachusetts and Connecticut. This similarity in administration produced, from that time, more harmony between the colonies.

The executive power, by the last charter, was represented by a governor, a deputy governor, and six councilors, elected and appointed by the municipal councils.

The legislative power was intrusted to a *General Assembly*, composed of a governor, a deputy governor, ten councilors, and a given number of members sent directly by the towns. The town of Newport sent six delegates; Providence, Portsmouth, and Warwick, each four; and two were sent from each of the less populous towns.

The *General Assembly* made laws, admitted citizens to the right of voting, appointed the public officers, established and regulated the courts of justice. It also had absolute control of the defence of the colony, and of the disposition of its resources for that purpose.

But what especially characterizes the administrative progress of this colony is the tolerant spirit which it exhibited; a spirit that has ever remained the fundamental rule of that happy country. The charter granted by Charles the Second contained this remarkable clause: "No one shall be called to an account, troubled, or punished for his religious opinions." Probably the first instance, by a royal act, of the introduction of the principle of religious liberty in the laws and institutions of the English colonies; an act which certainly does honor to the sovereign from whom the charter was derived.

Nevertheless, the colonists sometimes swerved from this spirit of tolerance. It was decreed, for example, by the legislative assembly, *that the Sabbath should be kept holy, and that no kind of labor or public amusement should be allowed on that day.*

The charter of Charles the Second remained in full force until the Revolution, and now serves as the fundamental basis of the new constitution of this State.

CHAPTER VIII.

1623—1700.

ENGLISH AND DUTCH COLONIES—NEW AMSTERDAM, NEW YORK, NEW JERSEY.

New Holland founded by Calvinists in New York Bay—Cromwell, the Protector, forms the project of taking possession of it—First popular assembly—The people retain the right of making laws—Rapid growth of New Amsterdam—A refuge for the persecuted and strangers from all parts of the world—Introduction of slaves—Tendency of the inhabitants of New England to emigrate, with the object of improving their condition—Charles the Second grants a part of the American territory, which he has already disposed of in favor of particular companies by letters patent, to his brother, the Duke of York—The English take forcible possession of the Dutch colony—The conquest insured to the crown of England by the treaty of Breda—Population of New England; of Boston—New Amsterdam takes the name of New York; Orange that of Albany—Territorial extent of the New York colony—Colony of New Jersey; its government organized on the model of those of the colonies of New England.

COLONY OF NEW HOLLAND—OF NEW YORK.

New Holland was founded, in 1623, on the shores of New York Bay, by Dutch Calvinists. Their habits of order, economy, toleration, and, above all, their love of commerce, were powerful agents in favor of the rapid growth of this colony; and its capital, then known as *New Amsterdam*, became, from its earliest foundation, so important a mart of commerce on the coast of America, that it greatly excited the jealousy of the Anglo-Americans of Virginia and of the New England coast. As the crown of England had ever refused formally to acknowledge the rights of the Dutch to settle on the Hudson or its adjacent shores, claiming priority of discovery by Cabot, under Henry the Seventh, it always anticipated the future possession of this colony.

In 1653, the Protector Cromwell formed the project of taking forcible possession of New Holland, but failed to put it in execution. His son entertained the same wish, but also failed to accomplish any result.

In 1653, the Dutch colony had so developed itself, that the inhabitants commenced to establish a regular government. A popular assembly met, which recognized the sovereignty of the people, and their legitimate and imprescriptible right to make their own laws.

New Amsterdam had, in fact, become, under the influence of the mother country, the general rendezvous of emigrants from all parts of Europe, the place where the persecuted of every creed congregated. Then, as now, English, Dutch, French, Belgians, Germans, Swiss, Piedmontese, and Italians, were to be found in New Amsterdam—all led there by the same spirit of independence and commercial enterprise. New Amsterdam, the city of strangers, already gave indications that, at a future day, it would become the great commercial emporium of America—the European bazaar of the New World.

After the capture of La Rochelle by the troops of the king, in 1656, the emigration of French Huguenots to New Amsterdam was so considerable that it became necessary to present the official publications both in French and Dutch.

Let us remark that, near this period, the importation of African slaves contributed to introduce that odious system of slave labor, and that African race, whose unfortunate seal is so indelibly impressed on the national history of the Americans.

In 1661, the Puritans of New England, finding in the social situation of their New Holland neighbors an aliment so favorable to their speculative and commercial instinct, entered into friendly intercourse with them, and soon, by their greater enterprise and ambition, compared with those of the quiet Dutch proprietors, possessed themselves of the most valuable offices among them.

The influence of the English became so great in the Assembly, that it was decreed that the public acts should thereafter be written and published both in English and Dutch.

This was the first and the most serious grasp at power, for the government of the colony had fallen into the hands of the Anglo-Americans. All that now remained for them to do was to substitute the flag of Great Britain for that of Holland; which act was but a matter of form that could not long be postponed.

In 1664, Charles the Second issued letters patent in favor of his brother, the Duke of York and Albany, by which he ceded to his royal highness, in fee, all that portion of the American continent which extends from the Kennebec to the St. Croix River, and all the territory between the western shore of the Connecticut River and the eastern shore of the Delaware, including *Long Island.* Hence, by the simple application of his signature to a piece of parchment, Charles the Second arrogated to himself the right of disposing of the legitimately acquired property of three nations—the French, Dutch, and Swedes.

These patents conferred on the Duke of York all the powers necessary to a civil and military government; that is to say, he could administer, pardon, or punish according to such laws as he felt disposed to establish, provided they did not conflict with those of England. In short, he could, according to the necessities of the case, proclaim martial law, the crown alone reserving to itself the right of appeal.

The English government was so considerate as to publish these laws both in Dutch and English, the better to inform the colonists of the royal prerogative. But the Dutch did not submit to these new royal pretensions without opposing all the resistance in their power to so iniquitous an encroachment on their rights of property. Their efforts proved fruitless.

Charles the Second appointed commissioners to act as a court of appeal in cases of dispute arising between the colonial government and the colonies. These commissioners visited Plymouth, Rhode Island, and New Amsterdam. They were authorized to treat for the cession of the latter colony to Great Britain, and to raise troops in the English colonies to strengthen by force her claims, should they be resisted.

At the same time, the Dutch establishments and vessels were simultaneously attacked without any other declaration of war than the publication of the royal letters of Charles the Second. In the month of August, an English squadron, under the orders of Richard Nichols, anchored on the coast of New Holland, and summoned the capital to surrender, which, as it had no means of defence, immediately yielded. His conquest was insured to England by the treaty of Breda in 1667. The Republic, however, regained its freedom in 1673; but a second treaty, concluded in 1674 between England and Holland, confirmed the clauses of the treaty of Breda, and restored to Great Britain those territories of which she had been for a short time deprived.

Thus did England become definitively possessed of that splendid colony, whose creation was due to the powerful genius of the aristocratic Republic of Holland in its palmy days, and which, from its origin, had united all the elements of grandeur and prosperity. Under the auspices of popular institutions, it was destined to attain its present supremacy, to which its Dutch origin contributed most powerfully.

The population of New England, at this period, amounted to one hundred and twenty-three thousand inhabitants, sixteen thousand of whom were able to do military duty. Boston alone contained a population of twelve thousand. It did not contain a single profane house, nor even a dancing school.

After the English had taken possession of New Holland, New Amsterdam received the name of New York; and Orange, at the head of navigation of the Hudson, that of Albany, which is now the capital of the State of New York. The Duke of York, doubting the validity of his first letters patent, applied for new ones, which were granted to him. These confirmed the powers with which he had already been vested, and prescribed, besides, that the colony should not carry on commerce without the express sanction of the crown, nor import English goods, except by submitting to the duties established in the mother country.

The province was governed by the Duke of York under this charter, until he ascended the throne of Great Britain.

Long Island and *New Jersey* were then included in the territory of New York, as well as the Swedish colonies on the Delaware, which had fallen into the power of the Dutch in 1655.

NEW JERSEY COLONY.

When the Duke of York became proprietor of the colony of New York, in 1674, he divided the territory which had been annexed to it between his two favorites, under the name of *New Jersey*.

The eastern portion was conceded to Sir George Carteret; the western portion to Lord Buckley. These gentlemen sold this property to speculators, who, with great energy, commenced the foundation of new settlements. The administration of the colony, however, remained under the authority of the two first proprietors, and of their heirs; but they soon became tired of so unfruitful an enterprise, and, in 1688, restored their rights to the government of Great Britain. The crown accepted the restitution.

In the course of this year, the council appointed by the proprietors, but not the elect of the people, resolved to restore the government of the colony, with its archives, to the Secretary-General of the Possessions of New England.

By this act of the superior council, the New Jersey colony passed under the control of New York, during the period of the Revolution in England. It was thus placed for nearly twelve years under the direct administration of the crown.

In 1703, this colony was definitively constituted, under a government of its own choice. It adopted, in all respects, constitutions similar to those of the other colonies.

CHAPTER IX.

1628—1700.

ENGLISH AND SWEDISH COLONIES—DELAWARE, PENNSYLVANIA, MARYLAND, AND NORTH AND SOUTH CAROLINA COLONIES.

Swedish colony of Delaware, projected by Gustavus Adolphus, founded by Oxenstiern, and established upon the liberal principles which especially characterize religious toleration—Brief existence of this colony—Its invasion by the Anglo-Saxons of New England—Colony of Pennsylvania founded by William Penn; it receives a popular government founded on religious toleration.—The *Delaware colony* organized and administered by English laws.—The *Maryland colony* founded by Lord Baltimore and Catholic emigrants; adoption of a popular government, based upon religious toleration and instruction—Conspiracy of the Protestants—Persecution of the Catholics—Situation of the colony in 1763.—*Colonization of North Carolina*, founded principally by emigrants from New England—Lord Clarendon, prime minister, proprietor of a vast domain in America, projects the creation of a landed aristocracy; consults the celebrated philosopher, Locke, relative to the form of a constitution adapted to his new empire of America—The emigrants select for themselves a popular government, and the system of Locke is abandoned.—*Colony of South Carolina;* founded by Joseph West at Beaufort—Popular government adopted by the first emigrants—Introduction of the representative system—Charleston founded—Scotch emigration—Intestine difficulties—Governor Colleton wishes to enforce martial law, but the inhabitants resist—William and Mary recall Colleton, and the representative system prevails—Consequences deduced from this chapter, and precedents relative to the progress of the English colonies on the American Continent, to the exclusion of the rival nations who had there established themselves, with rights based on a more equitable foundation.

SWEDISH AND FINLAND COLONIES—COLONY OF PENNSYLVANIA.

In the early part of the seventeenth century—near the time that Dutch industry was about to point out, with its rare commercial perspicacity, the spot on the New Continent destined to be, at a future day, the great commercial emporium of the New World—Gustavus Adolphus, King of Sweden, conceived the generous idea of creating in America a colony that should serve as a place of refuge to the proscribed of all nations. But the honor of realizing this noble conception was reserved for the celebrated Oxenstiern. In 1638, an expedition, under the command of Captain Minnits, a very experienced Hollander, who had already resided in America, was fitted out to transport to the shores of the Delaware a number of emigrants, for the most part Germans, of all denominations, and a certain number of Swiss families, with positive injunctions to purchase the land they required from the natives.

The expedition landed on the shores of Delaware Bay, then known as the *South River;* the Hudson was known as the *North River.* Captain Minnits, according to his instructions, purchased lands from the Indians, near Trenton, on which he founded an establishment; he formed another at the mouth of Christina River, in Delaware. A fort was built at the latter point for the protection of the colony, called Christiana, in honor of the young Queen of Sweden. He afterwards formed a third settlement, called Elzimburgh; and a fourth, Gottenburgh. All these establishments are now within the State of Delaware.

The Dutch, who claimed the right to these lands on the Delaware, founded on prior discovery and establishment, protested against these new arrivals; but beyond these representations their demonstrations of resistance did not extend.

The Swedish charter was exceedingly liberal. Above all, it was marked with a rare spirit of toleration; consequently, the Swedish establishments soon acquired importance. Some Dissenters, from New England, finding they could satisfy their ardent passion for gain more easily among the German, Swiss, and other emigrants who had taken refuge on these shores, than among their fellow-citizens of the North, incorporated themselves with them; and, as far back as 1646, an entire quarter of the city of Philadelphia was already settled by a mixed population of Swedes and Anglo-Americans.

The Swedish colony was governed by the first charter of Gustavus Adolphus for nearly seventeen years, notwithstanding the opposition of the Dutch, and especially that of their more active neighbors, the emigrants of the Anglo-Saxon race.

In 1655, the Swedish establishments on the Delaware passed under the authority of the Dutch. Their government was also made directly dependent on that of the Dutch, then in possession of New York.

When New York became the property of the English, the establishments on the Delaware became subject to the new government, notwithstanding this territory was held directly by a grant from the Maryland colony. This state of things lasted until Penn established his colony of Pennsylvania, and purchased directly from the Duke of York the territory of the present State of Delaware.

Such was the short duration of the second Scandinavian colony planted on the Continent of America, which, more fortunate than the first, left more durable traces of its presence in the commercial history of the State of Delaware, but especially in that of the rich State of Pennsylvania, where the imprint of the Scandinavian and German races has been indelibly preserved.

PENNSYLVANIA COLONY.

In 1681, Charles the Second conceded to William Penn all the establishments on the Delaware, and all the lands claimed to be under the jurisdiction of the government of New York. The principal conditions embodied in the charter granted to William Penn were, that the new province should be called Pennsylvania; that its proprietor and his successors, in their functions as governor, with the consent of a majority of the free men of the colony, or of their representatives assembled, might lay taxes to meet the public expenses; and that they might establish tribunals, appoint judges, and make laws, always provided these laws should not come in conflict with those of England.

The representatives had also the power to lay duties on importations. The transfer of property was free. In short, the crown engaged not to lay taxes or duties without the consent of the popular assembly, or without a special act of Parliament.

The territory conceded by this charter embraced all the country along the Delaware, extending from a point fifteen miles to the north of Newcastle to a line drawn from the sources of this river to the forty-fifth degree of north latitude, and extending to the west five degrees of longitude from its eastern boundaries.

William Penn purchased portions of the territory of New Jersey from Lord Buckley and the heirs of Sir George Carteret, which he incorporated with his own domain.

Desirous of giving his colonists a government in conformity with the wishes of the majority, he acknowledged, in 1682, a fundamental compact between them and himself, by which he perpetuated the rights and liberties of the people.

By virtue of this constitutive act each emigrant who became possessed of property acquired the same rights and privileges as the oldest inhabitants. He was an elector and eligible to office, without regard to his birth or religion.

The government was composed of a council of state and a popular assembly. The governor was president of the council. The members of the assembly were annually elected by the people. No tax could be raised without the consent of two-thirds of the members of both houses. The popular assembly fixed the time of the elections, the duration of the sessions, and that of the offices. The judiciary body was also subject to the legislative assembly.

Hence, the people were the source of all power, of all office, and absolutely governed themselves even before the grantee had given his sanction, in conformity with the charter derived from the king.

In 1690, Penn returned to the colony. He approved all these new dispositions; but to secure the spirit of the charter, a new constitution was to be formed, adopted, and approved by the proprietors.

This new constitution restored the executive power into the hands of a governor and a council of state, appointed by the proprietors. The governor remained president of the council.

The legislative power, with the right of first proposing laws, was confided to a popular assembly, annually elected by the people. The time of the elections and commencement of the sessions were fixed by law. The length of the sessions depended on the will of the assembly.

The people elected their sheriffs and coroners.

Questions concerning the right of property were decided by the parties in conflict, or by the council.

The judiciary remained dependent on the legislative assembly.

Liberty of conscience was assumed as a principle. The offices were free to every citizen professing Christianity.

Thus did Penn improve the government of his colony.

He instituted an executive power, emanating from the people, since all the minor officers were elected by the people. The judiciary power depended upon the people for its existence; from them also was derived all legislation. He would have neither an armed police, forts, militia, an established church, nor difference of rank. An entire freedom of opinion existed upon all subjects. In short, he had truly created an asylum—a place of refuge for the proscribed of all nations.

Thus, towards the end of the seventeenth century, did Penn raise the most splendid social monument which it was in the power of man to create. He founded a popular government on the true principles of liberty, to which the inhabitants of Pennsylvania owe the happiness and prosperity which they at present enjoy.

Still, the political organization of Pennsylvania presented the singular spectacle of a mixture of the principles of feudalism and democracy. The colonists acknowledged the right of the founders and their heirs to be their governors and proprietors. They admitted a right paramount, and of transmission; but they required, for the creation and execution of the laws, the sanction of the people, the only source of power, and the sole means of legalizing rights and harmonizing their action.

It is an interesting fact, that the first public mail was established, in Philadelphia, in the year 1695. At that time, letters were transmitted three times a year from Philadelphia to the south of the Potomac.

DELAWARE COLONY.

At the time of the invasion and occupation of the New Holland colony by the English, in 1664, the settlements founded on the shores of the Delaware by the Finlanders and Swiss, under the protection of the charter of Gustavus Adolphus, were considered part of the government of the New York colony. The claims of the crown of England to this territory, and to the establishments formed on it, were maintained by the Duke of York, who had become its proprietor. The government of New York, which had made careful preparations with the view of encroaching on the Delaware, had obtained direct influence on the inhabitants through the medium of numerous emigrants who had incorporated themselves with them. It took advantage of this influence to introduce a provincial government at Newcastle, dependent on that of New York. By this means English laws, vigorously put in operation, eventually became the laws of the colony of Delaware.

In 1683, William Penn, who had succeeded in establishing himself on the banks of the Delaware, purchased this territory from the Duke of York; thenceforth it became subject to an administrative government, dependent on the Pennsylvania colony.

In 1691, the Delaware colony constituted itself into an independent government, acknowledged by William Penn. Thus, towards the close of the seventeenth century, was the Delaware colony, nearly at the same time as that of Pennsylvania, organized as an independent democracy, having its own executive power, its popular legislative assembly, and a judiciary subject to this assembly.

MARYLAND COLONY.

The present State of Maryland formed a part of the Virginia colony until 1632, when, by a royal charter granted on the 20th of June, it was detached from it. This grant was made to Cecilius Calvert, in the name of his father, George Calvert, Lord Baltimore, in Ireland, who had formed the project of founding a colony in America, as an asylum for his persecuted co-religionists. This colony received its name from Henrietta Maria, daughter of Henry the Fourth, and wife of Charles the First.

The extent of country ceded by this charter, under the name of Maryland, was much greater than the present territory. It was bounded to the south by a line drawn from a headland on the Chesapeake, called *Watkin's Point,* to the ocean; to the east, by the ocean and the western shore of the Delaware Bay as far as the fortieth degree of latitude; to the north, by a line drawn from this parallel westward to the meridian of the principal source of the Potomac River; and from this point, following the west banks of this river, to *Smith's Point,* and finally to *Watkin's Point.*

It will, therefore, be seen that these boundaries included the present State of Delaware, a part of Pennsylvania, half of Chester county, as far as the Schuylkill River, and a considerable portion of Virginia.

The question concerning the limits of this colony was the cause of many troubles and violent strife between its inhabitants and those of the adjacent settlements; and these disputes were not finally settled until 1818.

The expedition for colonizing the lands ceded to Lord Baltimore was confided to Leonard Calvert, one of his sons. On the 22d of November, 1633, he sailed from the Isle of Wight with two hundred emigrants of note and fortune, principally Catholics. On the 24th of February, he landed at Point Comfort, in Virginia, where now stands the fortress which commands the entrance into Hampton Roads.

The expedition again put to sea for the purpose of exploring the Chesapeake Bay; ascended the Potomac a distance of forty leagues (one hundred and twenty miles), as far as an Indian village called *Piscataway;* returned and anchored at the mouth of the Potomac in a splendid bay, which they named St. Mary; and, on the 22d of March, 1634, they finally landed on a spot where they determined to found a permanent settlement, near an Indian village *Yaocomaco*, to which they gave the name of St. Mary. The proprietors of the Maryland grant spent, in less than three years, more than four hundred thousand dollars (two million francs) on this establishment.

The population of Maryland, in 1660, amounted to twelve thousand inhabitants, most of whom were planters of tobacco. This product served the colonists as a medium of exchange for all the necessaries of life. But, in the year 1686, the legislature of Maryland authorized a new monetary standard, which was received through all the colony instead of the English pound sterling. The other colonies followed this example; and a colonial thus replaced English currency.

The colonists who had sailed with Calvert belonged, for the most part, to a class of emigrants distinguished for knowledge, and for elevated and liberal ideas. Hence, they adopted a form of government modeled on that of England. They instituted a council, resembling that of the House of Lords, composed of the most distinguished members of the colony; and a lower house, composed of members appointed directly by the inhabitants of each district.

It was declared, by law, *that no individual should be tried, troubled, or molested on account of religious opinion.* Thus, the Maryland emigrants, by making their colony a real place of refuge, where each individual could render homage to his God according to his belief, provided always that he was a Christian, gave the first striking testimony of religious toleration in the New World. A beautiful and great example, which does honor to the Catholics of those times, against whom all the other sects had combined; a circumstance, too, the more remarkable, because in New England the Puritans, who had fled from their homes in consequence of their religious opinions, persecuted themselves their Protestant fellow-citizens. And in Virginia the Episcopalians exhibited the same severity towards the Puritans—their associates in the great task of enlightening the New World.

In consequence of these persecutions, a great number of dissenting Protestants from New England and Virginia removed to Maryland, where they felt extremely happy in escaping the intolerance of their fellow-citizens, and increased the resources and prosperity of the new colony.

Another circumstance, which does equal honor to the enlightened spirit of the founders of Maryland, was the immediate adoption by the legislature of a resolution which set apart a certain portion of the colonial domain to create a school fund, out of which all the children of the colony were to be gratuitously educated.

Thus, the same men, who had just established for themselves and their descendants liberty of conscience and of opinion, did not overlook instruction—the most important of all wants of the citizens of a democracy!

In 1689, the Maryland colony was powerfully convulsed by a Protestant insurrection against the Catholics; and, in 1692, it passed under the authority of the crown of England. Sir Lionel Copley was appointed its governor. The first acts of this new political chief were to establish the supremacy of the Anglican Church, and to impose a tax on the inhabitants in favor of the clergy. At this period, both Catholics and Quakers were persecuted.

St. Mary then contained from sixty to seventy houses, and a Catholic church which had been suffered to fall in ruins. The construction of this edifice, then an imposing monument for America, had cost forty thousand pounds of tobacco—a very considerable price at that period. This church was replaced by an Episcopal chapel.

In 1710, the seat of government, which had always been at

St. Mary, was transferred to Annapolis, whose foundation, as well as that of mail establishments, dates from that period. The population of the colony was then about thirty thousand. In 1763, it amounted to one hundred and sixty-five thousand, twenty thousand of whom were convicts from England.

The colony produced about twenty-eight thousand hogsheads of tobacco, valued at three and a half million francs (seven hundred thousand dollars). Its importations may be estimated at four million francs (about eight hundred thousand dollars). At this early period, the manufacture of iron was commenced. Eight furnaces and nine forges were built, which produced annually three thousand five hundred tons of pig and six hundred tons of bar iron.

Such was the situation and such the resources of the Maryland colony when the famous struggle with England for civil liberty commenced.

NORTH CAROLINA COLONY.

The Anglo-Saxons established in New England had brought with them that spirit of emigration which so eminently distinguishes them from all other races of men—a spirit which had powerfully contributed to make that colony the parent, as it were, of all the establishments of America.

In 1663, a small colony of emigrants from New England had settled near Cape Fear, on a river of that name, and entirely beyond all the English settlements in Virginia. Carrying with them the principles of liberty and independence, these colonists claimed the right of self-government and self-administration upon lands which they had purchased directly from the natives.

The Virginians, stimulated by the same spirit of emigration, had also extended their explorations, immediately after their arrival in America, to lands known as Southern Virginia or Carolina; and, in 1663, they had founded, on Albemarle Sound, establishments under the direction of a certain George Callmaid.

In June, 1665, Clarendon, the famous historian, and the devoted minister of Charles the Second, though hated by the people, obtained a royal charter, which granted to him and his associates all the territory extending from the Atlantic to the Pacific oceans, and ranging from the twenty-ninth to the thirty-sixth degree of north latitude. This territory included all North and South Carolina, Georgia, Tennessee, Alabama, Mississippi, Louisiana, Arkansas, a great part of Florida and Missouri, and nearly all Texas, with a large portion of Mexico! This vast empire became their immediate property. They had the power to make laws, but not without the consent of the freemen, the future inhabitants of the colony. Their privileges were the same as those conceded to the proprietors of Rhode Island and Connecticut.

An important clause in the charter acknowledged the liberty of conscience. Another had reference to the advantages attached to the introduction of the colonial system into the ports of the colony. The proprietors were at liberty to create titles, constitute domains, counties, baronies, and to establish a nobility with titles different from those in England. In short, everything indicated the foundation of a vast empire in America.

The celebrated John Locke had been requested by Shaftesbury, one of the proprietors, to draft a system of government for the colonists; but the speculations and doctrines of that eminent philosopher, the fruits of elaborate labor in the closet, were found to be totally at variance with the requirements and exigencies of those for whom they were prepared.

Locke's visionary dream was the creation of an aristocracy upon American soil; but this soil could only be made to develop a pure democracy. Therefore the new constitution, adopted by the eight proprietors in 1670, could never be put in force in the colony.

The inhabitants of Albemarle, at that period, more numerous than at any other point, adopted simple forms and laws, strictly in harmony with their necessities. The first popular assembly was held in 1667, in the county of Albemarle.

North Carolina was, for a long time, considered the rendezvous of all who had good reason to fly their country. Emigrants were found there from all countries—English, Scotch, Irish, French, Germans from the Palatinate, and Swiss. The latter founded the town of New Berne, upon the River Neuse.

The government of the colony remained for a great number of years subject to that of South Carolina, from which it originated. Notwithstanding the difficulties under which this colony labored in establishing an independent and stable form of government, and notwithstanding the turbulent spirit which long characterized its inhabitants, who were strangers to each other, it still increased more rapidly than South Carolina.

COLONY OF SOUTH CAROLINA.

The first settlements of this colony owed their origin to the speculative spirit of its proprietors; but increased only after the inhabitants had established for themselves an independent administration.

In 1670, a certain number of emigrants, under the guidance of Joseph West, had settled at Beaufort; but, not finding this locality advantageous, they had abandoned it, and founded another establishment on the nearest highlands of Ashley River. They immediately formed their administration upon the basis of liberty and independence, and inaugurated their representative system in 1672.

But Shaftesbury had not renounced the hope that the principles of the constitution drawn up and revised by Locke would yet prevail in the colony. The result proved the error of his judgment; for, while the superior council in London approved this constitution, the popular representation in the colony opposed it strenuously. Hence, South Carolina owed its political existence to a rupture between the partisans of the Established Church and the Reformers.

In 1680, the emigrants, finding that the position of their settlement on Ashley River was very unfavorable in a commercial point of view, determined to form an establishment at the confluence of Ashley and Cooper Rivers. To their new town they gave the name of *Charleston,* in honor of King Charles the Second. The population of this town increased rapidly, by reason of the influx of white emigrants and slaves, which had left Barbadoes under the guidance of Sir J. Yeamans.

The growth of this colony was greatly favored by the political and religious intolerance which, about this period, weighed so heavily upon Scotland, as well as by the arrival of a number of Dutch emigrants from New York, after its conquest by the English.

England and Ireland also furnished their quota of emigrants; and France, where the revocation of the edict of Nantes had just given to the Huguenots a fresh blow, furnished this colony, as well as other quarters of the globe, and even England, with its choicest blood, in relation to industry and intellectual culture.

At all points of the American Union, we can at this day see living proofs of the fatal emigration which impoverished France, and enriched other nations; but this emigration was most considerable in South Carolina and Virginia, where its influence was mostly exerted over the morals of the country, in preserving the intelligent, impassioned, and liberal stamp of their French origin.

The population of this colony was further augmented, at a somewhat later period, by inhabitants from Acadia, who were transported to Charleston by order of the English government, which had despoiled them of their property.

From 1685 to 1690 the colony experienced great internal difficulties in consequence of the pretensions and fiscal exactions of the proprietors, through the medium of Governor Colleton. But though disposed to employ military force to compel the execution of his will, he could not find in the country, fortunately for the colony, any organized troops, except the citizen soldiers; and these, strongly opposed to such acts of violence, took part with the people.

Upon the accession of William and Mary, Colleton's powers were revoked, Seth Sethell was appointed in his place, and the representative system was re-established. This form of government ever after prevailed without interruption.

In 1691, the government of the colony established a system of national defence, to protect the inhabitants from the incursions of the Indians and Spaniards in Florida, founded arsenals, created a revenue, and admitted the French Huguenot refugees to a participation of all the rights of citizenship.

In 1693, it was decided that the legislative assembly should meet twice a year—a system which, with slight modifications, exists at the present day.

The form of the governmental administration resembled that of Maryland.

The proprietors appointed the members of the superior council. The people elected the members of the assembly. The defence of the country was confided to the militia.

The people rejected the principles which the Revolution of

1688 had still preserved in England—namely, the recognition of a nobility, and the legitimate right to power, conferred by property.

The rights of political franchise were granted to all the inhabitants, indiscriminately, and without reference to their religious opinions; but the Established Church was recognized as that of the province.

The cultivation of rice, by slave labor, which became one of the principal productions of the soil, was introduced into the colony towards the end of the seventeenth century.

We may conclude, from the preceding remarks, that it is in the seventeenth century that the English made the most fortunate and persevering efforts to colonize the New World—where, starting from a single point, affording them scarcely a foot of soil, they gradually extended their influence from Maine to Florida, a territory including twelve degrees of latitude, founding, in their progress, twelve distinct colonies: Portsmouth, New Hampshire, Massachusetts Bay, Connecticut, Rhode Island, New York, New Jersey, Pennsylvania, Delaware, Maryland, Virginia, and North and South Carolina—and that each of these movements has been marked, first by the invasion of the soil of the natives, then by the invasion of the territory of the French, Dutch, and Swedes.

At the close of the seventeenth century, the population of the New England colonies amounted to one-half of that of all the other English colonies, then estimated at about two hundred and fifty thousand, and was ten times more numerous than that of New France, with which it was in a constant state of contention.

The consequence of these contests, provoked as much by the desire of obtaining the navigation of the St. Lawrence and the fertile regions of the west, as by hatred of the doctrines and principles professed by the Canadians, was that the three colonies of Massachusetts, Connecticut, and New York formed an offensive and defensive compact, in which the Governor of Massachusetts took the initiative. This congress was held at New York.

Hence, Massachusetts, which has given birth to several States, now very justly claims the honour of having given the first idea of the *American Union.*

The question of the conquest of Canada was discussed, during this congress, as a measure in which the prosperity of the three colonies was equally interested; and a plan of campaign was devised.

Thus, these colonies, whose governments were based upon the principles of pure democracy and of liberty of conscience and opinion, found in themselves, and in their organization, means not only to maintain order within their own limits, but also to project the conquest of a foreign colony without the assistance of England.

CHAPTER X.

1660—1671.

FRENCH COLONIES—CANADA, OR NEW FRANCE.

Parallel drawn between the origin of the French and that of the English colonies—La Mothe-Cadillac—Zeal and courage of the missionaries—Levying of tithes by the clergy—West India Company—M. de Tracy—Renewal of hostilities by the Iroquois; by the Anglo-Americans—Attack on Port Royal—Freedom of trade restored to Canada—New coin put in circulation—It is replaced by paper money—Marquette establishes the post of St. Mary—Convocation of the Indian nations at St. Mary—The intendant Talon—Posts founded on Lakes Ontario and Erie—French names designate the principal geographical points of the northwest—Establishment of Fort Cataracouy, also called Frontenac.

We conceived it necessary to suspend the historical summary of the colonization of New France in 1660, that we might exclusively take up that of the English colonies, the history of which we have brought down to the close of the seventeenth century. We shall now continue our narrative from the point at which we left off, and bring it down to the same period. Preliminary to this, however, we shall briefly contrast the methods of colonization pursued by the English and French, relative to their respective establishments.

What particularly strikes us, in the progress of the English establishments in America, is that England has always granted her people full liberty to emigrate to her colonies, by themselves and for themselves, whatever may have been their religious belief. Hence, among these colonists private interest has, from the commencement, induced a degree of enterprise and industry wholly unparalleled. This energy secured the success of the colonies, and was the primary cause of the present prosperity of the American Union.

France, on the contrary, had long deliberated upon the plan of an establishment in America, before she took any active part in colonization: she assumed to foresee everything, to order everything, to regulate everything. She could not be induced to rely upon the conduct and intelligence of the colonists, whom she reproached with narrow-mindedness. Catholics only were received in her colonies.

The Anglo-Americans at first devoted themselves to agriculture, which they constantly extended and improved, despite the spirit of conquest, invasion, and even of spoliation, which so often impelled them against the natives, or Europeans, whose rivalry they feared. Their commercial enterprises began at a later period.

The French government, which, from its immutable principles of administration, directed everything in America as in France, instead of encouraging the colonists in cultivating the soil, thought only of the advantages to be derived from the fur trade, and of the means by which that trade might be augmented. The only port in France which received direct profit from this source was Marseilles.

Hence, the establishments of New France were created in a spirit altogether military, with the avowed object of obtaining the greatest possible monopoly of the fur trade with the natives. As a consequence of this system, all the colonists, without exception, owed blind obedience to a purely military authority.

The progress of laws being unknown among the colonists, the arbitrary will of a governor, of his lieutenants, or of his commanders of posts, was an oracle from which there was no appeal. Entire submission was expected and enforced.

The government held the power of pardon and punishment, of advancement and dismissal; so much so, that it could make the people believe that its caprices and even tyranny were acts of justice.

Absolute power extended not only to subjects belonging to the military service or to the political administration, but to the civil jurisdiction. The governor arbitrarily decided every case that came before him, without appeal. This authority was maintained until 1663, when a judicial tribunal was created at Quebec.

Parisian customs, modified by a few local combinations, served as a code of laws for the colony.

It may easily be conceived that, under such a system, it was difficult for these establishments to flourish: hence, notwithstanding the zeal and courageous devotion of a few individuals, New France made but little progress. While a military despotism and religious fanaticism paralyzed the activity and industrial energy of the French colonists, freedom of conscience and opinion gave a powerful impulse to the adventurous spirit of the English, who were soon able to wrest from the French the fisheries on the grand banks, and their fur trade, even at their very doors.

In 1660, the enterprising and intelligent La Mothe-Cadillac established a post at Detroit, whose advantages, he foresaw, were so great as to insure the trade with the Indians of the interior, and control that of the lakes. The Jesuit missionaries had already a perfect knowledge of the admirable communication presented by this chain of lakes. They had, in their indefatigable zeal, planted the cross upon the borders of the Wabash, named by them St. Jerome, and upon the Mississippi; and numerous tribes of natives came in crowds to listen to their persuasive words. Wherever these pious soldiers of the cross penetrated, they installed a *mission*, and raised a chapel, which served also as a boundary to the vast domain conquered for New France. It was at this period, and in this manner, that the posts and missions of Michilimakinac, the Bay of St. Joseph, Fond du Lac, and the Sault St. Marie, were founded.

By means of their zeal and perseverance, they succeeded in creating among the Indians a marked predilection for the French. On the one hand, the missionaries studied the language of the Indians, and adapted themselves to their character and inclinations; in a word, they used all proper means to gain their confidence. On the other hand, the French colonists, far from teaching their savage brethren the manners of Europe, assumed those of the countries they inhabited—their indolence in time of peace, their activity in a state of war, and their love of a wandering and vagabond life. In short, a great number adopted their habits of life, and continued to dwell among them.

The colony of New France owed its origin, in a great measure, to religious influence; consequently, in 1663, the clergy demanded and obtained of the ministry in France *one-thirteenth of all the benefits of the land*, the *produce of the soil, and of the labor of the colonists.* This taxation, intolerable in a country still so sparsely settled, lasted four years, when the superior council of Quebec, in 1667, assumed the responsibility of reducing it to *one-twenty-sixth.*

The titles of the company created by Richelieu expired in 1663. *Their lordships of New France* then tendered their resignation to Louis the Fourteenth. They had enriched themselves, but had done little for the real advancement of the colony; and New France, the child of monopoly, was only relieved from this incubus to be pressed down by another under the form of the West India Company, created, in 1664, with privileges extending over a period of forty years. Louis the Fourteenth, however, consented to take the country under his royal protection. He sent a regiment to protect the colony from the attacks of the Indians, and appointed Tracy viceroy, Courcelles governor, and Talon intendant of civil affairs.

The king's troops arrived very opportunely; for the Indians, instigated by the English, greatly alarmed the several French establishments on the St. Lawrence, and on the shores of the lakes. They pillaged and destroyed everything that lay in their route. Falling suddenly upon a few huts, they massacred all their inhabitants. The panic had reached its height among the French establishments. So great was the daring of the Indians that they had several times boarded small vessels, laden with merchandise, even under the walls of Quebec.

The Governor of Canada, resolving to attack the Mohawks during the winter of 1665, marched into their country amidst the greatest privations and fatigues. But the Indians had abandoned their forests, and the expedition was unattended with any important results. Fort Chably was founded during this march.

But this augmentation of force restored the advantage which the French had lost over the Iroquois, who were thus compelled to make peace. By the treaty concluded with this nation, it was stipulated that their territory should remain forever attached to the domain of New France.

War having been declared, in 1666, by Louis the Fourteenth against the English, in favor of Holland, the commencement of hostilities completely checked the commerce of Canada. The

Anglo-Americans, profiting by the opportunity this circumstance afforded to enable them to appropriate to themselves the trade with the Indians, managed their operations with exceeding adroitness. They offered the natives for their furs merchandise of better quality and at lower prices than the French factors could afford. In fact, with the French, the monopoly of buying and selling was in the hands of the agents of the West India Company, whilst with the English trade was entirely unrestricted, that is to say, all the colonists participated, in an equal degree, in its benefits. Competition produced a fall in the price of merchandise, and liberty thus killed monopoly.

Port Royal was again attacked by a considerable force, and taken; but it was restored at the peace of Breda in 1667.

In 1668, the West India Company, not having complied with the obligations attached to their prerogative of monopolizing the commerce of the French possessions in America, was constrained to renounce this privilege, and from that day commerce, thus opened to all Frenchmen, soon received a salutary impulse.

But the colonies were then almost without financial resources; for, if the monopoly had enriched a few chiefs, the mass of the colonists were without means. To relieve them from a condition so disadvantageous, it was proposed to manufacture a new coin for all the establishments in America, with an ideal value one-fourth higher than the specie circulating in the metropolis. This expedient did not realize the advantage it promised; and paper money was necessarily substituted for the payment of the troops, and for other expenses of the government.

In 1668, the missionary, James Marquette, established the mission of St. Mary. By reason of his relations with the Indians on the shores of the Mississippi, and the information furnished him by his companion, Father Allouez, he formed the project of the discovery of this river, which he executed in 1669.

The natives called this river *Messipi*, or *Meschasipi*, which signifies *river everywhere*—from the word *missi* or *minsi*, everywhere, and *sipi*, river; because, when this river overflows its banks, its waters inundate the whole valley. According to the Illinois, this river also bore the name of *Meschagamisi*, or more frequently *Messesipy* or *Meschasipy*, all river, or great river. The French named it, alternately, Colbert River, St. Louis River, and Barbauches River.

In 1670, under the administration of the intendant Talon, and through the intervention of the agent Perrot, a meeting of the native tribes was called at the St. Mary's mission. Its object was to propose a vast plan for the extension of French domination to the most distant points of the American continent. It was announced to the various tribes which met there from the borders of the Missouri, Mississippi, Wabash, and Arkansas, that thereafter they would be under the protection of the great king. Thus was determined by the action of the military chiefs, assisted by the Jesuits, their zealous companions, the extension of the French empire in the New World from the mouths of the St. Lawrence to the mouths of the Mississippi. At this grand epoch in the history of France, the feeling of national honor was all-powerful among the people and chiefs of the State! Military posts were established at Detroit and at Michilimakinac; and the Indian trade on the borders of the Mississippi was insured against the depredations and attacks of the Iroquois.

New establishments were founded during this year on Lake Ontario and Lake Erie, which had been explored some years before. The French officers and missionaries had been particularly struck with the advantageous position of Lake Erie, as the centre of communication between the St. Lawrence and the chain of upper lakes, by the occupation of which they would have the control of the trade as well as of the native hordes who lived on their shores. At this period in the history of the French colonies, every effort tended to the same object—the extension and strengthening of French domination in America.

At that time, France had attained a rank and an ascendency among the European powers which gave to the national feeling an energy which animated all classes of men. The effect of this feeling upon the chiefs of the colony of New France was highly salutary.

Every new step they took in these unknown regions was marked by an honorable seal of their conquest. French names everywhere marked the places they had surveyed, and the points where they made settlements.

In this way, the names of *St. Louis* and *Frontenac* were given to Lake Ontario, and that of *Conti* to Lake Erie. *Ontario*, in the language of the Iroquois, signifies beautiful lake. They also named it *Skenin-Donig*, very beautiful lake. *Erié*, or *Erigé*, or

Erické, which they sometimes designated by the name of *Tciæ-harontiong*, signifies Cat, the name of the nation that lived on its borders.

The name of *Orleans* was given to Lake Huron,* also called *Kenegnondi*, or *Algonkin Michigauge*.

Lake Michigan, named *Dauphin*, was also known as Lake of the Illinois or of the Illinouach, or of men—the word Illinois signifying a mature man. The Miami nation, who frequented the borders of this lake, often gave it the name of *Mischigonong*, or Great Lake.

During the entire period of French domination, Lake Superior was known as *Lake Tracy* or *Condé*.

In 1671, the post of Frontenac, at the mouth of little Catarocouy Bay, was founded. It is situated where Lake Ontario empties into the River St. Lawrence, and was designed to protect the commerce of the lakes, and that of the St. Lawrence; to cover a communication from the lakes with Quebec; and to defend an excellent anchorage, where the boats and canoes could take shelter. These small vessels formed, at that time, all the merchant marine and navy of those countries.

Kingston is now built upon this post, one of the most important cities of Upper Canada, communicating directly with Montreal by the Rideau Canal and the Ottowa River. The distance between these two cities is two hundred and forty miles, and may be accomplished by steamboats; while by the St. Lawrence navigation was only practicable for small boats.

* Huron is of Canadian origin, and was given to the Indians living on that lake, because of their burnt hair, which made the head look like that of a wild boar.

CHAPTER XI.

1671—1700.

FRENCH COLONY—NEW FRANCE.

Discovery of the Mississippi by Marquette and Joliet—Voyage of Robert Cavalier de la Salle—Discovery of the mouth of the Mississippi—He establishes the post of the Illinois, and indicates the line of posts necessary to unite his new discoveries with the Canadian domain—Critical situation of Canada; M. de la Barre assembles the notables—Policy of the Indians towards the Europeans—M. de Denonville—M. de Champagny—Montreal almost destroyed by the Iroquois—The English colonies project the conquest of Canada—Attack and fall of Port Royal —Montreal and Quebec are also attacked, but resist—Port Royal retaken by the French—Post of Nekoat on the St. John—M. de Frontenac governor; he finally compels the Indians to make peace—Territorial extent of the French and English possessions—Population of these colonies.

We now come to one of the most interesting periods in the history of the colonies of New France, to that when the majestic Mississippi, until then unknown, was explored through its whole course by one of those brave and zealous missionaries, whose faith led them daily to expose their lives for the salvation of a soul.

Great and brilliant period, when religious faith, combined with patriotism, induced the sons of France to undertake the most laborious enterprises with the utmost disinterestedness!

In 1673, Father Marquette, a Jesuit, with soft and bland manners, and the Sieur Joliet, an inhabitant of Quebec, a very intelligent and brave man, undertook their expedition for the discovery of the Mississippi. These two gentlemen, equally active, enterprising, and devoted, left Green Bay, on Lake Michigan, accompanied by five Frenchmen and two Miami Indians, acting as guides and interpreters. On the 10th of June, they entered the Fox River, which empties into the lake, ascended it to its sources, and embarked on the Wisconsin, through which they reached the Mississippi. Descending this river, they passed the *Moingona*, now the Des Moines, in Iowa territory, some leagues below the mouth of the Missouri, known by the Algonquins as *Pekitaroni*, and, after sailing to the south several days, they passed the mouth of the Ohio, then known as the *Wabash*, after the Indian tribe which inhabited its borders. This magnificent river was also called *Hohio*, *Oua-Bous-Ki-Qua*, or *Akou-Ssa-Sipi*, the beautiful river.

They continued their navigation of the Mississippi, in the midst of innumerable islands, which often led them to doubt whether they were not in a great lake instead of a river. They at last reached the mouth of a large river, flowing from the west, the Arkansas, when, their provisions growing short, they were compelled to retrace their steps. They reascended the Illinois River, which Father Marquette named *Divine*, so astonished was the party with the stillness and smoothness of its waters. At a later period, it received the name of Governor Seignelay. They reached Green Bay in the month of September. Two years after this intrepid adventure, Father Marquette, already advanced in life—his constitution broken by long and excessive fatigues, privations, and abstinences—but ever zealous in his faith, undertook a journey from Chicago, on Lake Michigan, to the post of Michilimakinac. When this venerable father placed his foot on the shore, he advanced a short distance into the woods, according to his pious custom, to offer his tribute of devotion to God. When his companions approached him, to continue their journey, he had ceased to live. He had calmly expired in the midst of prayer, in the presence of his God! The river, on the shores of which Marquette ended his pious and laborious career, is in Michigan, and to this day bears his name.

About this period, Robert Cavalier de la Salle conceived the project of journeying overland to the Gulf of Mexico. Through the intervention of M. de Seignelay, and the favor of the minister Colbert, the king gave his consent to the enterprise. In this memorable journey, he was accompanied by his devoted friend M. de Tonty, an old tried soldier, who had lost his hand in Sicily. These bold and fearless explorers left Fort Frontenac, on Lake Ontario, the 7th of August, 1679, on board of a decked vessel of sixty tons, the first sail vessel that had ever ploughed the waters of this inland sea. After having overcome innumerable difficulties, and escaped the great dangers that the traveler must necessarily encounter in an unknown country, among Indian hordes, on whose dispositions no dependence can be placed, they at length arrived, on the 7th of April, 1682, in sight of the Gulf of Mexico, at the mouth of the Mississippi. About the 15th of July, of the same year, they had returned to Michilimakinac.

In the course of this expedition, they erected Fort Crevecœur on the borders of Lake Pimiteoni, part of the Illinois River, which was afterwards called *Fort St. Louis.* Fort Prud'homme was constructed one hundred and eighty miles above its mouth. The post of Arkansas was founded by M. de la Salle; Fort Chicago on Lake Superior; and Fort St. Louis upon the Chicago River, near the Aramoni. Finally, the post of Kaskaskia, or Conception, the seat of a Jesuit mission, became an important station in the progress of the French towards the west.

While the French were extending their conquests over the vast solitudes of the western countries, there was a complete stagnation of all kinds of business in the colonies. The resources of the country were not sufficient to cover the expenses of merchandise received from Europe, which was of the last importance to the colonists.

The extreme activity of the inhabitants of New England, and their intimate knowledge of business, induced them to venture wherever they could realize a profit; consequently, they anticipated the French everywhere in their trade with the natives. Hence, resulted the great indebtedness of the Canadian colonists to the mother country.

In this critical situation, the Governor-General De la Barre consulted the country upon the measures most likely to obviate these difficulties. He convoked a provisionary legislative council called the *Notables*, submitted to them the languid condition of the colony, and asked an expression of their opinion. Under such circumstances, it might have been expected that the colonists would have prayed for franchises and commercial freedom, as means of giving new life to their society. But no! After long deliberation, *they decided upon addressing a petition to the king, praying for a stronger garrison in Canada!*

Strange conclusion! which singularly contrasts with the examples of independence and courage set them by the inhabitants of the English colonies, even from the very infancy of their social and political life in America, and especially with that act of independence and strength which marked the history of the English colonies. At the period these colonies were projecting the conquest of Canada, without the assistance of the mother country, the French were imploring the power of the metropolis to protect them against a few Indians!

In fact, what could be expected from men, transplanted from the European to the American soil, with ideas of military hierarchy, administrative subordination, dependence upon a chief, and religious submission? These, it is true, made them enlightened subjects, but not enlightened citizens!

With the English emigrant, the principle of political liberty had been imbibed before departing from his native land, and on his arrival upon American soil, his institutions naturally assumed a democratic form. With the French emigrant, the principles of absolute power, military and religious despotism, had been transferred, in all their vigor, from the metropolis to the colony of New France. England had left her colonies to organize themselves more or less according to their pleasure. France had fashioned Canada after its own image, and had bestowed upon it its manners, laws, language, and temper.

Canada could, at that time, place at least three thousand men under arms, a number almost equal to that of the Iroquois warriors; but the Iroquois were freemen, while the inhabitants of New France were crushed by despotism and monopoly. The Iroquois recruited their force by adopting prisoners taken from other nations. No foreigner or heretic could settle in Canada. Hence, the war with these warlike natives had continued from the first settlement of the French on the continent, and did not cease till about a century afterwards, when this brave tribe had almost entirely disappeared.

On the arrival of the Europeans, the Indians, without distrust, had hailed them as friends, brothers, and guests; they soon perceived, when it was too late, that these guests became their masters, and could not be driven away; that, besides, they were constantly menaced with the dispossession of their heritage. Nevertheless, they discovered that these guests belonged to two different castes, very jealous of each other. From that instant, they determined to profit by the hatred which divided the two rival nations, and resolved that, since they could not succeed in expelling the *Manetonakis*, Europeans, they would at least manfully oppose their future encroachments. With this object in view, they ceased to employ their own strength favorably or adversely to either party. Thus, in 1684, observing that the French were gaining too great an ascendency over the English, they detached themselves from the former, and joined the opposite party.

Governor de la Barre, with the object of chastising the Iroquois, placed himself at the head of six hundred soldiers, four hundred followers, and three hundred garrison troops, and made an expedition to Fort Sable, which occupied a position near the outlet of the present Rideau Canal. But the diseases incident to the month of August, in those marshy and swampy countries, so decimated his little army, that he was obliged to abandon this post, and treat with the Indians.

In 1685, M. de Denonville succeeded M. de la Barre, and arrived in Canada with fresh troops. The animosities existing between the inhabitants of New England and those of New France daily increased, and soon reached to such a pitch that the conquest of Canada became clearly the design of the Anglo-Americans. Their desire to possess this beautiful country was stimulated by their hatred of legitimacy, and of the ancient forms of Christianity of which the Canadians were the representatives in the New World. These various passions of the inhabitants of New England were so violent, that they served as a common tie between the mother country and its colonies, relative to the aggressive projects which had long been entertained by the crown of England against the French possessions in America.

In 1686, M. de Champigny succeeded M. de Denonville as Governor of Canada. Under his administration, the post of Niagara was established, for the purpose of controlling the movements of the Iroquois upon the lakes; and the post of St. Charles, at the mouth of the Illinois River. These two forts completed the system of occupation of the newly-conquered territory of the Indians. Champigny's object was, first, to furnish advantageous positions against the Indians. Secondly, to protect and extend the fur trade. Thirdly, to circumvent the English colonies, to confine them to the shores of the Atlantic, and prevent them from making a descent upon the tributaries of the great Valley of the Mississippi, and thereby keep them from advancing towards the west.

This system had been adopted and pursued from the first occupation of the country. For this plan, the French were principally indebted to the superior genius and rare intelligence of La Salle, who, having anticipated the future state of New France, attempted, from the commencement, to secure his dominion upon the two great valleys of the St. Lawrence and Mississippi, and consequently, upon the most beautiful and important portion of the American continent.

These views were certainly very expansive. The plan was vast, the dispositions judicious; but the colony needed a population capable of sustaining so extended a line, and the garrisons of regular troops at those posts were so weak that the English traders dared to penetrate into the French territory, and traffick with impunity in sight of the post of Michilimakinac.

They had been obliged to abandon Fort Bourbon upon the River Thérese, in Hudson's Bay. This place, by the private enterprise of the English, had been immediately re-occupied in 1689, and named Fort Nelson.

In August, 1689, a very numerous party of Iroquois made a descent upon Montreal, which, being feebly defended, was taken and almost entirely destroyed.

This irruption was instigated by the colonists of New England, whose every thought and act had immediate relation to the conquest of Canada.

Finally, the English colonies, with the object of putting their plan in execution, conceived the idea of a congress. This congress was suggested by the Governor of Massachusetts, and was held in New York. Its object was to secure an alliance of the colonists against the Indians, to protect their frontier.

At this congress, it was resolved to undertake the conquest of Canada; and that, for this purpose, an attack should be made upon Montreal, through Lake Champlain, while an expedition by sea should be directed against Quebec.

In 1690, Port Royal was attacked, and, being poorly defended, was easily taken. The establishment of *Cheboucto*, now Halifax, was also seized, and settled by freebooters. But the attack by land on Montreal, as well as that upon Quebec, resulted less fortunately for the English colonists. The combined fleets of Boston and of England, composed of thirty-two sail, carried two thousand men, recruited in New England. Boston had also sent a land expedition, guided and supported by the Iroquois. When these forces arrived in sight of Quebec, the Indians, by a return of their capricious policy relative to the two rival nations, suddenly refused to second the views of the Anglo-Americans. The withdrawal of the Iroquois determined that of the Boston militia, and Quebec again escaped the covetousness of the Anglo-Americans.

In 1691, a single French man-of-war succeeded in retaking Port Royal. The post of Nekoat was established upon the River St. John; and the French government projected the recapture of Newfoundland, by sending some vessels and fresh reinforcements to the posts in Acadia.

In 1696, the English attempted to capture the post on the River St. John; but were repulsed with loss.

This year was equally fortunate for French domination in Canada. M. Louis de Buade, Count de Frontenac, then Governor-General of New France, undertook an expedition, in the month of July, against the Iroquois, and succeeded in reducing them to complete subjection. At length, the peace of Riswick, signed in 1697, caused a cessation of calamities in Europe, and of hostilities in America.

Thus, at the close of the seventeenth century, France had the incontestable right of property, not only to New France, Acadia, Hudson's Bay, and Newfoundland, but also to one-half of Maine, Vermont, and New York, to all the valley of the Mississippi, and Texas as far as the Rio del Norte, by reason of the discoveries of La Salle. After the peace of Riswick, she retained all Hudson's Bay, and all the places in her possession at the commencement of the war. That is to say, with the exception of the eastern half of Newfoundland, France retained one-half of all the coast from Maine to Labrador, Hudson's Bay, Canada, and all the valley of the Mississippi.

Upon the coast, England claimed as far as the River St. Croix, and extended her supremacy to the capes of Florida. The French claimed a part of Maine as far as the Kennebec.

The boundaries of the province of New York were more difficult to settle. The French claimed all the western part of the territory, which they had conquered from the Iroquois, the original proprietors of the land.

In fine, the preponderance of French arms extended over three-fourths of the American continent, that is to say, over a territory

9

comprising more than four hundred and fifty million *hectares*,* which communicated directly by the St. Lawrence with the Atlantic, through the Mississippi, to the Gulf of Mexico, and extended from the chain of the Apalachian or Alleghany Mountains, on the east, to the borders of the Pacific Ocean.

The territory occupied by the English, including about ninety-one million *hectares*, was situated between the principal chain of the Alleghanies and the shores of the Atlantic, and extended along the coast from Maine to Florida.

The territory of Florida, included in this estimate, was, however, occupied by the Spaniards; but its population exercised only a feeble influence.

The domination of France was based upon the occupation of a few posts scattered over this immense territory, with a population of about twelve thousand inhabitants. That of England was firmly settled upon a territory three times less extensive, but with a population twenty times greater than that of the French.

In short, the principle of absolute monarchy had succeeded in founding, in the course of a century, through the influence of the army and of the clergy, a colony of twelve thousand inhabitants; while the democratic principle had, by its mighty moral influence, created, in the same time, twelve distinct colonies, with a population numbering two hundred and fifty thousand, united by the same social tendencies, and the same desire for conquest.

* A little more than two French acres.—Tr.

CHAPTER XII.

1700—1750.

FRENCH COLONIES—NEW FRANCE.

Settlement of Detroit by M. la Mothe-Cadillac—The Canadians refuse to pay the tithe—Governor Collières—De Vaudreuil—Canal near Montreal—Renewed hostilities in America—Attack on Port Royal—Expedition against Acadia—Capture of Port Royal—Attack on Quebec—Peace of Utrecht—Commencement of the wars for commercial advantages—Settlement of Breton, or Royal Island—Brotherhood of St. Sulpicius—Sieur Vincennes—Colony of the Isle St. John—Fortifications of Louisburg—Lewistown—Charlevoix in America—Posts of Toulouse, Dauphin, and Névieka—Bed of coal in Acadia—Quebec and Montreal; their importance—M. de Varendry crosses from the borders of the St. Lawrence to the Pacific coast—Foundation of Halifax—The people of New England contemplate the conquest of New France—Capture of Port Royal—M. de la Galissonnière adopts means of resistance against the encroachments of the Anglo-Americans—Ohio officially taken possession of—Colonization of the western countries—Population of New France; its resources; its revenues.

The colonization of New France, under the Count de Frontenac, advanced with rapidity. Emigrants were principally sent to the western regions, the importance of which had just been appreciated.

In fact, nothing can be found, in Europe, comparable with these regions, as to richness and fertility of soil. Situated in the temperate zone, they are watered by numerous rivers, for the most part navigable for great distances, and connected, through an inland sea, with the Atlantic by the New York canals, and with the Gulf of Mexico by the Mississippi and its tributaries. This country abounds in vast prairies, immense forests, and wild fruit trees. Luxuriant vines form a dense shade, which shelters the bison and the wild bull, deers, hinds, and a multitude of the feathered tribe, such as the pintado or guinea fowl, the pheasant, the lark, the partridge, the woodcock, the turtle dove, and green parrots, smaller than those of the islands.

The rivers are covered with swans, wild geese, ducks, teal,

and bustards. It is a chance if these aquatic birds will get out of the way to allow your boat to pass.

The forests produce trees of an immense and majestic growth, and as straight as an arrow, the pecan tree, the white oak, the red oak, the hickory, the ash, the cotton tree, the tulip tree. The proud eagle soars incessantly over these giants of the forest.

Detroit received a garrison of one hundred men, and its government was confided to M. la Mothe-Cadillac, then commandant of Mackinaw, who had a direct grant of it, on condition that he would there form a settlement. To appreciate the importance of this grant, it must be known that it extended from Lake Erie to Lake Huron, running one hundred and sixty-five miles along the Detroit River. In addition to the French, he invited some Indian tribes, which he had had the address to attract around him and bind together, to settle on his territory, so as to secure his authority over the Indians as well as the body of his colonists.

He had, according to their number, made different grants to his settlers. For example, to a large family he gave from four to six acres fronting the Detroit River, and twenty-five acres extending into the woods; to lesser families, two acres front by twenty-five in depth.

The land thus granted to the Indians was to belong to them only so long as they should remain on it. Should they change their residence, the property was to return to the domain of M. de la Mothe-Cadillac.

M. de la Mothe also possessed in fee simple the Island of Mount Desert, on the coast of Maine, nearly forty-two miles in circumference. It was wrested from him by the English, as well as his fisheries, hunting grounds, commerce, and his freehold of Port Royal.

This system of apportioning lands existed throughout New France. The lords had the large, the laborers the small shares. Moreover, the conditions entered into with the working classes were such, that these gifts offered poor encouragement to settlers; because they were, for the most part, liable to fines, and trammeled with innumerable and varied charges that equaled the exactions of a lord from his vassal in the palmy days of the feudal system.

For example, the farmer was required to pay his lord, at his castle or principal residence, on the 20th of March, an annual rent of five livres,* and ten livres in furs. He was obliged to till his lands within the first three months after he had received his grant, under penalty of losing his rights. Every year he was obliged to erect, or assist in raising, a May-pole in front of the principal manor house, or pay three livres either in specie or in furs.

His grain was to be ground at the liege lord's mill, and toll to be paid for it. He could not sell his property without the permission of the lord of the manor. The duties and expenses of sale were paid by the farmer.

During the first ten years of this grant, no mechanic, such as a locksmith, blacksmith, armorer, or brasier, could settle there without a special permit from his lord.

The State reserved to itself all the building timber, for fortifications, ships, or boats.

The farmer or landed proprietor could not sell merchandize, as this monopoly was reserved for special agents. The sale of brandy to Indians was expressly prohibited.

Such were the principal conditions attached to the possession of property—that fundamental basis of the prosperity of a country. Hence it followed that such a system, so discouraging to purchasers, attracted but few settlers.

A system of military despotism was also imposed on Canada—a most effectual means of crushing the seeds of prosperity, which were one day to convert that country into so rich an empire.

As a result of this untoward system, France sent to her colonies subaltern agents to trade for furs, instead of actual settlers, an immeasurably superior source of wealth, by which France might eventually have acquired immense power in the New World.

The threats of the people of New England, and their frequent attacks on the possessions of New France, at last provoked, among a people generally so mild and indolent, the determination to make reprisals against their ambitious aggressors. M. de Chivy proposed to direct an expedition against Boston; and its execution was several times pressed upon the government, which, always too weak for its own defence, was far from being able to second any plan of attack upon its neighbors.

Of all the onerous charges imposed upon the colonists of New

* A livre is about the fifth of a dollar.—Tr.

France, the tithe was the most intolerable. The clergy of Canada, although rich and powerful, urged their claims by all the means in their power; and the Bishop of Quebec issued an ordinance, threatening to refuse to administer absolution or the communion to the refractory.

The king's minister, on becoming acquainted with these difficulties, interposed and secured an arrangement by which the prelate was to receive but one-half in cash. The other half was to be paid, at the end of the summer, to the parish curates, thus relieving the colonists of the necessity of directly taking it to the episcopal see.

Collières, appointed Governor of Canada in 1700, had always desired to establish friendly relations with the English. On the 1st of August, 1701, he collected together deputations from the Ottowas, Abenaquis, Iroquois, Hurons, Algonquins, Miamis, Sacks, Illinois, Outagamis, and other tribes; he explained to them his conciliatory views, and concluded a treaty of peace, which was invested with the different signs that characterize these nations.

Canada soon lost M. de Collières, the pacificator of the Indians. M. de Vaudreuil succeeded him in 1703.

The Sieur de Brulay, in the course of 1704, commenced a small canal near Montreal.

The hostilities between France and England, during the War of the Succession, soon extended to their American colonies.

On the 2d of July, 1704, an English squadron, sailing from Boston, appeared in the basin of Port Royal, and summoned the place to surrender; while another squadron, penetrating into the Bay of Fundy, entered Beau Bassin, to secure a diversion. The advantage was on the side of the French, and the enemy was compelled to re-embark.

Two more formidable expeditions were formed, in 1707, by the Governor-General of New England.

A fleet of eighty vessels appeared, in June, in sight of Port Royal. Three thousand men invested the fortress, but experienced such heavy losses that they were obliged to retire, after having carried off a number of animals, and burned the dwellings outside of the place.

During the same year, a second expedition was attempted

against Port Royal, and was also victoriously repulsed by the Governor of Acadia, the brave Subercaze.

England then formed the project of invading Canada. For this purpose, an army from the English colonies was to be seconded by a naval force, equipped either in America or in England. But Governor Vaudreuil had taken all the measures necessary to cover the threatened points. The land expedition failed, while the squadron, which was to have been sent into the St. Lawrence, received in Europe another destination.

Each year fresh enterprises were formed against the French possessions in Canada. While the English colonies continued to be powerfully seconded by the mother country, the French colonies did not even receive assistance.

Finally, in 1710, a naval expedition, much superior to the former, was directed against Acadia. It consisted of six English and thirty American vessels, with three thousand four hundred soldiers on board. The force of Subercaze consisted only of three hundred.

The courage of a handful of men was ineffectual against such an overwhelming force. After thirteen days of courageous resistance, they were forced to capitulate; but they evacuated the place with the honors of war. Only fifty-six of their original number remained. The name of Port Royal was then changed to *Annapolis*, in honor of Queen Anne of England.

In the following year, Viscount Bolingbroke projected an expedition against Quebec. The combined fleet collected at Boston, whence it sailed on the 13th of July, 1711, and anchored in the Bay of Gaspé. On the 3d of September, it weighed anchor, with the object of attacking Quebec; but it experienced such dense fogs that it was impossible to manœuvre. Eight vessels of the fleet were wrecked upon the rocks on the coast near the Seven Isles, situated at the mouth of the St. Lawrence, where nearly nine hundred men perished. Hence, the attack was abandoned.

At length, the peace of Utrecht, signed in 1713, put an end to the abasement to which France had been reduced during the reign of Louis the Fourteenth.

England, by a single blow, wrested from the French the establishments on Hudson's Bay, Newfoundland, and Acadia, with its ancient limits; in a word, all the outlets of New France upon the ocean. By that means she obtained supremacy over the fisheries.

In Europe, she obtained, by the same treaty, Gibraltar and Port Mahon, with the whole island of Minorca.

These various conquests were of immense advantage to her present and future commercial superiority, a supremacy to which her merchants already aspired.

Wars of religion had, for the last two centuries, armed the nations of the globe one against another. The object of the struggle had just changed. Henceforward, wars for commercial advantages were about to commence. The treaty of Utrecht may be regarded as the starting-point.

At the period of the treaty of Utrecht, Canada was in an inconceivable state of weakness and wretchedness. An attempt had been made to send to it a population; but this population was composed of runners, agents of the government, and a number of religious communities.

The comparative competency which some of her people had acquired was lost in consequence of unfortunate wars.

In 1713, the bills of exchange drawn upon the exchequer of the metropolis, to meet the expenses of the colony, were not paid; and from that moment, paper fell to the lowest state of depression.

The exportations from Canada, in 1714, did not exceed three hundred thousand francs (about sixty thousand dollars). The whole of this sum, with an equal amount from the government, was required to pay for the merchandise sent from Europe.

Nevertheless, after the peace of Utrecht, attention was again called to the French settlements in America. The isle of Cape Breton, situated at the entrance of the gulf, which had been left to France by this last treaty, was settled. Its name was changed to Royal Isle. Port Dauphin was founded, but was very soon abandoned for Louisburg, which presented a beautiful harbor, and was settled by the fishermen of Newfoundland.

The French who had abandoned Newfoundland retired to Cape Breton, whose population was further augmented by some refugees from Acadia. Other settlements were formed, or grew up in the Isle St. John, in the archipelago of the Madeleine, and in the Isle Miscou, situated at the entrance of the bay *des Chaleurs*. These different posts, advantageously situated for the fisheries in the Gulf of St. Lawrence, gave a fresh impulse to this industry.

In 1714, the brotherhood of St. Sulpicius had already constituted eighty-five parishes in Canada, forty-two of which were within the government of Quebec, thirteen within that of Trois Rivières, and twenty-eight within that of Montreal.

In 1715, the Sieur de Vincennes, a Canadian officer, visited the country of the Miamis, and founded a post, bearing his name, at the mouth of the Wabash. It is from this period especially that we can date the establishment of a line of posts from the lakes to the Mississippi.

The post of Vincennes was also called *Fort St. Ange*, or *Fort Pineguichicas.*

The command of Royal Isle was given to Major de Ligondes in 1710. In 1719, settlements were commenced on Isle St. John; and, in 1720, MM. de Vaudreuil and Noyan formed establishments below the division of the Niagara. The French were also engaged, this year, in fortifying Louisburg upon an excellent plan. The greater part of the materials were imported from Europe. More than thirty million livres (about six million dollars) was expended on the works. This position became important as a protection to the French fisheries and commerce in America. It formed the key to the navigation of the St. Lawrence.

In 1720, the bills drawn upon the metropolis by the agents of the State were paid with a loss of five-eighths. A specie currency was then restored for two years. After that, paper money was again put in circulation to the amount of a million livres (two hundred thousand dollars).

In 1721; La Jencaire founded Lewistown on the Niagara. This year, the historian Charlevoix visited the mission posts of Cataracoüy, Niagara, Detroit, Michilimakinac, and Puants Bay.

In the spring of 1722, he visited the mission established at the bottom of the Bay of St. Joseph, on Lake Michigan, where he was detained five weeks by sickness. Thence he went to Kaskaskias, from which place he descended the Mississippi to its outlet in the Gulf of Mexico. He wished to return by the same route; but, finding no one in Louisiana disposed to accompany him, he took passage for St. Domingo, and was wrecked on the southern cape of Florida. Returning to Louisiana, he took passage for Havana, whence he sailed for France, and arrived after a passage of ninety-three days.

It was supposed that the Acadians, for whom the right had been reserved to establish themselves at Cape Breton, would settle at the new establishments which had been formed at that place; but they preferred retaining their property under English rule. Royal Isle was therefore peopled, in great part, by a few European emigrants. At one time, nearly four thousand inhabitants were settled there; but they returned to Louisburg, Fort Dauphin, Toulouse, and Névieka.

The entire attention of these people was directed to the fisheries. The severity of the climate prevented them from attempting agricultural pursuits.

They found coal mines, but knew not how to work them to advantage. These mines, at the present day, are of immense importance for the supply of the steamers on the Halifax station.

In 1727, Quebec was defended by a fine citadel, built to the south, on a position commanding the city and the shores of the river; and by Fort St. Louis, in which a castle had been built. It was also covered by a certain number of batteries connected by an underground work. The city was divided into the upper and the lower town, and contained a palace for the governor, a bishopric, a cathedral, a Franciscan convent, a Jesuit convent, a church, situated in the lower town, and a convent for the females of the Congregation. There were also, at this time, thirty missions among the Indians on the borders of the lakes. Five of these were among the Iroquois, on Lake Ontario, on the south side; one at the extremity of the lake; and two near the rapids of the St. Lawrence; three on the borders of Lake St. Clair, near Detroit; one at the outlet of Lake Huron; one in Saguemine Bay; seven on the northern borders of Lake Huron; five in Puants Bay; two on the Wabash; one on the Miami; and one on the Kikapous.

Montreal, at the same period, contained a parish church, a seminary, a convent of Jesuits, one of Franciscans, a Hotel Dieu, a convent for females of the Congregation, a hospital of the chapter of *Bon-Secours*, a prison, and a parochial chapel, St. Anne.

In 1731, active measures were taken to fortify the outlets of Lake Champlain, upon the St. Lawrence, in order to cover Montreal, from that side, against the incursions of the Anglo-Americans.

The fisheries had received so fresh an impulse since the settlement of Royal Isle, in 1713, that, twenty years later, the annual yield, as well in codfish as in oil, amounted in value to three million two hundred thousand livres (about six hundred and fifty thousand dollars). These returns varied but little for several years.

In 1734, M. de Varendry traversed the American continent from the shores of the St. Lawrence to the Pacific Ocean, a distance estimated by him to be about nine hundred miles; and, in 1743, Louis Fornel discovered Esquimaux Bay, known by the natives as *Kenessakion.*

Halifax was founded by the English in 1743, near Chibuctou Bay. This city became the capital of Acadia, which then took the name of Nova Scotia, and was looked upon as a new centre of colonization. Four thousand colonists arrived from England and the European continent. The town of Lunenburgh was shortly afterwards founded by seven hundred Germans.

Notwithstanding all the concessions which France had been compelled to make at the treaty of Utrecht, the jealousy and ambition of the people of New England were not satisfied. Having once conceived the project of appropriating to themselves the possessions and the commerce of New France, they never would abandon it. Whenever an opportunity to make aggressions upon the French settlements presented itself, they seized it with avidity; and when no occasion correspondent to their wishes arose, they created one.

The renewed life which animated the northern settlements had given great pain to the people of New England. The importance of Royal Isle disturbed them. They resolved to take possession of it. The plan of invasion was formed in Boston in 1745: New England bore all the expenses of the expedition. A Mr. Pepperel, a merchant of that city, was its chief agent and instigator. He obtained the command of six thousand men, raised for that purpose. This army was conveyed in nine ships of war. The fleet, composed of one hundred sail in all, anchored in sight of Louisburg, in Chapeau Rouge Bay, since named Gabarus by the English. The attack was commenced on the 28th of April. Louisburg was in a condition to offer considerable resistance. Unfortunately, the military governor mistrusted the militia, which composed his principal disposable force for defence. They requested permission to make sorties, and attack the enemy on landing; but in the fear that they would pass over to the enemy, this request was refused. By reason of this fatal distrust, the garrison was compelled, after a vigorous resistance of fifty days, to capitulate. The fate of the whole island soon followed that of Louisburg.

The entire population of the colony amounted to two thousand souls. All embarked in the fleet, and were transported to Brest!

In 1747, M. de la Galissonnière was appointed Governor of New France, at which period, the Anglo-Americans were again desirous of extending their Nova Scotia boundary to the southern shores of the St. Lawrence. He resolved to repel their unjust pretensions, and restrain them within the peninsula, which the last treaties had assigned as their boundary. Moreover, the people of Pennsylvania, and particularly those of Virginia, made frequent attempts to extend their possessions westwardly as far as the shores of the Ohio. They had already examined the country beyond that river, and had explored the fertile plains of Indiana, and the rich territory of Ohio, which they ardently coveted. The governor of New France, whose attention was thus drawn in that direction, sought to resist their encroachments by constructing a line of forts along that frontier.

All the efforts of France to resist the onward march of the Anglo-Americans were unavailing. All past or future treaties were unable to check the progress of American democracy, destined to govern the New World. Nothing could prevent its triumph over feudal principles, military despotism, and papal authority.

The nations of Europe at length became fatigued with long and unproductive wars. A congress was assembled at Aix la-Chapelle in 1748, where a treaty of peace was signed after an eight years' contest.

Royal Isle was, at this period, restored to France. According to this, and the preceding treaties, the settled boundary of the French possessions in America was declared to be the Ohio River, and its tributaries; that is to say, the crest of the Apalachian or Alleghany Mountains was assumed as the boundary of the English colonies.

The greatest difficulty, however, was not to define the boundaries by treaties, but to resist the invasions of the Anglo-Americans—invasions the more threatening, because they were not the result of conquests by force of arms, but of the *isolated* though *sure* encroachments of agricultural emigrants, who were advancing as the pioneers or vanguard of those millions destined at a later period to go forth from the bosom of New England to the conquest of the great valley of the Mississippi, their object and their certain prey!

In 1749, the Acadians, no longer able to bear the yoke of the English, gave up their property, and emigrated, to the number of about three thousand, to the Isle St. John. Most of these emigrants were farmers. The residence of the fishermen on that island was Tracadia, St. Pierre, and the port *la Joie.*

The French then built Forts Gasparaux and Beauséjour, as outposts to their possessions between the Gulf of St. Lawrence and Bay of Fundy. They also formed settlements on the River St. John, which empties into this bay.

But Great Britain coveted all that region of country situated between Acadia and New England, and attacked Beauséjour with three thousand men. That fortress, after sustaining a siege of fourteen days, capitulated. Its capture involved that of Fort Gasparaux, which had a garrison of but forty men.

The English afterwards attacked Fort St. John, whose entrenchments were formed merely of palisades. The commandant set fire to it, and retired into the interior of the country.

During the same year, the French again took official possession of the country watered by the Ohio, and took occasion to bury, on several points of that river, plates of lead upon which the arms of France were engraved; that is to say, on the right shore, at the mouth of the Ohio; at *Chino-Dachito;* at *Venaugoukanon;* at *Ronanoara;* and lastly, below the *pointe coupée*, or *Kanonouangon.*

In 1750, the extension and consolidation of the western settlements were attempted. Those of the strait became the especial object of the solicitude of the government. None but men of good morals, and, according to the expression of the day, real *terriers*, that is to say, determined to settle as agriculturists, were received into these settlements.

To each settler a gun, a mattock, an axe, a ploughshare, a scythe, a sickle, and an auger were given, besides one sow, six hens and a cock, six pounds of powder, and twelve of shot. The State also undertook to feed him for eighteen months after his arrival at the place of his destination.

Unmarried men enjoyed equal prerogatives, with the exception that their support at the expense of the State began only on the day that they contracted a marriage. Every two inhabitants were provided with a cow and a yoke of oxen, which they were bound to replace after the first year.

The State also supplied the colonists with seed for their cleared lands for the first year, which were not to be replaced till the third year.

These dispositions on the part of the French government to colonize as actively as possible their north-west possessions did not prevent the English government, according to their praiseworthy habits, from disposing of a portion of this territory in favor of their own subjects. In 1750, England granted lands west of the Ohio River to a company which assumed the name of the *Ohio Company*, with permission to found a colony there. A few emigrants repaired to these lands, and attempted to establish their rights to them; but they encountered so much resistance on the part of the French, who had long been settled among the Indian nations in those countries, that they were obliged to retire. This new attempt to encroach on the territory of the French in the west determined M. de Galissonnière to establish a military communication between Fort Presqu'Ile on Lake Erie, and the Ohio along the course of the Alleghany River.

If the condition of the French possessions in America at the close of this half century be examined, it will be found very satisfactory, as well in a territorial point of view as with respect to the progress of colonization. France still held nearly all the territory which she had possessed at the close of the seventeenth century. She had lost Acadia, but had acquired Louisiana; and her right to the entire possession of the great regions of the West, the finest portion of the American continent, remained acknowledged and incontestable.

The population of New France, which, at the close of the seventeenth century, amounted to twelve thousand, was estimated, fifty years later, at sixty-three thousand. Therefore it had quintupled in half a century.

This population was distributed as follows:—

Quebec	8000
Montreal	4000
Trois Rivières	800
Interior country	42,000
In the west and at the Upper Lakes	8000

Of these sixty-three thousand inhabitants, those of the west were more especially addicted to hunting and the fur trade than to agricultural pursuits.

It was estimated that, throughout the whole of this colony, there were, at the period referred to, one hundred and eighty thousand acres under cultivation, and twenty thousand acres of prairie land. The annual crops amounted usually to four hundred thousand rations of wheat, five thousand of Indian corn, one hundred and thirty thousand of oats, three thousand of barley, six thousand bushels of beans, one hundred thousand quintals of tobacco, twenty thousand of flax, and five thousand of hemp.

Such were the resources and productions of the French North American colonies in 1750.

CHAPTER XIII.

1750—1763.

FRENCH COLONY—NEW FRANCE.

Marquis Duquesne is appointed Governor of Canada—He undertakes an expedition with the design of checking the encroachments of the Anglo-Americans in the west—He builds several forts—Fort Duquesne at Pittsburgh—Forts Machaut and Lebœuf—Braddock's defeat—Advantages of Pittsburgh as a manufacturing city; its present condition—Disposition of the military posts occupied by the French, and by the English—Renewal of hostilities between the two nations—Removal of the inhabitants from Acadia—Attack and capture of Forts Oswego and George by the French—The Anglo-Americans attempt to retake Fort George, but fail, with a loss of four thousand men—Attack of Louisburg—Heroic defence of the garrison, in which Governor Drucourt and his wife take an active part—Siege of Quebec—Death of Generals Wolf and Montcalm—Capitulation of the Canadian forces—A handful of troops and Canadians, attempting to retake their capital, surrenders to three armies sent to surround it—New France falls into the power of the English.

THE Marquis Duquesne, a distinguished naval officer, was appointed Governor of the French possessions in Canada in 1752. On his arrival at Quebec, he directed his attention to the means necessary to check the Anglo-American encroachments on all the settled boundaries between the English and French possessions. He accordingly organized an expedition, of which he took the command the following year. He erected a number of forts upon the shores of the Ohio, which had been diligently explored during the four preceding years.

The largest of these forts was erected at the confluence of the Monongahela and Alleghany Rivers, whose junction forms the Ohio. This fort was projected upon the model of Fort Frontenac. It was a square protected by bastions, and somewhat smaller than the former. Upon this plan, all the fortifications built for the same purpose in America were mostly constructed.

The position selected for this fort, which received the name of Duquesne, in honor of the governor, was admirable, as well in relation to military operations as to commerce and manufactures. It formed the centre of communication, by water, with Canada, with Illinois, with the lakes, and Louisiana. This point was, therefore, excellently adapted to check the movements of the Anglo-Americans of Pennsylvania and Virginia, should they attempt to descend into the valley of the Ohio. With the forts at the lower part of the Ohio, this position commanded the great valley so much coveted by the Anglo-Americans. Below Fort Duquesne was Fort Beauséjour, commanded by the Sieur Duplessis.

This disposition of the French was looked upon with apprehension, especially by the people of Virginia, for it evidently threatened to circumvent the English colonies in their projects of aggrandizement towards the west, the avowed object of their desires. The Virginians were, therefore, the first to pass beyond the limits of the Alleghany Mountains, and to dispute the possession of the valley of the Ohio with the French. But their first attempts were unfortunate. Their detachments were beaten on several occasions; and the forts they attempted to build upon the Ohio were destroyed.

The mother country resolved to avenge the affront cast upon her by these reverses of her colonists. For this purpose, she sent to their relief a considerable force, under the command of General Braddock. In the summer of 1755, this general proceeded to attack Fort Duquesne with thirty-six pieces of cannon and six thousand men. But he was surprised in his march, at about twelve miles from this post, by two hundred and five French troops, and one hundred and fifty Indians, and his army was almost exterminated. These unexpected reverses checked the march of the three numerous corps destined to act against Canada.

I delight in recording here that brilliant action on the part of our fellow-citizens, as much on account of the historical importance attached to it, as by reason of the fact itself, for we were then masters of those rich western countries, which I could never look upon without indescribable emotions of regret for their loss! And Fort Duquesne was the key of the Ohio!

In 1817, I visited the site of Fort Duquesne, and the scene of Braddock's defeat. The former now bears the name of Pittsburgh. The other yet retains its name, and will stand an imperishable monument of the heroic courage of a handful of Frenchmen, despite the furrows which periodically stir up the ashes of those who there left their mortal remains.

I could still trace the bastioned square, which had been defended at that time by eight cannons, four of which were three pounders. One of the bastions was in a perfect state of preservation; but now, these monuments of our passage into the valley of the Ohio, as children of the warlike France of that period, have disappeared to make room for a new city, containing a population of twenty-one thousand three hundred inhabitants,* which rather resembles a small manufacturing republic, advancing with giant strides towards its full development. Its inhabitants manufacture iron, lead, and all kinds of metals; wood-work, glass, paper, linen, and cotton. Their cut glass can compare with the richest of Europe. Their nail factories are probably the best in the world. The quality of the iron is excellent, although inferior to that of New Jersey.

The coal mines which abound everywhere, and are found almost at the surface of the earth, facilitate all their enterprises, in which fuel is an element of the greatest importance. A great number of workshops of all descriptions have been established. But the principal industry of this locality is the manufacture of steam engines for all purposes, but principally for steamboats. Pittsburgh is the great emporium of the west for the construction of steamboats. Out of four hundred steamboats, built in one year

* At this time, November, 1849, Pittsburgh has a population of over seventy thousand.—T.

on the western waters, seventy-five were constructed at Pittsburgh. The annual value of exports from that port is fifty millions.

In 1755, France occupied the following military posts: 1. Niagara, on Lake Ontario. 2. Detroit. 3. A post at the head of Lake Puants. 4. Presqu'Ile, on Lake Erie. 5. A post on the River *aux Bœufs*. 6. Duquesne. 7. Ouiatanon, on the St. Jerome, or Wabash. 8. Vincennes, fortified only by palisades, at the mouth of the Wabash. 9. Kaskia. 10. Chartres. 11. Escauslen, at the mouth of the Ohio. The Anglo-Americans had one fort at Oswego, on Lake Ontario; one at Pikkivatina, on the Miami of the Ohio; and, lastly, a post at Wheeling, on the Ohio, below Pittsburgh.

During this year, the English captured three hundred French vessels on the coast of Canada, without having made any declaration of war. Hostilities commenced anew in North America in April, 1755.

The unsettled question relative to the boundaries of the French and English possessions was the ostensible pretext for the war; but the real object sought to be gained by a renewal of hostilities was the conquest of Canada.

Under these circumstances, the British government exhibited an utter want of consideration for the French in Acadia, whose settlements, dispersed within the interior, were considered neutral. It determined to transport the entire population; and twelve thousand men were thus condemned to seek an asylum out of Acadia. The greater number of the expatriated were even necessitated to bear the expense of their transportation to other colonies.

A great number repaired to different parts of English America. Fifteen hundred Acadians landed in Virginia, where they were treated as prisoners of war, transferred to England, and thrown into prison at Bristol and Exeter. Twelve hundred arrived in Maryland; other detachments landed upon the coast of Carolina; while a great number perished on the American coast.

Several vessels landed a number of these unfortunate people at the island of Cape Breton, where they were received with heartfelt sympathy by their fellow-countrymen.

In the month of August, 1756, the French, although few in number, repaired to one of the most important points of the English lines on the borders of Lake Ontario. They attacked Fort Oswego, defended by a garrison of eighteen hundred men and by one hundred and twenty pieces of cannon. This post, which served as a sort of depot, contained a great quantity of ammunition of every kind. After a few days' energetic resistance, it was carried by three thousand Frenchmen. During the same year, several French parties, supported by the Indians, made various incursions within the limits of Pennsylvania, Virginia, and Carolina, and killed or disabled seven hundred men.

Nevertheless, the Anglo-Americans still pressed on the settlements of the west. They had already erected a fort at the mouth of Cumberland River, from which point they continually threatened the French possessions. It was even difficult to carry provisions to Fort Duquesne, where a garrison of eleven hundred men was stationed under the orders of M. de Lignery.

The Anglo-Americans had also erected strong positions upon the lakes, by means of which they were enabled to interrupt the communications between the St. Lawrence and the western settlements. Fort George was one of those points. It occupied an important position on Lake Champlain, in the direct line of communication, through the Hudson River, with the St. Lawrence. It became urgent to dislodge the Americans from this position, as well to preserve relations with the western country as to protect the capital of Canada.

In 1757, five thousand five hundred men, supported by eighteen hundred Indians, attacked this post, defended by two thousand two hundred and sixty-four Anglo-Americans. In a few days, the besieged were forced to capitulate. The French hastily raised a redoubt upon the ruins of the fort, to which they gave the name of *Carillon*. The Americans, appreciating the strength of this position, with respect to their projected attack upon Montreal, determined to retake it, and made prodigious efforts to effect this object. The redoubt *Carillon* was unfinished when it was attacked; but an abattis had been thrown upon its exposed front, which made the approach to it quite formidable.

On the 8th of July, 1758, the Anglo-Americans, who had collected their forces at Fort Edward, presented themselves in front of the redoubt, to the number of six thousand three hundred regulars, and thirteen thousand militia furnished by the colonies. They threw themselves upon this demi-bastion with rare intrepidity, and, undaunted by any obstacles, continued the assault for four hours! They lost over four thousand men, and were finally obliged to retreat from before these ramparts, hastily constructed, it is true, but defended by three thousand five hundred Frenchmen.

These brilliant exploits were, for some reason, the last which were destined to crown the courageous efforts of our brave troops in Canada. England had sent considerable forces to hasten the issue of the definitive establishment of its power in America. On the 2d of June, 1758, a fleet, composed of twenty-three ships of the line and eighteen frigates, carrying sixteen thousand troops under the command of General Wolf, anchored in Gabarus Bay, half a league from Louisburg.

Louisburg was then garrisoned by two thousand eight hundred men. Its fortifications were of wretched construction. The casings of the different curtains had entirely tumbled down. At that time, there was but a single casemate, and a small bomb-proof magazine.

Despite all these disadvantages, the besieged offered the most obstinate resistance. They were directed by able chiefs, at the head of whom were Governor Drucourt and his heroic wife, who emulously disputed with each other the sacred duty of defending the honor of their country.

Finally, after all its resources were exhausted, the city made an honorable capitulation. Its intrepid defenders received the esteem of their conquerors.

The capture of Royal Isle was of great importance. It was the key of Canada. To that point the war was carried the very next year.

About the end of June, an English fleet of three hundred sail, commanded by Admiral Saunders, made its appearance in the waters of the St. Lawrence, a few miles from Quebec. On a dark night, when the wind was favorable, the defenders of Quebec launched eight fire-ships, in the hope of reducing this fleet to ashes. But notwithstanding the circumstances which favored this attempt, it was unsuccessful. Its failure is attributable to the impatience of those who had charge of the expedition.

During this time, an army ten thousand strong attacked Point Levy, opposite Quebec, and commenced the bombardment of the city.

On the 13th of December, five thousand English soldiers landed at the foot of the heights which command the citadel, and fearlessly began the assault under the direction of General Wolf. In this assault, that brave general was slain. One part of the city was taken; but the citadel still remained in the power of the French, who performed prodigies of valor under the orders of General Montcalm. This great chief, to repulse the enemy, issued an order which unfortunately was not obeyed, and lost his life in defending the last demi-bastion in which he had entrenched himself.

The Chevalier Levy then assumed the command, conscious of the fault which had been committed relative to the orders of the brave Montcalm; but it was too late. The city capitulated on the 17th. Quebec then contained ten thousand inhabitants.

The capture of the capital of Canada was the signal of defeat at other points. Fort Niagara was taken on the 28th of July, 1759, after a siege of twenty days. This loss, and that of Fort Frontenac, surrendered to Colonel Bradstreet by its commander De Noyan, left open to the English the navigation of Lake Ontario, and permitted them to send fresh troops to Montreal. Fort Duquesne was also abandoned by its commandant, after he had destroyed its intrenchments.

Notwithstanding these reverses, the sentiment of honor and courage, so enduring in Frenchmen, still remained. A small corps of regulars and Canadian colonists determined to recover Quebec, the seat of government of their province, and on the 20th of April, 1760, descended the St. Lawrence upon the ice, and arrived within a short distance of the city before the English were aware of their approach. But a fortuitous accident revealed the presence of this Spartan band. One of the party fell into the water, and saved himself upon a cake of ice. Carried on shore at Quebec by the current, he was perceived by the garrison, who immediately spread the alarm. The English had thus time to prepare for the defence of the place. The French had calculated upon a surprise to insure the success of the enterprise. But they did not abandon this bold attempt, expecting a supply of provisions from Europe. But on the 16th of May they were obliged to raise the siege, and regain Montreal.

Unfortunately, this city, the last refuge of the troops and authorities of the colony, was not susceptible of defence. It was surrounded only by one wall, built for protection against the Indians, and not adapted to resist European forces.

Meanwhile, three armies were marching to encounter this heroic remnant of the French forces. One was descending, another ascending, the St. Lawrence; and the third, arriving by way of Lake Champlain, appeared before Montreal on the 8th of September, 1760. The besieged were obliged to capitulate in their own name, as well as in that of the entire colony!

Thus was solved the question concerning the boundary between the French and English possessions, by the conquest of the whole country, as sanctioned by the treaty of Paris in 1763.

All Canada was thus lost to France, with that Louisburg which had cost so much treasure and so much care, to be so often the prey of the English. All the lands east of the Mississippi were conceded to the English.

In the course of this fatal war, France lost its most flourishing youth, more than one-half of the ready money circulating in the kingdom, its navy, its commerce, and its credit.

The annual expense of governing Canada until the year 1750 had never exceeded one million seven hundred thousand francs (three hundred and forty thousand dollars). At the peace, it amounted to eighty million francs (sixteen million dollars)! Such was the result of the habitual prevarication of the all-powerful agents of the government in that country, who had only their own particular interests to subserve. The inhabitants were nothing but a species of animal, worked by a few individuals, whose avarice was as great as their ignorance and turpitude. This state of things was perceived too late, and was due to the negligence and apathy of the government of France, and especially to the system adopted in the administration and colonization of Canada.

CHAPTER XIV.

1700—1763.

ANGLO-AMERICAN COLONIES.

English Revolution of 1688—Its character and influence; slave trade decreed by Parliament—Introduction of slaves into the American colonies—Violence of the Puritans against the Catholic priests—Fresh quarrels between the English and French colonies relative to the boundary line of their respective frontiers—The American colonies project the conquest of Canada—Renewed attack upon Port Royal, which fails—Destruction of the French settlements upon the Penobscot, in the province of Maine—Difficulty of adjusting the frontiers between Spain and England—Hostilities which follow—Creation of the *new colony of Georgia*—Its object; form of its administration—Oglethorpe, principal founder of this colony—He attacks St. Augustine, and is repulsed—Attack of the Spaniards upon the English settlements of St. Simon; their complete route—Introduction of African negroes as slaves—Georgia changes its government—Captain John Reynolds—Adoption of a new administration, founded upon principles of liberty and independence—Relative forces of the French and English colonies on the renewal of hostilities—Result of that last conflict—Canada and the north-western territories become the property of England—Occupation of the north-west by the Anglo-Americans—The Indians take up arms to drive the Americans from their territories, and maintain their allegiance to France—The chief, Pontiac; failure of his project—Prosperity of the American colonies secured.

The conquest of the liberty which England enjoys dates from the Revolution of 1688, when the crown of King James passed to the Prince of Orange, by the decision of the British Parliament.

This revolution secured freedom of thought, the right of resistance, the power of the Parliament, and the influence of the commercial classes. It respected that which was established, while it conquered the liberty of the subject. It maintained the superiority of the aristocracy, but nevertheless increased the influence of the middle classes. It modified those vices which could not be entirely destroyed, and increased the guarantees of individual liberty, of political opinions, and of the freedom of the press, and asserted the responsibility of the executive power. In this manner, without violence, but also without serious reactions, constitutional liberty was permanently and definitively established in

England. And if England has not, since then, made marked progress, her constitutional rights yet remain intact.

We may remark that the essential object of the Revolution of England was English interests, English rights, but not those of humanity; that, in the end, the policy of its government has always been that of material interests, directed with a view to individual aggrandizement, and not by a feeling of reciprocity and justice, in this respect differing from our glorious Revolution of 1789, so generous, so great, so expansive in its natural interpretation of the immutable principles of liberty, which are destined one day to rule the whole civilized people of the globe.

The American colonies were the first to experience the fatal influence of these contracted and egotistical views. The English merchants, judging that it was their interest to maintain the colonies in a state of dependence upon them for manufactures, advocated the doctrine that slave labor, and the introduction of African slaves, were *advantageous to Great Britain and to her colonies!* The influence of this party was so great in England, at that time, that it induced William and Mary to secure the passage of a law by Parliament in favor of the *slave trade;* and the opinion of the king and of the Parliament, favorable to that iniquitous trade, was registered, even in the text of the law, in 1695.

Such were the principles which then directed English policy, and such have they remained! Now that England has conquered another empire in India, where she labors to find the means of supplying the raw material for her manufactures, and consequently to dispense with the products of the American soil, which is no longer her own, the slave trade has ceased to be useful. Emancipation may serve her interests. Hence the English merchants, to subserve their own interests, as in 1690, preach a contrary doctrine, immediate manumission, in order to strike a heavy blow at a powerful rival. And if the interests of her merchants required it, England would go to war to enforce a measure thus dressed in the garb of *humanity.*

At the commencement of the eighteenth century, in 1713, England, by the Treaty of Assienta, obtained the privilege of importing negroes, not only into her own colonies, but into those of Spanish America. She also had the monopoly of this odious traffic, of which she took advantage to people her southern colonies. From that day she protected, recommended, and encouraged the slave trade, and the introduction of the black race in America, that infectious leprosy which threatens to shake even to its foundation the splendid edifice of American democracy. But a great good must one day grow out of this great evil. At least such is our hope of the future; for, if America has received from Africa the heavy burden of slavery, Africa, in her turn, must one day receive from America the precious blessing of liberty.

At the time of the English revolution, three political systems were in existence in America—absolute despotism, aristocratic privileges, and pure democracy.

France represented absolute despotism in the New World, with the three orders in subjection to its laws: the power of the clergy, by a treaty with the Pope; the feudal power, by its standing armies; and the civil power, or commercial institutions, by the influence of the patronage of office and a vigorous police.

England, by the power of its Parliament, presented the ideas of aristocratic liberty—its privileges, its immunities, corporations, &c.

The Anglo-American colonies, by their social institutions, their separate existence, and by a government of their choice, represented the fundamental dogma of the sovereignty of the people.

The struggle between these three principles lasted nearly one century, thus affording scope for the practice of democracy, and terminated in the complete triumph of the sovereignty of the people in thirteen independent States, under the denomination of the United States.

Nevertheless, the English system did not cease to exert a strong influence on the exigencies, the actions, and even on the character of the Anglo-Americans; an influence which, in many respects, is still felt, though they have existed for more than fifty years as an independent nation. In fact, nothing is so indelible as the seal of our origin, especially when it accords with our interests.

But it is particularly in the conduct of the Anglo-American populations towards their rivals on the continent that the spirit and egotism of the English have been exposed in all their nakedness and deformity.

Thus, as it was well known that the advantages obtained by the French in their intercourse with the Indians proceeded from the influence which the missionaries had obtained over the minds of that credulous people, the Anglo-Americans, in their grasping jealousy of the same advantages, resolved to check this influence at its source. It was decreed, in 1700, by the government of the province of New York, *that any Catholic priest found in the province should be hung.*

We can judge by this official act of the spirit of cruelty and selfishness which in those days animated the inhabitants of the provinces bordering on New France—that is to say, of the Puritans against the Catholics. Therefore, the greatest animosity always manifested itself whenever a question relative to the settlement of a disputed boundary arose. And too often has it been necessary to record the barbarous treatment inflicted by the people of the frontier on the peaceful missionary.

France claimed that part of western New York, occupied by the Iroquois nation, which she had conquered. When it became necessary to regulate that frontier and to establish its boundaries, it was impossible to come to any definite understanding. The pretensions of the Americans were beyond all bounds. They wished to have access to Lake Erie and Lake Champlain, to be masters of the communication of the Hudson with the St. Lawrence, and the lakes! In their correspondence with Canada relative to this question, New York manifested great eagerness for the conquest of that colony. This was, in fact, a certain means of cutting short the question; a means not only warmly approved by the other colonies of New England, but in which they afterwards participated. Therefore, from that time, that conquest became the dominant thought of the Anglo-Americans.

In 1711, this project was so popular in New England that the means of putting it into execution were discussed in the Legislature of Massachusetts. The result of the discussion was that an expedition was afterwards organized and assembled in Boston, and even sailed with the design of attacking Port Royal.

Providence fortunately interposed to save this settlement. A storm defeated all the calculations of these rapacious aggressors, who were thus compelled to renounce their projects. But in 1723, they attacked the little colony and mission of Penobscot, founded above Bangor, in Maine. All the inhabitants were murdered, and the mission destroyed; and a fatal blow was thus given to the last French settlement in Maine. This was the third time that these establishments had been ruined by the fire and sword of the Anglo-Americans. This event was decisive; the French were expelled from the colony of Maine.

From that time, the twelve English colonies, founded in the seventeenth century, held undisputed possession of the whole Atlantic coast, from the River St. Croix to Florida.

Nevertheless, the boundary line between South Carolina, an English colony, and the Spanish possessions in Florida, was not established. The English, in consequence of their usurpation of the rights of the French, who, under John Ribaut and René de Laudonnière, in 1564, had formed a colony upon the territory in dispute, claimed possession as far as the River St. John. The Spaniards claimed priority of possession as far as the Bay of St. Helena, in Carolina. The pretensions on either side were great; but the power to enforce them was all on one side, that of England. To gain her point was, therefore, inevitable.

But the government of Florida adopted a policy which might seriously have compromised the peace and tranquillity of the planters of Carolina. Under the pretext of seeking to convert the negroes to the Catholic religion, an appeal had been made to them to repair to St. Augustine, the seat of government of Florida. The Africans, thus liberated, were soon incorporated into a regiment, to be employed afterwards for the purpose of menacing an invasion of the settlements of the English in Carolina.

In this state of things, and to prevent the desertion of their slaves, the Carolinians constructed a fort upon the Altamaha; but, in a short time, this fort was destroyed by a party of Spaniards and Indians. The planters then petitioned the government of the mother country for the means of protecting their frontier, a circumstance which, in a great measure, originated the new colony of Georgia.

COLONY OF GEORGIA.

The charter granted by George the Second, for the foundation of a new colony to the south of Carolina, is dated the 2d of June, 1732, and contained the following principal features:—

"His Majesty, having taken into consideration the distresses of a great number of his subjects, who are represented to be in a starving condition; that a great number of strangers are ready to expatriate themselves to escape oppression; and wishing also to protect the southern frontier of South Carolina from the dangers to which it is exposed, in consequence of its limited number of white inhabitants, has been graciously pleased to grant a charter of incorporation to a certain number of gentlemen, under the title of *Administrators of the Colony of Georgia in America.*

"The administrators are authorized to collect offerings and subscriptions, the proceeds of which are to be applied to clothe, arm, send out, and maintain a colony of poor English, or foreigners, to Georgia.

"His Majesty has granted, for this purpose, all the lands comprised between the Savannah and Altamaha Rivers, upon the coast, and included between two straight lines drawn from these rivers to the shores of the Pacific ocean, to fifteen administrators, as the domain of the province that is to bear the name of Georgia, to be governed for twenty-one years in the name of, and for the interests of, the poor."

We must remark that, at the date of this concession, the rights of the French and Spaniards, on the west side of the Mississippi, were generally established and acknowledged. Nevertheless, the crown of England, according to custom, did not hesitate to grant rights of property over domains to which it could have no possible pretensions.

"The administrators of the property are to receive no remuneration for their services, nor are they to enjoy any exclusive rights or privileges."

Besides, the charter contained provisions for the administration and government of the colony, in which the acknowledgment of *the principle of liberty of conscience* was assumed as a fundamental basis.

But, while Jews were received into the colony, Catholics were excluded!

This spirit of intolerance towards the Catholics was manifested in all the colonies. But this need excite no astonishment when we reflect that the English emigrants who had left their homes to establish these colonies were animated by a puritanical fanaticism. Even in Virginia, the Catholics remained until 1753, under the greatest political restrictions.

The colony of Georgia was therefore created to strengthen the Carolina settlements, and to relieve the poor classes of England, and persecuted foreigners.

The administrators, determining to transport, free of expense, the poor who wished to emigrate to the colony, made an appeal for funds for that object. Five hundred francs (one hundred dollars) entitled a colonist and his wife to a passage, an establishment, and support. The expense of a child was two hundred and fifty francs.*

Shaftesbury and Oglethorpe were among the administrators, of which body the latter was one of the most active and devoted members. Placing himself at the head of the colony, he sailed, in January, 1733, with thirty-five families, whom he established temporarily upon the present site of Savannah. He then made an extensive reconnaissance of a great part of the interior of the country; contracted a treaty of peace and alliance with the natives; and definitively established himself upon the site temporarily occupied by the colonists, where there was an Indian village called Yamanaw, the cession of which he had obtained from an old chief, Thoma-chi-chi.

These emigrants immediately adopted municipal institutions, and from that day the little community advanced legally and prosperously towards its destiny.

To protect this new colony from the incursions of the Indians or Spaniards, Oglethorpe built Fort Argyle in an advantageous position on the banks of the Savannah River.

It is a remarkable fact, in the first administrative constitution of the colony of Georgia, under the direction of the delegated commissioners, that the use of ardent spirits and the introduction of slaves were prohibited by special provisions, although in full

* Twenty *hectares* (about forty acres) were allowed to each emigrant, who was required to put a part of it immediately under cultivation, under penalty of losing his rights.

No proprietor could give away or sell his lands without the special permission of the administrative commissioners.

The right of inheritance existed only in the male line. In case of default of male issue, the lands reverted to the company. This restriction as to the right of property was founded upon the necessity of founding a military colony, where each person was to be a soldier and a farmer.

The rich were allowed to purchase lands in Georgia, individually, to the amount of two hundred hectares (about four hundred acres), half of which, however, was to be cultivated within a given time.

As these clauses appeared too onerous to the new colonists, the government was compelled to modify them.

vigor in almost all the other English colonies. In South Carolina, there were forty thousand slaves to five thousand whites.

This restrictive measure against the introduction of slave labor was adopted for the purpose of securing the object for which the colony had been created—provision for the necessities of the poor of England. To encourage their emigration and their labor, it was indispensable that the labor of the blacks should not be put in competition with that of the white colonists. Again, the administrative commissioners did not possess sufficient means for the purchase of slaves; and, finally, the vicinity of the Spaniards led to apprehensions that the latter might use their influence to decoy their slaves, and, by holding out to them the prospect of liberty, to induce them to desert.

For these reasons, the introduction of slaves into Georgia was for a time prevented, though the influence of the English traders, then protected by the royal assent, and by Parliament, was constantly exerted to force this colony to submit to the same rule which governed the other English provinces in America.

In 1734, Oglethorpe entered into an alliance with a Choctaw chief, named Red Slipper, who afterwards became a very useful ally of the Americans in their attacks against the French settlements in Louisiana.

In 1735, during Oglethorpe's temporary visit to England, numerous emigrations from Scotland furnished Georgia with valuable colonists. This colony was further augmented by emigrants, who were compelled to flee from the blind fanaticism of the Bishop of Salisbury. In 1737, Savannah already contained one hundred and forty houses. After the lapse of a century, its population amounts only to eleven thousand inhabitants.

In 1737, Oglethorpe returned with troops to protect Georgia against the attacks of the Spaniards.

In 1740, he made an attack upon St. Augustine, in Florida, and was repulsed with loss. Three years later, the Spaniards advanced upon the territory of Georgia with the intention of checking its colonization. Landing in St. Simon's Strait, they marched upon *Frederica,* a small, newly-formed borough at the head of the island of St. Simon. Oglethorpe advanced to meet them, attacked them at the head of a very strong detachment of Scotch Highlanders, and cut them to pieces. The field where this action was fought has since been known as the *Bloody Swamp,* in consequence of the great number of men who were driven into it and destroyed.

The generous and virtuous Oglethorpe had founded the colony of Georgia in the hope of witnessing its prosperity under the influence of free labor. So long as he remained at the head of affairs, he used all his influence to resist the introduction of slaves, demanded by a majority of the people, who had accepted a regulation whereby slavery was expressly prohibited. This wise regulation, adopted by Oglethorpe, was, in 1751, unfortunately rescinded.

At the same period, a great number of slaves, coming from the coast of Africa, were introduced into the colonies of Virginia and Maryland.

At the expiration of the term of the grant, the proprietors resigned their rights of administration, and Georgia was from that day governed directly by the officers of the crown. Captain John Reynolds was appointed governor by the king in 1754.

In 1761, the boundary difficulties between the Spaniards and English, on the Carolina frontier, were at length settled at the general peace. The Mississippi became the western boundary of the province, and St. Mary's River the common boundary between Georgia and Florida.

Georgia was then governed by a council of twenty-four members, who resided in England. This state of things did not harmonize with the necessities and exigencies of the colonists, who changed this mode of administration for a popular government, which was definitively installed in 1776.

Such was, from the commencement, the administrative progress of the colony of Georgia, the youngest of the thirteen colonies which existed at the Revolution of 1776.

During the first half of the eighteenth century, the English colonies made rapid progress under the happy influence of their local institutions, despite the circumstances which had never ceased to place them in opposition to the mother country. When, in 1755, hostilities again commenced between France and England relative to the boundary line of Acadia, of that part of the Iroquois territory included in the western part of New York, and of the valley of the Mississippi, the population of the English colonies amounted already to one million forty-six thousand inhabitants, while that of New France did not exceed sixty-five thousand. It will therefore be observed that the relative population of the English and French possessions was as sixteen to one, and that of New England and New France, the object of hostilities, as eight to one.

The struggle which commenced between these two powers was consequently unequal with respect to numbers, and not less so in the efficiency of their troops, ammunitions of war, and the moral influence of the political institutions by which the belligerent powers were swayed. The courage of the one party was stimulated only by the emulation attached to the career of arms in a warlike and honorable nation; that of the other by Puritan principles, by the hate of monarchy, and by the hope of possessing an object which they ardently coveted, the splendid territory of the west.

The result could not be doubtful; and the question of boundary must necessarily be decided against the interests of France, by the occupation not only of the contested territory, but also of all the contiguous country—or, rather, by dispossessing France of its legitimate rights, acquired by the discovery and colonization of the country.

Such, in fact, were the results of the war of 1760. The treaty of peace, at Paris, in 1763, surrendered to Great Britain all the rights of France to Canada, comprising the immense and beautiful country of the north-west, of the lakes, and all the territory east of the Mississippi, a territory more than six thousand miles in extent. This act consolidated the prosperity of the American colonies; and if, at that period, England had known how to appreciate the grateful feelings entertained by the American colonists towards her for terminating the war with France so advantageously for them, she might for ever have preserved their loyalty and their submission.

In 1760, an English garrison, under Major Roger, arrived to occupy Detroit, the chief town of the north-west settlements, the principal trading-post of the Indians. From that time, the adventurous American pioneer penetrated with greater boldness into those rich countries which he had already so long known how to appreciate. He darted on these lands, as it were, as on a prey which belonged to him, and drove from the soil its weak and indolent proprietors, whether Indian or Canadian.

The Indians, however, failed not to perceive shortly the difference of character between their new landlords and their old allies.

The French had been the friends of the red man, who, in return, had remained at peace with them. Nothing in their pacific and quiet manners appeared formidable. This state of things ceased to exist on the arrival of the Anglo-Americans, who were more turbulent, more active, and exhibited a more ardent desire to appropriate to themselves the territory of the Indian.

Under these circumstances, these children of the forest manifested a daring spirit. They conceived the bold design of driving the usurping race back to its original limits, and of thus, as it were, avenging their ancient and faithful allies, the French. Pontiac, chief of the Ottoways, was the skillful author of this project. Equally remarkable for penetration of mind and for cunning, he visited in person all the tribes which dwelt within an area of more than six hundred miles. Calling their chiefs together, he communicated to them his plan. He proposed that they should march to the frontier of their common enemy, and simultaneously attack all the English posts on a line extending more than twelve hundred miles. This plan was adopted by all the combined tribes, and on the day fixed for the general assault, the Indians, faithful to their engagements, suddenly fell upon all the posts on the frontier. The important station of Michilimackinac was taken, the fort burnt, and all the white residents put to death by the tomahawk.

Pontiac commanded the attack upon Detroit in person, as this was the most important post on the frontier. The fort was captured after a dreadful slaughter of the besieged. All the other posts suffered the same fate, with the exception of Niagara and Pittsburgh, which almost miraculously escaped the terrible vengeance of the red man. Doubtless, had it not been for the timely assistance of the English reinforcements, which had arrived in haste under the orders of Colonel Bouquet, the vast project of the brave and skillful Indian warrior might have had an issue fatal to the dominion of the Anglo-Saxon race in that part of the New World. Still, notwithstanding the result, the period was one of cruel reprisals made by the Indian to satisfy his hatred of the white race.

This bloody episode in the war of the aborigines, undertaken through hatred of the Anglo-Americans, and as a proof of the fidelity of the Indians towards their first allies, was the last act of this long drama of battles, as cruel as they were sanguinary and unjust, fought between France and England upon American soil. It terminated that seven years' war which decided the fate of the French possessions in America, the whole population of which passed over to the domination of Great Britain. But though Canada was thus made to change masters, it has always been found impossible to change the sympathies of its people, or their deep and jealous hatred of their conquerors, and especially of their Anglo-American neighbors.

It was my determination to record, in a historical inquiry, the signal conception of the Ottoway warrior, which is so directly connected with the influence which my compatriots so long exercised in America. It should have found a place in a work in which I have had at heart the desire to claim the credit which belongs to France in the civilization and occupation of the New World.

CHAPTER XV.

1763—1783.

ANGLO-AMERICAN COLONIES.—UNITED STATES.

Occupation of the western countries by the Americans—Recollections of the French settlers in those countries—Visit of General Lefebvre Desnouettes to St. Genevieve—Struggle between England and her colonies—The metropolis attempts to impose restrictions on the commerce of the colonies—Stamp Act—Ferment which it occasions—Convocation of a congress in New York proposed by the Assembly of Massachusetts—Repeal of the Stamp Act—New custom house bill—American associations against English commerce—Military occupation of Boston—The Assembly of Virginia and other colonies vote remonstrances—Ferment of the people, and the crisis which it produces in Boston—Symptoms of irritation rapidly disclosed in all the colonies—A cargo of tea thrown overboard at Boston—Closing of the port of Boston—Formation of a general congress in Philadelphia—Composition of this first assembly—Resolutions adopted by it—Restrictions of the commerce of the provinces of New England by the English Parliament—Climax of the causes of dissension between the mother country and her colonies—Levying of troops in New England; battle of Lexington; of Bunker Hill—Second session of Congress in Philadelphia—Manifesto published by this assembly—A levy of twenty thousand men voted by Congress—George Washington, a member from Virginia, elected commander-in-chief of the forces of the Confederation—Washington's arrival at Cambridge—Attack and capture of Montreal by the Americans under General Montgomery—Quebec attacked—Death of Montgomery—Thomas Paine—His "Common Sense"—Sitting of the Federal Congress on the 8th of June, 1776—Declaration of Independence—Act of Confederation—Treaty of alliance and commerce between the United States and France—Powerful co-operation of this great ally—Capitulation of Yorktown—England acknowledges the independence of the United States—Definitive treaty of peace between France, England, and the United States—Respective boundaries fixed by this treaty—Advantages reserved by the contracting parties.

England, at the close of the war with France in 1760, occupied, almost without opposition, all the territory in North America, with the exception of Florida, still in the possession of Spain, and Louisiana, reserved to France by the treaty of Paris, but already ceded to Spain by the secret treaty of the 3d November, 1762.

France, by the treaty of 1763, ceded to England all the country on the left bank of the Mississippi which she either occupied or claimed, and the American colonies, which extended to the shores of this river, thus became consolidated in their political existence.

The period of occupation, by the French, of the western countries, and of the borders of the lakes, had just terminated. A second commenced, that of England.

The first had endured almost a century, since the discovery of the territory by the missionaries and the brave La Salle. Nevertheless, the French adventurers had settled nothing, had created nothing. They arrived as voyagers and hunters; and as voyagers and hunters they lived. Their assimilation to the mode of life of the Indians was more complete than that of the Indians to the morals and manners they brought among them. Consequently, what is left, at this day, of the residence of our compatriots in these countries, undoubtedly the most beautiful on the continent of America? Some ruins of fortifications—scarcely a reminiscence! Here and there, and at great distances apart, a French family, often mixed with Indian blood, cultivating with indifference, and without forethought, a small square of land, on which a few fruit trees from France recall the memory of home.

Nevertheless, we should remark that, although our unfortunate compatriots have proved themselves indifferent to their interests upon American soil, still their lively recollection of their country, their love of glory, and their devotion to all that is French, do them infinite honor.

Enter the dwelling of a Frenchman in Illinois, Michigan, or Missouri. Let him discover by your accent that you come from the old country, from his *dear France;* and this man, who just before had appeared stupid, without feeling, and indolent, becomes as eager and zealous to testify his joy and pleasure as he had before been slow to accost you. He seems animated with a new life, which he derives from traditionary recollections. He will inform you that his grandfather was a Frenchman, with that frankness, that accent which convey so much meaning! "I am a Frenchman!"—and his eyes will fill with tears. He thinks of the land of his fathers, and in seeing you, he is reminded of the glories of France.

In 1817, I traveled through the Western States, accompanied by the brave General Lefebvre Desnouettes, a chevalier of the Empire without fear and without reproach. We had traversed Ohio, Indiana, Illinois, and were proceeding from Kaskaskia to

St. Genevieve, on the Mississippi, in the State of Missouri. An old Canadian, assisted by two Indians, had conveyed us across the river in the ferry boat which plies between these two towns, situated on opposite shores. While crossing, we had spoken of the country we were visiting, and of France, which we had left after her days of mourning. The name and title of the general had several times been mentioned in the course of conversation. The old master of the boat had heard and comprehended everything. He saw a living wreck of those glorious phalanxes, the fame of whose lofty deeds had reached even the shores of the Missouri, and had even excited the admiration of the red man. His enthusiasm was at its height.

St. Genevieve is not immediately on the banks of the river. The prudent inhabitants of that town had built it a short distance from the shore, that it might not be exposed to the rise of the Mississippi, which, at each overflow, carries away a portion of its banks. It required several minutes to reach the town; but our arrival had already been announced. One of our Indians had given the information to the inhabitants, who came in crowds to welcome the general. They seized him, touched him as the man of miracles. He had seen and spoken to the Emperor; they fancied they saw and conversed with Napoleon. Country, honor, Napoleon, all these feelings were blended in the sight of an illustrious Frenchman. In fine, obliged to alight from our horses to gratify the generous impulses of these old Canadians, we reached the town as they were firing a salute in honor of a general of Napoleon.

I had determined not to interlard this historical summary with any narrative that related to my personal feelings or to my recollections. But I could not resist the temptation to record this incident. It is a very bright flower among many striking reminiscences!

The strife which had already commenced between England and her colonies at the close of the seventeenth, continued through the whole of the eighteenth century, and was only kept in abeyance by an object equally dear both to the mother country and to her colonies—the defence of their frontiers against the Indians, with the dispossession of a rival nation whose vicinity and influence were inconvenient. But England was evidently gradually losing her claims to the fidelity of the American colonies. The great day when it was to become the sacred duty of the people to protect themselves by force was approaching. The Divine hand had marked it.

The American colonies had sprung up in the midst of a long series of trials. They discovered that they possessed within themselves a principle of existence. They wished to take advantage of the restoration of peace to improve their condition, and to place their prosperity upon a more solid foundation.

The mother country had observed their continued growth. She wished to direct them at pleasure; and sought every available means to preserve that ascendency over them by which she might continue to retain them in a state of dependence.

She at first attempted to impose restrictions upon their commerce as compensation for the expense of their protection. The Americans never formally acknowledged the legitimacy of this right; but they did not refuse the payment of the impost.

The war which England had maintained in America against France had considerably increased her debt. She therefore wanted her colonies to bear a part of this burden. For this purpose, in 1764, a proposition was made in Parliament to establish stamp duties in the American colonies. This impost was to apply to all the acts of courts of justice, of chancery, whether civil or ecclesiastical, of universities, or of courts of admiralty. It applied to the sentences of a court, to commercial licences, to insurances, to letters of marque, to the transfer of payments, to all contracts relating to the transmission of property by inheritance, by sale, or by grants. It even extended to pamphlets, to almanacs, to all daily publications. The proceeds of this duty were to be applied to meet the expenses required for the protection and defence of the colonies.

England was anxious to convert the proposition for a stamp act into a law; and when the bill was again brought forward in 1765, before the House of Commons, by Grenville, then prime minister, General Conway was the only one that dared to protest against the measure, declaring that it exceeded the powers of Parliament, as the colonies were not represented.

This law alienated all minds; and the ferment increased so rapidly in the colonies that they no longer hesitated to show their resentment.

As soon as the news reached America that the Stamp Act,

which had passed the House of Commons on the 7th of February, 1765, had afterwards been approved by the House of Lords and received the royal sanction, the legislative Assembly of Virginia declared that that colony was not bound to obey any law imposing taxes, unless such law had been passed by its own authorities. The governor dissolved the assembly, and ordered new elections. But all the members who had voted against the Stamp Act were re-elected; while none were re-elected who had voted in favor of it; so that the declaration became unanimous. It was on this occasion that Patrick Henry first made himself conspicuous for his rare and transcendent talents, and his heroic eloquence in support of the liberties of his country.

The same resolution was passed in the province of Massachusetts; and one of the most distinguished members of the legislature, James Otis, had the courage to propose a combination to resist encroachment upon their rights and their prerogatives as English citizens. He proposed to convoke a congress on the 1st of October, 1765, to which deputies from all the colonies should be invited to devise measures of public interest, required by the exigencies of circumstances.

This generous resolution was favorably received by a majority of the colonies; and Massachusetts, Rhode Island, Connecticut, New York, New Jersey, Pennsylvania, the governments of the counties of Newcastle, Kent, and Sussex, in Delaware, and the provinces of Maryland and South Carolina, hastened to send to the assembly their representatives.

The governors of the other colonies opposed this measure and refused to send representatives. The assembly convened at New York. It proclaimed the right of the colonies to resist the imposition of any taxes except such as were authorized by themselves; and at once resolved to send a petition to the king and to both Houses of Parliament to revoke the odious law, and to permit the free exercise of domestic legislation.

These representations, and this unanimous resistance, produced a deep sensation in England. In 1766, Parliament repealed the Stamp Act. While it asserted its right to maintain its legislative authority, it admitted that this should be exercised with caution. As the right to establish a revenue tariff had not been so actively contested, this species of taxation was resorted to.

Consequently, in 1767, the ministers presented a new bill in

Parliament, imposing a duty upon tea, glass, paper, and paints, exported from England into the colonies. The proceeds were to be applied to the salaries and pensions paid by the government in America, whether for the administration of the colonies or for their defence; and the surplus was to remain at the disposal of Parliament.

This law was to take effect on the 20th of October, 1767. As soon as the colonies were informed of this new attack upon their privileges, they exhibited the most violent opposition.

The Legislature of Massachusetts, which met at the beginning of 1768, addressed a protest against this new impost to the king, to the two Houses of Parliament, and to the principal persons who had advocated the repeal of the Stamp Act. It also addressed a circular to the other legislatures of the colonies, in which their attention was called to the dangers which threatened them, and to the encroachments of the crown upon their rights and privileges as English citizens. In consequence of the publication of this address, the governor ordered a dissolution of the assembly. A new one was convoked; but it confirmed the resolutions of the preceding one.

At this conjuncture, associations against English commerce were formed. The people of the colonies resolved to abandon the use of tea; and sumptuary resolutions were passed.

In 1768, Boston was occupied by the English troops, with the object of enforcing the execution of the custom laws. Parliament even declared that violators of the law should be removed to England for trial.

The Assembly of Virginia immediately addressed remonstrances to the British government against these proceedings; but, as these met with no success, the citizens resolved, by means of associations gradually formed in all the colonies, to break off all commercial relations with England, and to receive none of her importations.

The Legislature of Massachusetts declared that it could not deliberate freely so long as the city was occupied by a garrison. It refused the subsidies demanded for the support of the English troops. The same declarations were made by the. Legislatures of New York, Maryland, and Delaware.

The British government, at length renouncing in part its demands, consented to revoke the duties on glass, paper, and paints; and to retain only the duties on tea.

The continuance of this last tax, induced, in 1770, stormy discussions in Boston, where the excitement was much greater than at any other port. In the month of March of this year, a contest took place between the troops of the garrison and the citizens. A post was assailed by the multitude, and several men were killed in the bloody encounter. The excitement of the people became intense, and the removal of the garrison was required. It retired to Fort William in the harbor.

Two years passed by, in partial measures and in useless endeavors at conciliation between the two parties. The commerce of the metropolis with the colonies was checked by associations which refused to receive its productions. The administration of customs fettered in turn the intercourse of the colonies with other nations; and this state of things induced active smuggling.

In the meanwhile, other symptoms of irritation began to appear. A central committee, established at Boston, corresponded with several principal committees; and these with other bodies. This organization was followed in all the other colonies. Public opinion everywhere, and its influence in the councils of state, daily gained strength. The people were resolved to resist the encroachments of the British government.

The arrival of several cargoes of tea, which the English East India Company had shipped from London to Boston, soon presented the opportunity of a manifestation of public feeling. The people would not allow it to be landed; they demanded the immediate departure of the vessels. The demand was refused. The people then boarded the vessels, and threw the tea overboard. The same refusal was extended to other shipments arriving at New York, Philadelphia, and Charleston.

This long series of acts of resistance on the part of the Americans against the authority of Great Britain determined the English ministry to treat the city of Boston with severity, as they considered it the focus of the rebellion. Lord North, then prime minister, on the 14th of March, 1774, presented a bill in Parliament, which closed the port of Boston, and transferred its commercial privileges to Salem. A second bill deprived the colony of Massachusetts of the privilege of appointing its judges and magistrates, and transferred the right of their election to the crown. And finally, by a third bill, all individuals accused of acts of violence against the public officers were either to be tried in other colonies, or to be transported for trial to England.

In the same year, Parliament passed the "Quebec" bill. This bill augmented the privileges of the Canadians, and restored to them the administrative organization they enjoyed under the rule of France. It also recognized the supremacy of their religion. By this means, Parliament sought to conciliate the affections of the people of a colony recently acquired, who might still regret the domination of France.

These new laws were to take effect on the 1st of June, 1774. At the news of their sanction by Parliament, a deep and general feeling of grief was manifested throughout all the colonies. The Legislature of Virginia decreed that that day should be devoted to mourning, fasting, and prayer. The Assembly of Massachusetts called for the formation of a general congress. The same wish was expressed by all the other provinces. All appointed their delegates to this congress, whose opening session was fixed for the 4th of September, in Philadelphia.

This assembly was composed of fifty-one members, who chose for their president Peyton Randolph of Virginia, of which the following is a list:—

New Hampshire: John Sullivan and Nathaniel Folsom.

Massachusetts Bay: Thomas Cushing, Samuel Adams, John Adams, and Robert Treat Paine.

Rhode Island: Stephen Hopkins and Samuel Ward.

Connecticut: Eliphalet Dyer, Roger Sherman, and Silas Deane.

New York: Isaac Low, John Alsop, John Jay, James Duane, William Floyd, Henry Weisner, and Samuel Bocrum.

Pennsylvania: Joseph Galloway, Charles Humphreys, John Dickenson, Thomas Mifflin, Edward Biddle, John Morton, and George Ross.

Newcastle, &c.: Cæsar Rodney, Thomas McKean, and George Read.

Maryland: Matthew Tilghman, Thomas Johnson, William Paca, and Samuel Chase.

Virginia: Richard Henry Lee, George Washington, Patrick Henry, Jr., Richard Bloud, Benjamin Harrison, and Edmund Pendleton.

North Carolina: William Hooper, Joseph Hewes, and R. Coswell.

South Carolina: Henry Middleton, Thomas Lynch, Christopher Gadsden, John Rutledge, and Edward Rutledge.

The province of Georgia did not send its delegates till the following year. This assembly discussed, in the most deliberate manner, the civil, political, and commercial interests of the two countries, and adverted to the natural ties by which they were united, the advantages to result from perseverance, unanimity, and good feeling, and the unfortunate consequences of a rupture. It recapitulated all the grievances which the colonies had endured; asked satisfaction for them; and addressed a touching appeal to the people of England, reminding them of the ties which bound them to the Americans.

It also made an appeal to the Canadians, warned them of all the dangers to their liberties involved in the practical operation of the "Quebec" bill, and invited them to unite with the American party.

In short, the assembly addressed a proclamation to the colonies, portraying, in the most vivid colors, the infractions of their privileges, and encouraged them to resistance, and warned them against all attempts at disunion.

It was necessary that several months should elapse before the result of the deliberations of this congress, which adjourned on the 26th of October, to meet on the 10th of May, 1775, could be appreciated. The resolutions it passed were approved by all the colonial assemblies; and the colonies prepared to resist by force of arms. Pennsylvania, Maryland, Delaware, and Virginia raised militia. In New England, the zeal of the people appeared still more exalted.

In 1775, a parliamentary law restricted the commerce of the New England colony to the British possessions in Europe, and to the West Indies. The right to fish on the Banks of Newfoundland, an essential element in their prosperity, was prohibited. By the same parliamentary measure, the commerce of the southern colonies was confined to England alone.

This act constituted the climax of the causes of dissension between the mother country and her colonies. The insurrection assumed a threatening aspect. Munitions of war were collected. The New England States ordered a levy of troops, and the other colonies followed their example. Finally, an armed strife commenced; and the battle of Lexington, which took place on the 19th of April, 1775, became the signal for war.

This battle was soon followed, on the 17th of June, by another not less memorable, that of Bunker Hill, where the brave General Warren was killed.

The national Congress was holding its second session in Philadelphia, according to adjournment, while these manifestations of courage and patriotism, on the part of the people of New England, were taking place. Its first care was to consider the means of resisting the common enemy. The necessity of general co-operation was most sensibly felt. Each member saw the necessity of conferring the strength of all the colonies, and the power of acting in their name, on a federal head. Fortunately for the great object proposed, this legislative assembly was remarkable for the number of its talented men, accustomed to business, possessing legislative knowledge, and distinguished especially by entire and disinterested devotion to their country.

The proposition to assume a confederative organization was preceded by a manifesto. In this manifesto, all that the colonies had suffered was in a solemn manner proclaimed: the attempts made to deprive them of their privileges; the necessity which had compelled them to take up arms in their defence; and their determined resolution to lay them down only when the perils of their country had ceased.

This assembly also voted to raise an army of twenty thousand men, at the expense of the confederation, and gave the command of it to George Washington, a member from Virginia, who desired no other pay than his necessary expenses.

General Washington took command of the army in the month of July, 1775, and repaired to head quarters, then at Cambridge, Massachusetts, where the war had already commenced.

In the meanwhile, to divert the English from concentrating their forces upon the coast of New England, Congress resolved to send an expedition into the province of Lower Canada. An American division, embarked on Sorrel River in August, 1775, was rapidly carried to its mouth, with the object of cutting off all communication between Upper and Lower Canada. Another division, led by General Montgomery, crossed from Fort St. John to Montreal, landed without opposition at the island on which the city is situated, and took undisputed possession of it in September. General Montgomery then proceeded to attack Quebec, which he attempted to carry by main force, in the December of an excessively severe winter, amid a very heavy fall of snow. The American general braved all obstacles, and was about to take possession of the last battery which held out, when he was struck down by a discharge of grape and canister, bequeathing to his fellow-citizens the name of another hero to be enrolled among the patriots who had died in the cause of liberty and independence.

The death of Montgomery was the cause of the failure of the attack upon Quebec; and the severity of the winter induced a mutual cessation of hostilities, to be renewed with vigor in the spring.

The condition of affairs day by day assumed a graver aspect. The unequal struggle between England and her still growing colonies gave a decided preponderance to ideas of independence. Several remarkable productions seemed to favor this enthusiasm. That of Thomas Paine, entitled "Common Sense," exerted an overpowering influence. It rendered the sentiment of independence national; and Congress, being the organ of public opinion, soon prepared to adopt this sentiment. By the resolution of the 8th of May, 1776, each colony was requested to reject all authority emanating from the British crown, and to establish a form of government that would accord with the particular interest of each State, and with that of the whole confederation.

At the memorable session of the 8th of June, Richard Henry Lee, of Virginia, proposed the solemn proclamation of the independence of the colonies. He was seconded by John Adams, of Massachusetts. On the 14th of June, a committee was appointed to report upon this great question. This committee was Thomas Jefferson, John Adams, Benjamin Franklin, Roger Sherman, and Philip Livingston.

On the 2d of July, the Declaration of Independence was submitted to Congress, discussed, and unanimously adopted. The 3d was a day of fasting and prayer. On the 4th, the great resolution was officially promulgated. The Republic of the United States thus prepared to resist the oppressive acts of the mother country, in this first act of nationality, by a preliminary religious manifestation.

The constitutional form of government recommended for the

adoption of the confederation was not submitted to Congress by its committee until the 12th of July, 1777. It was proposed by this assembly on the 15th of the following November, and definitively approved by all the delegates from the States in March, 1781.

Three or four years were spent in discussing the important question, what rights and powers each State should vest in the federal government, to enable it to act most efficiently for the common defence.

Meanwhile, war, with its burdens, and its alternations of reverse and success, raged throughout the country. A treaty of commerce and alliance had, it is true, in 1778, been concluded between France and the United States. The intervention and efficient assistance of this powerful ally had thus been obtained in favor of the cause of liberty in the New World. Finally, on the 18th of October, 1781, Yorktown capitulated; and Lord Cornwallis, with the English forces, surrendered to the combined armies of America and France. A day for ever glorious and memorable, which terminated, so advantageously for the Americans, the war of Independence!

In 1782, the independence of the United States was acknowledged by England; and in 1783, a definitive treaty of peace was concluded between France, England, and the United States. By this treaty, the boundaries of their respective territories were fixed. That of the United States was separated from the British possessions in America by the River St. Croix towards Nova Scotia, and from Lower Canada by the chain of highlands which separates the waters which flow into the Atlantic Ocean from those which empty into the St. Lawrence. This line, extended to the sources of the Connecticut River, whose course it was to follow to the forty-fifth degree of latitude, was to take a westerly direction to the St. Lawrence; then to ascend the bed of this river, cross all the great lakes from east to west, and extend to the north-west of the Lake of the Woods. Thence it was to be prolonged to the Mississippi, which was to serve as a line of demarkation to the thirty-first degree. The boundary between the United States and Florida was to be fixed by a line drawn west to east from the Mississippi to the Apalachicola. Descending this river to its junction with the Mississippi, the line was to extend direct to the sources of the River St. Mary, whose course it was to follow to the Atlantic Ocean.

The United States held possession of all the islands within sixty miles of the coast, excepting those which heretofore had been comprised within the limits of Nova Scotia.

They also retained the right of fishing on the Banks of Newfoundland and in the Gulf of St. Lawrence, and wherever, in fact, the English and Americans had been in the habit of fishing. France retained the same right to the north and west of Newfoundland, from Cape St. John to Cape Raye. She had entire possession of the islands of St. Pierre and Miquelon. Lastly, the navigation of the Mississippi was declared to be free to France, England, and the United States, from its sources to the ocean.

CHAPTER XVI.

1783—1800.

THE AMERICAN UNION.

Financial condition of the United States on the return of peace—Congress enacts a law for the settlement of the country to the north-west of the Ohio—Weakness of the General Congress to administer the affairs of the United States—New constitution proposed and adopted—Congress of 1789; General Washington elected President of the Union—Amendments to the new constitution—First official census of the United States—Secretaries of State, of War, and Treasury, constituted—The courts of justice organized—Supreme court—District courts—Organization of the public revenue—Collection of customs—Building and support of light houses, signals, &c., for the security of navigation—Alexander Hamilton presents his celebrated report upon the finances—Creation of a national bank—Monetary system—The United States select a federal district, and found the city of Washington, which becomes the seat of the principal federal authorities, of Congress, and the capital of the United States—Recapitulation of the historical summary of the English colonies—The principle of independence as old as the colonies—New History of the United States by George Bancroft—History of the American Revolution by Jared Sparks—The principle of the Union very ancient; its strength drawn from the variety of the elements which compose it—Great example furnished by the American democracy.

At the restoration of peace, the United States found themselves in a very disastrous pecuniary situation. When they embarked in that struggle, which terminated only after a seven years' war, the colonies were ill prepared to sustain so weighty a burden. The misery of the country was therefore complete, its commerce annihilated.

Every mind was then directed to the perfection of the social organization, to the means of repairing the evils of the war, of reviving domestic prosperity, of co-ordinating the relations of the States of the confederation, and of combining their strength in a single sheaf. The desire of cementing their union and harmony, and of concentrating their means of defence, animated the minds of all the members of Congress; but this great object became much more difficult to accomplish, in consequence of the great national territory, including all the country to the north-west of the Ohio, acquired by treaties of peace.

On the 18th of July, 1787, Congress passed an act in which the basis of the new colonies to be established in this new territory was traced. But many difficulties between the United States and England still remained unsettled, the origin of which dated from the war of independence; for all the clauses of the treaty of peace had not yet been fulfilled. The principal of these concerned the commercial relations of the United States with England, because, by the first constitution, each State reserved to itself the right of regulating its own commerce. The correspondence which took place on this subject between the English government and the special agent of the United States was productive of no satisfactory result. England pretended that the laws of the confederation had neither sufficient harmony nor stability to ensure their execution in a manner both consistent and complete.

This was a powerful obstacle. The United States saw the necessity of adopting a more regular system in all their foreign transactions, and of founding the stability of their new relations on a constitution which would give more strength to the Federal Union and to the power charged with its maintenance. Under these circumstances, feeling conscious of its own weakness, Congress officially declared, on the 24th of February, 1787, its own inability to regulate the interests of the confederation with their granted powers, and appealed, in their emergency, to the people, whence these powers were derived.

A committee of twenty-five members was then appointed,

among whom were Washington, Madison, Hamilton, Jefferson, and Morris, to draft the American Constitution, which still exists as the fundamental law of the American Union. In presenting this constitution to Congress, Washington announced with what views it had been drawn up. It was the conviction of legislators that it was impossible to assure an independent sovereignty to each of the different States, and at the same time to provide for the interests and security of all. They had looked upon their union as necessary to their prosperity, to their strength, and probably to their national existence; and this opinion, deeply impressed upon their minds, had disposed all the States to a mutual deference, and to concessions necessary to the prosperity of the whole confederation.

Congress took no action itself relative to the constitution proposed by the committee, but referred it to the different States of the Union, each of which was invited to call a convention of its own citizens to discuss it. If the constitution should be ratified by nine States, the people were immediately, according to the forms it prescribed, to proceed to elect a President of the United States.

The deliberations of a special convention, which had taken in view all national interests, and of thirteen distinct conventions, occupied solely in discussing the same questions, and in examining the relations of the common interest to that of each State, were the result of the most luminous and impartial mode of discussion that can be conceived. This method assured, from the beginning, a general concurrence of opinion relative to the constitution that was adopted. North Carolina and Rhode Island were the only States that at first refused to ratify it. A new Congress was convoked at New York on the 4th of May, 1789; and when the two houses were completely organized, they proceeded to count the votes that had been returned from the general assemblies of all the States for the election of President of the United States. For this office, Washington received their unanimous vote; and John Adams, who had received the next highest number of votes, was proclaimed Vice-President.

Thus ended the acts of the Federal Congress, which, after having laboriously and honorably overcome all the difficulties of war and domestic agitation, at length saw firmly established, by treaties and by wise institutions, the independence of the United States.

Two years elapsed between the presentation and the positive adoption of the new constitution of the United States. During this interval, the views of all the legislatures, and the opinions of all the most enlightened men in the country, had been obtained concerning it. Several amendments, which appeared necessary, were discussed in the new Congress and adopted. They were then, like the articles of the constitution, submitted to the examination of the different States, and approved. Subsequent experience led to the adoption of a few additional modifications relative to the powers of the judiciary, and the manner of electing the President.

The States, by this constitution, conceded to the central government the right of watching over the general interests of the confederation; of providing for its necessities by levying taxes, and imposing duties on imports and exports; of regulating commercial relations with foreign powers, as well as between the several States of the Union, and with the Indian nations. The year 1789 must, then, be regarded as the period whence dates the third period of American history, that of the Union, which, since that time, has been in complete practical operation.

The Congress of 1790 ordered the first census of the United States to be taken. The white population in the thirteen States then amounted to 3,231,930, and that of the slaves to 697,897; total, 3,929,827.

From the very commencement of the session, Congress was employed in organizing the various departments of the government. The secretaries of state, of war, and of the treasury were instituted. To these eminent offices Washington appointed Jefferson, General Knox, and Alexander Hamilton. The navy was at that time under the control of the State Department, and was not separated from it until the year 1801.

The courts of justice of the United States were organized by a law of the 24th of September, 1789. The Supreme Court was to hold its sessions annually at the seat of government; and the district courts were to be held within the jurisdiction of the several States of the Union. Between these two jurisdictions, several circuit courts were established, as appellant tribunals, in a given range of cases. From the decisions of the circuit and district courts, an appeal could be made to the Supreme Court under certain restrictions.

This great tribunal formed, with the circuit and district courts, an independent judicial hierarchy, in its action and object, apart from the tribunals established by each State for the ordinary administration of justice. And the line of demarkation is so very distinctly drawn, that no judicial conflict can ever arise between them. The one class of tribunals is intended to defend the interests and to maintain the bonds of the association; the other to protect the life and property of the citizens of each State.

The federative form of the government of the United States required the establishment of this complex authority, not only in relation to the judicial order, but with respect to the administration of the public revenues; one of which belongs especially to the States, the others to the whole confederation. Thus, Congress was empowered to regulate customs duties, and the duties on tonnage and navigation—the sale of the public lands—and to execute all the laws whose object is to increase the revenues and pay the expenses of the United States.

A law determined the different ports where custom-houses were to be organized and duties collected, and where captains of vessels should declare their importations. This law established collectors, inspectors, and the other agents attached to this service. It embodied a code of regulations, with the penalties attached to their transgression.

The expense of maintaining light-houses, signals, buoys, and beacons placed for the security of navigation, was defrayed by the federal government. Other laws had reference to the fisheries, to the coasting trade, and to the regulations of ports. All parts of the marine service were subjected to common regulations, in all that concerned foreign relations, and the collection of public revenues.

In 1790, Alexander Hamilton, Secretary of the Treasury, presented to Congress his famous report on the debt of the United States, and on the means of paying it, and thus improving the public credit. The public debt then amounted, in foreign and domestic loans, to over sixty-four million dollars.

The debts of individual States, which had been incurred in maintaining and paying the expenses of the war, were placed on the same footing as those of the confederation, and the public treasury was equally charged with their payment.

Hamilton's report was discussed in Congress; and, on the 4th of August, 1790, a law was passed providing the means of discharging this debt.

The President of the United States was authorized to borrow twelve million dollars, for the payment of the arrearages, the interest, and a part of the capital of the foreign debt.

The proceeds of the sale of the public lands, situated in the western country, were assigned as security for the loans made for the payment of the debt of the United States.

At that time, Hamilton, desirous of establishing the public credit upon a more extended basis, proposed the establishment of a national bank with a capital of ten million dollars.

The creation of this institution met with strenuous opposition; but, on the 4th of March, 1791, the bill finally passed. The bank was chartered for twenty years. During its existence, no other bank could be established by a law of the United States.

On the 8th of May, 1791, a law was passed, regulating the money of the United States. The dollar was assumed as the basis, to which the larger and smaller coins were to bear a specific relation. The dollar is divided into one hundred parts. The mint was established in Philadelphia.

The leading object of the legislators of the United States was to secure domestic peace by strengthening the federal compact. That their deliberations might be removed from all local influences, they resolved to select a site for the seat of government which should be under the sole jurisdiction of the United States. The situation selected was on the banks of the Potomac, near its eastern branch, and in a district ten miles square, ceded to the United States by Maryland and Virginia. Washington there commenced the establishment of a city which bears his name. Ten years subsequently, it became the principal seat of the federal authorities, to which Congress removed to hold its regular sessions.

Such are the principal features of the governmental organization of the American Union.

The two first periods of American history doubtless abound with scenes of great interest, since they exhibit to us the slow but progressive operation of a self-constituted society, from its infancy to mature age; marked, of course, by the revolutions and the struggles inseparable from this condition. But humanity must be far more interested in the third period, for it presents a spectacle as grand as it is novel, of which history furnishes no antecedent—that of the American Union, composed of sovereign and independent States, acting as a single and great nation, by the power of governmental centralization.

If we now retrace our steps, in relation to the principal facts contained in this brief historical summary, exhibiting the origin and primary organization of the American colonies, we shall be struck with the vast difference in the mode of colonization adopted respectively by the French and English in their American dependencies. The French, by prolonged and destructive contests, conquered from the Indians, the country in which they established themselves. Penetrating into the interior, they were attracted by the fur trade, lived among the Indians, and adopted their manners instead of imparting to them their own.

The English, or rather the Anglo-Americans, built up their colonies by their industry, their activity, and their labor. They pushed forward their clearings, and thus drove the Indians before them by the force of their civilization. Then, in the progress of the political organization of the English colonies, an important fact, arising even from their constitution, strikes the attention: that is, at the close of the seventeenth century, the colonies were as much disposed to claim their independence from the mother country, as at the close of the eighteenth. But they were not sufficiently prepared for this step. They required all the time that elapsed from the former to the latter period to complete their preparations.

In America, the principle of independence gradually arrived at maturity by a series of struggles with the mother country. Above all, it was through these legitimate struggles between England and the new systems of government introduced by the emigrants of New England, that the colonies received their practical education in democracy.

It does not accord with the plan I have traced out for myself to present the history of these struggles in detail. While judging it prudent merely to indicate the period of their occurrence, and to exhibit their results, I refer the reader to the excellent works already published upon the subject. He will there obtain information, the value of which would be weakened if separated from the causes and circumstances under which it has been produced.

I shall take this opportunity to recommend a work from the pen of a distinguished gentleman of Boston, Mr. George Bancroft, the first volumes of which have just appeared in the United States. The favor with which his new *History of the United States* has been received by an American public is a significant guarantee of its excellence.

I will also add that one of the ablest of American writers, the celebrated editor, commentator, and annotator of the writings of Washington, Mr. Jared Sparks, is now preparing an important work upon the second period of the history of the United States, that of the Revolution, during which the spirit of independence was sustained by force of arms. This book, interesting to the American, will not be less so to the French reader, in consequence of the noble support which France, at that period, gave to the American patriots.

Another fact, neither less striking nor less important, to be taken into consideration in our endeavors to appreciate the power of the United States, as a nation, is, that the principle of the Union took its birth from the earliest period of the political organization of the English colonies as distinct societies. Thus we see that, so far back as 1637, the colonies of New England formed a local coalition to protect themselves against the attacks of the savages.

These colonies were Massachusetts, Connecticut, New Hampshire, and Maine. Rhode Island was not received into that confederation, the principles of which were, that the four contracting parties should be united by a league of amity, offensive and defensive; that the cost of maintaining this league should be proportioned to the number of the male inhabitants of each colony; that, on hearing of the invasion of any one of the colonies, the three others should render it assistance; that all matters relating to peace and war should be examined by commissioners, who should assemble in turn at Boston, Hartford, New Haven, and Plymouth.

In 1690, all the English colonies formed a compact mutually to assist one another. They even assembled in congress at New York, deliberated upon the measures which circumstances required them to take, and projected, independently of the mother country, *the conquest of New France*, a colony belonging to a powerful nation. This certainly was a very serious act of independence and sovereignty, which might from that day have laid bare the political character and ambition of the Anglo-American nation!

The principle of union, from that time in practical operation, has marched forward in silence, imperceptibly, its progress even unperceived by the colonists themselves, who, in their feeling of sincere loyalty to the English crown, appeared not to appreciate the character of this federative idea. No one could foresee whither all these things tended, nor the great results they were to bring forth.

In short, this principle made the American colonies equal to the circumstances in which they were placed at the second period of their history, that of contest by force of arms. It passed through this struggle victoriously, and thus created the *American Union*, which, to the present day, has proved to the world that a great and enlightened nation, possessing religious faith and principles, may exist in peace and prosperity under a purely democratic government.

But let us also remark that, with the Americans, the principle of union has not been the result of chance, nor the consequence of a preconceived plan or of fixed design. It is the child of necessity. The union became necessary by the augmentation of its strength, as well as of the elements which composed it. And Providence has so directed all its distinct classes of people—springing, nevertheless, from the same origin, and united by the same religion, the same language, the same principles—that they have become inextricably blended in one and the same power, thus securing the better protection of the whole.

Since that time, the wisdom of man has foreseen and accomplished everything necessary to extend the principle of union, and to embrace in a single network of individual interests the immense territory of the American Republic. Individual interest is the most powerful element in this union; in fact, the one reciprocally imparts life to the other.

CHAPTER XVII.

1678—1717.

FRENCH COLONIES—LOUISIANA.

Discovery of the Mississippi by Fernando de Soto; by Robert Cavalier de la Salle, who settles Texas; his unfortunate end—M. Iberville, founder of Louisiana, establishes a post at Biloxi; isle of Massacre; Baton Rouge; returns to Louisiana —Attempt of the Anglo-Americans to forestall the occupation of the Mississippi by the French—M. de Bienville—Louis XIV. refuses to grant the Protestants permission to settle in Louisiana—M. de Tonty—Foundation of the post of Balize; of Natchez; of Baton Rouge—Journey of M. de St. Denis to New Mexico—Settlements on Dauphin Island—Intrigues of the Anglo-Americans of the Carolinas among the Indians of Louisiana—Arrival of the missionaries; prostitutes destined to people the colony—Construction of Fort Condé at Mobile—M. la Mothe-Cadillac—M. Crozat becomes proprietor of Louisiana, and of its commerce for a period of fifteen years—Description of the settlements on Dauphin Island in 1716; visit to the same place one hundred years later—M. Crozat renounces his privileges.

The honor of the discovery of the Mississippi belongs to Fernando de Soto, as we have already stated in the second chapter. This ambitious companion of Christopher Columbus spent four years in Louisiana in search of treasures; traversed the course of the Mississippi for several degrees; even surveyed it to a certain extent, and finally died upon its shores on the 21st of May, 1542, after having examined the Red River, and the Brazos de Dios, in Texas. With the discovery of these countries was connected that of Florida, anteriorly made by the Spaniards; whence it follows, from the principle then admitted among nations in reference to their respective titles to unknown lands in the New World, that Louisiana should have belonged to Spain, as part of *New Mexico*, then in possession of the Spaniards, the name of which included the whole territory of Louisiana to the shores of the Pacific.

But other destinies awaited this beautiful and rich province, watered by the father of rivers. The adventurous genius of the

French sowed the first germs of that fecundity and immense prosperity which distinguish, at this time, the richest State of the American Union.

A Norman, Robert Cavalier de la Salle, distinguished by great enthusiasm and rare courage, became the Columbus of the western portions of North America. By virtue of the reports of Marquette and Joliet, his two predecessors, he conceived the project of exploring the mouth of the Mississippi, and of thus opening towards the south an outlet from New France, which had been, so to speak, in the possession of the English, since their occupation of Newfoundland, Acadia, and the vicinity of the St. Lawrence. He wished to enrich his country with a new conquest. He saw honor and profit in its execution, and was guided in his determination by an instinct for great deeds, the privilege of superior minds, and an intuitive knowledge of the secrets of the future, which never abandoned him.

To render the accomplishment of this plan useful and permanent, it became necessary to secure the countries which separated the Mississippi from the French settlements in Canada. This design was impracticable, unless posts could be established at certain distances along that immense line, so as to permit safe, if not easy, communication. Above all, it was necessary to gain the affections of the Indian nations inhabiting these countries.

It was with these views and inclinations that La Salle, in 1678,* made the preparations for his expedition, in which he was accompanied by the Sieur de Tonty, a distinguished, active, and enterprising officer. Four years elapsed before he was enabled to navigate the great river which he aspired to reconnoitre. On the 9th of April, 1682, he planted at its mouth the arms of France.

In the spring of 1683, he had returned to Quebec, whence he immediately sailed for France to propose the discovery of the Mississippi by sea, and the settlement of a large colony upon the fertile lands which it watered. He obtained the desired permission, and, at the same time, four small vessels, commanded by M. de Beaujeu.

He missed the mouth of the Mississippi by an error in his calculations, and was thrown into the Bay of San Bernardo, distant from it three hundred miles.

* Manuscript Memoirs of M. de Tonty, Archives of the Navy.

The hatred existing between M. de Beaujeu and La Salle rendered this error more melancholy than it ought to have been. Impatient to separate from each other, these two proud men determined to attempt a landing upon the point where chance had thrown them.

La Salle remained upon this coast with one hundred and sixty men; and the Sieur de Beaujeu sailed for France, thus abandoning his unfortunate companion to a wretched fate.

La Salle did not despond. Assuming personally the entire management of affairs, he founded an establishment on what he thought a favorable point in the bay, and afterwards resumed the pursuit of his favorite project, the discovery of the mouth of the Mississippi.

It was on this voyage of discovery, that the brave and unfortunate Frenchman perished, the victim of a cowardly assassination by two of his own men, on the 19th of March, 1687.

From all the information collected relative to the settlement founded by M. de la Salle to the westward of the Mississippi, and in the present State of Texas, it is evident that this rich territory rightfully belonged to France; and, but for his violent death, and especially for the circumstance that his murder was concealed for two years, and which, consequently, prevented the interference of France during this time, the Spaniards who then occupied Mexico would not have taken possession of the settlement, nor would they have destroyed, at its outset, the germ of the new colony. The Spaniards who destroyed the establishment of La Salle had traveled overland from Coahuila, upon the River Caldeo, in the kingdom of Leon. It is plain, from these facts, that the government of the United States, by its treaties with France, having inherited the right to the French possessions in America, entitled the provinces and governments of Louisiana, as well as the claims to discoveries made by the French in the name of France upon this continent, might show a valid title to the territory of the new State of Texas.

In 1697, M. d'Iberville, a Canadian gentleman, son of Charles Lemoine, an emigrant from Normandy, who had distinguished himself in 1695 and 1697, at the capture of Fort Bourbon, in Hudson's Bay; at that of Pemmaquit on the coast of Acadia, in 1696; and in various attacks on the English colonies at the Island of Newfoundland, called the attention of the minister to the projects of La Salle, and to the establishment of a colony on the Mississippi. In 1698, this distinguished officer was put in command of a small squadron of two frigates and two small vessels, with a complement of seamen and two hundred emigrants. He sailed from Rochefort towards the end of that year.

He arrived in sight of Florida on the 27th of January, 1699, in the latitude of the Island of *Santa Rosa*, fifteen miles to the east of Pensacola; coasted along the shore; found Pensacola occupied by the Spaniards, sounded the bar, and ascertained the depth of the water to be twenty feet. This depth remains unchanged at the present day. He continued his course to the westward, keeping his vessels off shore. Two light vessels or smacks were used to range along the coast near the land, and two feluccas to explore the shores. With two small bark canoes, some of his party frequently ascended the bays and rivers.

The men who were in the canoes, having seen a vast quantity of game, landed upon an island which they named *Escalet*, since called *Ile à Corne*, now known as Horn Island. It is contiguous to the Island of *Massacre*, which they also explored, and to which they gave this name, because of the great number of bones they found on it. Having advanced a little further to the westward, they landed upon Ship Island, so called from its good anchorage. At this island, the little flotilla anchored.

This harbor being a very safe one, M. d'Iberville dispatched some of his men in search of the mouth of the Mississippi; while he visited the land which lies at a very short distance to the north.

A few days after this, he embarked on board of a small shallop with his brother, M. de Bienville, a Franciscan, and forty-eight sailors, in search of the Mississippi, whose mouth he discovered by the great quantity of floating trees issuing from it. On the 2d of March, 1699, he entered the river, which had never before been entered by sea. He ascended it as high as the small Indian village *Bayagoulas*, on the right shore, a little above the River *Manchac*, now bearing the name of Iberville.

He tried to ascertain from the Indians whom he found on the borders of the river whether he was on the Mississippi; but they could not understand him. In the language of these aborigines, this river bore the name of *Malbancha.* He nevertheless constructed a fort on the river, which he named *Pontchartrain.*

At Bayagoulas, he had the good fortune to find a letter, in the hands of an Indian chief, from M. Tonty to La Salle, written in 1684, which had been carefully kept by the aborigines. He had then no longer any doubt as to the identity of the river upon which he was sailing with that discovered by M. de la Salle.

He also visited the Indian village of *Oumas*, situated upon the slope where Baton Rouge now stands, ascended the river as far as Natchez, and returned to Ship Island, passing through Manchac Bay and Lakes Maurepas and Pontchartrain, before known by navigators as the *Baie du St. Esprit.*

After having encamped upon Ship Island, M. d'Iberville determined to explore the coast on the main land. He entered Pascagoula River, and chose an advantageous position for a fort, to which he gave the name of Maurepas. On the banks of this stream, near the site selected, were several Indian villages, known as *Pascagoula*, *Moetoby*, and *Bylochy;* and at the sources of the river several other Indian villages, *Quinipisa* and *Chicachas.*

In the early part of 1699, M. d'Iberville returned to France to convey the intelligence of his discoveries, and to carry back reinforcements for the establishment of a colony. He left his brother De Bienville in command of the colony during his absence, and his brother-in-law Sauvolle in command of the post of Biloxi. These two intelligent officers made a detailed reconnoissance of the outlets of the Mississippi, especially towards the sea, which they sounded with great care, and made a report on the varied resources which the country afforded for the settlement of a colony.

In the course of this year, two missionaries from Canada, accompanied by sixteen Canadians, descended the river to its mouth, and then sailed along the coast until they reached Biloxi, and thus opened the first communication between New France and Louisiana, which was afterwards kept up by means of the Mobile River, or by the lakes and the Bay of Manchac.

M. d'Iberville, preparing to return to Louisiana, was placed in command of the frigate *la Renommée* and the storeship *la Gironde.* He was requested to rear a number of wild young beeves near Fort Biloxi, and, if possible, to bring some of them to France. He was also desired, in his instructions, to seek to procure pearls, some samples of which he had brought with him on his return from his first voyage; to ascertain whence they were obtained; and to give his personal assistance to that fishery. He was further desired to ascertain whether the wild mulberry tree was adapted to the nourishment of silk worms; also to examine the quality of the timber suitable for ship building.

But the principal duty with which he was charged by the minister was to search for mines. Those possessed by the Spaniards on the same coast, in the same latitude, and in land of the same quality, led him to believe that mines equally rich might be discovered in the vicinity of the Mississippi. M. d'Iberville was to take possession of these mines in the name of the king, and to make correct charts of them. He was authorized to have them worked, if possible, by the natives.

In this second voyage, M. d'Iberville was accompanied by his brother-in-law, M. le Sueur, proprietor of the lead mines in the country of the Sioux, at the upper part of the Mississippi, who was to proceed thither by ascending the river; by M. de Remonville, an amateur traveler; by M. de Raucour, who was sent out to the colony as the *king's scrivener* or *naval storekeeper*, embracing the functions of *commissary-general of the king*—a position in the colony second only to that of governor; and by M. de la Ronde as port warden.

When M. d'Iberville left the colony, its inhabitants numbered two hundred. On his return, he found only one hundred and fifty. The remainder had fallen victims to diseases of the climate. But the arrival of reinforcements gave new vigor to the adventurers who had come to seek their fortunes; thus stimulated, they commenced their exploration.

In the meanwhile, the news that the French were seeking to found a new colony on the Mississippi had reached the ears of the Anglo-Americans, whose jealousy was again excited by apprehensions of their success. They immediately determined to pursue the same object, in order, if possible, to forestall the French in their attempts to make a settlement. A resident of New Jersey, named Cox, incurred the expense of dispatching a vessel under the command of Captain Barr. On his arrival in the Mississippi to take possession, he met M. de Bienville engaged in surveying it, who informed him that the French actually occupied the country, and that it would be useless for him to attempt to make any settlements there. The interview between these two officers took place on that part of the river which still bears the name of *English Turn*, the point which had been reached by the English, and whence they retraced their steps.

M. de Bienville, in the absence of his brother, received a petition from the French Protestants, victims of the revocation of the Edict of Nantes, praying to be admitted to the enjoyment of liberty of conscience, and to be permitted to colonize the shores of the Mississippi. This petition was transmitted to M. de Pontchartrain, who returned this answer: *The king has not driven the Protestants from France, that they may establish a republic in America.* Hence, the stupid superstition of Louis the Fourteenth deprived this colony of a most useful class of inhabitants, who, by their wealth, industry, and perseverance, would have been of all others the best adapted for colonization.

M. de Tonty descended from Illinois with a few Canadians. Leaving them with M. d'Iberville for the foundation of a settlement on this river, he returned to Fort Chartres and Kaskaskia.

In 1700, M. d'Iberville founded the post of Balize at the mouth of the Mississippi; and Fort Rosalie—thus named in commemoration of the Countess of Pontchartrain—at the point of the river where the city of Natchez now stands.

On the present site of the city of Baton Rouge, near the mouth of the Bay of Manchac, formerly stood the Indian village of *Oumas*, which took the name of Iberville.

In consequence of the positive instructions of M. d'Iberville to make strict search for the mines that the country might contain, M. Juchereau de St. Denis was engaged six months in exploring the whole country west of Louisiana as far as New Mexico. He performed this journey at that period in a shorter time than it can now be accomplished. M. de Bienville also made a reconnoissance to the west for the same object. He visited Red River, which received the name of the *Marne*, and afterwards *la Sablonnière.*

If, at that period, the French had continued to occupy the Bay of St. Bernard, discovered and settled by La Salle, they would have become masters of the whole interior of the country by the communication opened across the Red River by the Sieur St. Denis.

In 1702, M. d'Iberville, convinced that the Mississippi, in consequence of the shallowness of the water over the bar, was not a favorable position for a maritime port, determined to transfer the principal establishment of the colony to a point on the Mobile River, one hundred and eighty miles eastward from the Mississippi, and thirty-six miles to the west of Pensacola.

There was not, it is true, much depth of water in the river and bay of Mobile; but Dauphin Island offered an excellent harbor, easy to defend. Here the water, at low tide, was from twenty to twenty-one feet, affording a good anchorage for vessels of from forty to fifty guns. The communication from Mobile to the northwestern settlements was almost as easy of access as that by the Mississippi; and the road had already been opened and followed by Canadian runners.

Mobile is a Spanish corruption of the word *Movilla*, from a tribe of Indians living on these waters.

The French had already been in Louisiana three or four years, and had passed all that time in reconnoitering, instead of devising plans for the formation of permanent settlements. There were but one hundred and thirty-nine individuals in the colony, of which nine were officers, twenty-four sailors, fourteen laborers, sixty-four Canadians, twenty soldiers, and eight cabin boys, at an annual expense of forty-two thousand one hundred and twenty-six livres (about eight thousand five hundred dollars)—a sum received with great irregularity. It was, therefore, more of a military than an agricultural establishment, which had thus been founded. In the colony, there was not a single family, not a single woman. M. d'Iberville, to meet this exigency, sent to France for twenty or thirty women for the requirements of the colony. These were to be given in marriage to the Canadians. He recommended particularly that they should be *well-formed;* that it would be best to procure them at Rochefort, or from the *General Hospital in Paris!* He also proposed to send for some Sioux and Illinois Indians, who numbered about four thousand armed warriors. He recommended M. le Sueur, his brother-in-law, as the most capable agent to conduct these Indians to the colony.

He suggested to the government the propriety of forming two grand territorial and administrative divisions in the French possessions in America; one under the name of the *Mississippi* or the *Louisiana Colony,* comprising all the country tributary to the

Mississippi River; the second under that of the *Canada Colony*, comprising all the country tributary to the River St. Lawrence, including the lakes. This plan was ultimately adopted.

In 1703, the Anglo-American colonies of South Carolina had already commenced to intrigue among the Indian nations in the vicinity of the posts of Louisiana for the purpose of creating difficulties in these establishments. M. de Bienville proposed a plan to attack Charleston by land, which, however, he did not even commence to execute.

In 1704, the French government having assented to the requisition of M. d'Iberville, sent out three missionaries, twenty girls intended for colonization, one midwife, and one hundred soldiers.

The documents of those days inform us that these twenty future mothers of Louisiana were under the direct superintendence of Marie Jeanne Morbé, conductress. Their names were, Françoise-Marianne de Boisrenaud, Jeanne-Catherine de Berenchard, Elizabeth le Périteau, Marie-Noël du Mesnil, Gabrielle Sanart, Marguerite ——, Marie-Thérèse Brochon, Angélique Briard, Marguerite Tavernier, Elizabeth Deshays, Marie Philippe, Louise-Marguerite Housseau, Marie-Madeleine Duane, Marie Dufresne, Marguerite Guichard, Reine Gilbert, Louise-Françoise Lafausse, Gabrielle Binet.

The family of the Sieur Etienne Bure, composed of three persons, was among the passengers. The name of the midwife was Catherine de Monthon; and she was married.

The *matériel* and *personnel* of Fort St. Louis, at Mobile, the principal post in Louisiana, presented the following condition: One hundred and eighty men in garrison, twenty-seven families, seven children from one to ten years of age, six Indians from twelve to eighteen, five Indian girls from fifteen to twenty; eighty one-story houses, nine oxen, fourteen cows, four bulls, five calves, one hundred hogs, three goats, and four hundred fowls.

In 1706, M. d'Iberville, who had truly been the father of the Louisiana colony, died at Havana during his third voyage from France to America. His death brought on the ruin of the establishments in Louisiana, which were completely neglected by the government of France.

M. de Bienville commanded Fort Mobile at that time, but was relieved by M. de May. He proposed to the government the propriety of allowing a few Indian chiefs, among whom he had settled, to visit France; but his request was refused on account of the expense attendant on the measure.

Some of the colonists, desirous of commencing agricultural pursuits, petitioned the government for permission to exchange Indian for African slaves from the islands, resting their claim upon similar exchanges already effected by the Anglo-Americans. This proposition was also refused.

In fine, M. de la Salle, king's commissioner, was succeeded by M. Dartaguette, who brought with him more colonists.

In 1709, Fort Mobile was entirely rebuilt. It was a bastioned square, containing within its walls: 1. The governor's house. 2. The king's stores. 3. The powder magazine. 4. The barracks. 5. The prison. Beyond the walls, there were a church, an hospital, a seminary, and a cemetery; quarters for soldiers, and for the priests; the quarters of M. de Bienville, of MM. de Chateaugue, de Grandeville, de Boisbrillant, de Mandeville, de Blondel, de Valagny, de Paillou, de St. Denis, de Chelen; of the chief surgeon; of M. Duclos, commissary, charged with the sale of lands, and the administration of police; of M. Poirier, storekeeper; of M. Jean-Louis Mache, gunner; the lodging houses of several women; lastly, the residences of the people in the pay of the king, and dwellings for travelers.

All these buildings were beyond the fort; but, as they were exposed to the overflow of the Mobile River, the inhabitants were compelled to seek an asylum either on the Island of Massacre, or on Dauphin Island, which was entirely sterile. A guard of twenty-five men was stationed on the former island to watch the movements of the colonists, and to prevent those who had accumulated a little money from abandoning the settlement.

The fort on the Mississippi was commanded by the Sieur St. Denis.

The Indians, incited by the English, made an attack upon the small town near Fort Mobile, and carried off twenty-six prisoners, whom they held in slavery. One of these Indians had been taken prisoner, and was burnt by the Mobilians to "dry the tears of those who had lost their relatives in the battle."

In 1710, M. de la Mothe-Cadillac, former governor and proprietor of Detroit, arrived in Louisiana, of which he had been appointed governor. He selected Fort Biloxi as his residence.

During this year, some of the colonists who had settled between the heads of the Bayou St. Jean and the Mississippi, the present site of New Orleans, had planted corn with great success.

The war sustained by France, in 1711, had so completely exhausted her treasury that she was unable to send timely assistance to the settlements established in Louisiana. The government found it expedient to adopt some means of preserving this colony without incurring expense. In its penury, it was induced to accept the propositions of M. Crozat, a celebrated merchant, who agreed to continue the colonization of these countries on condition that for fifteen years he should possess the monopoly of their trade. This privilege was granted to him by letters patent on the 14th of September, 1712, delivered at Fontainebleau.

Spain, however, attempted to oppose the establishments of M. Crozat, and even seized some of the vessels he had sent to Louisiana. Permission was then granted to introduce African slaves into the colony to cultivate the soil. During this year, a number of young women, from sixteen to twenty years of age, taken from the French hospitals, were sent to Louisiana to bear the germs of a good population into that colony. But it appears that the selection of these girls was so bad, according to the report of the commissary Duclos in 1713, that, out of twelve, only two could get married. The rest were so ugly and ill shapen that neither the colonists nor Canadians showed any inclination to unite themselves to them. "It is to be feared," he added, "that the others will long remain unmarried." The year 1713 was one of great distress to the colony. The provisions promised by M. Crozat did not arrive. The colonists were obliged to obtain supplies from Havana; and when those expected from France at last reached them, they were found to be damaged.

In 1714, there were but two hundred and fifty inhabitants in the whole country, thirty-five of whom belonged to the garrison under the command of M. de Bienville, at Biloxi. Moreover, from the report of M. la Mothe-Cadillac, this population was but "a miserable collection of the scum of Canada, fit only for the hangman, insubordinate, without religion, addicted to all sorts of vice, and to the Indian squaws, whom they preferred to the French."

M. de Bienville undertook another journey on the Red River to explore the mines of the country.

The clearings on the Mississippi amounted absolutely to nothing, while those on the Mobile, more populous than the other colony, advanced but slowly, because of the state of uncertainty which existed relative to the intentions of the government to maintain itself in that country. Such was the opinion expressed by Duclos to M. de Pontchartrain. Thus, it is not from to-day alone that French ministries have marked their acts of colonization by a fickleness fatal to the interests of France!

The missionaries erected a church upon Dauphin Island, which had become the most important post of the colony. The cultivation of indigo was attempted, and with such success that three crops were annually gathered.

Dauphin Island, which, at an early period of the colonization of Louisiana, was the principal post, and, as it were, the capital of the colony, is now what it was then, a sterile sand bank, upon which grow a few pines, creeping vines, and stunted palm trees around the ponds. It is about seven miles in length (twelve thousand metres), and about one mile in width (fifteen hundred metres), containing a superficies of about nine hundred acres (eighteen hundred hectares). The harbor was at the east end, formed by a small sand islet, known as Spanish Islet. It was situated between this islet and Massacre Island. The depth of the water was from four to five fathoms, and afforded excellent anchorage. It could be entered from the westward, by keeping near the island. On approaching it, it was necessary to pass a bar, where, at the time of M. d'Iberville's visit, the water was from twenty to twenty-one feet in depth. But in 1706, it had fallen to fifteen or sixteen feet. This anchorage could also be reached by steering for Mobile Bay, and crossing the bar, where the depth of the water was but twelve feet; a depth which has not since varied.

In front of this port, vessels of a heavier draught could anchor in an open roadstead.

The port of Dauphin was defended by a fort, under whose protection the government houses and those of the colonists had been erected. These frame buildings were ranged along the shore, built on the sand, and surrounded by small palisade pickets. Nothing could give a more unfavorable impression of this colony and its future prospects than the appearance of these wretched cabins, which were no better than the temporary huts put up by fishermen. Nevertheless, this island at one time contained over two hundred houses inclosed in an entrenched camp, surrounded by palisades where the garrison was quartered. The town was burnt down in the same year as old Biloxi.

When I visited this island in 1817, it was a perfect desert. It had become what nature intended it to be, the rendezvous of sea birds, and the resort of crocodiles, so abundant on that coast. A single individual had built his hut among the ruins of the old fort. He was an old pilot, brave and intelligent, whose heart was the seat of those noble sentiments of French honor, which one is always happy to speak of wherever they are exhibited.

In the year 1814, during the last war with England, Damour, the Mobile pilot, had been sought after by the commanding officer of the English squadron then on the coast. His reputation was well known from New Orleans to Pensacola. He alone was able to pilot the ships of this squadron through the wretched islands and difficult channels that abound along the coast of Louisiana. The party in pursuit of him searched the whole of Dauphin Island. They found his hut, turned his humble furniture upside down, and, after having despaired of securing their object, set fire to his property. In the mean time, Damour, his hatred of the English unmitigated, remained concealed in the foul water of one of the ponds on the island, in the midst of rushes and crocodiles, his head alone above its surface. In this position, he witnessed the destruction of his dwelling, debarred the means of vengeance. But the brave Frenchman was afterwards revenged, for, at the attack of Fort Boyer, on the very point of Mobile Bay, the English met with a shameful defeat before the feeble bastions of a sand redoubt, defended by a handful of brave Americans under their intrepid commander, Major Boyer.

The post of New Biloxi was situated upon the point of land to the right of the Bay of Biloxi, immediately fronting Ship Island. Old Biloxi was abandoned for this new position, which was thought to be more healthy. The Bay of Biloxi was inclosed by Deer Island.

The site of New Biloxi was very well selected as a position on the sea coast; but it had no communication with the interior of the country, or with the large rivers. It was not, therefore, a suitable place for the establishment of a colony. Still, the inclosure of the new establishment had been projected upon a regular plan. It was bastioned, and formed upon a scale as imposing as though it had been built for the defence of a second class fort.

In 1715, M. de Bienville assumed the command of the colony in the absence of M. d'Epinay. He attempted to form alliances with the natives, undertook an expedition into the midst of their settlements, and erected a fort upon the borders of the Alabama, one of the tributaries of the Mobile, so as to keep the Indians in check in that direction, for they had already been tampered with by the Anglo-Americans of the south. In 1716, he marched against the Natchez tribe, and permanently established Fort Rosalie. This fort afterwards served as the foundation of the city of Natchez. He finally succeeded in placing all the native tribes under the protection of France, with the exception of the Choctaws and Chickasaws, who had already been secured in the interest of the Americans. The last named tribes occasioned as many difficulties in the south as the Iroquois had caused in the north.

In 1717, M. Crozat, disgusted with his projects and deceived in his hopes, yielded up his privileges to the king. He left the colony in a sad condition, having, as it were, done nothing for its advancement, or, at least, so little that, at the time he resigned his rights, there were, at Louisiana, but four hundred white colonists, not including the garrison, twenty negroes, and about two hundred head of cattle.

CHAPTER XVIII.

1717—1731.

FRENCH COLONIES—LOUISIANA.

Louisiana ceded to the West India Company—Company organized by John Law—His financial system—Colonial administration—Site of New Orleans selected by M. de Bienville—Military force of the province—A post founded on Red River—Distribution of the factories of the West India Company—Mouth of the Mississippi—New territorial division adopted by the Company—Distribution of posts—Chiefs placed in command of them—Their respective emoluments—Establishments of the Jesuits—Ursuline nuns—Missions and parishes—Intervention of the English in the war against the Indians—Massacre perpetrated by the Natchez—Destruction of that tribe—The remnant that escapes takes refuge among the Chicactas—West India Company.

The province of Louisiana, and the country of the Illinois, attached to its government, were conceded to the West India Company, also called the Mississippi Company, by the king's edicts of April and September, 1717. This company was organized by John Law, a Scotchman, who, at that time, was in the intimate confidence of the Regent.

This company, established for the colonization of Louisiana and Mississippi, was founded upon a nominal capital of one hundred million francs, the stock of which was raised upon State bonds issued at par, but only worth fifty per cent. in the market!

At that period, the most absurd falsehoods were circulated concerning the riches and resources of Mississippi. Plans and maps were freely distributed, upon which gold mines were marked at almost every point, in order to seduce the credulity of lenders and speculators. Two hundred thousand shares of five hundred livres (one hundred dollars) each were issued; and their nominal value immediately advanced beyond all conception. They were titles which speculators thought must produce unbounded wealth. The course of the river was marked out by imaginary lines, and divided according to the whim of the purchaser, and the value he attached to it. A square league of land in Louisiana, in the most unknown corners, could scarcely be purchased for less than thirty thousand livres (six thousand dollars). In short, the value of this territory was greater, in certain cases, than the best cultivated lands in France!

Immense domains to the west of the Mississippi, and in the prairies of Arkansas, were granted to companies, and to rich commoners and nobles. More than six thousand inhabitants were to be furnished by these grantees. Law had reserved to himself a vast prairie in Arkansas; and, for the cultivation of these lands, he had engaged more than fifteen hundred colonists, had incurred an expense of more than a million and a-half of livres (about three hundred thousand dollars), and had purchased three hundred negroes, notwithstanding the company of which he was a member had the monopoly of the introduction of slaves. He had engaged a great number of mechanics of all kinds, and a crowd of German emigrants, to populate prairies that were more suitable for public pastures than for the habitation of man. When ten years had elapsed, but thirty wretched inhabitants could be found in this Eldorado.

The desire to emigrate to the Mississippi was so enthusiastic, in the hope of finding gold mines, as to bring forth a crowd of emigrants, mechanics, and soldiers. More than eight hundred embarked on board the *Victoire*, the *Duchess de Noailles*, and the *Marne;* and as, at that time, the French were still ignorant that they could enter the Mississippi with vessels coming from Europe, and as Dauphin Island had lost its harbor during that year by a sand bank, the vessels anchored opposite Ship Island. It was necessary to crowd all these emigrants into Fort Biloxi, whence they were to be transported in coasting vessels to the Mississippi. But, as the buildings at Biloxi were put up merely for a temporary purpose, and were withal in bad condition, the poor emigrants, who preferred the open air to close confinement in miserable huts, took the fever, and perished by disease and wretchedness.

The deceptions practiced by the abettors of Law's project caused the Mississippi to be looked upon with horror. The name was thereafter used as a term of reproach. Hence originated the threat, on the occasion of any misdemeanor or fault: "I will send you to Mississippi."

Nevertheless, the Company in Paris governed the colony, and

directed and administered its affairs, without possessing the least idea of the country. Thus, it constituted a government composed of a governor, an intendant, and a royal council. Each was endowed with distinct prerogatives. The governor had the direction of military affairs, and the treaties of alliance and commerce with the natives.

The intendant, or commissary, had charge of the police, of the courts, and the finances. He was also president and chief judge of the superior council. All expenditures were submitted to his examination for approval; and in him, in conjunction with the governor, was vested the responsibility of the sale of land.

The royal council, created by an edict of the 8th of September, 1719, was composed of a chief justice, an intendant, a king's attorney, six of the principal inhabitants, and a clerk of the province. All civil or criminal cases were referred to this court. Each individual could make his own defence either verbally or in writing. Commercial disputes were decided by the intendant, who was at once marine commissioner and admiralty judge. His decisions, as well as those of the superior council, were without appeal.

Hence, the power of the intendant was a sort of check upon that of the governor; while the power of each was kept in check by the royal council.

In 1718, M. de Bienville selected the site of the present city of New Orleans, thus named in honor of the Regent. The plan of this city was drawn up by the Sieur Blond de la Tour, Knight of St. Louis, lieutenant-general and brigadier of engineers. It was one hundred and five miles distant from the Balize, and formed an oblong square, measuring fourteen hundred and forty yards (seven hundred and twenty toises) parallel to the river, and six hundred yards (three hundred toises) in breadth.

Four companies of troops were then sent from France, amounting in all to four hundred men. They were distributed as follows:—

100	men for the	garrison	at Dauphin Island.
10	"	"	at Mobile.
30	"	"	at Biloxi.
30	"	"	at the post of Alabama.
150	"	"	at the post of Arkansas.
40	"	"	at the post of the Wabash.
30	"	a post in the interior.	

No manorial lands were ever conceded in Louisiana, as had been done in Canada. Nevertheless, Horn Island was granted to M. de Bienville, in mean tenure, in virtue of his eminent services.

The governor of the colony directed his whole attention to the means of preventing the encroachments of the Americans, whose activity and enterprising spirit rendered their vicinity formidable. He made requisitions for colonists from Europe, and for money and troops to fortify Dauphin Island, the seat of the superior council of the colony.

In the course of this year, a line of posts was established along the Mississippi, in order to place Louisiana in communication with Canada, which, until that period, had furnished Louisiana with her most intelligent colonists. One of them, named Tissenet, crossed from Mobile to the lakes, and returned with his family from Canada to the shores of this river.

In May, 1719, the French took Pensacola from the Spaniards and destroyed the Fort of the *Barancas;* but were compelled, six weeks after, to surrender to a Spanish fleet which besieged them, and attempted vainly to destroy the settlements on Dauphin Island. In September, Pensacola was again taken by the French, and was not restored to the Spaniards until the 26th of November, 1722, in pursuance of a treaty of peace.

In the same year, Bernard de la Harpe ascended the Red River, and founded Fort St. Louis, four hundred and eighty miles above Natchitoches. The Sieur Diron also founded a post in the country of the *Padoucas*. These two officers penetrated the west to within a few days march of *Santa Fe.*

In 1720, Ship Island was still the first point on the coast where vessels landed on coming from France. At this place, a fort had been constructed which contained the stores of the Company, and the dwelling of an overseer who attended to its affairs. On the second line were the posts of Biloxi and of the Illinois. In that year, a hospital was erected on Deer Island.

Biloxi was the principal factory of the Company, and the centre of its affairs. A ship yard was about to be built there for the repair of vessels, as well as a store-house to receive rigging.

The transportation of the colonists was performed by the boats of the Company, which, starting from Biloxi, passed through Lakes Pontchartrain and Maurepas, and Bayou Manchac. At the outlet of the bay, there was a post which communicated directly with the upper part of the river, by means of points ranged all along its course, at which boats employed in carrying correspondence and conveying troops could obtain all necessary supplies.

The boats on the river stopped at the port of Manchac. Those of Biloxi only passed from Manchac to Biloxi.

The *personnel* of the administration of Biloxi, at that time, consisted of a storekeeper; a person who attended to the entry and export of merchandize; one who had charge of the rigging and tackle; one who acted as clerk; and a certain number of laborers. Another clerk had charge of the stores on the river, established at Manchac, and at English Turn, on the right bank.

Dauphin Island was the second establishment. Manchac became the third, and for some time bore the name of New Orleans, because of its importance on the river. At this post, there were a book-keeper and a chief clerk. Each post had a garden and a poultry yard.

The government of France had recommended the opening of a road by land from Biloxi to the country of the Illinois, to obviate the delays which the overflow of the river occasioned in the correspondence between these two extreme points of the colony! A bearer of dispatches left each of these posts once a month. Colonists were sent to Natchez to cultivate tobacco, and their labors were highly successful.

The post of New Orleans became the fourth factory of the Company. The city, in which a few brick houses had already been built, was covered on the side towards the river by a levee, and in the rear by a large ditch, which served the purpose of a drain.

There was a military post at the mouth of Bayou St. John, in Lake Pontchartrain, nine miles from New Orleans, which was occupied by a sergeant and six men; a second post at Cat Island by an officer and fifteen men; a third, one hundred and eighty miles above New Orleans, at Point Coupée; and a fourth at Natchez.

The mouths of the Mississippi had then been thoroughly surveyed, sounded, and buoyed. They were six in number, as follows: 1. The north-east channel, or the Loutre. 2. The east. 3. The south-east. 4. The south. 5. The south-west. And 6. The Sauvol.

The south-east was the only practicable channel for vessels drawing fourteen feet of water; and to preserve as well as to improve it, a mole built of piles had been thrown up, which preserved the channel from the extreme point of the main land to the sea. A water battery, a military post, stores, a powder magazine, and a chapel, were built upon the bank that had been formed by these piles. A garrison of fifty men was usually kept there, as well as pilots and a few sailors. This post was known as the Balize Fort. At first constructed on the edge of the shore, about seven hundred yards from the sea, the deposits of earth by the current of the river have been so great that, at the present time, its distance from the sea is nearly nineteen miles.

The engineer de Paugé, to increase the depth of that channel, proposed to inclose the waters between two moles built of drift wood, covering an extent of two thousand four hundred yards. This plan, which certainly would have improved the channel, was never executed. It is to be regretted that, up to the present time, no efforts have been made to increase the depth of water at the mouth of this majestic river, for this result would not only be of great advantage to commerce, but it would diminish the rise in the river, and prevent the damage annually done to those who live on its shores.

In 1721, the West India Company adopted a new territorial division for the administration of this colony. Nine divisions were created, namely: 1. New Orleans. 2. Biloxi. 3. Mobile. 4. Alabama. 5. Natchez. 6. Yazoos. 7. Natchitoches. 8. Kansas, or Arkansas. 9. Illinois.

Each of these divisions or quarters was under the immediate control of a chief who assumed the title of commanding-general.

M. de Bienville, commandant-general of the colony, was also in immediate command of the divisions of New Orleans, Natchez, Yazoos, and Natchitoches or Red River. His salary amounted to twelve thousand livres (two thousand five hundred dollars).

M. le Blond de la Tour, brigadier of the engineer corps, chief engineer of the colony, resided at New Biloxi, of which he had the command.

The first lieutenant of the king had command of Arkansas and Illinois.

The second lieutenant of the king commanded at Mobile and Alabama. In Louisiana proper, there were three stations: New

Orleans, New Biloxi, and Mobile. The salaries of the persons employed by the Company were as follows:—

The governor-general	received	12,000	livres,	$2500
" lieutenant-governor	"	5,000	"	1000
" principal director of the Company	"	12,000	"	2500
" chief clerk of the factories	"	5,900	"	1140
" store-keeper	"	1,500	"	300
" captain commanding at New Orleans	"	1,800	"	360
" " at Missouri	"	1,000	"	250
" " at Illinois	"	700	"	140
" " at Biloxi	"	700	"	140

The administrative seat of the colony remained at Biloxi until the year 1723, when M. de Bienville transferred his head quarters to New Orleans. Biloxi then contained: 1. The director's office. 2. A store-house. 3. The director's dwelling. 4. A hospital. 5. The abode of the girls from the Salpêtrière Hospital. 6. The dwelling of the soldiers, and of the convicts who lived within the same inclosure.

The transfer of the seat of the colony to New Orleans gave an impetus to this town, and several new houses were built. The colony contained, at that time, a population of five hundred whites and four hundred blacks, mostly employed in the indigo factories.

Three hundred Germans were settled on the right shore, the wretched remains of several thousand who had been decoyed from their country to take part in the colonization system of Law. They had arrived in Louisiana under the orders of a Swedish Captain d'Aremberg, a veteran of Charles the Twelfth.

That part of the river was called the Germans' Coast, a name which it has ever since retained. It is very fertile, and exceedingly well cultivated.

Renewed attempts were made to occupy St. Bernard's Bay, in Texas; but the new post was attacked, and entirely destroyed, by the Camanche Indians.

Above the Germans' Coast, a colony of eight hundred Acadians was formed, who had arrived in Louisiana after the peace of Utrecht.

Vessels from Europe, bound to the colony, did not yet enter the river, although the channels had been surveyed for some time. They still continued to anchor at Ship Island; and Biloxi long afterwards remained the port of entry of the province.

In 1723, several Capuchin missionaries arrived at New Orleans.

In 1724, the New Orleans colony was composed of eleven military posts, namely: New Orleans, Balize, Biloxi, Dauphin Island, Alabama, Natchez, Natchitoches, Yazoos, Attakapas, and Illinois.

In 1726, the Jesuits, who had established themselves at New Orleans, were accused and convicted of prevarication. The fact is, they concerned themselves more about temporal than spiritual affairs. They gave more attention to their personal interests than to the conversion of the natives, or to the education of the colonists. They aspired to the acquisition of great wealth by their trade with the Indians.

In 1727, an Ursuline convent was founded in New Orleans. The nuns established a school for the education of female orphans, and devoted themselves to nursing the sick in the military hospital. This institution, here as elsewhere, rendered great service to the cause of humanity.

The Jesuits, who, until this period, had been freely allowed to settle in the colony, were banished by a royal edict. They had already gained so great an influence in the country that the number of their missions amounted to eleven:—

1. At New Orleans, where they had a church, at which four of their order officiated: Fathers Raphael, Theodore, Hyacinth, and Cyrille.

2. At Natchez, confided to the care of Father Philibert. There was no church at this mission.

3. At the Balize, under the care of Father Gaspard, where a church had but recently been built. Previously, mass had been celebrated in the kitchen of the mission house.

4. At Mobile, where there was a small church, but no school or paid choristers. Under the care of Father Mathieu.

5. One at the Appalaches, under the care of Father Oritorien.

6. At Natchitoches.

7. At the Germans' Coast.

8. At the post of the Tonikas.

9. At Pointe Coupée, sixty miles above the Tonikas.

10. At the Chapitoulos, or Burnt Canes.

11. At English Turn.

England, whose constant aim it has always been to attain her objects, if not directly, at least indirectly, never renounced her iniquitous policy of employing Indian emissaries to keep the French settlements in a state of constant uneasiness. From the origin of the Louisiana colony, the English Governor of South Carolina had sought an alliance with a warlike and formidable Indian nation, whose territory extended from the waters of the Mississippi to those of the Mobile, and thence to the Gulf. By means of presents of money and merchandize, he had gained over the Chicactas nation, and had enlisted them in his projects against the French colony of the Mississippi. He had induced these Chicactas to incite the Natchez, a mild and peaceable tribe, who had been friendly to the French, to rise against their ancient allies, on the futile ground that the French wished to deprive them of their territories and drive them from their country. This subterfuge succeeded. The chiefs of the Natchez believed it, inasmuch as they saw French farms gradually occupying all the lands which they had for centuries considered as their own.

Fort Rosalie, occupied by the French, was situated beyond the Yazoos, and immediately above White River. It was separated from the village of the Natchez merely by a small rivulet. In the vicinity and under the protection of the fort were a few dwellings, where tobacco and cotton were cultivated.

The Natchez had recourse to an insidious stratagem to destroy the French without danger to themselves. They pretended that they were about engaging in a great chase; and, by appearing four at a time at the door of each habitation, under the pretext of borrowing, they obtained all the arms of the French. At eight o'clock in the morning, the chief of the Natchez, accompanied by a few of his warriors, repaired to the residence of Captain Chopart, commandant of the post, and offered some poultry for sale. He contrived to let several loose in the house. The officer, in the attempt to drive them out, stooped down, when the chief gave the signal of attack; and the commandant fell under the fire of the barbarians. This murder was the signal for a general massacre of the inhabitants, which did not cease until four o'clock in the afternoon.

The Indians carried the heads of their victims to their camp, where they divided their spoils. A few children and women had escaped the massacre; the former were received into the tribe, while the latter were held as slaves. More than two hundred persons perished in this terrible butchery, which took place on the 28th of November, 1729.

The news of this irruption, and of its disastrous results, produced great consternation among the inhabitants of New Orleans. Reinforcements were immediately marched to Fort Rosalie, with which, on the 28th of January, 1730, the Sieur de Chartres suddenly fell upon the camp of the Natchez, and cruelly revenged his murdered countrymen. By this bold stroke, the tribe was almost entirely destroyed, and those who escaped took shelter among the Chicactas, who had so inconsiderately urged them to this revolt.

The West India Company, after the lapse of fourteen years, finding that its expenditures, growing out of the aggressions made on the colony, exceeded its income, in July, 1731, gave up its charter. This surrender of the administration of the province of Louisiana, including the country of the Illinois, took effect on the 1st of July; and by a royal ordinance of the same date, the country was declared free to all who might wish to settle there.

Nevertheless, colonization, during the management of the Company, had made considerable progress. The settlements had assumed some degree of importance and stability. Tobacco, cotton, indigo, rice, and Indian corn were cultivated with success; while more than two thousand slaves were on the plantations of the colony.

CHAPTER XIX.

1732—1769.

FRENCH COLONIES—LOUISIANA.

Administration of Governor Perrier—He is succeeded by M. de Bienville—War against the Chicactas Indians—Defeat of a party led by M. d'Artaguette—Death of this worthy officer—Another engagement with the Chicactas—Establishment of Natchitoches—Depth of water found in the channels of the Mississippi—Population of Louisiana—Its military forces—Administration of M. de Kerlerek—Introduction of the cultivation of the sugar-cane by M. Dubreuil—M. de Kerlerek foils the projected attacks of the Anglo-Americans—Cession of Louisiana to Spain—Arrival of Governor Ulloa—The citizens refuse to submit to Spanish domination—Conspiracy to effect their expulsion—Decree issued by the superior council, obliging Governor Ulloa and the Spanish troops to leave the colony—Claims of the Louisianians on the French government—O'Reilly sent by the court of Madrid to take possession of Louisiana—The Louisianians, wishing to declare the independence of their country, apply to the English, then at Pensacola, to assist them—O'Reilly's arrival at New Orleans—He promises an amnesty, and forgetfulness of all that has occurred, but orders the execution of six of the principal conspirators.

Governor Perrier began to govern the province of Louisiana on behalf of the king in 1732. His first care was to provide adequate means of defence. He completed Fort Condé, at Mobile, which he garrisoned with sixty men. Nearly fifteen thousand Indians, in the vicinity of Mobile River, were tributary to this post.

For some time, the design to surround Mobile, which had been raised under the protection of Fort Condé, with a regular bastioned inclosure, was entertained; but it was abandoned on account of the expense that it would involve. The town increased according to the caprice of those who came there to settle; but at no time was it very considerable. M. Perrier rebuilt the fort at Natchez, its position on the river being important to keep in check the Indians of that quarter. He also built a fort at the point where the St. Francis empties into the Mississippi; and another, called

Assumption, on Margot River, now Wolf River, above the Chickasaw Bluffs. He also increased the garrison of Fort Tombeckbee, four hundred and eighty miles distant from Mobile.

In 1732, a powder magazine and barracks were constructed at New Orleans, the latter sufficiently large to accommodate three hundred soldiers.

In this year, M. de Verges, engineer of the province, proposed, by means of camels, to be kept at the post of Balize, to effect at slight expense the passage of vessels drawing eighteen feet across the bar of the Mississippi.

In 1735, M. de Bienville succeeded M. Perrier as governor of the province. This able chief was intimately acquainted with the country, and had completely identified his fortune with the success of colonization in Louisiana. He also thoroughly understood the Indian character, and appreciated the advantages and inconveniences attendant on their vicinity to the French settlements. One of his first acts, with the object of subduing the Chicactas, who had sold themselves to the Anglo-Americans, was to require the delivery of the Natchez Indians who had sought and obtained refuge among them at the time of the recapture of Fort Rosalie by the troops of the province. The answer they returned was an indignant and courageous refusal.

M. de Bienville then declared war against them, to meet the expenses of which he issued a paper currency, which was circulated in the colony.

His first step was to stir up several neighboring tribes, allies of the French, against them. In the mean time, while some of their chiefs attempted to approach the governor ostensibly to solicit peace, a party fell suddenly on a French post, killed eight soldiers, and carried the officer to their camp.

M. de Bienville then concluded that with such enemies but one course of action was available, a resort to main force. He immediately projected a powerful expedition into their territory, which he designed to take place in the spring of 1736. He sent orders to M. d'Artaguette, commandant at Illinois, to advance with his forces on the Chicactas, and to be, in March, on the Tombeckbee River, near a point where the Americans have since founded the small town called *Cotton-Gin-Port*, at the head of navigation of that river, where he would join him with troops from the post of Mobile. Unable to make his preparations for the time appointed, he sent another messenger to M. d'Artaguette to apprise him of his delay; unfortunately, the latter had commenced his march, and did not receive the message. D'Artaguette continued to advance at the head of a few brave Frenchmen, and a party of Illinois and Miami warriors, their allies, and was greatly surprised not to find M. de Bienville at the place appointed, and still more so at receiving no tidings concerning him. Nevertheless, as he had boldly penetrated into the country of the Chicactas, and was already in sight of their villages, he did not hesitate to attack them immediately. But scarcely had he made the first movement when he found himself surrounded by four or five hundred hostile Indians, led by Americans. These rushed with such intrepidity upon their assailants that a panic was produced among the Illinois and Miamis, who fled in every direction. M. d'Artaguette, seeing himself thus abandoned by his Indian warriors, who composed the majority of his force, resolved to fall back on the position where, under the charge of a few of his men, he had left his stores. But the Chicactas pursued him so rapidly that, despite the firmness and devoted courage of all the officers, soldiers, and citizens who had accompanied him in this unfortunate expedition, and who vied with one another in feats of bravery, he was entirely defeated, for the enemy was far superior in numbers. D'Artaguette had succeeded in checking his assailants with thirty-eight Iroquois, twenty-eight Arkansas, and five Frenchmen, who fought bravely to defend their flag, when, wounded in several places, this heroic officer, and the brave followers who covered him with their bodies, surrendered. A single officer and a Jesuit were the only prisoners taken by the Chicactas.

D'Artaguette had led forth fifty Canadian Frenchmen, and a thousand Indians of various tribes. He had been accompanied by Father Senet, who, with the brave Vincennes, was taken prisoner and burned. A city in Illinois was named after Vincennes, thereby transmitting his name to posterity.

This disastrous defeat occurred on Palm Sunday. The Chicactas, having taken all the baggage of the French, were apprised by means of the letter of Governor de Bienville to Artaguette of his intended attack. This information put them on their guard, and they made preparations for defence.

In this affair, the Louisiana colony lost one of its most distinguished officers, the unfortunate and brave Major d'Artaguette, and

M. de St. Ange, equally regretted for his zeal and courage. M. de Noyan, nephew of M. de Bienville, was among the wounded. The failure of the enterprise paralyzed the subsequent operations of the French in this country, where the Anglo-Americans—who had incited this war, and, by underhanded means, had directed the Indians—gained an ascendency, which increased from year to year, to the great detriment of the influence and of the establishments of the French.

In 1737, a hospital was founded in New Orleans.

The Anglo-Americans continued to arouse the Indian nations in the vicinity of the French, and even to incite the allies of the latter to attack the colony. They had already succeeded in gaining over Red Slipper, a Chicactas chief. They also tried to hire the Choctaw chief, Red Stocking. Nevertheless, the majority of the Choctaws remained faithful to the French. The latter was a very powerful tribe, and was spread over an extent of one hundred and fifty miles. It was distributed in fifty villages, under fifty chiefs, with a force of four thousand effective warriors. Its head chiefs were *Stiscohakko* (Blue Wood), and *You-lak-ti-ma-ta-ha*, the largest of his race.

In 1739, by a royal edict, the ports of Louisiana and of the Antilles were declared free.

In 1740, the Governor of Louisiana, having received assistance from Canada, again tried his fortune against the English and the Chicactas tribe; but was not more successful than he had been on previous occasions. When favorable circumstances at length brought about a reconciliation with the Indians, a treaty of peace was concluded by M. de Bienville. After that period, the tranquillity of the colony was no longer disturbed by them. These two expeditions cost France more than one million livres (two hundred thousand dollars).

In 1743, the settlement of Natchitoches, two hundred and sixteen miles above the mouth of Red River, and three hundred and ninety-six miles from New Orleans, received a fresh impulse by the arrival of new emigrants.

In 1747, the principal channel of the Mississippi, where the post of Balize was established, and which had undergone no change for a period of twenty-eight years, suddenly became closed. Its depth was only seven or eight feet. On the other hand, the depth of the east channel increased to *seventeen feet.* A French frigate, the *Chameau*, entered it without difficulty.

When the wind blew seaward, the tide sometimes rose three feet four inches at the lower part of the river. The gradual elevation of the ground near the mouths of the river caused a rise in the tides when certain winds prevailed. This fact was noticed by M. Duverger, who had carefully made observations on the rise and fall of the waters at the Balize.

In 1750, the population of Louisiana amounted to about five thousand whites, and two thousand five hundred slaves. The military strength of the colony was two thousand men, fifty of whom were Swiss, distributed as follows:—

1000	men in	the garrison	at New Orleans.
500	"	"	at Mobile.
300	"	"	at Arkansas.
50	"	"	at Natchez.
50	"	"	at Natchitoches.
50	"	"	at Pointe Coupée.
50	"	"	at the Germans' Coast.

Thus, Louisiana, after half a century, was still a colony without a name, without productions, without industry, without inhabitants, and exposed to the insults and depredations of the Indians.

In 1751, M. de Kerlerek was appointed governor-general. He favored the trade of English interlopers, thus causing much trouble and discord. The colony at that period had equal reason to regret the serious conflicts between the governor and the commissary De Rochemore.

At this period, the inhabitants began to think seriously of the necessity of commencing agricultural pursuits, the sole resource of these rich countries. The introduction of the sugar cane was contemplated. As far back as 1742, the Jesuits had succeeded in preserving a few stalks which they had obtained from St. Domingo. Several experiments had been made to grow the cane on a small scale, when M. Dubreuil, one of the richest men in the colony, as well as one of those most interested in everything connected with its prosperity, undertook to cultivate it extensively. Having sent to St. Domingo for the cane, he succeeded, in 1757 and 1758, in making brown sugar of an excellent quality, several samples of which he transmitted to the minister of France.

The death of this zealous colonist suspended, for a time, these experiments. But at length M. de Mazan, an old retired officer, and one of the richest inhabitants of the colony, with the object of prosecuting them on a large scale, obtained very ripe cane, which he ground upon his own plantation, and succeeded in producing a beautiful article, which, for quality and quantity, equaled the product of the St. Domingo and Martinique cane.

In 1760, M. de Kerlerek baffled the projects of the Anglo-Americans, who, with the purpose of attacking the colony, had succeeded in detaching a portion of the Choctaw nation from the interest of the French. He afterwards constructed a continuous inclosure, composed of a battlemented palisade and a ditch, and flanked it by five redoubts, which completely protected New Orleans against any sudden attack. The citizens were then enrolled and organized as militia. The command of these was given to old retired officers, among whom were MM. d'Aremberg, Favrost, Pontalba, the Chevalier Macarty, De Mazan, Leblanc, Olivier, Duverger, father and son, Bienvenu, sergeant major of militia, and Beauré, Lavergne, and Trudeau.

The administration of M. de Kerlerek had been fortunate for Louisiana, which was just commencing to rise from her state of lethargy, when, at the close of the war between France and England, a shameful peace was purchased by the cession of our possessions in Canada to the English crown. However, this peace might have operated to its advantage. The Louisianians believed that the future would bring with it better times, and that their fur trade would be augmented by a part of that which had formerly passed through Canada. Commerce with the French islands became more brisk after the peace of 1763. As intercourse with Mexico, which had been interrupted by the war, was renewed, the arrival of French vessels upon the shores of the Mississippi became more frequent. Canadian emigrants arrived in crowds from Canada to increase the resources and productive strength of the colony. In fine, at the very time the future seemed to open with a smiling and unusually encouraging prospect, the French government officially announced to the people of Louisiana, on the 21st of April, 1764, through the medium of M. Dabbadie, director-general and commandant of the province, that, by a secret convention of the 3d of November, 1762, Louis the Fifteenth had ceded New Orleans, and all the country extending along the right bank of the Mississippi, to the crown of Spain. Thus did France, in a single day, resign the work of a century—a work which had cost so much trouble, so much generous blood, so much treasure. Thus did she renounce her rights, and disinherit her children of a place of rest and of refuge in the New World! Strange fatality, which always directs the actions of governments against the interests of the governed!

The history of French colonization in the province of Louisiana would conclude with the cession of this colony to the crown of Spain, and all interest which attaches to it would cease as far as relates to the French, if the atrocities subsequently inflicted by the Spaniards upon our fellow-citizens did not require our notice, in connection with important facts concerning the colony of Louisiana.

The Louisiana colonists manifested the greatest aversion to Spanish dominion. This disposition, well known to the mother country, had no influence upon the arrangements concluded between the Courts of Versailles and Madrid. On the fifth of March, 1766, M. d'Ulloa arrived in the colony with eighty soldiers. Nevertheless, he did not take immediate possession of the country in the name of his master; and the colony continued to be administered in the name of the King of France, under M. Aubry. M. d'Ulloa asked permission merely to establish a few posts on the river. His desire was accomplished; and from the mouth of the river to the Illinois, three distinct flags were seen to wave in the breeze—those of France, Spain, and England. Everything remained perfectly quiet.

Nevertheless, from that time, the expenses of the government and administration of Louisiana were borne by the King of Spain; and no vessel could arrive there from France unless furnished with a Spanish passport.

M. d'Ulloa only awaited the arrival of the forces necessary to take ostensible possession of the colony when the revolt of the 29th of October, 1768, broke out.

The inhabitants could not believe that Spain wished to secure possession of this province, because of the few advantages to its government such possession would be likely to produce. They thought rather that M. d'Ulloa and his officers were agents sent out to ascertain the resources of the country; and, as they seemed to be but ill satisfied, the people of Louisiana concluded that the reports made to the Spanish government must have been very unfavorable.

Such was the feeling of the Louisianians when the King of Spain issued a law which interdicted all commercial relations with those markets which had heretofore received their produce. Instead of attempting to quiet the feelings of the colonists, and thus inducing them to conform to the views of the Spanish government, Ulloa manifested intolerable haughtiness, imposed heavy taxes upon the people, and, by repeated arbitrary measures, excited their hatred.

The Louisianians were goaded to desperation. They could not reconcile themselves to the idea of being subject to foreign laws; and they requested the council of their colony to inform the Spanish government that it must retire.

This decree was issued on the 28th of October, 1768; and M. d'Ulloa was compelled to yield to it, notwithstanding the representations made by M. Aubry to the general council, and to the principal leaders of this movement.

This manifestation of loyalty on the part of the Louisianians towards the government of the mother country who had abandoned them, and of hatred to that of Spain, was conducted with ability and all the outward signs of legality. No acts of violence were committed. Deputies were sent to the government of France; but they did not reach their destination till six weeks after the arrival of Governor d'Ulloa. The public sympathized with the colonists; but the ministers manifested towards them the greatest displeasure! Nothing could change the decree against the poor colony. The Spanish government ordered General O'Reilly, an Irishman by birth, in the service of Spain, to sail from the Island of Cuba, with three thousand regular troops, to Louisiana, whither he arrived in a frigate, with twenty-three transports, on the 12th of August, 1769.

The excitement of the Louisianians, on receiving the news of the return of the Spaniards, is beyond description. They were anxious to oppose their landing, to burn their vessels, to declare a republic, and to place themselves under the protection of England. MM. de Bienville and Mazan had made advances to the authorities of Pensacola, then in possession of the English, to ascertain their feelings upon the subject; but their overtures had been received with coldness. It is, moreover, authentically proved by the records of the criminal trials of that period, by published memoirs, and by the publication of a pamphlet entitled "Reflections of a Citizen," that the principal chiefs of the superior council of Louisiana, and a great part of the leading men of that colony, had entertained the idea of declaring their country a *republic;*[*] that this bold enterprise had been quietly contrived, through the medium of commissioner Foucault, at the residence of the widow Pradel, where the conspirators met nightly; that from this house MM. de Noyan and de Mazan repaired to the English authorities at Pensacola, with the object of obtaining their recognition of the important act declaratory of their independence. Hence it appears that, but for some unimportant circumstances, New Orleans would have robbed Boston of the honor of being the cradle of American liberty!

Such were the sentiments of the people when General O'Reilly issued a proclamation, in which he promised peace and tranquillity to the people. The commandant Aubry,[†] successor of M. Dabbadie, who died miserably in New Orleans, played a part in this affair unworthy of a Frenchman, and of an old defender of Fort Duquesne. Interposing in behalf of the Spaniards, he made declarations to the inhabitants which induced them at length to permit the entrance of the Spanish ships and troops into New Orleans.

But Spanish vengeance soon displayed itself, and French blood was the first to flow for liberty on American soil as a pious offering, as the first fruits of a still greater tribute to be paid to it, some years later, by our compatriots, the allies of the immortal Washington.

On the very day of O'Reilly's reception, after a dinner to which all the persons of distinction, military and civil, had been invited, twelve of their number were arrested, and immediately tried and executed! Five of these citizens were beheaded for their religious devotion to their country and to liberty, namely: MM. Nicholas Chovin de la Fresnière, king's advocate (this patriot would not consent to utter a single word in his defence, so sacred did he consider his cause, so vile did he regard his enemies

* Extract from official documents in the Naval Archives.

† Captain Aubry, after O'Reilly had taken definitive possession of Louisiana, sailed for France, was wrecked on the coast, and perished.

the judges); Jean Baptiste de Noyan, a half pay captain of cavalry; Pierre Carresse, merchant; Pierre Marquis, an old Swiss officer; Joseph Milhet, merchant. M. Villeré died of his wounds before he was brought to trial.

MM. Joseph Petit, merchant; Balthazar Mazan; Julien Jerome Doucet, lawyer; Jean Milhet, merchant; Pierre Poupet, merchant; and Pierre Hardi de Boisblanc, counselor, were sent to languish in the dungeons of Havana.

M. Foucault was the only one of the accused who was permitted to return to France to be tried by his government.

This horrible tragedy, ordered by the Spanish minister, created no feeling of indignation in the French ministry. But it will never be forgotten by France any more than the new proofs of attachment which the people of Louisiana have manifested towards her.

CHAPTER XX.

1512—1821.

SPANISH COLONIES—LOUISIANA, FLORIDA.

Discovery of Florida; its settlement—St. Augustine founded—St. Joseph's Bay—St. Mark—Pensacola—Conduct of the Spaniards towards the natives—Occupation of West Florida by the English—Louisiana ceded to Spain—The English driven from their posts in West Florida—Situation of the colony at that period—Form of the government and of the administration—New boundary treaty between Spain and the United States—The Americans obtain the free navigation of the Mississippi, and the right to store their produce in New Orleans—Difficulties arising from the execution of this treaty—Louisiana re-ceded to France; subsequently sold by the French Republic to the United States—Importance of this acquisition to the United States—Spain for several years keeps possession of East Florida—Definitive cession of all Florida to the United States—Its political advantages to the American Union.

The discovery of Florida by the Spaniards, as we have already stated in Chapter I., dates as far back as 1512; consequently, this discovery is anterior to that of any other point on the continent. Its settlement also preceded that of the North American colonies.

According to the histories of that early period, it would appear that this country, at the time of the arrival of the Europeans, was as populous as Peru or Mexico. It was supposed to be exceedingly favorable to colonization; for the earth was strewn with flowers, and the climate was delightful. These advantages are real—they have not changed. No part of the territory of the United States presents conditions so favorable to man; but the soil is by no means so generous as the spontaneous growth of flowers, so very seductive to the eye, would seem to indicate. The vegetation and bloom are owing rather to the soft temperature of a climate uniformly warm, than to the richness of the soil, which is composed chiefly of sand.

But the real advantages of Florida were not the objects which the Spaniards sought when they discovered it. As their insatiable thirst for gold, and their hope of finding treasures in the bosom of the earth, or fountains which would impart eternal youth, found no encouragement, they confined themselves to the establishment of military posts along the coast, by means of which they might easily maintain intercourse with the natives of the interior, and with their principal station in the Gulf at Havana.

It was thus that, in 1565, they founded St. Augustine on the shores of the Atlantic, St. Joseph and St. Mark on the Gulf, and, in 1696, Pensacola, also on the gulf. Neither of these posts rapidly increased. Their existence depended entirely on the necessities and expenses of the garrisons, or agents of the government, who composed nearly the whole population.

St. Augustine, which appears to have been the most considerable, has never had, at any time, more than from fifteen to eighteen hundred inhabitants, notwithstanding it is situated in the midst of orange groves, at the bottom of a splendid bay, in proximity to a fine river, the St. John, and in a most temperate and healthy climate. This little town has, in consequence of these advantages, been the resort of all strangers, or colonists from the Antilles, whom sickness has compelled to seek, under a serener sky, the restoration of their broken health; but it has never been a commercial or a manufacturing city. Nevertheless, its importance as the chief town of the Spanish colony, and its proximity to the Anglo-American settlements, frequently rendered it an object of envy to the latter, who several times attacked it, though without success.

The Bay of St. Joseph, on the gulf, had, at an early day, been noticed, by Spanish, English, and French navigators, in consequence of the good anchorage it afforded; the safety of its harbor, permitting the entrance of vessels drawing eighteen feet of water; and its proximity to the Antilles. Several temporary, but no permanent, establishments had been formed there. In 1708, the French made the attempt, but soon abandoned it. It devolved on the Americans to give a commercial and political existence to this place, and to insure its permanency. Their active and penetrating mind enabled them to appreciate the advantages which so admirable a position, now a part of Georgia, must develop in the future.

St. Mark was settled in a more permanent manner by the Spaniards. Here they raised a fort, to which the Indians of the interior came to exchange their furs for other commodities. The port still serves as an outlet to Tallahassee, the capital of Florida; but all its advantages are nearly destroyed by the proximity and superiority of St. Joseph.

Pensacola, after St. Augustine, was the principal seaport of the Spaniards in Florida with respect to population; but for the extent and safety of its roadstead, where frigates can enter, it ranks first. After Havana, it is the best harbor in the Gulf of Mexico. It was known to De Soto and his companions, in 1558, under the name of *Anchosi* or *Achusi*. In 1693, the Spaniards named it St. Mary; and in 1696, St. Mary de Galvez.

In 1700, Pensacola contained a population, including the garrison, of only two hundred inhabitants, who depended entirely upon Havana for their provisions. This condition, moreover, has never varied at any period. Its inhabitants have never manifested sufficient industry to provide for their own necessities.

Florida was settled by Spaniards stimulated by religious fanaticism, which prompted the Catholic missionaries to make proselytes among the numerous Indian nations of the New World. But we must, at the same time, acknowledge that the Spaniards have always treated the natives with more loyalty, deference, kindness, and justice than any other of the European nations. From the first, they adopted the principle never to arm the Indians. They afterwards made attempts to convert them to Christianity, and finally completely amalgamated with them.

The Franciscan missionaries have been the principal agents of the Spaniards among the Indian nations into whose country they penetrated. They boldly advanced among the *Appalaches*, also named *Apalates*, *Appelatche*, and *Palassi*. These Indians, the mountaineers of North America, lived among the Alleghany Mountains, which, indistinctly known under the name of these tribes, have, from that time, retained the characteristic name of the *Apalachian* Mountains. The missionaries converted so many of these Indians to the Catholic faith that, when they were driven from Carolina by the Anglo-Americans, a great number sought refuge under the walls of St. Augustine, and others around the settlements of Mobile, Pensacola, and Spiritu Santo Bay. Under the name of Florida, the Spaniards claimed a great portion of American territory, including a part of South Carolina, Georgia, Florida, Mississippi, Alabama, Tennessee, and all Louisiana and Texas.

As France had settled the shores of the Mississippi, and colonized Louisiana, the territory included in this province was acknowledged as French property.

In 1760, the people of the English colonies, who had been encroaching on the domains of Spain in the Floridas, obtained a settlement definitively establishing the boundary between the Anglo-American and the Spanish possessions. It was then that the River St. Mary became the line of demarkation between Georgia and Florida.

Governor Oglethorpe, of Georgia, who had taken Havana from the Spaniards in 1762, restored it to them in 1763, in exchange for Florida, which thus passed to the possession of the English. The principal settlements, at that time, were St. Matthew, St. Augustine, St. Mark, St. Joseph, and Pensacola. The British government, wishing to establish planters in Florida, offered, the following year, 1764, one hundred acres of land to any head of a family that would settle there, and fifty to each person he would take with him, on condition that he would pay an annual rent of one cent per acre. Notwithstanding these advantageous conditions, the colony did not increase rapidly.

Louisiana, ceded to Spain by a secret treaty in 1762, passed under the rule of that power in 1769, as we have already stated in treating of the colonial history of that French province. General O'Reilly was charged with the consummation of this act, in which he displayed great cruelty and an odious spirit of vengeance. In order to remain peaceful master of this colony, he expelled the Anglo-Americans and Jews, and instituted a military government, which insured to Spain the supremacy of her laws and principles.

He bequeathed his administration to Don Luis Unzaga, who was himself replaced, in 1780, by Don Bernard de Galvez, an able and enterprising man, whose administration was more popular than that of his predecessors.

In 1780, Governor-General Galvez set on foot an expedition against the Anglo-Americans settled on several points of West Florida. He marched on Baton Rouge and Mobile, which he succeeded in taking. The surrender of these posts was followed by that of Pensacola in 1781; and thus all West Florida fell under the power of Spain. East Florida remained in possession of the English.

General Galvez, after the successful issue of his expedition, sought to introduce order in the administration of his government. The colony recovered a little tranquillity while this able governor remained at the head of affairs.

The military resources of the colony, at this period, consisted of a single regiment of regular infantry, whose effective force did not amount to more than twelve hundred men, instead of two thousand and two hundred, the full complement; of one battalion of militia, whose contingent was indefinite; one of the *Germans of the Coast;* and one of *colored people:* in all, about five or six thousand men.

The population of New Orleans was, at the same time, from eight to ten thousand inhabitants; and that of the whole colony about one hundred thousand.

In the governmental organization of the colony, as modified by Galvez, the military governor was also president of the courts of justice and of commerce.

The intendant, or civil governor, had under his control a *contador major*, and royal officers, who formed an admiralty court and a chamber of accounts.

The court of justice was subordinate to the supreme jurisdiction of the royal audience of Mexico.

The bishop resided in New Orleans, and was assisted by a numerous clergy, distributed throughout the parishes according to the necessities of the colony.

The public revenue was raised from the proceeds of the customs. The duties imposed were six per cent. on exports, and on importations from Spain; and fifteen per cent. on foreign importations.

The custom-house employed a great number of agents; but the revenue was far from covering the expenses of the administration. The deficit was generally estimated at about one hundred and fifty thousand dollars.

At that period, this colony was prized only for the value of its hides, which, in the markets of Europe, it was thought, could compete with those of Buenos Ayres.

The Rio Bravo, according to the Spaniards, was the boundary line between the province of Louisiana and that of Texas.

At the general peace in 1783, East Florida was restored to Spain, which thus again possessed both Floridas, as well as Louisiana.

In 1795, the Americans concluded a treaty with the government of Spain, by which they obtained a new boundary line on their Florida frontier. All the Spanish settlements to the south of the thirty-first degree of latitude were evacuated and passed under the dominion of the United States; and the free navigation of the Mississippi, as well as the right of storing merchandize in New Orleans, was granted to American vessels. But the Spaniards did not respect the articles of the treaty, and the United States made preparations to compel compliance by main force. For that purpose, troops were assembled on the Ohio in readiness to descend to New Orleans.

In 1800, Bonaparte, then first consul, obtained from Spain the retrocession of Louisiana. This treaty was concluded on the 1st of October, more than one year previous to the unfortunate expedition that had been fitted out to retake St. Domingo, and the day after the convention signed with the United States relative to the right of neutrals. But the treaty had remained a secret, and Bonaparte had deferred taking possession of Louisiana until he could effect his purpose with more safety. If he could have recovered St. Domingo and Louisiana, he would thus have elevated anew, in the islands and on the continent of America, the colonial power of France.

The disaster of St. Domingo prevented the realization of this great scheme.

The right granted to American vessels to store goods in New

Orleans had been tacitly prolonged since the expiration of its first limit; but the Spanish intendant, Morales, subsequently suppressed it by a proclamation of the 16th of October, 1802. This unexpected prohibition aroused the discontent of the Americans, who could not dispense with the free navigation of the Mississippi, nor with the commercial facilities that the right of deposit gave them.

Threats of invasion were renewed in the Western States. In the meanwhile, President Jefferson demanded of Spain the fulfilment of her treaty of 1795, and commenced negotiations with France for the cession of New Orleans, and a part of the left shore of the Mississippi.

Bonaparte, however, had made preparations for the occupation of Louisiana. M. Laussat had been appointed maritime prefect of the colony, and General Victor governor.

But on the approach of the war which was so soon again to rekindle Europe, the first consul, wishing to collect all his disposable forces around him, renounced his intention of sending troops to America, as they would be much more essential to him at home.

On the other hand, the Americans solicited from the French government the cession of the city of New Orleans and the lands adjacent. Their negotiator, Chancellor Livingston, even proposed that the territory belonging to the colony, situated to the north of Arkansas, should be added to the cession. From that time, the first consul gave up all idea of occupying Louisiana, and determined to cede to the United States a possession which he at first felt desirous of securing for France. He hoped, by such an arrangement, to oppose a counterpoise to the maritime power of Great Britain; for he saw in this rivalry of interests, and in this balance of power, a new means of resisting the monopoly and exclusive pretensions of a single nation.

The decree of the 3d of April, 1803, fixed the terms of this cession; and the Americans, for the small sum of fifteen million dollars, acquired the rights of France over that magnificent colony and its dependencies, agreeing, on their part, to indemnify their fellow-citizens for the losses they had sustained by the illegal capture of their vessels and cargoes, losses amounting to upwards of five million dollars.

Though this colony had been separated from France forty years;

though the first generation had passed away; and though the interests, manners, and laws of the people had been modified, the ascendency of old associations and of early affections still remained; and when the people learned that they were about to be governed once more by the laws of their fatherland, their emotions were profound.

To accomplish the cession of Louisiana, it became necessary, in the first place, that the Spanish authorities should restore it to the French, who had been commissioned to receive it. Accordingly, on the 30th of November, 1803, the government of Louisiana was transferred to M. Laussat, who had for several months resided in New Orleans, though not in the employment of government, by M. de Salcedo and the Marquis of Casa-Calvo, brigadiers in the Spanish army, and commissioners of his Catholic majesty.

For the most important facts here related, we are indebted to the *Moniteur de la Louisiane*, the official journal of New Orleans; and we refer our readers to the proclamation addressed to the Louisianians, on that occasion, by M. Laussat, in the name of the French Republic.

This new functionary only temporarily performed the duties to which he had been called. Nevertheless, he appointed a new municipal council, and adopted several important internal regulations, then of the utmost importance to public tranquillity. The municipal council was composed of twelve members and a secretary, as follows: MM. Boré, mayor; Derbigny, secretary; Destrehan, first assistant to the mayor; Sauvé, second assistant; Livaudais, sen., Petit Cavelier, Villeray, Johns, sen., Fortier, sen., Donaldson, Faurie, Allard, jun., Tureaud, John Watkins, and Labatut, treasurer of the city.

M. Bellechasse was appointed colonel of the New Orleans militia, and instructor of the companies of free men of color.

With the object of preparing the second transfer of sovereignty, the American general, Wilkinson, advanced, on the 20th of December, with a body of troops towards New Orleans, and issued an order of the day. On the same day, the government of the colony was transferred to W. C. C. Claiborne, United States commissioner, who was appointed to take possession of it. Mr. Claiborne, on this occasion, addressed a proclamation to the Louisianians, published in English, French, and Spanish, and delivered an address in the great hall of the court house.

The French flag had waved for twenty days over the public buildings of New Orleans. It was delivered with military honors into the hands of the French commissioner, and saluted with the most enthusiastic acclamations by the whole population.

Thus passed under the dominion of the Anglo-Americans the colony of Louisiana, the last possession of France on the American continent, founded amid the most brilliant expectations, called to the most imposing destinies, and for which the French government only obtained a few million francs, not even an equivalent for the free entrance of the *American Nile*, thus abandoned to the United States, and thus insuring to them the entire possession of all North America at no very distant period.

As territory, the acquisition of Louisiana was in many respects a substantial advantage; for, by the treaty of cession, the United States inherited the same rights, titles, and claims to the whole extent of country to the east, and principally to the west of the Mississippi, that Spain and France enjoyed. The French had pushed their settlements west of the Mississippi as far as the river *Aux Cannes*, in the Bay of *San Bernard*, the *Red River*, and the *Arkansas*, in the province of Texas. The frontiers between the Spanish colony of New Mexico and Louisiana had never been officially settled. Hence, the Americans took possession of things as they found them, and could thus claim rights of property to a great portion of Texas.

The destiny of the Louisianians had again changed; but they were no longer dependent upon the caprice, will, or ignorance of their government. They at once became invested, by the act of occupation of the United States, with the rights and prerogatives of a constitution, and of a free government. In fact, the Louisianians, when they became free citizens of the United States, immediately entered into the enjoyment of all the rights belonging to freemen, and participated directly in the prosperity of their country by constituting a government for themselves. And, certainly, the happiness they have since enjoyed, and the miraculous prosperity of their adopted country, need never cause them to regret a political change to which they were forced to submit, though they had not even been consulted in relation to it. Should bygone times have been unprofitable to them, their recompense both for the present and the future consists in their singular position, destined to be the outlet to the labor and industry of the millions of freemen who shall people the rich and immense western territory of America!

From 1800 to 1819, that part of Florida lying between St. Augustine and Pensacola remained in the possession of Spain. Spain took no pains to secure her territory against the encroachments of adventurers, who, on several occasions, profiting by its vicinity to the United States, attempted to annoy the latter government.

The Americans were not the people quietly to tolerate such a state of things. The government of the United States, as far back as 1811, fearing that Spain would cede this country to some European power, adopted the necessary measures to prevent such a result. It perseveringly and skillfully negotiated with the court of Madrid for its acquisition. To a country already so rich in lands as the Union, Florida was of but little value with respect to its soil; but it was of immense importance in a national point of view, as completing the maritime frontier of the United States on the gulf, and, above all, as withdrawing from an enemy of the United States all means of aggression, by depriving him of the only point where he could land on their territory.

At the same time, and to rest their negotiations on a tangible basis, the Americans, having been compelled to punish the outrages committed by several Indian tribes upon their citizens on the borders of Alabama and Georgia, took possession of St. Mark and Pensacola, in 1810, under the plea that the Spaniards had not sufficient force at these two points to prevent the incursions of the Indians, who continued to obtain munitions of war from these two posts. Nevertheless, Pensacola was restored to the Spaniards after the Americans had taken vengeance on some of the foreign agents who had instigated these savages to attack the borderers. But they held possession of St. Mark.

By the treaty of the 22d of February, 1819, Spain at length definitively ceded Florida to the American government for the sum of five million dollars, the amount of the claims of American merchants on the Spaniards for the property that had been condemned by them in the ports of Spain. The Spanish government also renounced all her rights, prerogatives, and claims over the territory north of the forty-second degree of latitude, starting from a line intersecting the Arkansas River.

Transfer of possession took place in 1821. Since that period, the territory of Florida has been permanently attached to the American Union. Its purchase from Spain, under the presidency of James Monroe, is undoubtedly in American history an event of the greatest importance in a political point of view, and does as much honor to the diplomatic talents of this chief magistrate as to his profound knowledge of the true interests of the United States.

Thus was the maritime frontier of the Union completed. But one national jurisdiction has thenceforth extended from Passamaquoddy Bay, in the east, to the Sabine River, west of the Mississippi, on the Gulf of Mexico. Hence, there has been no further reason to fear the aggressions and internal dissensions which a foreign enemy could stir up on this territory by assuming the garb of neutrality, or, rather, by reason of the weakness of the Spanish government, which was unable to enforce respect for its laws.

CHAPTER XXI.

OREGON TERRITORY.

Description of Oregon territory—Historical summary of all the partial or complete expeditions to the north-west coast of the Pacific, and Oregon territory—Expedition of Captains Lewis and Clarke—Settlement of the Columbia by J. J. Astor—Occupation of the American establishments by the English—Convention of 1818—Hudson's Bay Company—Its organization—Sandwich Islands—Treaty of 1823 between Russia and Great Britain — Negotiations commenced, in 1827, between England and the United States—Treaty of 1828 between the United States and Mexico—Measures adopted by the government at Washington relative to the occupation of Oregon—Emigrations of Americans towards the western regions—Final settlement of the Oregon territory.

DESCRIPTION OF THE OREGON TERRITORY.

The United States attain the western coast of North America through the Oregon territory, and thus extend their domain from the Atlantic to the Pacific Oceans. This remarkable geographical position must powerfully contribute towards the brilliant destinies which await the American Union. It favors, in fact, on its own soil, the prodigious development to which its inhabitants, in their insatiable activity, are tending; insures to them the means of participating in the great commercial interests which attract all the nations of Europe towards the regions of the Pacific Ocean; and places them in a condition to take an active part in the great struggles which must eventually occur for commercial supremacy on the ocean—struggles whose causes, in my opinion, are continually augmenting, each day threatening more and more the peace of the world.

Under the denomination of *Oregon Territory*, the Americans include all that portion of territory lying west of the Rocky Mountains to the shores of the great ocean, and extending along the coast from parallel 42° to 54° 40′ north latitude. The forty-second degree has been established by treaty between the United States and Mexico as the southern boundary; and 54° 40′ has been assumed by the Americans as the boundary line between their possessions and those of the English.

The treaty concluded in 1846 between the United States and Great Britain definitively established the fifty-fourth degree of north latitude as the boundary line between these two powers.*

Long and protracted negotiations had been held before the conclusion of this treaty, in consequence of the claims of England to the territory. In this chapter we purpose to give a summary of the political and diplomatic points on which both nations based their pretensions to the disputed territory.

The immense territory of Oregon is as yet but very imperfectly known. Nevertheless, since the different explorations made by order of the United States government, we have been enabled to

* It is scarcely necessary to inform the American reader that this is an error. By the treaty between the United States and Great Britain, ratified by the Senate of the United States on the 18th of June, 1846, the boundary line of the United States and British territories was declared to be on the parallel of the *forty-ninth* degree of north latitude till it reaches Queen Charlotte's Sound; thence, through the Straits of Fuca, to the Pacific Ocean. Vancouver's Island was thus yielded to Great Britain. This treaty secures to the Hudson's Bay Company, during the continuance of its charter, the free navigation of the Columbia River up to its intersection with the parallel of the forty-ninth degree of latitude; and to the citizens of the United States the privilege of freely visiting the rivers and harbors north of the forty-ninth degree.—Tr.

fix our attention on some facts relative to the agricultural, commercial, and manufacturing resources of that vast region.

Among the documents published in 1843 and 1844, by order of Congress, we find very interesting information in the report of Lieutenant Wilkes, of the United States Navy, relative to his explorations of the coast of the Pacific and of the Oregon territory.

This country is generally mountainous and thickly wooded, though containing a few prairies. It is remarkable for the number of its rich and fertile valleys, formed by two almost parallel chains of mountains, which divide this territory, from the shores of the ocean to the Rocky Mountains, into three regions or zones of almost equal size, but different with respect to climate, nature of soil, and productions.

But what most essentially characterizes the natural appearance of these countries, is the manner in which these high mountains, not less than from twelve to fourteen thousand feet above the level of the sea, are perforated, north and south, east and west, by the Columbia and Oregon Rivers, thus affording means of communication through them, without which they would have ever remained almost insurmountable barriers.

The most western chain is called the *Cascades.* It ranges parallel with the coast at a mean distance of about one hundred and sixty miles, and is formed of a succession of peaks, rising far above the level of perpetual snow, which, in these regions, is about six thousand feet above the level of the sea. The second chain, between the *Cascades* and the Rocky Mountains, is that to which the name of *Blue Mountains* has been given. It is composed, so to speak, of lesser chains and buttresses detached from the principal chain of the Oregon.

The Columbia is a deep river, with numerous tributaries. Its course is almost as extensive as the Mississippi, but not so favorable for navigation. The northern sources of this river flow from the midst of the Rocky Mountains in 54° 40′ north latitude, and in longitude 118° west of Greenwich, and nearly five thousand metres (fifteen thousand feet) above the level of the ocean. From this point to Wallawalla, in latitude 45°, its course is four hundred and forty miles from north to south. It then receives the southern branch, known also as the Soptin or Lewis River. The latter runs for a distance of five hundred and twenty miles, taking its rise in the Rocky Mountains, in latitude 42°, and longitude 110° west of Greenwich, near the heads of the Yellow Stone, the Platte, the Arkansas, and the Rio Colorado of Texas.

From Wallawalla, the point of bifurcation, the course of the Columbia to the ocean is from east to west, and its length two hundred and forty miles, only one hundred and twenty of which are navigable for sailing vessels.

The Columbia at its mouth is but twelve feet deep; but the common tides rise six feet. The entrance of this beautiful river is obstructed by sand banks, constantly changing their position, and by breakers caused by southerly and westerly winds, which on this coast blow very hard, and render navigation very dangerous to those unacquainted with the river.

But if the mouth of the Columbia does not afford a large and convenient port for American vessels, compensation is found in the Straits of Juan de Fuca and Puget Sound, included within the limits of the Oregon territory, where there are safe and spacious harbors, of easy access to the largest class of vessels. Here the tides rise eighteen feet, and are hence favorable for ship-yards and naval depots. There is no doubt that, in a short time, the United States will establish on these waters a military and naval arsenal, and an important naval station, where their navy and commercial marine will find a safe and convenient harbor.

This western coast, however, for the most part obscured by thick and dense fogs, is not abundantly provided with havens, ports, or harbors, to which vessels can at all times with safety retreat; and the only two points on this part of the American continent which afford all the advantages and conveniences of large and commodious harbors are the port of San Francisco* in Upper California, and the Gulf of Juan de Fuca or Puget's Sound. The other ports are only of third rate importance, the depth of water at their entrance not exceeding from ten to twelve feet.

Along the coast, the climate is remarkable for its mildness and evenness, the mean temperature being 12° 23′ centigrade (about 53° Fahrenheit). In summer, the prevailing winds are from the south-west and west; in winter, from the south, west, and south-west. The winters continue from December to February. The rains commence in November, and continue until March; they

* Now in the possession of the United States, by the late treaty of peace with Mexico.—Tr.

are frequent, but not abundant. There is but little snow, and even this rarely remains on the ground more than three days. The frosts commence in August; the nights are cold. Indian corn does not come to maturity. But this region is nevertheless adapted to all sorts of culture. It is, above all, well wooded, and favorable for all kinds of fruit trees.

The atmospheric conditions of the second region are different; the summers are dry and warmer, and the winters colder. The extremes of heat and cold are also more frequent, the thermometer varying from —7° 78′ in winter to +42° 23′ centigrade (—45° to +107° Fahr.) in summer, and in the shade. Notwithstanding these great changes, the country is considered healthy and very favorable for raising cattle, in consequence of its vast prairies, and its well-wooded valleys.

In the third region, approaching the Rocky Mountains, the temperature is still more variable, and frequently, within the twenty-four hours, all the seasons of the year are felt. The cold is very severe in winter, and the heat in summer very intense. Rain very seldom falls; and snow is still more uncommon. This region is particularly arid, except in very deep valleys, where the flocks find nourishment, or where they are attracted by salt licks, and therefore is of little value in an agricultural point of view. This aridity, sterility, and extreme temperature of climate exist only within the chain of the Rocky Mountains. Upon the two declivities, nature is more kindly, and vegetation resumes its empire, with all the conditions propitious to the existence of man.

From all these facts, we may draw the conclusion that these countries are favorable to agriculture only in a moderate degree, but exceedingly well adapted for the propagation of cattle and other animals which afford such an abundant supply of hides, tallow, and furs to the hunters of those regions. Future explorations may develop the natural resources of the country, such as the precious metals, with more certainty; since, on the coast, coal has already been found in great quantity, and of very combustible quality. Regions bearing such striking marks of the convulsions caused by subterranean fires must contain within their bosom treasures not less precious than those found in Arkansas, Missouri, Iowa, and Wisconsin, whose geographical positions are almost identical. They present also an equally wide field of industry. Besides, the physical disposition of the country presents numerous sites for the establishment of manufactories that require great water power.

Another resource, which must not be overlooked, is the abundance of all kinds of fish found on the coast, and in the bays and rivers of this territory; and particularly the quantity and quality of the salmon of the Columbia River. The salmon fisheries supply nourishment at present to more than twenty thousand Indians, and to all the colonists of those regions, besides furnishing a large exportation to the Islands.

HISTORICAL SUMMARY OF ALL THE EXPEDITIONS MADE TO THE NORTH-WEST COAST OF THE PACIFIC, AND TO THE TERRITORY OF OREGON.

1500—1846.

Now that we have described the physical aspects of Oregon territory, and shown its resources and advantages for a population that may one day inhabit it, we shall present a short summary of all the partial or complete expeditions to this portion of the American continent.

We can vouch for the authenticity of all the facts we are about to relate, inasmuch as we have carefully collated all the official historical documents published on this subject by the various nations interested in extending the field of geographical discovery in those distant countries with the object of establishing a fur trade, at one time so highly lucrative. We have freely consulted, and with great interest, the beautiful work of Mr. R. Greenhow, published in 1844, by order of the government of the United States, at Washington, from which we have obtained much valuable information.

Christopher Columbus, who made the first discoveries in the New World, in the name of Spain, was also the first to visit the western coast of Mexico. In his fourth voyage, in 1500, he discovered the coast of Honduras, the Mosquito Shore, and the coast of Verragua, descending along the isthmus as far as Porto-Bello and the River Belen.

The expeditions of Ponce de Leon to Florida in 1512, of Cortes to Mexico in 1517, and of Fernando de Soto to Florida in 1537, put the Spaniards in possession of the country between the Capes of Florida on the Atlantic and the coasts of Mexico and California on the Pacific Ocean, to which they gave the name of New Spain.

Cortes had scarcely become master of the rich empire of Mexico, when, desirous of extending the field of his discoveries, he sent an expedition composed of two vessels, in 1526, to the Molucca Islands. In 1528, Pedro Nuñez Maldonado examined, under his orders, the west coast of Xalisco from Zacatula to Santiago.

In 1532, he fitted out an expedition composed of two other vessels, the command of which he gave to his relative Diego Hurtado de Mendoza, and to Juan de Mazuela. They sailed from Tehuantepec. One of these vessels was lost; the other reached the port of Xalisco. It was not till one year after the loss of this vessel that Cortes heard of the occurrence. He immediately fitted out two others, and gave the command of them to Ferdinand Grijalva and Diego Bacerra. These vessels sailed in company from Tehuantepec, on the 30th of September, 1533; but they soon parted.

Grijalva proceeded towards the west, and discovered a group of islands known, at this time, under the name of the *Revilla gigedo*. Bacerra sailed along the coast of Xalisco, and was murdered by his crew. His vessel was seized by Nuño de Guzman, who had settled at Guadalaxara, in California.

Cortes, determined himself to reconnoitre the countries discovered to the west by Ximenes, sailed with three vessels from Chiamatla, in 1535, and united his forces in the Bay of Santa Cruz, whence he intended to march for the conquest of a new kingdom in Mexico, with the expectation of realizing immense wealth. But in this expedition, he encountered nothing but difficulty and misery. It was during this long absence from his government that Don Antonio de Mendoza was appointed by the court of Madrid Governor and Viceroy of New Spain.

Nevertheless, Cortes succeeded in founding a permanent settlement on the peninsula which has since received the name of California, and thus established the incontestable rights of the crown of Spain to that portion of the continent. The bay named Santa Cruz by Cortes is probably the same as that which has since received the name of *Port la Paz*, situated on the twenty-fourth degree of latitude, and about one hundred miles from the Pacific Ocean.

The new Viceroy of Mexico was not less jealous than Cortes to advance his fortune by attempting new discoveries in the west. He had obtained information respecting this country from a certain Alvaro Nuñez de Cobeza-Vaca, and from two other Spaniards, and a negro, who, detached from the expedition of Paufilo Narvaez, in 1537, to the Floridas, had traversed these vast regions from Tampa Bay, where they had landed, to the shores of California.

These travelers gave the most extravagant accounts of the wealth of the countries they had crossed, and of the number of cities and inhabitants they had seen. Mendoza determined to satisfy himself concerning the truth of these statements, and, advised by his friend, the celebrated Bartolomé de Las Casas, he sent an expedition, in March, 1539, to Cullacan, under the orders of a Franciscan, named Marcos de Niza, accompanied by Honorato and the negro Estavañico, who had crossed the continent with Cobeza-Vaca.

About this period, the last expedition of Cortes was fitted out. It was commanded by Francisco de Ulloa, who sailed from Acapulco with three vessels, in July, 1539.

One of these vessels was lost near Cullacan; but with the other two Ulloa continued his voyage towards the Bay of Santa Cruz. Thence he proceeded to the west, made a complete examination of the two shores of the Gulf of California, and ascertained that this long peninsula was attached to the main land at the thirty-second degree of latitude, although he did not discover the Colorado River, which empties into the sea at the head of the bay. To this bay, Ulloa gave the name of the *Sea of Cortes*, although on the Spanish charts it is generally denominated *Vermillion Sea*, and in others as the *Gulf of California.*

In October, 1539, Ulloa again sailed from Santa Cruz, advanced westward towards Cape *San Lucas*, which forms the southern extremity of California, and then, with a fair wind, moved towards the north. In January, 1540, he discovered an island in latitude 28°, to which he gave the name of *Cedar Island.* His crew being almost worn out by privations and disease, was compelled to return to Santiago, in Xalisco.

In the meanwhile, the expedition, under the orders of the

Franciscan Marcos de Niza, had attained, according to report, in the interior of the western regions, the thirty-fifth degree of north latitude, and had crossed an extremely rich country, well cultivated, and abounding in mines of gold, silver, and precious stones, whose inhabitants were represented to be more advanced in civilization than those of Mexico or Peru.

Notwithstanding the evident exaggeration of these reports, the Viceroy Mendoza did not hesitate, for a moment, to send immediately two corps of armed troops, one by land and the other by sea, to prepare the conquest of these new countries.

Fernando de Alarcon received the command of the sea expedition, and, in May, 1540, sailed from Santiago with two vessels. He reached the head of California Bay the following August, and discovered the River *Colorado*, which he named *Rio de Nuestra Señora de Buena Guia.*

Alarcon ascended this river for more than two hundred and forty miles, and afterwards returned to Mexico with the intelligence that he had been unable to discover any country resembling the descriptions he had received.

The land expedition, composed of cavalry and infantry, was commanded by Francisco Vasquez de Coronado, lately appointed governor of New Gallicia, in the place of Nuño de Guzman. This intrepid chief, not in the least addicted to exaggeration, advanced boldly towards the north, following the directions he had received. He penetrated far into the country, despite all the difficulties he had to surmount, and reached that part of the territory now known as *Sonara*, situated on that great chain of mountains, to the east of the head of the Bay of California, where the River Yaqui and Gila take their rise; and, after having passed two years in vain attempts to explore the interior of the country, and in seeking the cities and treasures promised by Francisco Marco, he returned to Mexico.

In 1542, Mendoza fitted out another expedition for the exploration and conquest of the north-western territory. This was led by Juan Rodiguez de Cubrillo. He sailed from Navidad in June, doubled Cape San Lucas, and reached the forty-fourth degree of latitude; but was soon driven back by head winds, and was forced to take shelter in a port of one of the islands of Santa Barbara, in latitude 34°, where he died. The pilot Bartolomé Ferrelo, who had accompanied him, then took command of the expedition, and pushed his discoveries to the north-west as far as Cape Blanc. In February, 1544, he discovered a cape, in latitude 41°, which he named *Cabo de Fortunas.* In March, he reached latitude 44°; but head winds soon drove him to the south, where his crew, completely broken down by fatigue and privations, was compelled to take shelter in the port of Navidas.

The cape newly discovered by Ferrelo was, within a short period, named *Cape Mendocino,* in honor of the viceroy.

The Portuguese, during this period, had succeeded in opening a profitable trade with India; and their vessels accomplished these voyages by the Cape of Good Hope. The Spaniards, with the same object, attempted to form establishments in Asia; but their expeditions had failed up to the middle of the sixteenth century.

However, in 1542, Ruy Lopez de Villalobos succeeded in crossing the Pacific, with a small squadron from Mexico, and took possession of the Philippine Islands in the name of his sovereign; but, a short time after, his forces having been dispersed, all his vessels were destroyed.

In 1564, the Spaniards, under Miguel de Légazpi, again attempted to found an establishment on the Philippines, and were successful. That navigator, accompanied by Andrès de Urdoñeta, sailed from Mexico, and crossed the Pacific Ocean. On his return voyage, he steered from the Philippines to the north-west, and reached the fortieth degree of latitude, where the variable winds permitted him to approach the coast of California, and thus to return with ease to Mexico.

Since that period, a brisk trade has been established between Acapulco and Manilla, capital of the Philippines, and Macao in China, in which the precious metals and European merchandise have been exchanged for silks, spices, and china, either to be consumed in America, or transported to Europe. An important commerce has also been established between Panama and the ports of Peru and Chili.

The existence of this trade, and the wealth accumulated in the American cities on the shores of the Pacific Ocean, soon came to the knowledge of the English, who did not hesitate to surmount the difficulties of so distant a navigation, when they could secure to themselves, in any wise, participation in the plunder.

The first appearance of the English in the Pacific was in 1575. A party of freebooters, headed by one John Oxenham, crossed the

Isthmus of Panama, and, having constructed a vessel on the southern shore, succeeded in capturing a great number of important prizes before they were overcome by the Spaniards, who put all of them to death at Panama.

Sir Francis Drake, three years later, signally avenged the death of his fellow-citizens. This celebrated navigator sailed from Plymouth in 1577, and passed through the Straits of Magellan in September, 1578; he then proceeded, with a vessel of one hundred tons burden and a crew of sixty men, to execute the project he had formed, the pillage of the Spanish cities on the west coast of America.

Having attained the object of his voyage, plundered the city of Guatulco, on the coast of Mexico, and filled his vessel with precious spoils, he was about to return to England in the spring of 1579, when, fearing that he might fall in with the Spanish vessels while passing through the Straits of Magellan, he determined to seek a northern passage to the Atlantic. Consequently, in sailing from Guatulco, he doubled the cape towards the northwest, and, having sailed about four thousand two hundred miles in that direction, he found himself, in the beginning of June, near the forty-second degree of north latitude. The severe temperature he encountered having induced sickness among his crew, he was unable longer to keep at sea, and he determined to seek the shore. He soon hove in sight of the coast, and attempted to approach it; but, finding no harbor where he could safely anchor, he sailed along the shore until he reached the thirty-eighth degree of latitude, where he entered a large and beautiful bay. This was probably the Bay of San Francisco, or of Bodega, a few leagues to the north.

Drake remained some time in this harbor to refresh his crew, and to refit his vessel. The natives having offered him the sovereignty of the country, he took possession of it in the name of Queen Elizabeth, and gave it the name of *New Albion.*

Having renounced his intention of seeking a northern passage, he returned to Europe by sailing directly across the Pacific as far as the Philippines, and by following the ordinary route of the Portuguese navigators across the Indian seas, and doubling the Cape of Good Hope. He reached Portsmouth in September, 1590.

On this pretended discovery of Drake, which was nothing but

a flagrant usurpation of the rights acquired by the Spaniards through their navigators, the English now rest their right of property in the Oregon territory, assuming that Drake had examined the north-west coast as high as the forty-eighth degree of north latitude; and that he had, besides, taken possession, in the name of his sovereign, of the country in the Bay of San Francisco, the right to which he had acquired from the Indians.

Now, it is fully proved that Drake never sailed beyond the forty-third degree of north latitude; and the act of taking possession of the lands in the Bay of San Francisco was a violation of the rights of the crown of Spain.

In the voyages constantly made by the Spanish galleons from Mexico to India, the vessels were invariably carried by easterly winds directly across the Pacific Ocean in three months. But their return voyages generally occupied twice that time. The vessels sailing from Macao generally directed their course towards the west coast of California, which, from that period, became very familiar to the Spanish navigators.

In one of these voyages, in 1584, Francisco Gali touched the coast of California in north latitude 37° 35′. Documents of that period, preserved in the archives of the India Company, even show that the point of the coast he examined was situated in the fifty-seventh and a half degree of north latitude.

In 1595, Sebastian Cermenon, returning from Manilla in the ship San Augustin, examined the north-west coast, by order of the Viceroy of Mexico, with the object of discovering, if possible, a port where vessels coming from India might stop. This vessel was lost near the Bay of San Francisco, to the south of Cape Mendocino.

Drake's success encouraged a great number of his fellow-citizens to pursue the same adventurous voyages across the Straits of Magellan, and to seek a passage to the Pacific Ocean by the north-west.

Thomas Cavendish or Candish acquired some celebrity by the terror which his name inspired among the Spaniards, during his voyage around the world in 1587. He anchored for some time near Cape San Lucas, the southern extremity of California, and then captured the galleon Santa Anna, coming from India and bound to Acapulco, pillaged it, burnt it, and abandoned the crew upon the coast. The Santa Anna having providentially been cast upon the shore, the crew succeeded in putting her in a condition fit for sea, and were thus enabled to reach the opposite shore of the Gulf of California. Among the crew were Juan de Fuca and Sebastian Vizcaino, who afterwards acquired some reputation.

From the report of the Greek pilot Juan de Fuca—who died in Venice in 1602—and which was published in 1625 by Michael Lock, we learn that that pilot had, in 1589, been employed by the Viceroy of Mexico to undertake a voyage in search of the supposed Straits of *Anian*, concerning the existence of which various versions were then prevalent; that, this voyage having resulted in nothing of importance, he had, in 1592, been again sent to explore the north-west coast; that, between the forty-seventh and forty-eighth degree of latitude, he discovered an inlet; and that in this inlet he had sailed more than twenty days, of which, moreover, he reported a description so faithful, that, at a later period, it served to prove not only the truth of his account, but the authenticity of his discovery.

In 1595, Philip the Second ordered a complete exploration of the north-west coast, to determine its exact position relative to the Spanish settlements in New Mexico intersected by the *Bravo del Norte*, and extending to the fortieth degree of latitude.

Accordingly, in the spring of 1596, Count de Monterey, Viceroy of Mexico, sent three vessels from Acapulco, under the command of Sebastian Vizcaino, who, we have already seen, was one of the officers of the Santa Anna, destroyed by Cavendish at Cape San Lucas.

This voyage was confined to attempts to form establishments at St. Sebastian, and at La Paz or Santa Cruz. Cortes, sixty years before, had himself wished to found such establishments, but had failed in his endeavors, as much because of the sterility of the soil, as on account of the ferocity of the natives.

Philip the Third, having succeeded to the throne in 1598, immediately sought to carry out the plan of his predecessor. He ordered the Viceroy of Mexico to equip a small squadron, that it might continue the reconnoissance that had already been commenced.

Sebastian Vizcaino took command of this new armament, composed of three vessels. He sailed, on the 5th of May, 1602, from Acapulco, accompanied by Toribio, Gomez de Corvan, and Martin de Aguilar. This little squadron anchored at San José, to the east of Cape San Lucas; resumed its voyage of exploration on the 2d of July; entered the Bay of the Madeleine, between the twenty-fourth and twenty-fifth degrees of latitude; visited a port on Cedar Island; another in 31° north latitude, to which the name of *Port San Quintin* was given, and farther to the north *San Miguel*, discovered by Cabrillo, the name of which was then changed to *San Diego*.

After having thoroughly examined this port, the flotilla sailed through the archipelago of Santa Barbara, visited by Cabrillo sixty years before; doubled the Cape Galern of that navigator, since known as Cape Conception; and anchored in the *Port des Pines* of Cabrillo, but to which the name of *Monterey* has been given in honor of the viceroy of that name.

In January, 1603, Vizcaino had proceeded as far as the forty-second degree of north latitude, and discovered a cape which he named San Sebastian; but his crew having been considerably reduced by sickness, he consented to return to Mexico, and arrived at Acapulco in March.

The vessel commanded by Martin de Aguilar continued its voyage of discovery alone. He recognized Cape Blanc in latitude 43°, and thought he had discovered the mouth of a large river, which the strength of the current prevented him from entering. This vessel returned to Mexico after the loss of the commander Aguilar, the pilot Flores, and the greater part of the crew.

Vizcaino, after having returned from his expedition, obtained permission from Philip the Third to found trading establishments at the points he had examined; but he died before he could accomplish his projects.

At the period of Vizcaino's expedition, the Spanish government was very much interested in the discoveries made in the Pacific. Several expeditions were sent out; and in one of them, undertaken in 1595 by Alvaro de Mendona du Pesu, the Marquesas group of islands was discovered. It received this name in consequence of the beauty of its females. In 1605, Pedro Fernandez de Quiros performed another voyage from Mexico, and visited other islands in those seas, namely: *Otaheite* and *Owyhee*. He also believed that he had discovered another southern continent, which he named *Australie del Espiritu Santo*.

For one hundred and fifty years after that period, the Spaniards seemed to manifest no further desire to found new settlements on the western coast of California, or to increase their possessions on the Continent.

In 1608, Henry Hudson, in a voyage in search of a passage to the north-west of America, discovered the strait which now bears his name. Eight years subsequently, William Baffin noticed the same strait.

In 1608, John Wright visited the coast of America in the fifty-sixth degree of latitude, near Cape Grimugt, on the coast of Labrador, and perished in the enterprise.

In 1612, Nelson River was discovered by Button and James Hall.

In 1616, William Baffin discovered the bay which has since borne his name.

But, without contradiction, one of the most important discoveries of this period was that of the possibility of sailing around the southern extremity of the New World, accomplished by Lemaire and Van Schouten, two celebrated Dutch navigators, in 1616, who passed from one ocean to the other by doubling Cape Horn, thus named in honor of their native city. This discovery rendered the voyage into Oceanica much less difficult.

From the period of this discovery, Dutch privateers frequently visited the north-west coast of America, and established their cruizing-ground along the coast of California, whence they intercepted the Spanish East India traders.

This condition of things again drew the attention of the Spaniards towards the north-west coast of America. To protect their trade and to destroy these pirates, they formed settlements on the eastern coast of the Gulf of California, and, for this purpose, sent out various expeditions, from 1631 to 1667, under the command of Vicuña and Ortega; Barriga and Portes; Piñadero, and, lastly, Lucenilla and Arondo.

As far as relates to the colonization of California, these expeditions were without any result. It was reserved for the persevering and intelligent spirit of the Jesuits to overcome all the difficulties which the hostile nature of the natives and the sterility of the soil presented.

As far back as the year 1643, two Dutch navigators, Martin Geritzin de Vries and Hendrick Shaep, had explored the coast of Japan up to latitude 48° north, and entered the Gulf of Ochotsk

16

between the main land on the west and the Kamtschatka and Kurile Islands on the east.

In 1673, Thomas Peche, an English corsair, while in search of the famous Straits of Anian, visited the same coast and the same gulf, which then bore, on some charts, the name of Straits of *Vriés* or *Anian.*

Hudson's and Baffin's discoveries on the north-west coast of America renewed the hope of finding a north-west passage; and for this object a company, under the immediate protection of Prince Rupert, was formed in England. Charles the Second, in 1669, granted to an association called *Company of English Commercial Adventurers in Hudson's Bay,* the exclusive rights of trade and property to all the lands watered by Hudson's Bay and its tributaries.

This royal concession, which gave birth to the celebrated Hudson's Bay Company, was made in favor of those courtiers who were seized with a desire for speculation. It gave to the company exclusive possession of the seas, bays, straits, lakes, and rivers, and all the lands adjacent to Hudson's Bay. This enormous monopoly insured the prosperity of the company, and greatly contributed to the consolidation of its authority and power in those countries.

The charter of this company compelled it to pursue the discovery, so ardently desired, of a north-west passage. The same obligation was also imposed on vessels engaged in the whale fisheries.

The Jesuits, having at length obtained permission from the crown of Spain to establish themselves in California, by founding settlements there in the name of the King of Spain, began that immense work in 1697. Father Salvatierra assumed the direction of this important mission. He was followed by Fathers Kuhu (a German), Piccolo Egeste, and other associates, as zealous as they were learned and devoted to the cause of civilization among the natives of the New World. The settlement of *Loreto* was founded on the eastern shore of the peninsula; shortly after, *La Paz, Santa Cruz,* and *San José,* near Cape San Lucas. In a few years, sixteen missions were created, which formed, as it were, a chain of posts, by means of which the authority of the Jesuits, and the influence of the Roman religion, were extended over California. But having been driven, in 1767, from the states of

Spain by the decree of Charles the Third, issued at the solicitation of the celebrated Count Aranda, the Jesuits were also expelled from California by Don Gaspar de Portola; and the fruits of their long and toilsome labors were thus lost to civilization.

As early as 1711, the Russians were complete masters of all the north of Asia, where the fur trade yielded them immense profits. They had examined the northern coast of Asia for a considerable distance to the eastward, and had formed settlements on the peninsula of Kamtschatka. But they had not yet ascertained whether or not the continent of Asia was united to that of America.

In 1728, Vitus Behring, a Dane, and a very able navigator, was employed by the Empress Catharine to make a voyage of discovery. He sailed in a small vessel that had been built at the mouth of the Kamtschatka River, and was accompanied by Alexei Tchisikof, a Russian, and Martin Spangbug, a German. He examined the whole coast up to 67° 18′ north latitude, the north-eastern extremity of the Asiatic continent, and returned to the port of Kamtschatka. The following year he attempted to discover the coasts of the American continent; but, prevented by head winds, he put into the Gulf of Ochotsk.

In 1732, Krupischef made a voyage in which he examined the position of the American coast.

In 1741, Behring commanded another expedition, composed of two vessels, the *St. Pierre* and *St. Paul*. He was accompanied by Tchisikof, in charge of the *St. Paul*. He discovered the coast of the American continent at the sixtieth degree of north latitude, on *St. Elias'* day, and named the promontory formed by the land in honor of this saint, by which name all subsequent navigators on this coast have since designated it.

The Russians observed the peninsula of Aliaska, the Island of Kodiak, landed on one of the islands of the Schumagin group, passed the *Aleutian* archipelago, which extends, to the west of Aliaska, as far as the fifty-third degree of latitude, and wintered on an island in latitude 55°, where Behring died, on the 8th of December, 1741. In 1742, the survivors of the crew, having built a frail vessel from the wreck of their ship, returned to the port of Avatscha.

Tchisikof also discovered the American continent, and, with his celebrated companion, thus assisted to extend hydrographical and geographical information with respect to that portion of the American continent, as well as with respect to the relative position of the coasts of Asia and America.

These expeditions and consequent discoveries awakened the attention of France, England, and Spain, and stimulated their governments to fresh enterprises, several of which were principally directed to the discovery of a north-west passage.

A short time after the peace of 1763, colonies were planted by France and England on the sterile and desolate Islands of Falkland, in Oceanica, near the entrance to the Straits of Magellan; but, on the representations of the Spanish government, the French consented to recall their colonists. The English government took no heed of the claims of the Spanish government, and continued to maintain its settlements. Towards the year 1770, however, Don Francisco Bucareli succeeded in driving the English from their establishment at Fort Egmont.

In 1766, Lieutenant Synd, of the imperial navy of Russia, by order of the Empress Catharine, made a voyage to the north of the coast of Kamtschatka. He advanced as far as the sixty-sixth degree of latitude, and examined the American continent the following year, where he debarked.

Captains Krenitzin and Levaschef, in 1769, determined the geographical position of several points of the chain of the Aleutian Islands.

It is a curious fact, in the annals of voyages at that time, that the first direct voyage by sea between the new discoveries in the north Pacific Ocean and China, in the prosecution of the fur trade, was undertaken and accomplished by the Poles, under their national colors. These had been exiled to Kamtschatka.

The attention of the Americans, about the same period, was also directed to the exploration of the western countries by land; and, after the peace of 1763, they no longer confined themselves to visiting the regions simply beyond the Alleghany Mountains, but advanced towards the west, and attempted other discoveries to the north-west.

Captain Jonathan Carver, of Connecticut, was one of the first to undertake a journey in that direction. He left Boston in 1766, explored Lake Michigan and Green Bay, crossed Fox River (*des Renards*) at Wisconsin, sailed to the Upper Mississippi, where he examined the mouth of the St. Croix, and returned to that of the

St. Pierre, which he ascended to the heart of the country of the Naudaumessis. Carver also made a similar exploration along the left shore of the Mississippi. He entered Chippewa River, and traversed a country which the Indians of the north-west were in the habit of visiting, from whom he received information of the existence of a large river, called the Oregon or Origon (river of the west), said by the Indians to empty into the Pacific Ocean, near the pretended Anian Strait, and to take its rise in the chain of the Rocky Mountains.

The celebrated Captain Cook made his first voyage to the South Sea in 1768. His object was the determination of astronomical observations relative to the passage of Venus over the sun's disk in 1769.

Captain Bougainville made a voyage of discovery to the South Sea in 1767, and returned to France in 1769.

Immediately after the expulsion of the Jesuits from Mexico in 1767, the Viceroy de Croix, and the *visitador* Galvez, devoted their attention to the foundation of colonies and garrisons on the west coast of California. It was ordered that the first troops should be sent to *Port San Diego*, or *Port Monterey*, which had been previously settled by Vizcaino. Consequently, a few colonists and soldiers were called together at *La Paz*, on the west coast of California, and, in the spring of 1769, marched towards *San Diego*, in two parties, one commanded by Gaspar de Portola, and the other by Fernando de Rivera.

Rivera arrived at San Diego, with his party, on the 11th of May, 1769, where he found two vessels that had anticipated him by several days. Portola took a more difficult route, and did not rejoin his companions till after the lapse of two months. The choice of a site having been made on the Bay of San Diego, Portola advanced with his party towards Monterey; but, missing his way, he was obliged to retrace his steps to San Diego, in consequence of scarcity of provisions, and the advanced state of the season, the vessel that was to have carried provisions to Monterey never having been seen.

The colonists of San Diego experienced great suffering, as well for want of provisions as on account of the hostility of the natives; but supplies having at length arrived in March, 1770, Portola continued his expedition to Monterey, where he succeeded in founding a settlement. Fresh colonists, sent from Mexico, settled at various points between San Diego and Monterey, soon provided abundant means of subsistence, so that, before 1771, the settlers of Upper California were enabled to buffet all the casualties of their position.

From 1769 to 1772, Samuel Hearne, agent of the Hudson's Bay Company, starting from Fort Prince of Wales, the principal station of the company on the western shore of Hudson's Bay, in nearly the sixtieth degree of latitude, performed three journeys across the countries of the west and north-west, a distance of nearly a thousand miles. In his last journey, Hearne discovered the *Great Slave Lake*, and other lakes in the direction of the north-west. He also followed the course of a stream which has since been called the Coppermine River, and examined its mouth, which he judged to be in latitude 72° north, and in longitude 20° west of the last post of the Hudson's Bay Company. He supposed that this river emptied into a kind of inferior bay, similar to that of Hudson.

Captain Cook made his second voyage to the South Sea in 1772. His object was to ascertain the existence of the southern continent, to which the attention of most of the maritime powers was then drawn.

From 1771 to 1779, the Spanish government made strenuous efforts to found permanent settlements in California. For this purpose, the assistance of the Franciscans was invoked, who devoted themselves with perseverance and disinterestedness to the pious work of converting the natives to Christianity. Farms were established, and cultivated by Indians engaged for a period of ten years, who were subjected to an equitable, though not severe, discipline.

In 1775, the Franciscans Font and Gazzes traveled from Mexico to the mission of San Gabriel, in California, on the Rio Colorado. In the same year, Dominguez and Escalonté, belonging to the same order, attempted to penetrate from Santa Fe, in New Mexico, to the shores of the Pacific Ocean; but they soon retraced their steps.

In 1774, Perez sailed from San Blas, with orders from Bucareli, then Viceroy of Mexico, to reconnoitre the north-west coast. He first visited San Diego, then Monterey, and, on the 18th of July, landed on the coast in latitude 54°: this point he named *Cape Ste. Marguerite*. The snow-covered mountains were in sight, and were called *Sierra de San Cristoval.* A few Indians approached the Spaniards in their canoes, and made some exchanges for otter skins.

The land observed in this voyage was the western coast of the island now known as Queen Charlotte's Island, and Cape Ste. Marguerite, the extreme north-west point, marked on the English charts as North Cape, at the entrance of the channel or pass of *Dixon.*

On the 9th of August, Perez anchored in a wide bay in latitude 49° 30′, and established a communication with the natives. He named this bay *Port San Lorenzo*, the same afterwards designated by Captain Cook as King George's Strait, or Nootka Strait.

Continuing his voyage to the south-west, Perez discovered, in latitude 47° 47′, a high mountain covered with snow, which he named *Sierra de Santa Rosalia.* This corresponds with the *Mount Olympus* of the English charts.

On the return of Perez to Mexico, Bucareli ordered a new exploring expedition, of which he gave the command to Captain Bruno Heceta, under whose orders Perez was again to go to sea, as well as Juan de Ayala and Antonio Morelli.

This expedition, composed of two vessels, sailed from San Blas, on the 15th of March, 1775, in company with the schooner San Carlos, bound to Monterey. The commander of this schooner, having become delirious, was succeeded by Ayala. Juan Francisco de la Bodega y Quadra assumed the command of the schooner *La Sonora.*

Having passed the *San Carlos*, the two vessels of the expedition steered a westerly course, and, on the 10th of June, anchored in a bay beyond Cape Mendocin, in latitude 41°. This bay received the name of *Port de la Trinité.*

Heceta and Bodega continued their voyage on the 19th of June. They lost sight of land for three weeks; but again perceived it in latitude 48° 27′. Wishing to reconnoitre the coast, they sent a boat with seven men on shore, who were all murdered by the natives.

Having resumed their course, the two vessels were separated by a violent storm. Heceta returned to Monterey, while Bodega pursued his voyage of discovery.

On his return voyage, Heceta landed in latitude 50°, on the south side of the Island of Vancouver and Quadra, and, passing through the port of San Lorenzo, (Nootka Strait,) discovered the previous year by Perez, he arrived in sight of the main land, in latitude 48°, without having observed the Straits of Fuca. Running a southerly course, he arrived, on the 15th of August, 1775, in front of an outlet, whence flowed a current so rapid that he could not enter it. He mistook this outlet for the entrance of the Straits of Fuca, of which he was in search. He remained in these waters for the purpose of making more minute observations; but, unable to overcome the strength of the current, which carried him along with it, he determined to continue his voyage.

Heceta named this entrance the *Débouché de l'Assomption* (outlet of the Assumption), and the two points forming its entrance, *Cape St. Roch* and *Cape des Feuilles*. The charts published in Mexico at that period bear the names *Débouché d'Heceta*, and River St. Roch. This outlet was the mouth of the Columbia or Oregon River, which Robert Gray entered in 1792.

In the mean while, Bodega and Morelli were laboriously pursuing their voyage to the north-west, and had at length reached, in latitude 56°, King George's archipelago, Mount Edgecombe, the Bay of Islands, and the Straits of Norfolk, according to English navigators, but to which they respectively gave the names of *Port Remedios*, *Port Guadaloupe*, and *Mount San Jacinto*.

The Spaniards landed in Port Remedios, and took possession of the country in the name of their sovereign, according to the usual formalities; but they were attacked by the natives, who forced them to re-embark. They then determined to return to Monterey. In latitude 55° 35′, they entered a harbor which they named *Port Bucareli;* this port is on Prince of Wales Island. They afterwards reached the north-eastern extremity of Queen Charlotte's Island, which Perez named *Cape San Marguerite*, and examined the channel which separates this island from Prince of Wales Island, which they named *Entrado de Perez*, afterwards named by the English *Dixon's Channel.* They successively examined several points on the coast; passed Cape Mendocin; entered a small harbor in latitude 38°, to which Bodega gave his own name, and at length reached San Blas, on the 20th of November, 1775.

From the foregoing details, it is clear, even omitting the voyage of Perez, that the Spaniards, so far back as 1775, had reconnoitered and examined with care the whole west coast of the American continent, from Monterey, in latitude 37°, to latitude 48° north, and had determined the general direction of the west coast of the islands which line the continent between the forty-eighth and fifty-eighth degrees of north latitude.

The third voyage of Captain Cook was performed in 1776. His object was to discover a passage either to the north-west or north-east. He sailed from Plymouth, on the 12th of July, 1776, on board of the ship *Resolution*, accompanied by Captain Charles Clarke in command of the *Discovery*, furnished with all the instruments required for such a voyage. He displayed great skill on this occasion, and exhibited a spirit of enterprise and perseverance which has justly entitled him to great celebrity among the navigators to whom geographical science owes many of its important discoveries.

Captain Cook's instructions from the board of admiralty explicitly prove that the only object of his voyage was the discovery of a more direct route to India than that by the Cape of Good Hope or Cape Horn, through a supposed passage uniting the two oceans, and not the foundation of new settlements in Oregon. His instructions, in fact, were very precise: That he should sail as directly as possible for the *coast of New Albion*, which he was to make in latitude 45°, without deviating from his course with the object of discovering new lands, or putting into any of the Spanish ports; that he should anchor in any one of the ports of New Albion that might be most convenient in his route in order to procure refreshments; that he should then continue his voyage to the sixty-fifth degree of latitude, or even farther north if not prevented by land or ice; but, above all, that he should not lose time in reconnoitering or exploring any river, bay, harbor, or inlet, until after his destination should have been reached, which he was enjoined, if possible, to arrive at in June, so that he might have full time to examine the rivers, bays, or inlets, which, from their dimensions, might appear of sufficient importance to be considered as means of communication between Hudson's and Baffin's Bays.

The orders of Captain Cook ended by an injunction to take possession, in the name of Great Britain, of the country he might discover in this inlet, provided that it should be uninhabited, or that it had not previously been discovered or visited.

We must also remark that the name of *New Albion*, cited in these instructions, is used merely to designate that part of the west coast of America towards which the expedition was to shape its course, and not to imply the property claimed by Great Britain.

Cook arrived in the Pacific Ocean by the South Sea and the Cape of Good Hope. He spent nearly one year in examining Van Diemen's Land, New Zealand, the Friendly and Society Islands, and other places in those latitudes. In the early part of 1778, he directed his course northward, and, on the 18th of January, made his first discovery, the Island of *Atooi* or *Kanoi*, in the twentieth degree of latitude. This was one of a group which he named the *Sandwich Islands*, in honor of the first lord of the admiralty.

On the 17th of March, 1778, he reached the north-west coast, in latitude 44° 10′. Driven to the south-west by head winds, he had an opportunity of more carefully examining several parts of these shores that had already been visited by the Spaniards.

The winds became fair. He then shaped his course towards the north-west, and recognized Nootka Sound, which had already been explored, in 1774, by Juan Perez, who gave it the name of *San Lorenzo*. Cook anchored in one of the ports, so abundant in this sound; visited the natives, who were represented as cannibals; and found among them several iron instruments, two silver spoons, and a few copper articles, clearly proving prior intercourse between these natives and Europeans. He changed the name of this sound to that of *King George's Straits*.

Having again put to sea, he sailed as far north as latitude 55°, where he observed the highlands seen by Bodega in 1775, and named by him *Mount San Jacinto*. Cook gave them the name of *Mount Edgecombe*. *Port Remedios*, of the Spaniards, he changed to the *Bay of Islands*.

He then pursued his course to latitude 57°, recognized Mount Fairweather, the *Mount St. Elias* described by Behring, and from this point commenced his search for a north-west passage. He visited the Shumagin Islands of Behring, and Unalashka Island in the Aleutian cluster; reached land in latitude 65° 46′, which he named *Cape Prince of Wales;* then sailed westward, and recognized Cape Tchuquetehoi, the eastern extremity of Behring's Straits. Having advanced, beyond this sea, to the north, he reached the American coast in latitude 70° 20′, and the coast of Asia in latitude 68° 56′.

Having been checked by the ice in his course northward, he

determined, in consequence of the advanced state of the season, to return to a more southern latitude. He re-entered Behring's Straits, and, on the 3d of October, anchored in the harbor of *Samagaouda*, on the north side of Unalashka.

He left Unalashka on the 27th of October, and in November discovered the Owyhee and Momee Islands (Hawaii and Manai), the two largest of the Sandwich Islands. Here, on the 16th of February, 1779, this brave and generous navigator was murdered by the natives.

We must here observe that the voyages of Captain Cook gave to England no basis for any new claims to any portion of the American continent; for the places he saw, to the south of Mount Edgecombe, had already been seen and examined by Perez, Bodega, and Heceta, as we have shown. The lands he recognized to the north had been designated by Russian navigators.

Nevertheless, Captain Cook incontestably deserves the credit of having laid down, with more correctness than any of his predecessors, the relative positions of the north-east and north-west coasts of the continents of Asia and America, as well as the precise configuration of their shores.

Before proceeding any farther with our summary, let us endeavor to ascertain what, at the period of which we speak, was the respective state of parties claiming titles to property on the north-west coast and its dependent territory.

France, as we have already had occasion several times to observe in the course of this historical summary, had taken possession of the St. Lawrence and of the Mississippi. She therefore extended her dominion over the vast territory watered by these two rivers, including the chain of lakes, having to the east only the Anglo-American provinces of the Atlantic, and then indefinitely extending towards the Pacific Ocean and the Spanish possessions.

England was, at that period, in possession of all the territory on the Atlantic coast, from the St. Lawrence to Florida. She also extended her pretensions indefinitely to the west, in conflict with the rights of France. She had also established herself in Hudson's Bay, asserting claims to the territory in the interior as far as the Pacific Ocean.

Spain, mistress of Mexico, California, New Mexico, and Florida, extended her claim of sovereignty over all the territory lying between the Pacific, the Gulf of Mexico, and Cape Florida on the Atlantic.

Such was the position of parties in 1783, when the Treaty of Paris, of the 3d September, usually known as the *Treaty of Peace*, introduced great modifications in their respective relations.

England then acknowledged the liberty, sovereignty, and independence of the United States. By this solemn act, she renounced all rights of sovereignty over the territory occupied by the American Union, as well as that dependent upon it. She thus virtually created the first title of the Americans to the possession of the western territories.

But let us here remark a significant act, showing the duplicity England has ever exhibited in her international relations. At the very moment she had renounced, by a solemn act, all title to the possession of the western territories dependent on the United States, she authorized, by legislative sanction, the creation of a new association at Montreal, under the name of the North-West Company, the object of which was to carry on the fur trade in these very districts; thus concealing, under the mask of the commercial operations of a company, any hostile intentions that she might be ready to back at a future period, should her interests require it, by force.

From that time, there were two powerful rival companies in the fur trade in America; but their operations were confined to distinct territories. For a time, the competition between them was exceedingly brisk; so much so as often to produce between the agents of the companies desperate contests. This state of things was disastrous to the interests of the Americans, whose frontier posts frequently became the theatre of violent and bloody scenes on the part of the Indians craftily excited against them. This hostility may be attributed as much to the jealousy and cupidity of these two companies, as to the hatred of England towards the United States.

The results of Captain Cook's voyage were published in 1781. At that period, the commerce of the Pacific was shared by two English companies—the South Sea and the East India Companies. The vessels of the former were permitted to enter the Pacific, on their fur trade or fishing expeditions, only through the Straits of Magellan or around Cape Horn; those of the latter were to reach the same destination by the Cape of Good Hope. All other vessels were excluded from these seas for either of these objects. The consequence was that a number of English subjects, anxious to engage in this trade, on account of the great demand for furs, and the heavy profits realized from them, were obliged to sail under foreign colors; in fact, to denationalize themselves.

Among the first English adventurers who, under foreign colors, traded in the Pacific, was James Hanna. In 1785, he visited Nootka Sound, under the Portuguese flag. His trade with the natives was very profitable; but a second voyage, in 1786, resulted less advantageously.

In the course of this year, several attempts were made to establish a direct trade between Macao and Kamtschatka; but they all failed.

Captains Lowrie and Guire made several voyages to the western coast of Bombay, and Meares and Tippling to that of Calcutta, under the flag of the East India Company.

Before recording the result of Meares' voyage, we shall call to mind the expedition of our unfortunate fellow-citizen Jean-François Garaup de Lapeyrouse, which took place in 1785. In June, 1786, he visited Mount St. Elias, and the American coast between latitudes 50° and 54°. Arriving at Monterey, he made a number of scientific observations; and, on the 24th of September of that year, he left that port never again to see land.

Captain Meares wintered in the Gulf of Nootka from 1786 to 1787. He obtained permission from the chief of the tribe that inhabited the coast to erect a few huts to shelter his men, and several store-houses to deposit his merchandise. During the winter, he lost one-half of his men by scurvy.

On the west coast, the principal places resorted to for the fur trade, at this period, were King George's Straits or Nootka Sound, the Straits of Norfolk, the port of Guadaloupe, near Mount San Jacinto, Prince William's Straits, and Cook River.

In 1785, a new company, having been formed in London, under the name of King George's Straits Company, sent an expedition, under the command of Captains Portlock and Dixon, to trade exclusively between the north-west coast and China.

In 1786, the ships of this company visited Nootka Sound; but the season being far advanced, they were compelled to winter at the Sandwich Islands.

In 1787, they visited Cook's River and Prince William's Straits.

Here they found Captain Meares, whose vessel had been locked up in the ice, and whose crew was reduced to one-half of its original number by sickness.

Captain Dixon then continued his voyage alone to the eastward of Mount Jacinto or Edgecombe, the Port Remedios of Bodega. He changed this name to that of Norfolk Straits, notwithstanding a narrative of Bodega's voyage, published in England in 1781, was known to him. He also claimed, with equal shamelessness, the discovery of the west coast of America to the south of the fifty-fourth degree of latitude, urging that Captain Cook had not himself seen it, though this celebrated navigator had awarded to the Spaniards the credit of its discovery.

Captain Dixon, having learned from the natives that the place at which he had landed was detached from the main land by an arm of the sea, gave it the name of Queen Charlotte's Island, and distinguished the northern entrance to the interior strait as *Dixon Canal.*

Captain Duncan, sent out by the same company in 1787, visited Prince of Wales Strait, sailed through every part of it, and discovered a considerable number of islands, which he named the Prince Royal Archipelago.

In the same year, Captain Berkeley, commanding a ship in the Austrian East India Company's service, anchored in the strait previously discovered by Juan de Fuca.

In 1788, the Portuguese, who were actively engaged in the fur trade between the north-west coast and China, sent two vessels to Macao under their own flag; but these were commanded by two English officers, John Meares and William Douglas, who had acquired some reputation in former voyages on the same coast.

These two navigators, from the fact of their bearing Portuguese commissions, and sailing under the Portuguese flag, had lost their nationality as citizens of Great Britain. Hence, during this period, all their official acts, in relation to their legal consequences, belonged to the crown of Portugal.

Douglas visited Cook River. Meares sailed directly for Nootka Sound, where his crew immediately commenced to build a small vessel suitable for trading with the natives along the coast. Desirous of profiting by this delay, to reconnoitre the southern shores, Meares effected an arrangement with one of the chiefs of the bordering tribes, and obtained permission to build a house for the use of the men he expected to leave behind him.

Meares, on his return, rejoined Douglas, and found his small vessel completed. He gave it the name of the *North-West America.* He returned to China with a cargo of furs, and left orders for the two remaining vessels to repair to the Sandwich Islands during the winter, and to return to Nootka Straits in the spring.

At this period, the Americans directed their attention to the rich trade thus carried on between the north-west coast and China. The city of Boston, always distinguished for its spirit of enterprise, fitted out a trading expedition, of which Joseph Barrell, Samuel Brown, Charles Bulfinch, John Darby, Growell Hatch, and John M. Pintard were the principal owners. This expedition, composed of two vessels, the ship *Columbia,* with a crew of two hundred and twenty men, Captain John Kendrick, and the sloop *Lady Washington,* of ninety tons, Captain Robert Gray, sailed on the 1st of October, 1787.

The *Lady Washington* first touched the north-west coast in latitude 46° in August, 1788. It came very near being lost on the breakers at the mouth of a river which Gray attempted to enter. At this point, he was attacked by the natives, in which contest one of his men was killed, and another wounded. Shaping his course to the south-west, he arrived, on the 17th of September, in Nootka Straits, where, after a few days, the *Columbia* joined him.

Meares, in obedience to the orders he had received, left this harbor, to winter at the Sandwich Islands, after the arrival of these two American vessels.

In the mean while, the Spanish government, at length discovering the importance which this trade had acquired, began to take umbrage at the various attempts of other nations to settle on this coast, despite the precedence of title to it which Spain enjoyed, and, in 1788, sent two vessels from San Blas, under the respective orders of Estevan Martinez, who had been a pilot of Juan Perez in 1774, and Gonzalo Haro. These vessels, on the 25th of May, 1788, anchored in the waters of Prince William's Straits. Haro visited the Russian establishments of Codiak; and Martinez explored Prince William's Straits. They then sailed in company along the eastern coast of the first harbor of Alieska as far as

Unalashka, the largest of the Aleutian Islands, and returned to the port of San Blas.

In May, 1789, Martinez, in the name of the crown of Spain, took possession of Nootka Straits, as well as of some vessels he found there, trading with the natives. He hauled down the English flag, and hoisted that of Spain. He thus maintained the supremacy of the rights of his Catholic majesty along the whole Pacific coast of America, from Cape Horn to the sixtieth degree of north latitude.

He at length returned to Mexico with his three prizes, the *Argonaut*, the *Princess Royal*, and the *North-West America*, then under the orders of Viana and Douglas.

This authoritative procedure took place in the Bay of Nootka, in presence of the American vessels *Columbia* and *Lady Washington*, whose officers were well treated by the Spanish commanders.

This circumstance created great difficulties between the Spanish and English governments, which were settled only by the convention concluded in 1790, called the *Nootka Convention.* By this convention, Spain agreed to restore all the property that had been wrested from the English, and to pay, in addition, an indemnity of a million francs (two hundred thousand dollars).

The following are the principal articles of the treaty:—

It was covenanted, by the first and second articles, that the buildings and lands on the north-west coast of America, of which English subjects had been dispossessed by a Spanish officer in the month of April, 1789, should be restored; that, besides, equitable reparation should be made for all acts of violence or hostility committed by citizens of either country against the citizens of the other subsequent to the month of April, 1789; and that, should the subjects of the parties in question have been, *since that period*, forcibly dispossessed of their lands, ships, or other property on the American coast, they should be reinstated in all their rights, and receive a just indemnity for their losses.

The third article stipulated that, for the future, the subjects of neither country should be molested in their navigation, whether with the object of fishing in the South Sea or Pacific Ocean, or of landing on the unoccupied shores for the purpose of founding settlements or trading with the natives.

The two governments appointed commissioners to proceed to

Nootka harbor, with instructions to determine the amount of indemnity to be allowed, and the extent of property to be restored, to English subjects.

The commissioner appointed by the English government was Captain Vancouver, who received special orders from the board of admiralty to examine the whole American coast from the thirty-fifth to the sixtieth degree of north latitude; to ascertain the number of establishments already formed on that coast by European nations; and, lastly, to endeavor to discover whether a navigable northern passage existed between the Atlantic and Pacific Oceans.

The Spanish government invested Quadra with full powers to settle the question at issue between England and Spain.

In the meanwhile, Captain Metcalf, an American from New York, accompanied by his two sons, visited this coast. He sailed with two vessels, one of which, a small schooner, the *Fair American*, he had purchased in Canton. This schooner was seized in Nootka Sound by the Spanish commander Martinez; but it was soon after restored to the owner. The destruction of the whole crew of the *Fair American* by the natives of Kawaihas, one of the Sandwich Islands, induced Metcalf to return to the United States.

About this period, Captain Billings made a voyage to the north-west coast on behalf of the Russians; Quimper and Alexander Malaspina on behalf of the Spaniards; and Captain Marchand, of Marseilles, in the employ of a French company. A great number of English and American vessels soon commenced a brisk trade in that quarter. Among the English, Captain Brown appears to have been the most distinguished for the useful information he furnished relative to that coast to Captain Vancouver himself.

The American expedition returned to Boston after a somewhat unfruitful voyage; but its intelligent projectors, far from being discouraged at this result, determined to repair the *Columbia*, and again to dispatch it to the north-west coast, as well for the purpose of trade as of new attempts at discovery.

Captain Gray again sailed in 1790. He was followed by Captain Joseph Ingraham, in a brig of seventy tons. Two other vessels, the *Hancock*, Captain Crowel, and the *Jefferson*, Captain Roberts, made part of the expedition. Captain Magee, of the *Margaret*, sailed from New York the same year.

Ingraham, while sailing in the Pacific, discovered a group of islands, lying between the eighth and eighteenth degrees of latitude, to which he gave the names of Washington, Adams, Franklin, Knox, Federal, and Lincoln.

Captain Gray arrived in the Pacific in the spring of 1791, and reconnoitered Cape Mendocino. He then directed his course along the coast towards Nootka Sound. In latitude 42°, he discovered what he supposed to be the mouth of a river, which he vainly endeavored to enter, in consequence of the force of the outward current.

On the 15th of June, he anchored in the port of Clycquet, in Nootka Sound; examined the coast between the fifty-fourth and fifty-sixth degrees of latitude; entered the strait, which he named Massachusetts Canal, for a distance of thirty miles; and then returned to Clycquet, where he passed the winter. At this place, he purchased land from the natives, erected Fort Defiance, and built the schooner *Enterprise*.

In the same year, Captain Kendrick, an American, also purchased land from several Indian chiefs in Nootka Sound. In 1793, the owners of the vessel he commanded made an unsuccessful attempt to sell this land in England. Captain Kendrick lost his life in one of the Sandwich Islands, and his vessel never returned to the United States.

In the spring of 1792, Captain Gray again put to sea on board the *Columbia*. While cruising towards the south-west, his companion, Captain Harwell, in the schooner *Adventure*, directed his course towards Charlotte Island. On the 29th of April, Gray met Vancouver near the mouth of the Straits of Juan de Fuca, who had sailed from England in January, 1791, on board the *Discovery*, accompanied by Lieutenant R. Broughton, in the brig Chatham. He communicated to him the details of his discoveries on the coast, along which Vancouver had sailed without making any observations, and informed him that he had entered a strait in latitude 54° north, and had ascended it as high as latitude 56° without reaching its termination.

Captain Gray, determined to ascertain the nature of the discoveries he had already made, sailed very close to the coast in a south-westerly direction. On the 7th of May, he again descried, towards the west, the same breakers he had observed in latitude 46° 58′. Assured that these indications of the mouth of a great river were real, he managed fortunately to effect an entrance, and soon safely came to anchor. The bay he entered received the name of Bulfinch Harbor, in honor of one of the owners of the vessel he commanded. On the 11th of May, at half past seven o'clock, he crossed the bar of the great river of Oregon, which he called the *Columbia*, the name of his vessel. Ascending this river a certain distance, he observed that it discharged an immense quantity of fresh water into the sea. He remained there until the 20th, during which time he effected several landings to ascertain the nature of the shores.

To Captain Robert Gray, then, belongs the honor of the discovery of Oregon, and of having been the first to navigate its waters. To him also is due the honor of having fulfilled all the conditions necessary to establish the title of the Americans to the discovery and possession of the Columbia River. Captain Gray gave a name to this river, surveyed its entrance, and designated the northern point of its mouth *Cape Hancock*, named *Cape Disappointment* by Meares in 1788. To the southern point he gave the name of *Cape Adams*.

Having effected this discovery, Gray sailed towards the eastern coast of Queen Charlotte's Island, where his vessel was much damaged by striking on a rock. He fortunately succeeded in reaching Nootka Sound, where Captain Ingraham arrived almost at the same time. Captain Gray officially communicated his discovery to the Spanish commandant Quadra, and in September, with Captain Ingraham, returned to the United States.

Quadra, with the view of executing the commission that had been intrusted to him by the Spanish government, questioned Captain Gray relative to the transactions that had taken place, to his knowledge, between the English and the Indian chiefs concerning the acquisition of lands, and the right of the former to erect buildings in Nootka Sound. Captain Gray answered that he and his men had had frequent intercourse with the chief of the Indian tribe Maquinna for more than nine months; but that he was not aware that the English had purchased lands from the Indians, and that the only building he had seen on his arrival was an Indian hut, which had been destroyed long before the arrival of the Spaniards.

The Portuguese commander Vienna confirmed these statements.

From this testimony, the Spanish commissioner thought himself able to maintain that the English had no right whatever to restitution of any kind. Consequently, as soon as Vancouver arrived in Nootka Sound, he made known to him the conclusion at which he had arrived. Nevertheless, to prove his desire to come to an amicable arrangement, he proposed, for the present, to cede to the English the lands on which Meares had settled in 1788, and to yield to them the buildings which had been erected by the Spaniards, and all the lands they had cultivated; and to await the decision of their respective governments with regard to the claims of the English.

Quadra could come to no understanding with Vancouver relative to the interpretation of Count Florida Blanca's letter. Vancouver maintained that England, from the very terms of the Spanish minister's orders, had the absolute right of dominion over all the territory watered by Nootka Sound. Quadra, on the contrary, maintained that England had no right to the restitution of any property, except the lands Meares had specially purchased from the natives, and the huts he had erected thereon.

The two commissioners, therefore, separated without coming to any understanding. Nootka continued to be considered a Spanish port; but England retained possession of it in fact!

Upon information received from Captain Gray, Vancouver, in 1792, sent Captain Broughton to examine the entrance of the great river which Gray had discovered. He examined Bulfinch Harbor, entered the Columbia, went on shore, and took possession of the territory in the name of his sovereign, as though the country had remained unknown until his arrival. He pretended, moreover, that Gray had mistaken a large bay for the mouth of this river, and therefore had not entered it.

Vancouver pursued his course to the north-west, and entered the Straits of Fuca, which he thoroughly examined. He thus ascertained the correctness of the descriptions of the Greek pilot Juan de Fuca. This circumstance tended to perpetuate the name of this celebrated pilot as the designation of the southern entrance into this strait.

Vancouver, nevertheless, named all the territory watered by the Straits of Juan de Fuca *New Georgia.* He took possession of all that portion of the American continent, and of the adjacent islands, in the name of his sovereign, all of which he named anew in commemoration of the royal family, the ministers, Parliament, and the army and navy of Great Britain.

From the circumstantial details just related, it is, I think, incontestably demonstrated that not one of the points on this coast, or on the adjacent islands, was ever occupied by the English anterior to the foundation by the Spaniards, in May, 1789, of the port in Nootka Sound.

The ulterior abandonment of Nootka Sound by the Spaniards, in 1795, according to the third and fifth articles of the convention, of which we have already spoken, merely gave the English the right, in common with the Spaniards, to land and trade on points of the coast to the north of the port of San Francisco.

We have scrupulously presented, in chronological order, the various expeditions undertaken with the view of reconnoitering, or of founding settlements on, the north-west coast. We shall, in the same order and in the same spirit, give a summary of the journeys made into the interior of the country.

We must here remark that, to insure the monopoly of the fur trade in the north-west territory of America, the celebrated Hudson's Bay Company had obtained new recruits, in 1784, from among the Canadians, under the denomination of the North-West Company of Montreal. It absorbed, in the same manner, several other associations, subsequently engaged in the same trade.

The North-West Company, however, retained its own constitution for several years. The capital of the company was at first divided into sixteen shares; it was then increased to twenty; and finally to forty. A certain portion of these shares belonged to *agents* residing at Montreal, who furnished the means necessary to carry on the business. The remainder of the shares was divided among proprietors or partners charged with the administration of the affairs of the company at the posts or forts in the interior, and clerks who directly traded with the Indians.

The assistants, or *clerks*, were, for the most part, young Scotchmen who had entered the service of the company for five or seven years. At the expiration of this term of apprenticeship, they were admitted into the company as partners.

The subordinate assistants, such as *guides*, *interpreters*, or *voyageurs*, were recruited from among the Canadians. The latter served at once as porters and boatmen on the rivers. All the assistants, stimulated by the hope of advancement, remained in the interest of the company.

The merchandise imported from England by the agents to carry on the trade with the Indians was generally packed in bales weighing from a hundred to a hundred and ten pounds. The packages of furs sent in exchange were of very nearly equal weight. Four years elapsed before a return could be made.

Alexander Mackenzie, one of the members of the company, commanding Fort Tchipionyan, a post on the lake of the Athabosca Mountains, undertook, in 1789, on behalf of the company, an exceedingly adventurous exploring journey, with the object of reaching the shores of the Pacific Ocean.

Lake Athabosca, on the shores of which Mackenzie resided, is nearly two hundred miles long, east and west; its mean width is about thirteen miles; and it is situated near the fifty-ninth degree of north latitude, and about midway between the Pacific Ocean and Hudson's Bay.

Mackenzie embarked, in June, on Slave River, entered the great Slave Lake, and discovered a large river, to which he gave his own name. He then descended this river for nearly nine hundred miles, in a north-west direction, until it terminated in the ocean, or what he supposed to be the ocean. In the course of three months, he returned to Fort Tchipionyan.

In 1792, Mackenzie undertook another journey in behalf of the North-West Company, with the view of extending the field of its commercial operations with the Indians beyond the Rocky Mountains, and of exploring the sources of the Columbia River. He set out on the 10th of October, and ascended the Unjegala or Peace River, as far as the foot of the Rocky Mountains, where he passed the winter. In June, he continued his journey, and ascended this river to its sources in about 54° north latitude. He then crossed a portage of half a mile, embarked on another river, called by the natives *Tacontahutessee*, or *Frasier River*, and descended it for a distance of two hundred and ten miles, mistaking it for the Columbia River; but so great became the difficulties of navigation, that he was obliged to abandon the river, and to seek, by land, in a south-westerly direction, the shores of the Pacific. He reached the coast on the 22d of July, 1793, to the north of Quadra and Vancouver's Island, and therefore about four hundred and fifty miles to the north of the mouth of the Columbia River, and about one year after Captain Gray had entered and explored it.

The river which Mackenzie mistook for the Columbia was Frasier River, which takes its rise farther to the north, and empties into the Straits of Juan de Fuca, near Puget's Sound.

Mackenzie, pursuing a more direct course on his return, reached his post in August.

Notwithstanding the authenticity of these facts, the English have never hesitated to affirm that Mackenzie was the first who discovered and explored the upper course of the Columbia.

In 1794, Trudeau, a citizen of St. Louis, performed a journey to the Rocky Mountains in behalf of the Spanish government. At about the same period, and under the same government, Manuel Lisas was carrying on a profitable trade in furs with the north-west.

The Russians began to turn their attention to the fur trade in America, then so profitable. In 1799, they attempted to found the celebrated establishment of Sitka. This was destroyed by the natives, but was rebuilt, as well as the establishments of Unalashka and Kodiak, in 1803. The Russian government then sent an expedition to America with the object of giving to their establishments as thorough a development as possible. The command of this expedition was intrusted to Captains Krusenstern and Lisiensky, who circumnavigated the globe, and returned to Cronstadt in August, 1806.

The Russians then claimed the sovereignty of all the north-west coast of the American continent, from Behring's Straits to the mouth of the Columbia River, and attempted to impose restrictions upon American navigators and traders who claimed the right of free trade with the natives on the coast. Negotiations were opened on this subject between the Russian government and Mr. Adams, the American minister at St. Petersburgh. But the American government would never concede any of its just rights to the government of Russia.

We now approach the most important epoch in the prosperity and advancement of the American republic—that at which, by a most inexplicable turn of fortune, France felt herself compelled to intrust to other hands the destinies of one of her most brilliant colonies. The cession of Louisiana to the United States took place on the 3d of April, 1803.

By this too celebrated treaty, the United States became legal inheritors of all the rights and claims of France to the vast regions of country west of the Mississippi.

Let us take a retrospective glance at the connection of events relative to the possessions of France on the American continent. The first thing which claims our attention is an edict, dated the 14th of September, 1712, by which Louis the Fifteenth granted to Antoine Crozat a commercial monopoly over the whole territory of Louisiana.

This decree is as follows:—

"We do, by these presents, signed by our hand, grant to the said Sieur Crozat the sole right of trading in all the lands in our possession bounded by New Mexico and by the lands of the English of Carolina; in all the settlements, ports, harbors, rivers, and especially the port and harbor of Dauphin Island, formerly called Massacre, the river St. Louis, formerly called Mississippi, from the sea-shore to the Illinois, together with the River St. Philip, formerly called the Missouri, and St. Hierosme, formerly called the Wabash; and in all the country, or countries, inland lakes, and rivers emptying directly or indirectly into this portion of the River St. Louis. We decree that the said lands, countries, rivers, lakes, and islands be and remain included under the title of the General Government of Louisiana, which shall be dependent upon the general government of New France, to which it shall remain subordinate; and decree, besides, that all the lands which we possess from the Illinois shall be united, as need may be, to the general government of New France, and shall make part of it. We reserve, however, the right of increasing, if we judge proper, the extent of the government of the said country of Louisiana."*

Crozat gave up this privilege in 1717. The Illinois country was joined to Louisiana, and ceded to the West India Company, better known as the Mississippi or Law's Company. This company retained its rights of possession until the year 1732, at which period Louisiana was restored to the crown of France. This entire country continued to be administered as a French province until 1763, when it passed under the dominion of Spain. Ceded

* Old French, and translated almost literally.—Tr.

again to France in 1795, it was, in 1803, finally sold to the United States.

Immediately after this important acquisition, the federal government of the Union directed its attention to the regions beyond the Rocky Mountains. To Thomas Jefferson, then President of the Republic, is due the honor of having first conceived the idea of extending the jurisdiction of the United States over the countries watered by the Pacific Ocean. Of the expedition thus projected, he drew up the plan himself. He wrote out the necessary instructions, which he placed in the hands of Captains Lewis and Clarke, who were enjoined to conduct the enterprise to a successful issue.

These bold explorers were directed to ascend the Missouri from its mouth to its sources; and then, by the most direct route, to reach the first navigable river on the western slope of the Rocky Mountains, and to follow it to the shores of the great ocean.

This journey, begun on the 14th of May, 1804, was accomplished with equal skill and success. Lewis and Clarke, accompanied by forty men, who were furnished with means of defence, and enjoined to commit no aggressions, diligently sought to obtain a thorough knowledge of the countries through which they traveled. They endeavored to win the confidence of the natives, many tribes of whom they met on their route. They informed the Indians that the United States had succeeded the French in the possession of Louisiana, and that they were charged by their government to bring them peace, support, and protection; and, as a guarantee of the new compact the United States government wished to form with them, to offer them assistance, and such presents as would be conducive to their comfort. They then gave them arms, uniforms, cloth, and a variety of useful articles, and hoisted the American flag in their midst, as the sign of sovereignty of the United States, of which, from that day, they became the adopted sons. Our travelers also represented the object of their enterprise as a visit their new father, the President of the United States, ordered to be made to his red children, and invited them, as a mark of gratitude, to send him a deputation.

During their journey, to the west of the Rocky Mountains, Captains Lewis and Clarke had frequent intercourse with the natives of the country. They spent the winter among the Classop Indians, with whom they left a written document, stating that they had been sent by "the government of the United States to explore the interior of the American continent; that they had journeyed up the Missouri River, and down the Columbia to its mouth at the Pacific Ocean; that they had arrived there on the 14th of November, 1805, and left on the 23d of March, 1806, to return, by the same route, to the United States."

On their return, the expedition separated into two parties. Captain Lewis ascended the north branch of the Columbia, which he named Clarke River. He made a detailed survey of it and its principal tributaries. Captain Clarke traversed the main branch of the Columbia, called also Lewis River, until he reached the Yellow Stone. Descending this river to its confluence with the Missouri, he joined the party of Captain Lewis, when they returned together to St. Louis. They arrived on the 23d of September, after having traveled, during this expedition by land, more than nine thousand miles.

Whilst Lewis and Clarke were performing this adventurous journey in the north-west, Major Zebulon Montgomery Pike, by order of the government, also made a reconnoissance of the countries west of the Mississippi. He ascended this river as high as Sandy Lake, in latitude 49°. In 1806, the same officer undertook another exploring expedition. Leaving the mouth of the Missouri, he ascended the Osage along its entire course; he then crossed to the Arkansas River, which he ascended to its source, whilst one of his countrymen, Wilkinson, descended the same river to its mouth. He afterwards reconnoitered the sources of the La Plata, and traveled beyond the mountains to the borders of the Rio del Norte, which he descended.

Dunbar, Hunter, and Dr. Sibley, towards the same period, explored the countries watered by the Red River and the Washita, which, flowing through Arkansas, take their rise in Texas.

The English North-West Company, on hearing of the expedition of Lewis and Clarke, attempted to anticipate its object; and, in 1805, sent M. Laroque to establish posts, and to occupy the basin of the Columbia River near its mouth. This expedition experienced so many difficulties that it was unable to penetrate, into the interior, beyond the tribes and villages of the Mandans of the Missouri.

In 1806, this company projected another expedition, and sent Mr. Simon Frasier, with a party, to found posts to the west of the

Rocky Mountains. Leaving Fort Tchipionyan, Frasier crossed the mountains near the gorge through which Peace River flows, and founded a post in the fifty-fourth degree of latitude, which still retains his name. This was, in fact, the first English post established west of the mountains. Other posts were afterwards successively founded in those western regions, which received the name of *New Caledonia.*

The successful expeditions of Captains Lewis and Clarke opened to the Americans a vast field for speculation in the fur trade, in which several citizens of St. Louis had already acquired large fortunes and some reputation. At that time, the Missouri Company was formed, under the direction of Manuel Lisa. This intelligent gentleman founded several factories near the sources of the Missouri, and to the west of the Rocky Mountains, on the borders of Lewis River, a branch of the Columbia. Mr. Henry, one of his agents, was at the head of the latter establishments, which the enmity of the Indians, incited by the rivalry of the English companies, and the difficulty of procuring provisions, forced him to abandon in 1810.

Enterprising travelers, interested in the fur trade, thus boldly advanced into these regions, until then, so to speak, unknown, anticipating, in return for the privations they endured, and the numberless dangers they encountered, a great increase of wealth.

Gradually, the inhabitants of the lower shores of the Missouri and Arkansas began to ascend these rivers, and spread throughout the intermediate countries, thus temporarily suspending their onward course towards the western slopes of the Rocky Mountains.

Other landmarks, to direct the course of American emigration towards the shores of the Pacific Ocean, yet remained to be planted across the chains of the Rocky Mountains by men of expansive views, who could grasp the realization, at a very early period, of the immense destinies of the American nation.

To John Jacob Astor, a citizen of New York, is due the honor of having first realized the idea of occupying, in the name of the United States, the mouth and shores of the great river of which Captain Gray had discovered the entrance, and Lewis and Clarke reconnoitered the course.

Another American citizen, Captain Smith, of Boston, also conceived the same project in 1810. He arrived by sea at the mouth of the Columbia River, and laid the foundation of a settlement at

Oak Point, on the southern shore of the river. The Indians destroyed this post, and Smith was compelled to abandon his enterprise.

John Jacob Astor, in 1810, founded the American Atlantic Company, for the prosecution of the fur trade. The seat of this company was in New York.

Two very remarkable circumstances, which here deserve our notice, have transpired relative to the intentions of its founder. In the first place, Mr. Astor selected the elements of his company, in great part, from among the English subjects or agents who had been in the service of the North-West Company of Montreal. In the second place, he feared the competition which this rich company might set up against his enterprise, and therefore made a proposal to its directors, through a secret agent, to become interested in one-third of the capital. This proposition was not accepted.

Mr. Astor projected two expeditions, one by sea and the other by land. In 1809, he sent his first vessel, the *Enterprise*, Captain Elbot, to the north-west coast. In September, 1810, the remaining one, the *Tonquin*, Captain Jonathan Thorn, sailed from New York, with all the persons on board requisite for the establishment to be founded at the mouth of the Columbia River.

In January of the same year, the land expedition, under the command of Wilson P. Hunt, and composed of seventy-three men, left St. Louis, and pursued as nearly as possible the route taken by Lewis and Clarke.

In October, 1811, Mr. Astor sent out, by a third vessel, the *Beaver*, Captain Sowles, the other managers and agents of the company, of which Mr. Clarke had been appointed director. He also took the precaution to send an agent to St. Petersburgh to enter into a commercial arrangement with the Russian Company.

Captain Thorn arrived at the mouth of the Columbia River on the 24th of March, 1811. He experienced great difficulty in crossing the bar, on which occasion he lost three of his crew. He immediately commenced, in conformity with his instructions, to build a house for the protection of the colonists he was to leave behind him. For this purpose, he chose the position previously designated, by the English Captain Broughton, *Point George*, on the southern shore. The necessary building materials had been brought from New York thoroughly prepared, and the house was soon constructed.

This small colony took the name of *Astoria*, in honor of the founder of the company.

Whilst this incipient colony was thus actively engaged in its organization, it was visited, in July, by a detachment of the North-West Company, under the orders of Mr. Thompson, geographer and astronomer of the company. This party was well received by the American colony under its commander Macdougal, who had formerly been in the employ of the English company. This company, when informed of Mr. Astor's project, had immediately resolved to prevent its realization by the prior foundation of an establishment at the mouth of the Columbia River. It had, for this purpose, sent out an expedition, which had miscarried. A second one arrived, under the orders of Mr. Thompson; but, as we have just seen, after an establishment had already been founded by the Americans.

Thus, Lewis and Clarke discovered the Columbia River in 1805, and reached its mouth on the 14th of November of the same year.

The English North-West Company did not found its first establishment to the west of the Rocky Mountains, in latitude 54°, and consequently, some distance from the basin of the Columbia River, till 1806.

In fine, the American establishments on the Columbia River were founded in 1809, 1810, and 1811; whilst Thompson, director of the English North-West Company, did not arrive among the *Flathead* Indians till 1811, after Astoria had been founded.

Such are the facts relative to the succession of European settlements in the western regions—facts which establish the precedency of the Americans.

Let us resume the thread of our narrative.

Mr. Thompson, after having given his men time to rest, and received all the provisions the Americans could spare, returned homeward. He was accompanied by a party of Americans, under the orders of Mr. Davis Stuart, who founded the post of Okenagan on one of the branches of the Columbia, indiscriminately designated as Thompson and Clarke River, about one hundred and fifty or two hundred miles above its mouth.

Towards the end of January, 1812, one-half of the American

party sent by land, under the orders of Mr. Hunt, arrived at Astoria in a most deplorable condition. A second detachment arrived, a short time after, in a condition equally miserable.

At length, on the 5th of May, the *Beaver*, commanded by Captain Sowles, arrived at the mouth of the Columbia River, with additional colonists and all kinds of provisions.

The *Tonquin*, Captain Thorne, had been wrecked on the coast, to the south, in June, 1811, and the whole party, with the exception of one man who had escaped and made his way to Astoria, had been murdered by the Indians.

The unfortunate Mackay was on board of this vessel. Mr. Hunt was then appointed on the mission to Russia, whither he sailed in the *Beaver* in August, 1812.

During the summer of 1812, the Americans were busily engaged in founding new posts. A third post was established at the head waters of the Kouskouski, a tributary of the Columbia, on the very spot where Lewis and Clarke, in their journey of discovery, had built boats to descend these rivers. Donald Mackenzie, John Reide, and Alfred Seton formed a part of this third detachment.

The post of *Spokan* was founded on the river, and among a tribe of Indians, of the same name.

The last post was established on the River Wallamette.

By means of these various posts or factories, all of which were connected by water communication, the American North-West Fur Company had extended its operations, and consequently its influence, over a territory more than seven hundred miles in extent.

As a result of the relations thus established, rich and numerous supplies of furs began to arrive at the central settlement of Astoria, to be shipped to China on board the *Beaver* on her return voyage to the coast, when, in January, 1813, information was received at Astoria that the United States had declared war against Great Britain in the preceding June.

Subsequently, Messrs. Mactavish and Laroque brought intelligence that the progress of the war was unfavorable to the Americans. Nevertheless, they were well received by the chiefs of the American posts, who, whether from a feeling of kindness for their former patrons, or from a spirit of speculation, or want of confidence in their new position, sold Astoria to the agents of the North-West Company.

This transaction had been concluded a few days before Captain Black, commanding his majesty's ship *Raccoon*, took official possession of the American settlement. This officer immediately changed the name of *Astoria* to that of *Fort George*.

When Mr. Hunt, on the 28th of February, returned to Astoria from his mission to St. Petersburgh, he found that the establishments and property of the company had changed masters.

But the Treaty of Ghent, signed on the 24th of December, 1814, left the respective rights of the English and Americans to the territory of Oregon, as well as their boundaries to the west of the Rocky Mountains, in an unsettled state. Things remained on the same basis of reciprocity, that is to say, simultaneous occupation and trade, that had been sanctioned in 1807.

The Americans, therefore, assumed the right of retaking and occupying the posts they had founded before the war. It would even appear that, on the pressing request of Mr. Astor, who proposed to continue his commercial relations with the north-west, the government of the United States officially informed the English government of its intention to resume possession of the posts on the Columbia. But, in consequence of highly censurable carelessness on the part of the federal government, no measures were resorted to to effect this object until the arrival of Captain Biddle, in September, 1817, in the United States sloop-of-war Ontario, at the mouth of the Columbia River.

From 1815 to 1818, Lieutenant Kotzebue, of the Russian service, made a very interesting voyage to the Pacific Ocean, in search of a north-west passage.

Captain Biddle took possession of the American posts on the Columbia River in August, 1818.

Mr. Provon, the commissioner appointed by the American government to obtain the restitution of the posts of the north-west, arrived at the Columbia, on board of an English vessel, in October, 1818. Thus, Astoria was restored to its founders and proprietors, through American officers, unconditionally. But the American Fur Company made no efforts to continue its operations in those distant regions. On the other hand, the English agents, continuing to reside there, have remained masters of these posts, thus securing the monopoly of the fur trade.

The English, since the period referred to, have founded Fort Vancouver, about ninety miles above the mouth of the Columbia, in a position which commands the navigation of the river. The surrender of the American posts on the Columbia was the result of a convention entered into between the governments of the United States and Great Britain, on the 20th of October, 1818, which contains the following clauses:—

Article second. It is agreed, between Great Britain and the United States, that the forty-ninth degree of north latitude, starting from the north-western extremity of the Lake of the Woods, and extending to the chain of the Rocky Mountains, shall serve as the boundary line between the two countries.

Article fifth. All the territory to the north-west and west of the Rocky Mountains, and all the harbors, bays, rivers, islands, &c., claimed by either party, shall be open and free for the term of ten years from the date of the signing of the present convention; this temporary arrangement being so understood as in nowise to prejudice the claims of either of the contracting parties to any portion of the Oregon Territory.

In 1819, the animosity that had for many years existed between the Hudson's Bay and the English North-West Companies was amicably brought to a close through the interposition of Parliament. The two companies were then merged into one, or, rather, the Hudson's Bay Company absorbed the other.

In consequence of this fusion, Parliament, on the 2d of July, 1821, passed an act "to regulate the fur trade, and to establish a civil and criminal jurisdiction, in certain portions of North America." The ostensible object of this act was to give more stability to the Hudson's Bay Company; but the true and not less apparent one was to justify its pretensions to jurisdiction and property in these regions.

The year 1819, like that of 1803, was an epoch in the political history of the United States; for that year was signalized by an act highly important to the prosperity and security of that great republic, the acquisition of Florida by a treaty which bears its name. The boundary line established by this treaty between the United States and the Spanish possessions in America was to commence at the sources of the Arkansas River in latitude 42° north, and to take a westerly course as far as the Pacific Ocean. Besides, his Catholic majesty ceded to the United States all his rights, claims, and pretensions to the territory north of this line, and for ever renounced all right and title to it in his own name and in that of his heirs and successors.

Mexico, at the ratification of this treaty, formed a part of the Spanish monarchy, and was thus bound by the same stipulation.

The only British possessions in America, in 1819, were the territories bordering on the St. Lawrence and Hudson's Bay. The remainder of the American territory, to the east of the Rocky Mountains, and to the south-west as far as the boundary of Mexico, had become the incontestable property of the United States, as heir of the titles and rights of France and Spain to the greater portion of the coast of the Pacific Ocean; the validity and priority of which rights we have already sufficiently established.

The exploring expeditions of Ross, Perry, and Franklin took place about the year 1821.

The Hudson's Bay and North-West Companies, as we have just stated, were merged into one, under the title of *Hudson's Bay Fur Company*, to which Parliament granted the entire monopoly of the fur trade in the terms of the concession made by Charles the Second, and invested it with civil jurisdiction over all the country it occupied.

By virtue of the privileges thus awarded, the Hudson's Bay Company extended its jurisdiction, not only over all the British possessions in Hudson's Bay, but also over all the territory of Oregon, and even over a part of California. It thus became, in relation to America, what the East India Company is to the mercantile and financial aristocracy of England, a means of extending its monopoly, and to its government an element of encroachment and usurpation.

This position, which, by the by, is not a novel one, and consequently should occasion no surprise, arises from the ordinary course of policy of that half-merchant and half-aristocratic power of Great Britain, which sought to oppose a barrier to the threatening extension of American democracy.

Let us briefly consider the present organization of the Hudson's Bay Company. This company possesses a large capital, divided into as many shares as there are proprietors, the greater number of whom reside in America, and personally watch over the interests of the company. The shares are not held as perpetual property, nor are they transferable as other shares. They are held for life, and transmissible only by substitution, that is to say, by transfers arranged beforehand with the consent of the parties, the new proprietor being placed in the same condition as his predecessor.

The chiefs or factors residing in America have the title of associates or *partners*. Each partner placed at the head of the factories has a salary equivalent to an eighth of a share, twenty-five thousand francs (five thousand dollars) a year; the subordinate agents are entitled only to the sixteenth of a share.

The principal agents hold an annual meeting at York, in Upper Canada, at which the reports transmitted by the subordinate agents are examined, and the administration purified. Here they deliberate, and discuss the plans of operation for the following campaign; the new orders to be given to trappers; in short, such general directions as will increase the profits of the company, and tend to the preservation of the beaver in the company's districts. Their report is then sent to the directors in London for their personal examination.

This company, by the power derived from its constitution, exercises a complete despotism over all its subordinates. It has absolute control of the liberty of all who are in its service, whether as sub-agents, employees, bondsmen, or slaves; for the slavery which exists in all the Indian tribes is also admitted throughout the domain of the Hudson's Bay Company. The chiefs have therefore the power of life and death over any individual who refuses to submit to the rules of the company. They regulate, determine, or withdraw at will the salaries of all their agents or employees. They fix the price of all provisions or articles of consumption, as also of the beaver skins sold by the natives. From these purchases, and from the sale of their merchandise, they realize a profit of not less than three hundred per cent.

The laborers, who are generally natives of the Orkney Islands or Canadians, are enlisted for a term of five years in the service of the company, and receive from three hundred and seventy-five to four hundred and twenty-five francs a year (from seventy-five to eighty-five dollars). The clerks at the posts are better paid. All are armed, disciplined, and subjected to a rule equal in severity to that of an army. Every act of insubordination is immediately punished with death.

Each trapper is accompanied by three or four slaves. The price of an Indian slave is from ten to twenty blankets; that of a female is higher. If a slave dies within six months after he has been purchased, the seller is bound to return half the price paid for him. The love of gain with respect to the sale of a native is such among the Indians, that the instances are frequent in which fathers sell their own sons.

The company has covered the Oregon Territory with factories and military posts, which serve as store-houses and rallying-points for their agents and for the Indians. The central factory or store-house is at Vancouver, on the northern shore, upwards of one hundred miles above the mouth of the Columbia, and at the head of navigation. At the southern portion of this river, the company has built Fort Umaqua, near the mouth of a river of the same name. It has invaded a part of California, and occupies an important post in the harbor of San Francisco, one of the best on the north-west coast of the Pacific, which vessels of all sizes can enter. It is now mistress of more than five hundred thousand square miles to the west, and of two million five hundred thousand miles to the east, of the Rocky Mountains.

In fine, as though the territory of Oregon were insufficient to satisfy the ambition of England, who aspires to become absolute mistress of the whole of the Pacific, and to be independent of the competition of Russia in the markets of China, the Hudson's Bay Company, in 1842, took a lease for ten years of all the Russian establishments in North America at an annual rent of from twenty-six to forty thousand dollars.

This treaty, however, does not include the post at the Island of Sitka, where Russia has a very large establishment.

The last circumstance we shall notice concerning the views of England relative to America—a circumstance which should justly alarm the Americans, from its tendency to menace their power—is that the Hudson's Bay Company has recently directed its attention to the permanent occupation of the Oregon Territory, by founding agricultural and manufacturing establishments, and practical schools for the education of a generation it is raising with its own ideas and under its own domination.

To insure its trade with these countries, the company has a small naval force at its disposal, composed of four vessels adapted for long voyages, two schooners which sail along the coast from

California to the Russian settlements, and a steamer. All these vessels are fully armed and equipped. Moreover, they have founded an establishment at the Sandwich Islands, where these vessels can take in refreshments and provisions.

The Americans, whose numerous whale-ships frequent these seas, have, with the consent of the local authorities, also established a station on these islands, which, being the most important in Oceanica, alone afford all the advantages of a provision station favorable to the commercial interests which attract to the Pacific Ocean all the maritime nations of the world.

The Sandwich Islands are destined to realize a high degree of commercial prosperity, because of their remarkable geographical position in Oceanica, midway between America and China, and in the direct track of European vessels bound to India or on whaling voyages. The native inhabitants of these islands understand the immense advantages of their position, and have therefore, for some time, been endeavoring to obtain the acknowledgment of their independence and of their neutrality. With this object they have sent commissioners to Washington, London, and Paris to negotiate, as a free nation, concerning their own interests. I doubt not that, already well received in the United States and in England, they will be equally well received in France, where the government should well understand the importance of the independence and neutrality of that portion of the globe, as a security that no foreign power shall exercise over it undue influence.

A new American association, the *Columbia Company*, was organized in 1822; but, in 1826, it was united to the North American Company.

In 1823, M. H. Ashley undertook a journey towards the sources of the Colorado in California, west of the Rocky Mountains. He visited the shores of the La Plata, and established a station near Lake Utah.

In 1824, the United States and Russia concluded a convention, establishing the boundaries of their respective territories in America. By the third article of this convention, it was agreed that no citizen should, without the authority of the United States, found any settlement on the north-west coast of America, or in any of the adjacent islands, north of 54° 40′; while Russia, on her part, engaged not to permit any of her subjects to settle to the south of that line.

In 1825, Russia concluded a treaty with Great Britain, by which both parties agreed to consider the same parallel, 54° 40′, and its intersection with the southern extremity of Prince of Wales Island, as the boundary between their possessions on the coasts and islands of the north-western portion of the American continent.

In 1824 and 1825, the government of the United States made a proposition to Great Britain to adopt latitude 49° north as their boundary from the west of the Rocky Mountains to the Pacific Ocean, admitted by the treaty of 1818 as the boundary line to the east of the Rocky Mountains. The English ministry refused to accede to this proposition, for which they substituted an offer to consider the forty-ninth degree as the line of separation, but only to the point where it intersects the sources of the Columbia River, the middle of which was to be followed as a boundary to the Pacific Ocean.

By this insidious offer, England aimed at securing to herself the most important military and maritime positions on the coast, in the Straits of Juan de Fuca, on Puget's Sound, and at the mouth of the Columbia River, and would have been certain, from that period, of remaining mistress of the commerce of that coast, and of the whole of Oregon Territory.

In 1827, the United States rejected this proposition, on the ground that it would thereby concede to Great Britain a territory to the south of the forty-ninth degree. The United States acted wisely in refusing to accede to this new claim of the British government; because in fact, as well as by right, the Americans have an incontestable title to the occupation of the north-west territory, at least as far as the fiftieth degree of latitude. For if, with the object of determining the limit of the rights which a nation claims, the discovery of a river and the formation of a settlement at a given time are assumed as the basis of the title to property and sovereignty to all the territory which this river waters, the deduction from this principle is that the United States should extend its claims to all the north-west territory at least as high as the fifty-third degree, the point where the Columbia takes its northern rise. If, however, we rest on the other principle, that every nation which takes possession of an unknown or unoccupied country has the right of sovereignty over one-half of the territory comprised between its settlements and those of another nation, we still conclude that, as the American posts of *Astoria* and *Clatsops* are situated very nearly in latitude 46° 20′, whilst the English post, supposed to be the most southern of the two founded by Cook in 1778, is in latitude 61° 30′, latitude 53° 54′ ought to become the northern limit between the territories of England and the United States.

The negotiations between the two countries relative to this question having produced no result, Mr. Gallatin received orders from the cabinet at Washington officially to notify the English government that the American government no longer held itself bound to abide by the propositions previously made, to settle the limits of the north-west territory, and that the United States reserved its full rights and titles to its possessions in this territory.

Nevertheless, by the convention of 1827, it was admitted by the two nations:—

1st. That the clauses of the convention of 1818 should continue in full force for an indefinite length of time, as though they had become the subject of new negotiations.

2d. That from the 20th of October, 1828, either of the contracting parties should have the right to recede from the terms of the convention, by giving to the other one year's notice, in the usual form.

3d. Finally, each of the parties maintained certain reservations relative to its respective rights, which each pretended to preserve in their integrity.

From 1824 to 1827, Ashley, having carried on a profitable trade with the posts to the west of the Rocky Mountains, entered into an arrangement with the company founded by Messrs. Smith, Jackson, and Sublette, to which he transferred his interests. At that time, a direct communication was established by large parties between the post of Lake Utah and St. Louis.

Pilcher undertook an expedition to the west of the Rocky Mountains in 1827, 1828, and 1829.

In 1828, the United States concluded a treaty with Mexico, which had then become a State independent of the crown of Spain. The boundary established between Spain and the United States was confirmed by the Mexican government. Thus, on this question, no difficulty can arise between the United States and Mexico.

In summing up the results of the treaties concluded between the United States and Spain, Russia, and Mexico, as well as of the convention with England, previously cited in their chronological order, we see that the American Republic established, by these acts, the boundaries within which it pretended to enforce its rights of property and sovereignty over the shores of the great Pacific Ocean. These limits were comprised between latitudes 42° and 54° 40′ north, and inclose a territory of *twelve degrees and forty minutes* in extent on the ocean.

Great Britain alone contested the validity of the rights of the United States to this extent of district, and raised claims to the greater part, if not to the whole, of it. The preceding analysis must have thrown light on this dispute, and shown in whom the rights inhere. They were, as we have said, incontestably on the side of the Americans.

Such, however, was the question to be settled between the two rival powers, in the solution of which each thought its honor and interests equally at stake ; although, in my opinion, the situation of England was the more embarrassing and dangerous.

We must here remark that England could not renounce her pretensions to the occupation of the mouth of the Columbia, and the posts depending on this river, without yielding to the Americans all the advantages of these maritime and military positions, whose importance, on account of the great commercial interests that attracted all the nations of Europe to these regions, had greatly augmented. Now, the grave feature of the alternative is this: If Great Britain, on the one hand, retains possession of this coast, her preponderance in the Pacific will become so great as to be highly detrimental to the Americans, the only rivals whom she fears. If, on the other hand, the United States is allowed free access to the western coast, the Americans will immediately assume preponderance in those seas.

The American Republic increases daily, rather because of the enterprising character and commercial ambition of its citizens, than of the intervention of the government. In the hands of Americans, a new station on the north-west coast would, in the pursuit of their destiny of commercial and manufacturing antagonism to Great Britain, soon become a powerful auxiliary.

This commercial enterprise Great Britain will strive by all the means in her power to check or altogether prevent; because it is that which she most fears.

But the Americans wisely appreciate their exceptional position, and the advantages it assures them, so long, at least, as they shall have the wisdom to maintain their constitution, to which they are indebted for their happy governmental centralization, the only strength and security of their national existence. They have always been accustomed to consider the whole continent as eventually their inheritance; and this consummation is rapidly approaching, through the miraculous progress of their system of colonization, which insures the gradual, but not less certain, occupation of the vast domain which has fallen to their lot. What can conventions, treaties, and even an armed resistance effect against the inevitable activity of their nature? Probably retard the result for a time. But, sooner or later, the Americans must become masters of the mouth of the Columbia River on the great ocean, as they now are of the mouth of the Hudson on the Atlantic; and, certain of this result, they await the force of events to place them in possession of the territory they claim, rather than by force of arms attempt to wrest it from an enemy that might be long able to resist their efforts.

We must not, however, be deceived by the apparent forbearance of the American people; this has its limits. Of their ability to secure respect, they have already given ample proofs. They are steadfast in their purpose. The claims which, for the time, they fail to urge, are merely held in abeyance until a suitable opportunity arises for reviving them.

The question of the occupation and colonization of Oregon is not of very recent origin. As far back as 1804, President Jefferson actively engaged in plans to extend the jurisdiction of the United States over this territory. President Monroe, adopting the views of Jefferson, in 1824 made a special message to Congress, recommending the establishment of military posts at the mouth of the Columbia River. The following year, John Quincy Adams, on his accession to the Presidency, recommended the adoption of the same measure, and, moreover, the establishment of a naval station on the shores of the Pacific Ocean. President Tyler, during his administration, renewed the recommendation.

In consequence of these several executive recommendations,

Congress at length took the urgency of this national measure into consideration: first, in 1821; then successively in the years 1826, 1838, 1839, 1843, and 1844. The committees to which this part of the presidential messages has been referred have uniformly reported favorably upon it, and have called the attention of Congress to the measures that would be most in accordance with the sentiment of the nation. But these reports, thus far, have remained without any effective result.

The committee to which this subject was referred, in 1843, expressed itself in much stronger terms than any previous committee, relative to the necessity of adopting measures to extend the jurisdiction of the American government over the Oregon Territory. Advancing the opinion that, by right, the United States was under no obligation previously to give the British government notice of its intention to extend its jurisdiction over a territory to which it was entitled, the committee urged an appropriation of two hundred thousand dollars to carry its recommendation into effect. The amount of the appropriation was certainly not the cause of the rejection of the proposal; nevertheless, the question was once more postponed. This last delay concerning the accomplishment of a measure daily gaining numerous partisans, grew out of causes which, on the election of Mr. Polk to the Presidency, ceased to exist.

In this election, the great democratic party triumphed throughout every portion of the Union. It was then enabled to express its opinions, in both Houses of Congress, with assurance amounting almost to certainty that a majority would support all the measures proposed by its official organ.

In his remarkable message to both Houses of Congress, on the 2d of December, 1845, the President, in clear and precise terms, expressed the determination of the government to occupy the disputed territory, not provisionally, but permanently. The President declared plainly, and with firmness, that the right of the United States to Oregon was absolute; that the American government intended to maintain it under all circumstances, and, if necessary, by force of arms; that there was no further occasion for compromise; that the term of the provisional convention would expire in one year; and finally, that, by extending over the disputed territory the laws of the United States, and by establishing a chain of posts to be occupied by American soldiers, it was thenceforth to become an integral portion of the American soil.

No document emanating from the chief magistrate of the United States was ever received with more approbation and enthusiasm; for no message had ever given a more frank and explicit exposition of the national will concerning all that affects the interests and honor of the people!

It must not, however, be understood that the American government intended, by its last message, entirely to reject all negotiation. In a laudable spirit of conciliation, and with the desire to avoid, as much as was compatible with the dignity and rights of the nation, any cause of rupture that might compromise the general peace, it confessed itself willing to forego its legal claims, and to accept the forty-ninth degree of latitude as the boundary between the two nations upon the Pacific coast, thus according *free entrance into all the ports of Vancouver's Island, to the south of that parallel;* that is to say, free entrance into the Straits of Juan de Fuca, or Puget's Sound.

The English government, not satisfied with this concession, still claimed the free navigation of the Columbia River. The American government peremptorily refused to accede to this new claim of the English diplomatists in favor of the interests of the celebrated Hudson's Bay Company in the Oregon Territory.

We think that the United States ought not to have recognized any such extravagant claims. By granting free entrance into the ports of Vancouver's Island, it has conceded a great right—a fact which must satisfactorily prove to all European politicians that the American democrats are not ambitious, and ready to sacrifice everything, even the peace of the world, in a spirit of propagandism or aggrandizement.

The Americans are not propagandists; they are only attached to their own institutions, which an experience of seventy years has proved to be, of all others, the best adapted for their situation; and, in consequence, they are animated by a spirit of obstinacy—a spirit which has been thoroughly proved on all occasions—where the maintenance of their rights has been necessary. Nothing can make them flinch on this point.

The British government, well knowing the character of the nation with which it was engaged on the Oregon question, and knowing all its resources in case of a rupture; knowing also the injury its commerce would suffer by the swarm of privateers that would infest the coast of the United States, should war be declared, hesitated not to renew negotiations, and immediately sent Lord Ashburton to treat directly on this subject with the government at Washington.

During these discussions, the American emigrant still pressed onwards to the regions of the west, by all the methods appropriate to his character. The American preacher, with his company of courageous and devoted followers, had already crossed the Rocky Mountains. Other missionaries, impelled by the same motives, have followed his footsteps, everywhere spreading the faith, the language, and the influence and authority of their country and government. These brave pioneers of American civilization have already founded seven missions in the Oregon territory: at Astoria; at Multuomia, or Wallamette; in the Puget district; on the Willamette; at Umpqua; and at Clatsop. The children of the forest collect around them to receive the first influences of civilization. A number of American families, impelled by the same spirit of proselytism, have also settled in those distant regions, where they are destined to become the nucleus of important agricultural colonies; for the valley of the Columbia offers irresistible attractions to the American. Its climate, soil, and natural productions are as favorable to man as those of the Mississippi. The Rocky Mountains alone form a repulsive and sterile barrier, which emigrants require energy and perseverance to overcome to reach the western declivities, where nature has been so bountiful.

It is not to be presumed that the progress of the American population towards the west—an advancement estimated, according to observation, at half a degree of longitude a year—will be checked by this barrier. This population must continue to advance by reason of causes inherent in the very nature of the American. The desire of this active and eminently colonizing race is one day to cover the whole of North America.

The occupation of Oregon can never be a subject of doubt. It is merely a question of time. In 1844, the population of those distant regions already amounted to more than eight thousand; and we daily see new trains of emigrants, from the Eastern and Western States, carrying large reinforcements to the American family already organized on the shores of the Pacific. There a regular elective government is constituted, composed of an executive magistrate, a supreme judge, and a legislative assembly composed of nine members, elected by the people. The laws in force are those which govern the people of the territories of the United States. In fine, to create a moral influence over a population composed of such diverse elements, the legislature of 1844 prohibited the use of ardent spirits under a penalty of one hundred and sixty dollars.

We may then predict that, ere long, the same flood of emigration which, from the shores of the Atlantic, emigrated beyond the Alleghany Mountains to the Valley of the Mississippi, will soon have gone beyond the barrier of the Rocky Mountains, to extend its influence on the shores of the Pacific. At a period not far remote, the American will find himself in front of India, with the same advantages that the people of the Atlantic possess relative to Europe. His active and enterprising spirit, aided by the marvelous power of steam, will render the American continent an intermediate link in the Union that will have been created between Europe and the East Indies.

1848. The Americans now have peaceable possession of the whole valley of the Columbia, and all the territory of Oregon. Their pioneers are already spreading over this admirable country, carrying with them their colonizing and dominant tendencies. Posts are established by which a regular chain of communication is kept up between Washington and Astoria, at the mouth of the Columbia River. A railroad twenty-six hundred miles long, destined one day to unite the Atlantic to the Pacific, is now spoken of, and will, ere long, be completed. It will cross the chain of the Rocky Mountains. The railroad is a vital artery of American nationality, of its power, and of its commerce in the Pacific and with Asia; and it will connect steam navigation on the Atlantic with that on the Pacific.

When this project shall have been realized, the Americans will have concentrated on their own continent the commerce of Europe with China and Asia—an immense and colossal work, but in harmony with the peculiar tendencies of their nature.

CHAPTER XXII.

CONCLUSION.

When we look back on the most prominent and characteristic facts contained in this historical and chronological summary of the first establishments, and of the various systems of colonization, of the Europeans in America, the first thing that strikes our attention is the violent act of usurpation by which the European displaced the red man on the American continent. Another circumstance, not less prominent, and not less deplorable for humanity, is the incessant disputes, the cruel conflicts, and the violent spoliations which sent abroad in the world the various civilized people who, in seeking to colonize the New Continent, arrogated to themselves, in the name of civilization and religion, which they abused in an equal degree, the right of reducing the natives to a state of slavery, and of appropriating the wealth of this unknown land to themselves. The third remarkable point—a point which certainly should not be lost sight of, as well for our immediate as for our future instruction—is the difference in the means adopted by Europeans of various origin in their systems of colonization, and especially the supremacy of the Anglo-Saxon race, which alone remained mistress of the American soil. The means by which this result has been accomplished, although in themselves unjust, have, nevertheless, produced useful results—results logically deducible from the conditions assumed. Let us examine the course of events, and their actual consequences. That the Europeans, when they arrived on the new continent, found proprietors of the soil, is an indisputable fact. But what were they? who were they? A roving race of people who lived by the chase, and wandered over their immense domains like the beasts against which they warred, without a single element of a social institution, or of a political organization. They existed in a sort of *negative community;* that is to say, they were in that primitive state in which all things exist prior to the civilization of mankind; in a state of nature, in which property is unimproved, and in which, consequently, man is not superior to the bird or beast of the forest.

By Negative Community, civilized man understands that state of things which is represented by accidental occupation; but by Positive Community, on the contrary, that state of things in which is recognized the common and permanent property of the many, of which, consequently, no one can take possession anew without the consent of the first occupants.

Such was the distinction on which the European founded his pretensions to dispossess the native American of his rights of property in the soil, which he had heretofore occupied without opposition.

By this simple preponderance, the European ranged the American race under the former class, and himself, the white man *par excellence*, in the second.

"It must be mine," said the European; "and the reason is that I am a *white man!*"

Addressing the Indian, he said, "Your state of community can exist only in the midst of immense deserts; it must yield to the strength and compact form of civilization; for the earth was given to man only to support the greatest possible number of people. Consequently, no nation, no caste can pretend to the right of abstracting from the necessities of others more than is *necessary* to its own *existence* or its *comfort!*"

Where, we ask, would the application of such logic lead us, if we extend it to its legitimate results? Where would be the limit of *necessity* and *comfort?*

Besides, what shall we now say of the results of this ruthless logic, the complete expulsion, to be soon followed by the entire extinction, of the red race? Nothing; unless force may be assumed to sanction, though not justify, violence!

The second fact, the sanguinary struggles which marked the arrival of the Europeans on the American continent, who violently contested the right of property over a few leagues more or less of this vast domain, as though a territory so immense was not sufficiently large to contain all of them, is naturally explained by the spirit of egotism and cruelty to which man is prone when moved only by instinctive avarice, and uncontrolled by honor.

Under these circumstances, everything is perverted. The laudable ends of civilization become a means of spoliation, and religion itself an arm which fanaticism renders even more terrible; as though an eternal Providence had been pleased to make us appear small in our own eyes in proportion as we believe ourselves elevated by the object we seek to attain!

The remaining circumstance to be considered deserves our especial attention, for thence we may deduce historical lessons for present and future application. Various people left the north and south of Europe to take possession of the great discovery of Columbus, each prompted by the desire of realizing, after its peculiar manner, all the advantages this discovery could afford.

The French colonized Canada; the English, Dutch, Scandinavians, and Germans the coast of New England; the Spaniards, the southern part of the continent.

The French, in accordance with the peculiar genius of their nation, planted a military colony on the shores of the St. Lawrence, and on the borders of the great Lakes. They settled upon a unitarian and feudal basis, under the Roman Catholic faith. They determined the vague limits of the immense territory of New France by the mere planting of the cross. Commerce was brought to the aid of this colony; but it proved a monopoly, yielding no profit to the colonists, and enriching only a few speculators in the mother country. No one thought of establishing real proprietors, and therefore inhabitants, in New France. To lead a military life, to follow the chase, and thus to enrich themselves by the fur trade, were the only occupations of those who emigrated from the shores of the Seine, the Marne, or the Charente to those of the St. Lawrence, and the Bay of Chaleurs.

The French had scarcely succeeded in establishing a permanent post on the St. Lawrence, when they commenced a roving life, and boldly attacked the warlike Iroquois. A whole century passed in unequal struggles, though reflecting equal honor on the bravery of all who participated in the contest. The arms of France appeared to cover the whole American continent, from Hudson's Bay to the head of the Lakes, and from the sources of the Mississippi to the Gulf of Mexico; but this vast space was occupied only by a few thousand men, distributed at detached points, pompously dignified with the name of forts, posts, or cities. Real inhabitants there were none; for every one was attracted by the charm of a roving and adventurous life, by the chances of realizing a fortune, though at the risk and peril of life. No one thought of preserving property. The improvidence of the French, their unqualified confidence in their government relative to all that pertained to their general interests, left them, after the lapse of a century, as ill prepared to constitute and to maintain a society as on the first day of their arrival on the American Continent.

The Spaniards discovered the southern part of the continent, but the foundation of their establishments was coincident with that of the French settlements. Under the sole guidance of avarice and religious fanaticism, they advanced boldly into the virgin forests, in solemn procession, with the cross and banner in front, seeking, by force of arms, to compel the natives to fall at their feet, and acknowledge them their masters! Thus, with true Castilian vanity, they overran the desert plains of Florida, Georgia, and Alabama, with all the pomp of a triumph; but, disappointed in the presumptuous hope of acquiring wealth without industry, they returned, dying with hunger and wretchedness, to the shores whence they had departed. Centuries elapse, and this indolent race, after having plundered the New World, to the natives of which it had ever been unmerciful, is compelled to abandon a territory into which it had never introduced the least germ of civilization.

Such was the result of the system of colonization pursued by the people of the south of Europe. They displayed heroic courage, great boldness and perseverance, in the dangers and sufferings inseparable from the belligerent attitude they assumed towards the natives of the country they sought to conquer; but they did not succeed in founding a permanent society, able to maintain itself by its own resources. Their failure is attributable to the fact that they adopted as the basis of their system of colonization the same principles by which the established order of things was regulated in their native countries. They did not comprehend that, in a new country, men inspired with new ideas, and animated with the holy fire of liberty and the spirit of a true religion, were required. They were unaffected by the sublime spectacle of nature presented by the splendid forests of the New World. Of the destiny of this world, they could form no conception!

But the case was different with the people who came from the north of Europe. Of these, the greater number were Anglo-Saxons, who colonized the shores of New England sixty years subsequent to the foundation of the Spanish and French settlements. These colonists also founded the colony of Virginia, and marked the outset of their career, as inhabitants of a new world, by claiming, for themselves and descendants, the title and prerogatives of *free citizens.* Liberty thus served as the starting-point of a colony whose inhabitants ever considered *labor alone* the security of an independent existence.

Other points of the same coast farther to the north soon became peopled with a great number of small distinct societies, composed of mere strangers to one another, or associated with different objects in view, but united by the same feeling of municipal liberty, the value of which they fully appreciated. Each of these communities became the centre of a compact body of people attached to the soil, whose first care was to obtain the necessaries of life by cultivating the earth, thus laying the foundation of their future prosperity.

The colonists designed to conquer the country, not by force of arms, but by means of their improvements, and the influence of their civilization. With the Bible in hand, the Anglican missionary founded at once the meeting-house and the factory. These pacific measures had a durable effect. But this course of conduct did not prevent the inhabitants from inflicting severe lessons on the Indians in their vicinity, when they became troublesome.

This important fact, that is to say, the difference in the means employed by different Europeans in the colonization of the New World, is associated with a circumstance equally remarkable—the struggle which took place between the two races from the north and the south of Europe, terminating in the extinction of the authority of the latter.

Let us trace the details of the history of the gradual development of the English colonies. We must remark, in the first place, that the early emigrants of New England, in addition to their British origin, were Puritans; that is to say, they desired liberty of conscience for themselves and their co-religionists. Still, they were animated by a spirit of the greatest intolerance towards others, and by excessive ambition. They carried with them the germ of the *Anglo-Saxon-American* character. Thus, the territory of New England, although containing comparatively few inhabitants when the French occupied Canada, the Dutch New York, and the Swedes the Delaware, already appeared too small, in the eyes of our insatiable Puritans, to suffice for their *necessities*, for their *existence*, and their *comfort;* hence they immediately coveted the annexation of their neighbors' domain.

They openly projected the conquest of New France; the forcible seizure of the Dutch colony of New York, whose inhabitants soon became confounded with the great Anglo-American family; and the extension of their jurisdiction over the Swedish colony of Delaware, whose German and Scandinavian settlers served as a nucleus of the magnificent philanthropic establishment of William Penn.

Before the close of the seventeenth century, the Anglo-Americans had already founded twelve distinct colonies, with a population of more than two hundred and fifty thousand inhabitants, and had become the real masters of the whole Atlantic coast, from the Bay of Fundy to Florida. The Massachusetts Bay Colony had been the central point of all this population, whence, as from a hive, it had spread with activity and indefatigable industry, guided by an instinctive colonizing genius, throughout this entire domain.

At this period, France claimed as a conquest of her arms the whole American Continent, from Hudson's Bay to the mouth of the Mississippi, west of the great chain of the Apalachian or Alleghany Mountains. She had planted over this immense line, more than three thousand six hundred miles in extent, a few military posts and trading stations, with a population not exceeding twelve thousand.

The presence of Spain in the southern part of the continent, in the territory of Florida, was indicated simply by a few feeble garrisons, occupying several points on the coast of the Gulf, and one or two on the Atlantic.

The relative influence of the three great powers engaged in the colonization of America is explained by the system each pursued. The Anglo-Saxons alone enjoyed, in reality, the rights of free citizens—an advantage due to the municipal liberty which had already marked their laws and their manners. With this people, therefore, everything was directed by an enlightened personal interest, which produced effects greater and more durable, and establishments more extensive, solid, and useful, than any produced by all the exclusive privileges accorded to the citizens of the other two nations.

But it was reserved for the eighteenth century to witness the accomplishment of still greater wonders by the Anglo-Saxon race in America! The English colonies, which, at the time of the Revolution of 1688, were somewhat disposed to assert their independence of the mother country, prepared for this great act of sovereignty by the practical application of the fundamental principles on which it was to be established. In the first place, they formed an alliance, offensive and defensive, against the attacks of the Indians on their frontier, and openly resolved the conquest of Canada, the better to insure the integrity of their territory. Thence a terrible struggle ensued between France and England for supremacy in America. Fortune decided in favor of England; and Canada, with the rich domain of the whole north-west territory, fell into her power.

During the course of these hostilities, the leaven of jealousy, which had, for a long time, been producing an antagonism between the Anglo-Americans and the mother country, seemed to be lost in the common desire of both to dispossess a powerful rival of property which each coveted with equal ardor. But, after the peace, the elements of collision between the English and their descendants began to produce their wonted effects. Great Britain, her self-love wounded, resolved to make use of her authority and power; but she lost both the one and the other. The Fourth of July, 1776, marked the commencement of a new era in the history of the world. On that ever-memorable day, the people of the United States, without any extraordinary provocation, moved by a sense of their own dignity, and determined to resist the arbitrary encroachments of the crown of England, strong in her acquired and acknowledged rights, declared themselves *free and independent* of British domination.

North America then became divided among four powers—France, England, Spain, and the American Union.

France still retained possession of Louisiana, in the colonization of which she had followed the same defective system she had pursued in relation to Canada. She had expended immense sums in the foundation of this settlement, where she kept, at heavy expense, strong garrisons, and a ruinous administrative *personnel*, from which she had never derived the least advantage.

England remained mistress of the province of Canada and all its dependencies, where she had taken the place of France, thus extending her rights and prerogatives over all that had belonged to the founders of Acadia, Canada, and Newfoundland.

Spain was driven still farther towards the Gulf shore by an American population, already advancing towards that latitude.

The American Union, composed of thirteen independent States, claimed all the territory between New Brunswick and Florida, and between the shores of the Atlantic and the chain of the Alleghanies, which some American pioneers had already crossed, to range the Valley of the Mississippi. Her population did not then exceed four millions.

From that period, the progress of the Americans towards the wilds of the interior is truly surprising. Though seventy years have scarcely elapsed, the Union is composed of *thirty* independent States, and of *twenty-one million* freemen. Extending their pacific conquests more than twelve hundred miles over the rich lands of the west, the American people have crossed the Alleghany Mountains, reached the borders of the great Lakes at the north, and the Gulf of Mexico at the south, and thus, after having bought Florida and Louisiana, occupy the vast Valley of the Mississippi from its sources to its mouth.

In a short time, the tide of successive emigrations will fertilize this immense valley, and all the rich country dependent on it, will reach the base of the Rocky Mountains, and, crossing them, advance towards the tranquil waters of the great ocean; and then spread along the Cordilleras which divide California from the *Rio Grande del Norte.* As a consequence of this last manifestation of their incomparable instinct for colonization, the Americans have extended the south-west frontier of the Republic from the shores of the *Sabine* to those of the *Rio Grande del Norte.* They have laid the foundation of a powerful State beyond the Rocky Mountains, and they regard the shores of the great ocean as the only limits the Republic can henceforth recognize towards the setting sun; whilst the north and the south present a vast field for the future! In fine, such are, in 1848, the gigantic proportions of the American Union—a Colossus, whose head we perceive coming out of the mists which cover the polar regions, whose feet extend as far as the Isthmus of Panama; while with one arm he threatens Europe by means of the Atlantic, and grasps with the other, through the great ocean, the rich archipelagos and the continents of Asia.

Thus, within a short period, the Anglo-American race has become firmly established on a territory comprising more than seventeen hundred million acres; consequently, exceeding fourteen times that of France. It has consigned its ancient rulers to a position beyond the St. Lawrence, where their situation towards the United States is similar to that which France, during her possession of Canada, occupied towards the English colonies; that is to say, on the left shore of the St. Lawrence, aristocratic and monarchichal principles are in juxtaposition with democratic principles on the neighboring shore.

Therefore, it is possible to predict the consequences of such a political and geographical position. The River St. Lawrence, essentially American, which must of necessity become the outlet into the Atlantic of that great line of communication and navigation opened by the Lakes and the Mississippi, will, ere long, be controlled by the American democracy; for it cannot be denied that American policy is identical with that of England, as well in its origin as in its objects. But English policy benefits only a small number of individuals, invested with all the power and all the wealth of the country. Whatever may be the result of a given foreign policy, the people always remain in the greatest wretchedness, the slaves of an oppressive oligarchy. On the other hand, American policy benefits the entire nation, which actively participates in all the projects of the government, as well in their accomplishment as in their results.

If we go back to the early history of the American people, we see the Anglo-Saxon race, from which they have descended, perseveringly pursue, from the day of its arrival on the American Continent, that policy of encroachment and violence which rendered its presence so dangerous to its neighbors, who, much more peaceably inclined, were far less skilled in the iniquitous science of spoliation. This policy has constantly shown itself egotistical and cruel, ambitious and despotic. It manifested itself under the banners of St. George, and, without any modification, has passed under the flag of the American Union. Let us not then be astonished at the prodigies it has enabled the Americans to achieve. Influenced by the dogmas of democracy, whose aim is individual interest, I see no limits to their progress but the ocean, the dominion of which they will one day dispute with England; no barrier but the influence of the principles of the Christian religion, which may yet exercise a certain control over the actions of a people so enlightened, and bring them back to the sound doctrines which alone enabled their venerable ancestors to triumph in the great struggle for liberty in 1776.

To the south and towards the west of the Mississippi, the only territory contiguous to the United States was the ancient Spanish province of Mexico. This was still under Spanish domination, when the cabinet of Madrid, in 1821, was compelled to cede to that of Washington the territory of Florida, where its authority was no longer respected. At the same time, an Anglo-American, Moses Austin, obtained permission to found a colony in a deserted territory belonging to Mexico. This was the first sign of invasion, by the Anglo-Americans, of the fertile regions watered by the Colorado, discovered by the unfortunate La Salle. Fifteen years later, in 1836, a new American colony was constituted, and conquered its independence by a brilliant victory!

The United States, at that period, considered it unadvisable to admit this State into the Union. The fear that it would disturb the political balance between the North and the South alone prevented its admission. In my opinion, consideration of the question was only postponed to a more opportune moment. But Texas was not the less an independent American State, destined to rival in prosperity the Southern States of the Union. With a territory comprising more than one hundred and twenty-one million acres, and extending from the twenty-sixth to the thirty-fourth parallel, it possesses extraordinary physical advantages. Richness of soil is combined with a climate adapted to every species of culture, from the grain of northern latitudes to the productions peculiar to the tropics. Texas, moreover, has had the wisdom to adopt liberal institutions, modeled on those of the United States, which, under the practical guidance of Americans, insure its independence and prosperity.

Texas was annexed to the American Union in 1846. By this act of profound policy, the Anglo-Americans have extended their dominion to the Rio Bravo del Norte. The war with Mexico, which followed this annexation, placed the destinies of the empire of the Montezumas in their hands, and enlarged the boundaries of the United States by the whole of Upper California, and a part of New Mexico. But it occasioned heavy expenses—a disadvantage, it is true, counterbalanced by a prospective augmentation of wealth exceeding the expenditure tenfold. Its immediate result has been the prevention of European interference on the American Continent. But, prominent above everything, is the fact that it has advanced, more than a century, the march of civilization throughout one of the richest portions of the world! Hence, we may now venture to predict that, at a time not far distant, the American race will cover the immense territory lying between the polar icebergs and the tropics, between the borders of the Atlantic and the shores of the Pacific Ocean.

Thus, it is proved by incontestable historical facts that the preponderance of the Anglo-Americans over all the other nations established anteriorly to, or simultaneously with, them in the New World, is attributable to the characteristics of the race from which they sprang, to their own distinctive genius, and, above all, to the religious and democratic principles which have at all times formed the fundamental basis of the American character.

If the various facts recorded in this historical summary have been attentively remarked, the difference in the policy respectively pursued by the two great nations which have ultimately shared North America must have been observed—a difference which is still stamped in all their acts, their form of government, their literature, and their religion. An immense void, then, separates these two nations, to fill which appears to me an impracticable task. But the sober reader must have found in this study an important subject for reflection relative to the struggles that may again arise to divide the world. That is, although the English and American nations are identical in their origin, and in relation to the objects each proposes to attain, yet are they essentially different in the vital principles of their political organizations.

In England, the landed aristocracy direct affairs. In the United States, the great democratic mass is agricultural. Between these two classes it is impossible to find a single idea, a single sentiment in common. The men who thus possess equal rights, who enjoy universal suffrage, and therefore a common responsibility, in all ranks of society—who have, above all, a sovereign contempt for hereditary right, and generally manifest but little confidence in the wisdom of their ancestors—can never live in harmony with the English. The legislation of the United States, and the method according to which intercourse with foreign nations is conducted, have an origin entirely different from those of England. The diplomatists of England and the United States have been raised in schools of diametrically opposite character. Should they meet, they would not be able to understand each other.

There is not the least affinity in the elements of these two forms of government. Their policy, however, is eminently pacific, and all occasions of hostility are carefully avoided. But should wars arise, they will be conducted with unusual energy, because the hatred of the Americans towards the English is more inveterate than towards any other nation. Thus, an immense void will one day separate these two commercial nations, which, springing from one stock, a community of origin, language, and religious opinions ought to bring together.

PART II.

MILITARY, AGRICULTURAL, COMMERCIAL, AND INDUSTRIAL RESOURCES OF THE UNITED STATES.

I HAVE exhibited the origin and the institutions of the Americans, and the struggles by which they have made themselves masters of the principal portion of the immense continent of North America.

I shall now describe their system of national defence, their military resources, and the influence which their origin, their geographical position, and especially their political institutions, have exerted upon them as an agricultural, commercial, and industrial people.

CHAPTER I.

NATIONAL DEFENCE.

GENERAL CONSIDERATIONS.

Origin of the national defence—First project of it embodied in the Constitution of 1787 — Circumstances unfavorable to its accomplishment — The fourteenth Congress orders its establishment—Arrival of General Bernard in the United States—Organization of a Board for the National Defence—Its labors—Military reconnoissance of the interior, and of the maritime frontier of the Union—General plan adopted for the defence of the coast—Elements of this American system.

IF we assume war to be the primary condition of mankind in the ages of barbarism, the science of defence, as a means of preserving and maintaining independence and internal tranquillity, must necessarily be the starting-point of an era of civilization where peace becomes a primary object. In order that man may profitably abandon himself to the inspirations of civilization, and to the progress of every department of knowledge his genius is prompted to develop, individual security is of the first importance. The first duty of a people, in their march towards civilization, is to secure their national independence. This duty becomes more sacred and imperious where a free people are concerned, because to retain freedom their territory must be placed in a condition to repel all invasion and all aggression. In this case, the measures adopted for common security must necessarily add to the strength of the links that bind together every part of the social body. Wholly directed against apprehension from abroad, these parts of the social system become mutually essential for the conservation of every interest.

Such were the views that directed the wise legislators who framed the ever-memorable Constitution of the United States. The necessity of a common defence served as the basis of the federal compact, and of the organization of the American Union. A combination of the active strength of the thirteen colonies was decreed, and a federal power created. Among the powers conceded to this general assembly by the Constitution of 1787, we find the following:—

"Congress shall have power to provide and maintain a navy; to raise and support armies; to organize a militia; and to provide for the common defence and the general welfare."

Nevertheless, these sound legislative provisions were not immediately carried out by reason of the exigencies of the times, and of the all-engrossing war in which the Confederation had been engaged against Great Britain. But the nation had come out of this great struggle triumphantly—a struggle for which it had been in no wise prepared. It had effected its independence, but its credit was considerably shaken by the immense debt necessarily incurred.

The Union profited by the peace so dearly bought by seeking, with the utmost perseverance, to attain the highest possible degree of prosperity. She was pursuing this course with rare intelligence when the war with England, in 1812,* found her in as un-

* The United States declared war against England on the 19th of June, 1812.

prepared a state as she was in the first war. She was again constrained to defend her immense territory against a powerful army, animated with the hope of repossessing Britain's ancient colonies, or at least firmly determined to inflict upon them all possible injury.

The courage of the Americans, sustained by a feeling of profound attachment to their institutions, as well as by hatred of British domination, supplied the want of preparation of means of defence. Victory remained with the defenders of liberty and independence; but it was dearly bought.

At the peace of 1814, the nation again found itself burdened with an immense debt; but its strength and resources had increased, and the national feeling acquired renewed energy: for the moral effect of a war is to strengthen the attachment of a free people to their institutions in proportion to the sacrifices these institutions have required; and the physical effect is to develop resources hitherto greatly neglected, or deemed unavailable.

Such, to the American Union, were the consequences of this war. Her treasury was seriously affected—soon, however, to be replenished by additional revenues.

The experience of the past had not been unfruitful to the Americans of the second period. In the event of another conflict with a maritime power, the nation resolved to be better prepared, not only to repel aggression on its territory, but to enforce the respect due to the United States as one of the great powers of the world.

The Congress of 1816 unanimously adopted the wise previsions of 1787, and thus presented to the world a great and noble example of what a free people can do when they will to accomplish any result.

We must acknowledge that this unanimity in the councils of the State relative to the accomplishment of so great a national act is attributable to the fact that free institutions had surrounded the cradle of the American people; that, consequently, as the intellectual faculties of this people had been early developed, they had turned their experience to the benefit of society, by instilling vigor into political action through the adoption of means of national defence.

In the first session of the fourteenth Congress, during the Presidency of James Madison, in 1816, Congress passed an act to establish a series of permanent fortifications; to organize the army; and to provide for the gradual increase of the navy. Appropriations were immediately granted for this purpose, which have been subsequently continued from year to year.

In consequence of these legislative proceedings, the President of the United States was authorized, by a special act, to employ a French officer of high grade, and of tried talents and experience—the protracted wars of the Empire affording a guarantee that such an officer could be found in the French army. General Bernard, aid-de-camp to Napoleon, and chief of the Topographical Bureau, was the person selected.*

Soon after the arrival of General Bernard in the United States, a board composed of engineers and officers of the navy was appointed to inquire into the means of determining the best system of national defence.

To fulfil the important task with which the nation had entrusted it, the Board immediately commenced a careful reconnoissance of the whole frontier of the Union, as well on the Atlantic as on the Gulf of Mexico; of its principal geographical and hydrographical peculiarities; of the existing means of communication between the vast regions of the west with the Eastern States; it surveyed, in fine, the chain of lakes which separates the northern portion of the Union from the British Possessions in America.

After this primary and indispensable labor, the Board began to combine, to study, and to apply on the spot the material means of defence, the general basis of which, after having been thoroughly

* General Bernard was appointed chief of the Topographical Bureau during the Hundred Days. The Emperor, at this memorable period, committed to his charge an important work, no less than that of drafting for active service, and in the shortest possible time, all the national guards of the empire. The Emperor believed, after having struck the first blow at the heads of the columns advancing towards the capital, that he could employ these citizen forces to drive back the hordes that had dared to pass the frontiers of France. The disasters of Waterloo prevented the consummation of this great conception, the tradition of which should be religiously preserved for future generations. General Bernard had the good fortune to find in the United States the elements by which the New World could realize all the benefit derivable from the conception of the Emperor. The plan is among the archives of the American Republic, and may readily be put in practice when the safety of the nation shall require it.

discussed by each member, was unanimously determined. To the principal members of the Board was confided the care of studying all these projects in detail.

The Board assumed, as the basis of the system proposed, that, in a free country, constituted like the United States, the national defence ought to rest on a foundation supported by the navy, by fortifications, by means of communication by land and water, and by a regular army and an organized militia.

That, after the navy, the militia should be called on for active co-operation; that, to render their co-operation effective, fortifications were required, as well for a place of shelter as for the means of checking the invasion of an enemy.

That all the points on the coast not being equally vulnerable or important, permanent defences ought to be commenced at points presenting at the same time the greatest inducements to an enemy, and the most important positions for the navy, as harbors of safety and rendezvous.

The Board also unanimously recognized the necessity of first employing the resources of the State to protect the coast by fortifications on the Gulf of Mexico, and especially on the delta of the Mississippi.

With the object, therefore, of drawing up plans for this frontier, General Bernard commenced his honorable mission. Heedless of exposure to the dangerous climate of Louisiana, and the sickly miasma of the Mississippi marshes, he repaired thither immediately on his arrival in the United States, and there remained two years, the better to perform his duties. The sense of duty in him assumed almost a religious character.

In the conception of the various projects concerning this immense system of defence and commercial communication, General Bernard had a splendid opportunity of developing his rare talents, and his deep and varied information as an engineer. He sought to direct his European military mind to democratic institutions, to the commercial habits of the nation which did him the honor to call him into its service, so as personally to contribute to one of the most gigantic works that had ever been conceived or executed.

He traced all the roads, canals, and means of communication which were to bind together every part of the Union. He projected the greater number of those fortresses which will place a frontier more than three thousand miles in extent beyond the power of invasion.

All the fortifications were planned with a view to render the defence as efficacious as possible without exciting the apprehensions of the people relative to the safety of their liberty, or interfering with their commercial habits. General Bernard gave them all the development strictly required for adequate defence, and so arranged the interior as to afford courageous defenders, in case of ineffectual resistance, the means of insuring an honorable capitulation.

By these dispositions, so ably combined, it cannot be denied that General Bernard saved the United States an immense sum, which it would have been forced to expend, had it not profited by the experience which the long wars of Europe had given to the engineers of the Old World.

The great merit of the system of defence adopted by the Americans is that it protects the great centres of population and commerce in the Union, and extends its protection over all the great water-courses, the outlets of commerce and of the rich productions of American industry, and turns to account all the resources of the nation. The elements of which it is composed are inseparable, for the numerous relations which exist between them are essential to form a whole, without which we could attribute no excellence to the system. Each part contributes to the general effect; each element is indispensable to the efficiency of the others. Suppress the navy, and the defence becomes passive. Cut off the lines of communication of the system, and the navy ceases to act effectively, since it will then suffer for want of supplies. Fortifications would offer but feeble resistance, if not provisioned in time, and supplied with men and munitions of war. Again, if the fortifications were abandoned, the navy, compelled to divide its forces to defend the coasts, would lose its unity of action.

It is thus evident that the work of defence would not be complete without the simultaneous concurrence of a given number of equally indispensable elements. But an immense advantage of the system adopted is its harmony with the civil and political institutions of the country, since, in constituting a material guarantee of the inviolability of the American territory, it contributes to extend the sphere of the usefulness of the Union both at home and abroad.

I purpose, in the following chapters, to treat separately and consecutively of each element of the national defence.

CHAPTER II.

NATIONAL DEFENCE.

NAVY OF THE UNITED STATES.

Its gradual organization, and present importance—Its effective strength—Yards for building and repairs—Ports of shelter—Roadsteads.

The Anglo-Americans did not possess a navy prior to the War of the Revolution. Their commerce was then naturally under the protection of the navy of England. Nevertheless, as the coasts of New England and America were, at this period, infested with pirates, and as some of the colonies were at open war with the French, in possession of Canada and Acadia, they had armed a few vessels with the twofold object of protecting their coast and annoying their neighbors.

When, in 1745, the colony of Massachusetts, assisted by the Connecticut and Rhode Island colonies, attacked Louisburg, the Anglo-Americans had thirteen armed vessels in their service.

In 1758, the commerce of New York supported forty-eight privateers, carrying in all six hundred and ninety-five guns and five thousand five hundred and sixty men. In 1776, it armed several ships to act against the commerce of the mother country. One of these vessels, the *Liberty*, commanded by Joseph Wheaton, became celebrated on account of the number of prizes it took from the English.

Petitions were, at this period, presented to the National Congress for the organization of a naval force. Congress ordered the construction of ten vessels, of which only five were built, and issued letters of marque. A number of privateers sailed from the ports of Massachusetts, New York, and Maryland, and thus increased the naval force of the Americans. The largest vessel in the navy carried only thirty guns.

However, Congress passed another act, authorizing the construction of three ships of seventy-four guns. Of these, only one was built, which was offered to the King of France as indemnity for one he had lost in the service of the United States.

In the third year of the War of the Revolution, when the naval force was at its maximum, there were only fifteen public armed vessels or privateers.

Notwithstanding this disproportion in the naval force, the Americans continued to cruize in all the seas where English merchant vessels were found; and even ventured on the coast of Africa. They succeeded in capturing a greater number of prizes than American commerce could afford the English.

Among the names of the brave men who distinguished themselves on the ocean in this protracted struggle, such as the Nicholsons, the Barneys, Tucker, Thompson, Whipple, Rathbone, Maters, Cunningham, and others, Paul Jones, the celebrated commander of the privateer *Alfred*, was justly the most distinguished. After cruising seven months in the seas of Europe, he returned to Rhode Island with sixteen prizes.

It would appear, from the annals of that period, that no national colors had been adopted by Congress until the 14th of July, 1777. It was then ordered that thirteen alternate red and white stripes, symbolizing the thirteen confederated colonies, and thirteen white stars in a blue field, as an insignia of the new constellation which was soon to rise in the midst of nations, should be the national colors of the American Union.

In the course of this year, Paul Jones sailed from Plymouth, in the *Ranger*, on a mission to France. This was the first public armed vessel, under the new national flag, that had ever entered a foreign port. Consequently, on its arrival at Brest, it was saluted as the flag of an ally and of a free and independent nation.

Paul Jones, having delivered his dispatches, immediately put to sea, and made a descent on the coast of England. He anchored at White Haven, landed, spiked the guns of the fort, and would certainly have set fire to and destroyed all the vessels in port, had his orders been properly obeyed. On leaving the harbor, he captured an English armed vessel of superior force, and returned to Brest with his prize.

France, about this period, conceived the idea of making a descent on the coast of England. Paul Jones was to have had command of the naval force, and General Lafayette of the troops, required for the enterprise; but unforeseen circumstances prevented the attempt. It was then that Paul Jones took command of a vessel of forty guns, the famous *Bonhomme Richard*, thus named in honor of the celebrated almanac of Franklin.

With this vessel, he captured the *Pallas* and the *Duchess of Scarborough;* but his vessel had been so crippled in his engagement with the former that it foundered a short time after he abandoned it. Congress, on his return to the United States, gave him the command of the seventy-four which had been presented to the King of France. The administration of the American navy was then in the hands of committees of Congress. This system being found defective, a single committee, named that of admiralty, composed of five members, three of whom were not members of the House, was entrusted with the management of naval affairs. In 1781, the system was again modified. A department of state or foreign affairs was then created, which was invested with the control of the navy.

After the Revolution, the sailors were discharged, and the Union was left without a navy.

But in a short time American commerce was again exposed to the depredations of pirates. The central government was therefore compelled to engage a certain number of armed vessels in its service, which were stationed on the coasts of New Hampshire, Massachusetts, Rhode Island, Connecticut, Pennsylvania, Delaware, Virginia, North and South Carolina, and Georgia. This force was composed of 365 vessels, of 66,691 tons burden, carrying 2,723 guns. It was manned by 6,847 sailors.

In 1800,* the administration of the navy was separated from the department of foreign affairs, and transferred to that of the treasury.

In 1801,† Congress organized a separate department for the administration of the navy; Benjamin Stoddart‡ was the first Secre-

* The navy department was established as a separate bureau in 1798. —Tr.

† See preceding note.—Tr.

‡ George Cabot was appointed 3d May, 1798, but declined, and Benjamin Stoddart was appointed in his place on the 21st of May, 1798.—Tr.

20

tary of the Navy. Upon his recommendation, the details of the service were entrusted to a Board of Navy Commissioners,* the senior officer being president of the Board. This Board often came in conflict with the Secretary of State. It could scarcely have been otherwise in a country where, by the spirit of its institutions, each public officer has legal rights by which he must be governed in the performance of his duty. The feeling of passive submission is unknown among individuals in American society. The law points out the relative position of each person in the various branches of the public service. Unless that is clearly defined, each functionary interprets it as he understands it, and consequently endeavors to make himself independent of his superior.

In 1809, the naval force of the United States consisted of seven frigates of forty-four guns, and two of thirty-two guns; two sloops of twenty guns; five brigs of sixteen guns; three schooners of ten and twelve guns; and one hundred and seventy gun-boats, with one gun on a pivot. The latter drew very little water, and were supplied with sweeps, for calm weather. They were recommended by Jefferson for the defence of the coast and the mouths of rivers.

The navy was the same in 1812, when the United States declared war against Great Britain.

Notwithstanding this apparent weakness, the largest vessel carrying only forty-four guns, American vessels navigated the North Seas, crossed the ocean, and frequented the shores of the Pacific, in defiance of the numerous English vessels that covered every sea.

War was declared on the 19th of June, 1812. Immediately, *forty-three* privateers left the ports of New York and Baltimore, carrying in all one hundred and ninety-four guns, and two thousand two hundred and thirty men.

During the continuance of the war, the number of vessels in the navy, exclusive of the gun-boats, was increased to fifty-eight. The largest ship then in service was a frigate of fifty-eight guns.†

* The author is in error. The Board of Navy Commissioners was appointed for the first time, by act of Congress, on the 7th of February, 1815.—Tr.

† The President, Constitution, and United States frigates were the largest, and carried only fifty-four guns.—Tr.

Congress ordered the construction of three ships of the line, to carry seventy-four guns; and four frigates of the first, and five of the second class.

In that great struggle sustained by the Americans against the English, their powerful enemy, in defence of their principle that the flag of a nation protects its merchandize, their navy performed prodigies of valor.

The brave Captain Hull began that series of victories so gloriously continued by Lawrence, Perry, Decatur, Porter, Morris, Warrington, &c.

This second war established the reputation, and consolidated the power, of the navy of the United States, which from that day received the fostering care of the nation. Congress was compelled to bestow attention on its permanent organization, and insure it the means of working out its high destinies.

In 1816, Congress passed a law for the gradual increase of the navy; from which time considerable sums have been expended, and still continue to be annually appropriated for this object.

The United States Navy is now composed of seventy-seven vessels of all classes, exclusive of those destined for the defence of the Lakes.

LIST OF VESSELS COMPOSING THE UNITED STATES NAVY.*

THIRTEEN SHIPS OF THE LINE OF THE FIRST CLASS.

	Guns.	When built.	Where stationed.
Pennsylvania	120	1837	Norfolk.
Franklin	74	1815	Boston.
Washington†	74	1816	New York.
Columbus	74	1819	Norfolk.
Ohio	74	1820	Pacific Ocean.
North Carolina	74	1820	New York.
Delaware	74	1820	Norfolk.
Alabama	74	On the stocks.	Portsmouth, N. H.
Vermont	74	1848	Boston.
Virginia	74	On the stocks.	Boston.
New York	74	On the stocks.	Norfolk.
Independence (Razee)	54	1814	
New Orleans	74	On the stocks.	Sacket's Harbor.

* We have inserted the above list from the Navy Register for 1849, instead of that given by the author.—Tr.

† Broken up as unfit for repairs.—Tr.

TWELVE FIRST CLASS FRIGATES.

	Guns.	When built.	Where stationed.
United States	44	1797	Norfolk.
Constitution	44	1797	Mediterranean.
Potomac	44	1821	Norfolk.
Brandywine	44	1825	Coast of Brazil.
Columbia	44	1836	Norfolk.
Congress	44	1841	Norfolk.
Cumberland	44	1842	New York.
Savannah	44	1842	Pacific.
Raritan	44	1843	Home Squadron.
St. Lawrence	44	1847	European Seas.
Santee	44	On the stocks.	
Sabine	44	On the stocks.	

Java, Hudson, and Guerriere—broken up.

TWO SECOND CLASS FRIGATES.

Constellation	36	1797	Norfolk.
Macedonian	36	1836	New York.

SIXTEEN FIRST CLASS SLOOPS OF WAR.

John Adams	20	1820	Boston.
Vincennes	20	1826	New York.
Warren	20	1826	Pacific.
Falmouth	20	1827	Boston.
Fairfield	20	1828	Norfolk.
Vandalia	20	1828	Norfolk.
St. Louis	20	1828	Coast of Brazil.
Cyane	20	1837	Norfolk.
Levant	20	1837	Norfolk.
Saratoga	20	1842	Home Squadron.
Portsmouth	20	1843	Coast of Africa.
Plymouth	20	1843	East Indies.
St. Mary's	20	1844	Pacific.
Jamestown	20	1844	Mediterranean.
Albany	20	1846	Home Squadron.
Germantown	20	1846	Home Squadron.

Boston, 20; Concord, 20; Peacock, 18—wrecked.

SIX SECOND AND THIRD CLASS SLOOPS.

Ontario	18	1813	Baltimore.
Decatur	16	1839	Coast of Africa.
Yorktown	16	1839	Coast of Africa.
Preble	16	1839	Pacific.
Marion	16	1839	Boston.
Dale	16	1839	Pacific.

FIVE BRIGS.

	Guns.	When built.	Where stationed.
Boxer	10	1831	Philadelphia.
Dolphin	10	1836	East Indies.
Porpoise	10	1836	Coast of Africa.
Bainbridge	10	1842	Coast of Africa.
Perry	10	1843	Coast of Brazil.

FOUR SCHOONERS.

Flirt	2	——	Coast Survey.
Phœnix	2	——	Coast Survey.
Petrel	1	——	Coast Survey.
Fancy	1	——	Mediterranean.

FOURTEEN STEAMERS.

Mississippi	10	1841	Norfolk.
Susquehanna	10	On the stocks.	Philadelphia.
Powhatan	10	On the stocks.	Norfolk.
Saranac	10	1848	Portsmouth, N. H.
San Jacinto	10	On the stocks.	New York.
Fulton	4	1837	New York.
Union	4	1842	Philadelphia.
Princeton	9	1843	Mediterranean.
Michigan	1	1844	Lake Erie.
Alleghany	2	1847	Mediterranean.
Vixen	3	1846	Home Squadron.
Water Witch	1	1845	Home Squadron.
General Taylor	1	1848	Pensacola.
Engineer	1	1843	Norfolk.

SIX STORE SHIPS.

Relief	6	1836	Coast of Brazil.
Erie	4	1813	Mediterranean.
Lexington	6	1825	Pacific.
Southampton	4	1845	Pacific.
Fredonia	4	1846	Pacific.
Supply	4	1846	Mediterranean.

These vessels, for the most part, carry more guns than they are rated to carry. The seventy-fours carry from 80 to 90 guns. The only three-decked vessel in the United States Navy is the *Pennsylvania*, which carries 120 guns. The first class frigates carry from 54 to 64 guns, and those of the second class 48 guns; the first class sloops carry 24, and the second class 22 guns. The brigs and schooners from 12 to 14 guns, and the others from 1 to 6.*

It must not be supposed, from the above list, that the navy of the United States presents no stronger force than 2166 guns ; this number is but nominal, as the real number may be estimated at double that rate.

The following is the armament of these vessels, according to the class to which they belong:—

FIRST CLASS SHIPS OF THE LINE.

Cannon.

8 eight-inch Paixhans.
28 forty-two pounders on the lower gun-deck.
28 thirty-two pounders on the main-deck.
24 thirty-two pound carronades on the spar-deck.
2 forty-two pounders (long) on the forecastle.

90 guns of every calibre.

Ammunition and Small Arms.

337,737 pounds of cannon ball.
18,794 pounds of hollow-shot.
46,556 pounds of powder.
320 powder flasks.
220 muskets.
220 pistols.
100 battle lanterns.
90 percussion locks.
300 boarding pikes.
280 cutlasses.

FIRST CLASS FRIGATE.

Its armament is composed of 52 guns, of which 4 are eight-inch Paixhans, 28 thirty-two pounders, and 20 forty-two pounders. Ammunition in proportion.

FIRST CLASS SLOOP.

Armament composed of 22† guns, of which 2 are eight-inch Paixhans, and 20 thirty-two pounders.

The Americans seem to march in advance of other nations, in the power and dimensions of their steamers. The Mississippi

* This is a mistake with reference to sloops and brigs. None carry more than they are rated to carry.—Tr.

† Only twenty guns, including four eight-inch Paixhans.—Tr.

and Missouri, lately built, are of 1680 tons burden, and 800 horse power. They measure 229 feet 8 inches in length, 41 feet 6 inches in breadth, and 24 feet 6 inches in depth. With the requisite machinery, armament, and provisions on board, 2700 tons are displaced. Each of these steamers cost upwards of 450,000 dollars. Their speed is superior to that of any sea steamers heretofore built, going, on the River Delaware, at the rate of twenty miles an hour.*

Each of these steamers carries 10 Paixhan guns, 8 sixty-eight pounders, and 2 one hundred and twenty pounders.

To this effectual force must be added that on the lakes; the armed steamers and sail vessels in the revenue service; five steamers of 2000 tons burden, running between Liverpool and New York; five of equal size between New York and Chagres, touching at Savermol and New Orleans; and the steamers intended for a regular line in the Pacific, between Peru and the new American provinces of Oregon.

But, independently of all the conditions which will henceforth place the navy in a respectable position, immense supplies of timber, iron, hemp, tar, and all other materials used for the construction and equipment of vessels, are collected in the principal navy yards of the Republic, thus affording ample facilities for the immediate augmentation of the navy at any given period.

If to all these disposable materials be added the advantages of constantly possessing, in the country, supplies of all kinds, and skillful mechanics for the execution of all its work in the public yards, we may judge with what facility the government can at all times be prepared for all the casualties of war.

Finally, if we compare the navies of England, France, and the United States, we shall, it is true, find that the latter is at present evidently inferior to both of the former; but, if we consider the immense advantage the United States possesses in its excellent nursery for seamen, that is to say its commercial marine, this inferiority will be seen to be more apparent than real.

In fact, the commercial marine of the United States is composed of 20,000 vessels, whose burden is estimated at 2,500,000 tons. It employs from 110,000 to 120,000 sailors. That of England is composed of 22,112 vessels, with a burden of

* A mistake both as to the dimensions and speed of these vessels.—Tr.

3,067,425 tons. This difference is more fictitious than real, and may be attributed to the different methods by which the tonnage of the two countries is determined. If these methods rested on the same basis, the tonnage of the two countries would prove to be very nearly the same.

The commercial marine of France consists only of 10,845 vessels, with a burden of 589,507 tons.

American commerce, then, secures the navy of the United States a marked relative superiority over the navies of England and France.

These circumstances are favorable to the navy, since they afford the opportunity of selecting men who not only enter a service with which they are familiar, but enter it voluntarily. The United States service is much less laborious than the merchant service, and is equally well paid; and its invalids, with their widows or orphans, are provided for. We may thus comprehend the advantage possessed by the government of selecting for this service only picked men.

The American marine employs 10,842 persons, of whom 10,142 belong to the navy, as I have shown in my work on *Democracy in America*, published by M. Gosselin in 1841, to which I refer for the details of the organization of this service.

In 1841, Congress passed an act establishing a Home Squadron for the protection of the immense coast of the United States.

This judicious measure, proposed by a Southern member of Congress, was unanimously adopted, without distinction of party, thus furnishing another example that the Americans unite in a solid phalanx relative to everything that tends to conserve the integrity of their country, or the safety of their institutions.

This squadron consists of eight ships of war, two of which are steamers. It is commanded by one of the most experienced senior officers of the navy. It must necessarily tend to give completeness to the national defence.

The United States constantly holds five squadrons in commission, viz.: in the Mediterranean; on the coast of Brazil; in the Pacific; in the East Indies; and on the coast of Africa. Each of these squadrons is composed of four ships, except that on the coast of Africa, which has but three.*

* These squadrons are not limited with respect to the number of ships. Their size varies according to circumstances.—Tr.

It has two foreign naval depots for supplies; one at Port Mahon in the Mediterranean; the other at Rio Janeiro, in Brazil.

At the present time, the Americans devote their attention to the augmentation of their navy, which is the only power that is not likely to wound the democratic susceptibilities of the people. The defects of its administration required a remedy. In 1842, Congress abolished the Board of Navy Commissioners, and established in its stead five different bureaus, under the control of the Secretary of the Navy. By this new organization, it is hoped that more economy will be introduced into the affairs of the navy, and that its efficiency will be improved.

The departments entrusted to the management of these bureaus are as follows:—

First—docks and yards.

Second—building, equipment, and repairs.

Third—provisions and clothing.

Fourth—ordnance and hydrography.

Fifth—medicine and surgery.

The chiefs of the first and fourth bureaus are taken from the captains of the navy, with a fixed salary of 3,500 dollars. An able naval constructor directs the second bureau,* whose salary is 3000 dollars. The chief of the third receives the same salary. A surgeon in the navy has charge of the fifth bureau, with a salary of 2,500 dollars.

Each bureau is provided with a number of clerks, proportioned to the importance of the labor it demands.

Congress also found it necessary to organize a branch of service corresponding to the development of the steam navy. In this, it has followed the example of Great Britain, which has recently adopted specific arrangements relative to steam navigation.

New regulations have been adopted to determine the capacity, the rank, and the duties of all engaged in the naval steam service. This department is placed under the control of an engineer-in-chief, who receives a salary of 3000 dollars.

Each steam frigate has a complement of eight engineers. The

* The chief of this bureau is also selected from among the captains in the navy.—Tr.

chief engineer receives a salary of 3000 dollars.* Associated with him are two first assistant engineers, with a salary of 900 dollars each; two second assistants, with a salary of 620 dollars each; and three third assistants, with a salary of 500 dollars each.

New regulations have also been adopted relative to the education of young men intended for this service. On board of ships, these are divided into four classes. They are admitted into the fourth class at from fourteen to seventeen years of age, rising gradually every year. After they have been examined, and admitted into the first class, they form a part of the active service, and are eligible to promotion.

By this spirit of foresight, the government has assured the supremacy of the influence and the continuance of the institutions of the Union.

The navy of the United States will one day play a great part in the destinies of the American nation. Hence it must ever be kept prepared to act with all its energy, so as to be able to take either the initiative or the defensive in the struggles which must necessarily take place between England and the United States relative to the monopoly of commerce and manufactures. To meet these exigencies, it became necessary to provide navy yards for the construction and repair of vessels, as well as stations and harbors, defended by the regular army or by the militia, and capable of being supplied with men, provisions, and materials of war by lines of internal communication.

All these objects are secured, thanks to the foresight of the American people.

There are nine navy yards in the United States, namely: Portsmouth, New Hampshire; Charlestown, near Boston, in Massachusetts; Brooklyn, opposite New York; Philadelphia, on the Delaware; Washington, on the Potomac; Gosport, near Norfolk; Pensacola, in the Gulf of Mexico; Sacket's Harbor, on Lake Ontario; Erie, on Lake Erie; and Memphis, on the Mississippi.

There are dry docks only at three of these yards, Charlestown, Brooklyn, and Gosport. These are constructed of excellent material, granite, from the quarries near Quincy. Mr. Baldwin,

* The engineer-in-chief alone receives 3000 dollars. Those attached to ships are chief engineers, with a salary of 1500 dollars.—Tr.

an able American engineer, was the first to introduce these splendid structures, which may bear favorable comparison with those of Cherbourg in France, or of Plymouth in England. Each cost 150,000 dollars.*

Their dimensions are as follows: Length, 341 feet 3 inches; breadth, 80 feet 4 inches; depth, 30 feet. As the tide at Boston does not ordinarily rise over thirteen feet, it became necessary to pump sixteen or seventeen feet of water into the dock, by means of a steam engine, to enable a seventy-four to float in it.

This toilsome and expensive operation was indispensable at all points of the American shore, where the tides rise very little compared to those of La Mancha, in Europe. It is only at Halifax, or at Saint John's, New Brunswick, a part of the British Possessions in America, that the tides rise sufficiently high to enable ships of the line to float in the docks.

The American coast presents a great number of harbors, adapted for shelter in storms, or as means of escape from the pursuit of a superior force. Fortunately, it is also abundantly supplied with roadsteads. For the defence of these, the government has already expended very large sums, and is still endeavoring to finish the works that will complete the system of defence so happily prosecuted since the last war.

The two most extensive roadsteads on the coast of the United States are Narraganset at the north, and Hampton at the south, at the entrance of the Chesapeake Bay.

Boston and New York are next in importance. Pensacola is the only roadstead in the Gulf of Mexico.

One of the greatest advantages of the Narraganset roadstead, independently of its excellent anchorage, where the water is from eight to twenty fathoms deep, with a very good bottom—and of its vast extent, where the largest fleets can anchor in safety, as did that of Count de Grasse during the Revolution—is that it is the only one on the American coast accessible with a northwest wind, from which quarter blow nearly all the winter gales, so violent and so dangerous on an iron-bound coast. Vessels can also beat in and out of it in almost any state of the weather, without scarcely ever needing a pilot.

* The cost of these docks is far greater than that stated in the text, being, on the average, at least 750,000 dollars each.—Tr.

The Boston and New York roads are always accessible when the wind blows from north-north-west, south-south-east by east, while Narraganset Bay can be entered by all winds from north-west to east by west. It is the immense advantage thus afforded to American fleets that gives so high a military importance to this roadstead. For this reason, moreover, the Board of National Defence has so strengthened this place by means of permanent fortifications as to give it the character of an American Gibraltar.

Hampton Roads is not less important, as well because of its proximity to the Gulf of Mexico as because it is the only harbor on the southern coast which ships of war can enter.

The Pensacola roadstead answers every purpose of the navy on that portion of the maritime frontier of the Union. It has consequently been fortified at great expense.

Sacket's Harbor on Lake Ontario, and Erie or Presqu'Ile on Lake Erie, are excellent naval stations, where the government has also collected supplies sufficient to insure the navy a decided advantage on the lakes.

CHAPTER III.

NATIONAL DEFENCE.

FORTIFICATIONS.

Their object—Character—Armament—Jurisdiction.

The Americans have erected no ostentatious ramparts, because they have felt and understood that the best defence of their country is its legions of freemen; still they have not neglected the construction of such permanent fortifications as were judged necessary for the numerous seaports with which their coasts are so abundantly provided, and which with their navy give them a commercial superiority over every nation of the globe.

Of all fortresses, patriotism, attachment to the institutions of a country, and perfect harmony between the people and the government, are undoubtedly the best. Now, all these elements the Americans possess. In trying emergencies, therefore, such as those in which liberty or property is at stake, they can be relied on with far more confidence than the most formidable of ramparts.

The engineers who were appointed to put these frontiers in a state of defence were strongly impressed with this consideration. They well understood that, in accordance with the true principles of strategy, the Americans required but few strong places of the first class. But they saw that fortresses sufficiently large to concentrate the forces, called to act, according to circumstances, on threatened points of the frontier, were required; that these should cross the great lines of communication, so as to secure a prompt supply of provisions; in short, to use a military word, that the points should be stragetic—that is to say, adapted to protect the country in the rear, and to cover the base of operations presented by the line of communications parallel to the coast, and that which connects with the interior where the magazines are established; an arrangement adapted to afford adequate supplies at all times along the whole base of operations.

The object of the American fortifications is to cover all the ports of the United States, and thus secure them for the navy, so as to deprive an enemy of any position where he might establish himself, during a war, under the protection of a superior naval force, and thus annoy the frontier. These fortifications protect those great centres of population, which influence in so high a degree the destinies of the country. They are designed to keep open, as much as possible, the great thoroughfares of internal navigation at their outlet, the ocean, by covering the various harbors, ports, and accessible points on the coast. In short, they secure the great naval depots from all aggression by land or sea.

The development and strength of these fortifications vary according to their relative importance in the general system of defence adopted along the coast.

The smallest of these fortifications would, in time of war, require a garrison of three hundred men; the largest, a garrison of from one thousand to twelve hundred men.

Fortresses of the first class require garrisons of from twenty-five hundred to three thousand men.

The armament for the lesser forts varies from fifty to two hundred pieces of every calibre. Forts of the first class require from three hundred and seventy to four hundred and thirty-eight pieces.

This armament is generally composed of twelve, eighteen, twenty-four, thirty-two, and forty pounders; field pieces, carronades, eight-inch howitzers; eight, ten, and thirteen-inch mortars, and swivels.

They are all furnished with furnaces to heat shot, an incendiary projectile so justly appreciated both by sail and steam vessels.

All the fortifications are casemated, and bomb proof. The interior barracks are so arranged as to afford a retreat and shelter against the incendiary projectiles of an enemy.

Such is the general character of the fortifications erected by the Americans to place their frontier in a state of defence, in the construction of which they have perseveringly labored since 1816. They are also distinguished by that beauty of finish and good condition characteristic of everything the Americans undertake. Except the fortifications of Holland and Belgium, I know of none more nicely kept.

American cities are not, like those in Europe, defended by walls. Moreover, the nature of the service this defence would necessarily require would ill accord with the institutions of the country, with the exigencies of commerce, and above all with the character of the inhabitants. A commercial port, like Havre, encased within fortifications, from which the inhabitants can have no egress except through crowded and narrow issues, and only at particular times, would be monstrous in the eyes of the Americans, who have their own interpretation of the liberty which society ought ever to enjoy.

The sea ports of the United States are rendered inaccessible to an enemy's vessels by fortifications, always placed at certain distances from the cities, on elevated positions, commanding the entrance into the roadsteads.

All these positions are essential parts of one general system of defence, and, in a measure, so allied to one another that each fortified point, besides its ability to act at the place of its location, can immediately co-operate with the other points of the line. They can thus afford security to the movements of troops on the various roads, railways, and canals of the country, as well as protect the stores and military depots whose location had been previously assigned by the Board of Defence.

The system of strategy adopted for the defence of the American territory may be considered the most complete application of the great conceptions of military science; and a tribute justly due by posterity to the memory of General Bernard is the title of the Vauban of America.

The fortifications erected for the defence of the great commercial cities on the shores of the Atlantic, such as Boston, New York, Philadelphia, Baltimore, and Norfolk, have no connection with the internal or municipal regulations of these cities, which always remain subject to the civil authorities and the common law.

The fortifications are, in some rare instances, the property of particular States; but they mostly belong to the general government. They are always under the jurisdiction of the respective authorities to which they belong; whence it results that the suppression of crimes or misdemeanors within the territory of a fort belonging to the general government comes under the cognizance of the federal authority.

The application of the common law is consequently the same with respect to the other fortifications as to individual property, the right of search and extradition not being available with regard to foreign property, without the consent of the local authorities. This law emanates from the right of sovereignty claimed by each State; for the general government is empowered to exercise control only over the property submitted to its special jurisdiction, such as that appropriated for the erection of fortresses, storehouses, arsenals, navy yards, and other useful public establishments.

CHAPTER IV.

NATIONAL DEFENCE.

MARITIME FRONTIERS OF THE UNION.

Description of the several maritime frontiers of the United States, and of their military organization—Ports of Portsmouth, Boston, New York, Philadelphia, Baltimore, Charleston, and Pensacola.

The American Union extends its jurisdiction over a territory estimated to contain about 1482,600,000 acres, about the twenty-third part of the habitable portion of the globe. This immense territory is situated between the Atlantic and Pacific Oceans. We shall only direct our attention to that which borders on the former, and that which is east of the Rocky Mountains. This territory covers a superficies of 1182,589,948 acres.

The maritime frontier of the United States extends from the twenty-fifth to the forty-sixth degrees of north latitude; that is to say, over twenty-one degrees of latitude and twenty-seven degrees of longitude.

The total extent of the coast, without including the sinuosities of the shores, and the large interior bays which form part of it, is about 3,245 miles.

The frontier is generally subdivided as follows:—

1st. *North-Eastern Frontier*, from Passamaquoddy Bay to Cape Cod.

2d. *Frontier* extending from Cape Cod to Cape Hatteras.

3d. *Southern Frontier*, extending from Cape Hatteras to Cape Florida.

These three divisions are the *Atlantic Frontier.*

4th. *Gulf Frontier*, extending from Cape Florida to the mouth of the Sabine, west of the Mississippi.

Although it might, at first glance, appear a gigantic and almost impracticable attempt to fortify so extensive a coast, yet a careful study of localities will readily show this to be possible. This we shall endeavor to explain, not in detail, but with sufficient precision to enable the reader to appreciate the merit of the system by which this result has been accomplished.

In the first place, we remark that a considerable portion of this frontier is not accessible to vessels of large draught, and consequently can be exposed only to attacks from small parties, in frail vessels. Against these, a few field batteries, manned by the militia, would in all cases suffice.

Those portions of the maritime frontier which have required permanent fortifications are precisely those where the great centres of population and commerce, navy yards, or the great outlets of rivers which lead to arsenals, foundries, &c., are found. In these cases, the necessary fortifications have an importance proportional to the interest the enemy might have in attacking them.

All the fortifications erected for the security of these various establishments, whether military or commercial, exhibit the excellence of the system pursued in their construction.

The following details of the military organization of these frontiers will clearly exhibit the security of the territory of the Union against future violation, a security based on the accomplishment of a plan judiciously proposed by the Board of Defence in 1816, and strictly followed since that time.

THE NORTH-EAST FRONTIER.

This frontier, remarkable for the ruggedness of its coast and the number of its ports, is equally celebrated for the thick fogs which, during certain seasons, cover it with an almost impenetrable veil. It extends about four hundred and eighty-four miles, and is lined with islands. Accessible to heavy vessels at all points, the navigation of this coast is no less safe to seamen acquainted with it than it is dangerous to those ignorant of it; for it is studded with high rocks which, when concealed by thick fogs, are highly dangerous to the inexperienced.

Mount Desert Island, at one time belonging to M. la Mothe-Cadillac, is the most important anchorage on this coast. There, ships of the line of the largest class find an excellent harbor, and are easily defended by batteries.

Penobscot Bay, immediately to the westward, is the outlet of a very brisk trade, and an important artery of the internal navigation of the State of Maine. Bucksport, on these waters, has been selected as a port of shelter.

Sheepscot, to the west of this bay, is another port of shelter, sufficiently deep and large for all classes of vessels.

The Kennebeck River is important because of the line of operations it presents against Quebec. This river, the reader must remember, was ascended, in 1649, by Gabriel Drouillet, one of those bold and adventurous missionaries who traced, in America, the first lines of communication of which future generations were to avail themselves. It is also the outlet of the flourishing commerce of a number of cities built on its shores, among which Bath holds the first rank.

Portland is a commercial city of the second class; but it is a useful port for fisheries, and susceptible of easy defence.

Portsmouth has been fortified in consequence of its good anchorage, and because it is the seat of one of the United States navy yards.

Between the last port and the harbor of Boston, there are a great many points which, though of less importance, bear a certain relation to the interests of commerce, and consequently form an integral portion of the system of national defence.

But the harbor of Boston is undoubtedly the most important military position on the north-east coast, on account of the excellence of its anchorage and its wealth. This harbor is nearly seventy-five miles square, and is completely land-locked. It affords perfect shelter to ships of war. There one of the most important naval stations has been established. In short, Boston is a commercial city of the first order, with a population distinguished for activity and enterprise, amounting to more than 93,452 souls. Nearly one thousand two hundred and ten miles of railroad radiate from this capital of New England to the north, east, west, and south, instilling fresh vigor into its intelligent and industrious inhabitants.

The fortifications of this harbor have been completed with so much judgment and zeal by the able engineer who has had charge of the work, that it may now be considered perfectly sheltered from all external invasion.

CENTRAL MARITIME FRONTIER.

This portion of the coast contains fewer harbors than the preceding. It is accordingly less rocky, but surrounded by sand banks. The climate is less severe and the atmosphere less charged with fogs. It is intersected by large inland bays, which, by means of numerous rivers, permit the tide to ascend a great distance into the interior. Its entire extent is about six hundred and thirty miles.

Narraganset harbor is the most important one on this coast. The celebrity it has acquired in consequence of the concentration of the French naval forces there, under the orders of Count de Grasse, during the War of the Revolution, would suffice to prove its advantages as a safe roadstead. For this purpose, it has been especially reserved by the Americans, who have incurred heavy expense in rendering it inaccessible tò an enemy's naval force.

New York, which, next to London, is the largest port in the world, is the harbor second in importance on this coast. Its rank and commercial reputation must justify the details we shall give of its immense resources.

The population of New York, in 1847, was 410,000. In the last ten years, it has increased one hundred and fifty per cent. The administration of the city costs its inhabitants the annual sum of 1,400,000 dollars. The value of real estate and personal property is estimated at 253,000,000 dollars.

Its tonnage has exhibited a corresponding increase. It now amounts to 618,186 tons. This does not include the coast and river trade, which amounts to 78,750 tons, nor the seventy-five steamers, constantly running, amounting to 30,760 tons. One hundred vessels of all classes are annually built in New York, with a total burden of about 17,000 tons. In this number are included sixteen steamers.

The value of merchandize imported and exported in the course of one year is estimated at 120,000,000 dollars.

The tonnage of New York, next to that of London, is greater than that of any other port in the world, and is equal to one-sixth of the tonnage of the whole United States.

When trade is very active, the number of vessels in port exceeds eight hundred, exclusive of steamers and coasters. More than two thousand foreign vessels annually enter, and nearly three thousand coasters annually leave, this port. In 1847, more than one hundred and seventy-five thousand foreigners arrived in New York.

In the year 1842, New York completed the greatest monument that the health and necessities of a people can require. Its inhabitants are now supplied with an abundance of pure and limpid water from the mountains. An aqueduct about forty miles in length, running nearly in a direct line, and costing about 12,000,000 dollars, conveys nearly 60,000,000 gallons of water a-day to the centre of this great American city; whilst the supply of London is only about 34,840,000 gallons.*

New York is situated on Manhattan Island, which is fourteen and a half miles long by three miles wide. It is in latitude 40° 42′ north, and 74° 2′ west from Greenwich. The city proper is ten miles in circumference.

Manhattan Island is watered to the east by the sea, which reaches it through Long Island Sound, and to the west by the Hudson River, which, as far as Albany, may be regarded as an arm of the sea, the tide extending up to that point.

The arm of the sea which bathes the eastern shore of the city of New York is now known as the *East River;* and the Hudson as the *North River.* It is the junction of these two great water-courses at the southern point of Manhattan Island which forms

* The Croton, which supplies New York with water, takes its rise in a group of mountains, connected with the chain of the Alleghanies, near *Sing Sing;* consequently, below the point where the Hudson crosses that chain, without forming any falls. Its water comes from a primitive basin, and is very pure. The following comparative analysis of the water of the Croton, and of the Schuylkill which supplies Philadelphia, was made by Messrs. James C. Booth and W. H. Boye of Philadelphia.

	Croton.	Schuylkill.
Carbonate of lime	45.86	53.67
Carbonate of magnesia	18.78	11.87
Alkaline carbonates	16.57	4.53
Alkaline chlorate	3.87	3.75
Oxide of iron	2.21	1.88
Silica	7.18	9.68
Organic matter	5.53	0.88
Alkaline sulphate		13.74
	100.00	100.00

the admirable bay or harbor of New York, which is without parallel in the whole world.

The Bay of New York is about ten miles long, and five miles wide. It communicates directly with the sea by a strait called the *Narrows*, which is twenty-seven hundred yards wide, and is formed by Long Island to the east, and Staten Island to the west. A line of permanent fortifications completely defends this narrow pass.

Beyond the Narrows, the coasts of New Jersey and Long Island form a sort of roadstead, which, from the Narrows to the outside bar near Sandy Hook, where it terminates, and where the water has a depth of only twenty-four feet at low tide, is not less than seven miles in length. The tide ordinarily rises five feet.

The projects of the Board of Defence embrace the protection of this roadstead by means of fortifications on the outside bar, and floating batteries or armed steamers adapted for the navigation of the sand banks in the vicinity.

I have no doubt that this profound conception of the authors of the system of national defence will be promptly and thoroughly realized. The future, pregnant with impenetrable events, makes this a duty. To postpone much longer the accomplishment of these works would be involuntarily diminishing the chances of success. So great a lack of foresight is scarcely presumable. Sandy Hook should be well secured, for on it the defence of New York essentially depends. The government has already commenced the construction of works at this point.

From New York to the Chesapeake Bay the coast is flat, and almost destitute of harbors, with the exception of the mouth of Delaware Bay, on whose waters the city of Philadelphia,* with a population of 258,922 inhabitants, is situated.† Delaware Bay, however, offered no shelter, and the sand banks which obstruct its entrance, like those of the Seine, rendered its access difficult and its anchorage unsafe. But an artificial harbor or breakwater, constructed at its mouth, under the direction of the Board of Internal Improvement, has entirely remedied this inconveni-

* Philadelphia is supplied with water from the Schuylkill River at the rate of 2,376,000 gallons a-day.

† Philadelphia is situated on the Delaware River, not on Delaware Bay.—Tr.

ence. Fortifications protect both the anchorage and the entrance to this bay.*

Chesapeake Bay, on the Atlantic shore, is the central basin of all the natural and artificial navigable waters of the Union. It is the great intermediate chain which binds together the northern and the southern coasts, and whence national fleets can extend their protection to foreign as well as domestic commerce.

This magnificent bay, extending into the interior one hundred and ninety-four miles, is navigable for the largest class of vessels, and contains a multitude of harbors and basins. It receives the waters of several large, and a great number of secondary, rivers. It is the outlet of the trade of the capitals of Virginia and Maryland, and of the celebrated Chesapeake and Ohio Canal.

The fortifications erected near the mouth of the Chesapeake, on Hampton Roads, are intended to defend the navy yard at Norfolk, which, next to that of Boston, is the most important in the Union; to prevent the invasion of an enemy at that point; to cover the navigable avenues of Virginia; in short, to secure thorough protection to the cities situated on the waters of this bay, against which no enemy would dare to venture, so long as he would have any occasion to fear the naval forces stationed in Hampton Roads.

These fortifications are of far greater importance than those constructed at other positions on the same coast. Their importance are the greater from their connection with the various parts of the system of national defence. The Board of 1816, having terminated the reconnoissance of all the shores of the United States, decided upon giving a development to the fortifications of Hampton Roads exceeding that of any of the fortifications yet erected in the United States—a development, nevertheless, strictly indispensable to the defence of so central a point of operations.

Hampton Roads and Narraganset possess equal stragetic advantages; it was therefore proper that both should be placed in a condition commensurate with their importance.

Notwithstanding the extent of the fortifications at the mouth, the Board also proceeded to protect the cities at the head, of the Chesapeake. With this object, *Hawkins' Point* and *Sollers'*

* These fortifications protect the entrance to the Delaware River, of which the bay is the expansion.—Tr.

Point were selected for the immediate protection of Baltimore and the Delaware Canal; and the shores of the Patuxent and of the Potomac were fortified to cover the federal city, the port of Alexandria, and the outlet of the Ohio Canal.

MARITIME FRONTIER OF THE SOUTH.

This portion of the American coast, more than eleven hundred miles in extent, is characterized by the presence of an immense sand bank, formed by the uniform motion of the Gulf Stream. Consequently, this frontier is inaccessible to vessels of war of heavy draught. It is accessible at few points to vessels of small draught, for the sand bank which covers the coast is pierced only at great intervals by canals or natural openings made by the flow of the waters from the interior on their passage to the sea. These channels are shallow, and mostly of difficult access. They lead to various interior bays, which communicate one with another, and admit an inland navigation along the coast.

Charleston, South Carolina, is the most important port on this frontier. It presents a sufficiently large basin; but the outside bar does not permit the entrance of vessels drawing more than twelve feet of water.

Port Royal, fifty-eight miles south of Charleston, and twenty miles north of Savannah, is the only harbor which will admit vessels of larger draught. The last points on the coast that afford a harbor for light vessels are Savannah and St. Mary's River.

The defence of the principal points on this frontier is secured by fortifications, and by the co-operation of armed steamers built in such a manner as to sail with facility through all the outside channels of the coast.

FRONTIER OF THE GULF OF MEXICO.

This frontier, in its general characters, very much resembles that we have just noticed. It has very nearly the same extent, eleven hundred and sixty-four miles, or about three-eighths of the entire extent of the maritime frontier. Its security, however, interests four-fifths of the Union; for the coast of the Gulf of Mexico forms the maritime frontier not only of Louisiana, Mississippi, Alabama, and West Florida, but also of Arkansas, Tennessee, Kentucky, Ohio, Missouri, Indiana, Illinois, Wisconsin, and Iowa, thus embracing three-fourths of the territory of the Union.

The importance of this frontier, and the impossibility of establishing a correlation between its means of defence and those of the Atlantic frontier, have rendered it indispensable to adopt a complete and independent system for the effectual protection of so accessible a part of the Republic. From the geographical position of the coast, and of the territory interested in its defence; from the insalubrity of the climate, the nature of the adjacent country, the varied interests of the inhabitants, and the character of the population on which the duty of repelling the attacks of a foreign enemy would devolve; it is, and will for a long time remain, too weak to perform alone this national task. The Mississippi River is the only outlet of these vast and wealthy regions; and New Orleans, established upon its shores, is the point where at present is concentrated, with the richest productions, the largest amount of disposable capital in the Union.

All these considerations must necessarily have exerted an influence on the minds of the Board, and led to the adoption of a system of defence, proportioned to the interest an enemy might have in directing its attacks on this portion of the Union.

Land and water communication formed an integral portion of this system, thus furnishing the means of enabling the militia of the interior at any given moment to defend the frontier of the Gulf. These means of communication are connected with the navigation of the coast, and are protected by military arsenals and depots of arms, placed at convenient distances along the navigable rivers. On the coast itself, fortifications are placed for the direct defence of the water avenues leading from the sea to the shores of the Mississippi, whether directly along its course, or through its western and eastern channels.

The important Bays of Mobile and Pensacola, the first as the outlet of the rich State of Alabama, the second because of its excellence in a naval point of view, are also embraced in this system of defence. Provided with permanent fortifications, these anchorages are secured to the American navy. The Board of Defence also judged it necessary to establish in these waters one of the great naval stations of the United States. Twenty-two feet of water can be carried over this bar; it is crossed with facility, and has remained unchanged for half a century. The inner harbor is perfect, and completely sheltered from every wind.

The United States cannot too soon carry out the plan, proposed by the Board of Defence, of erecting in the harbor of Pensacola a maritime arsenal and a navy yard. No point of American territory presents equal advantages; for the timber of Florida is celebrated for its superior quality. Described more than a century and a half since by our most able naval officers, it is now an object of considerable speculation in commerce, for the construction of vessels.

On no point of the American coast, perhaps, could steamers and floating batteries render more eminent service in the national defence. These could always thread a multiplicity of channels, and at any time find protection under forts built expressly for their special defence, in case an enemy with a superior force should attempt, by crossing them, to circumvent access to New Orleans and the delta of the Mississippi.

My firm conviction, founded upon my knowledge of the resources of defence, is that an enemy who would have the presumption to face so many dangers would find this frontier as strong as a wall behind which *two thousand cannon*, served by *ten thousand picked artillerists*, would always be ready to receive them.

In the event of a war, the defence of the entire coast of the United States by permanent fortifications is henceforward assured by more than *twenty-two thousand cannon*, of all calibres, manned by *sixty-four thousand men*, taken from volunteer companies, disciplined and trained to the use of siege pieces.

Such unparalleled means, entirely derived from the resources of the War Department, show, most conclusively, what foresight the government of the United States can exhibit concerning everything that affects the great interests of the country. No one can refuse to acknowledge that the Americans understand these interests as well as they know how to persevere in the accomplishment of whatever tends to consolidate them.

CHAPTER V.

NATIONAL DEFENCE.

INLAND FRONTIER.

Description of the Northern Line, and of its defensive organization—Hydrography of the great Lakes—Western Line.

The present inland frontier extends from Passamaquoddy Bay to Lake Superior, and from this point to the Sabine Bay, in the Gulf of Mexico. Its precise extent is not exactly known; but it may be estimated at about three thousand six hundred and seventy miles, forming two great divisions, namely, the *Northern* and the *Western.* The former extends from Passamaquoddy Bay to the head of Lake Superior; it divides the English Possessions from the United States, and is very nearly two thousand miles in extent.

NORTHERN LINE.

The chain of lakes to the north of the United States, communicating one with another, and with the Ocean through the River St. Lawrence, presents a line of navigation, which penetrates the interior of the American territory for a distance of nearly two thousand miles. This line is undoubtedly one of the characteristic features of the physical geography of America. It forms very nearly the line of demarkation between the Republic of the United States and the British Possessions.

This frontier, with reference to national defence, bears some resemblance to that of the Atlantic, by reason of the inland seas on which it rests.

A brief description of the lakes which compose this inland sea will show their importance relative to national defence as well as to the commercial prosperity of the country lying on their borders.

There are five great lakes: Lake Superior, the largest of all, and Lakes Michigan, Huron, Erie, and Ontario. The latter is separated from Lake Erie by the Falls of Niagara.

Lake Superior is about four hundred miles long, and eighty wide, with a superficies of thirty-two thousand square miles. It is nearly nine hundred feet deep, and five hundred and eighty-six feet above the level of the sea. It is the largest sheet of fresh water known, and may be regarded as the source of all the tributary rivers of the St. Lawrence.

This lake communicates with Lake Huron by the River St. Mary. This river is forty miles wide, and it has a fall of twenty-three feet in its entire course. Consequently, at present, it is navigable only for very small craft. But so easily can its depth be increased that, ere long, this improvement will be effected.

River St. Mary is entirely commanded by Fort Brady, an American post erected at the falls of the river.

Lake Michigan is three hundred and twenty miles long and seventy wide, with a superficies of twenty-two thousand four hundred square miles, without including Green Bay, at its northern extremity, which is one hundred miles long and twenty wide, and has a superficies of two thousand square miles. Lakes Michigan and Green Bay are five hundred and sixty-nine feet above the level of the ocean. The former is nearly one thousand and the latter five hundred feet deep.

Fort Howard, a military post belonging to the United States, is situated on Green Bay; and Fort Dearborn is situated at the southern extremity of Lake Michigan.

The shores of Lake Michigan are already populous. Michigan, Chicago, and Milwaukie are the principal cities.

This lake communicates with Lake Huron by the Straits of Michilimakinac, which of late years, as was predicted by the early Jesuit missionaries, those bold pioneers of French colonization in the New World, has become a position of great commercial importance. At this point the United States has established a military post, Fort Mackinaw, which commands the strait.

Lake Huron is two hundred and forty miles long, and eighty wide. Its superficial extent is twenty thousand four hundred square miles. It is nearly one thousand feet deep, and five hundred and sixty-nine feet above the level of the sea. It communicates with Lake Erie by the River St. Clair, which is thirty-five miles long, and by a small lake of the same name leading into Detroit River, which is twenty-nine miles in length. This communication is navigable for all classes of vessels.

Lake St. Clair has a superficial extent of three hundred and sixty square miles. It is twenty feet deep, and five hundred and sixty-one feet above the level of the ocean.

Fort Detroit, at the head of the river of the same name, completely protects the entrance of Lake Huron.

The city of Detroit, capital of the State of Michigan, is situated at the point where Lake Sinclair empties into Detroit River. This old French settlement has become a very important city, owing to its advantageous position for the trade of the lakes.

Lake Erie is two hundred and forty miles long, and forty wide, with a superficies of nine thousand six hundred square miles. It is eighty-two feet deep, five hundred and fifty-six feet above the level of the sea, and three hundred feet above the level of Lake Ontario. The bottom of this lake is rocky. It has a feeble current in the direction of Lake Ontario, which is checked by the action of the winds. During the winter, the lake is often obstructed by ice. The principal towns on its shores are situated on the American side: Portland, Sandusky, Cleveland, Erie, or Presqu'Ile, Ashtabula, Dunkirk, and Buffalo.

The Niagara River serves to discharge the waters of Lake Erie into Lake Ontario. It is thirty-seven miles long. The cataracts have a fall of one hundred and fifty-two feet. For a distance of seven miles above and below the Falls, the river is not navigable in consequence of rapids and whirlpools. Near its mouth, the celebrated Fort Niagara, now occupied by soldiers of the United States, has been built.

Lake Ontario is one hundred and eighty miles long and thirty-five wide, and has a superficial extent of six thousand three hundred square miles. It is navigable for vessels of the largest class. In some places, it is six hundred feet deep; but its mean depth is about five hundred feet. It is two hundred and thirty feet above the level of the ocean. Though farther north than Lake Erie, it is never closed by the ice.

On the English shore, the principal cities on its borders are Toronto, Kingston, and Niagara. On that of the United States, Oswego, Genesee, and Sacket's Harbor; the latter is a naval and military station, where a strong force is always kept in consequence of its proximity to Canada, and where ships can be built and launched with facility.

The natural communication presented by this American Mediterranean is interrupted, as we have seen, between Lake Erie and Lake Ontario, by the Falls of Niagara. This obstacle is now overcome by an artificial navigation on the two opposite shores. On the English side, by the Welland Canal; and on the American territory by the Erie Canal and a branch of the Oswego Canal.

Welland Canal is forty-two miles long, fifty-three feet wide at the surface and twenty-five feet at the bottom. It is about eight feet in depth. Unfortunately, it cannot be navigated by steamboats, an inconvenience which must soon be removed. Nevertheless, in its present state, it affords a communication between the two lakes for vessels of one hundred and twenty-five tons burden. It was commenced in 1824, and finished in 1829. It cost 1,350,000 dollars, more than thirty-two thousand dollars a mile.

The head of the Welland Canal is at the Port of Maitland, on Lake Erie. It terminates in a small river which empties into Lake Ontario, at Fort Dalhousie, and passes about five miles to the west of the Falls.

Up to the present time, the Americans have been contented with the facilities of communication between the two lakes afforded by the Erie Canal. Nevertheless, as the importance of the Lake trade has augmented through the improvements constantly taking place in the rich adjoining countries, they no longer feel willing to permit their Canadian rivals to monopolize all the advantages of sail navigation. Attention has been directed to the practicability of opening a direct canal on the American side, sufficiently large for steamers and sailing vessels. This splendid project has been examined by Major Bache, a distinguished officer of the corps of Topographical Engineers, who has proved that it is not only practicable, but that it would be, in relation to the defence of the country, and its commercial prosperity, an enterprise of the most useful kind.

Let us hope that this canal, so highly important to New York and the Western States, and consequently to the whole of the Atlantic coast, will not be considered merely a feasible project, but that it will be constructed with expedition.

The following table shows the principal dimensions of the

GREAT LAKES OF THE UNITED STATES.*

	Length in miles.	Breadth in miles.	Depth in feet.	Height above the ocean in feet.	Area. Sq. Miles.	Acres.
			ft. in.	ft. in.		
Lake Superior	400	80	885.9	586.7½	32,000	20,471,740
Green Bay	100	20	492.2	569	2,000	1,279,484
Lake Michigan	320	70	984.3	569	22,400	14,330,018
Lake Huron	240	80	984.3	569	20,400	13,050,735
Lake St. Clair	20	18	20	561	360	230,307
Lake Erie	240	40	82	556	9,600	6,139,522
Lake Ontario	180	35	492	230	6,300	4,030,374
					93,060	59,532,180

From this table, it will be seen that Lakes Michigan, Huron, and Green Bay are on the same level; that all the others are of different heights; that Lake Superior is the most elevated; and that this American Mediterranean may be considered the most vast collection of fresh water on the face of the globe, since it covers a surface equal to 59,532,180 acres, nearly one-half of the surface of France. The quantity of fresh water contained in the whole of these basins, including the River St. Lawrence, according to various authors who have investigated the subject, would appear to be equal to one-half of all the fresh water on the globe!

The total extent of coast watered by these inland seas is estimated at five thousand five hundred and forty-two miles, of which three thousand one hundred and ninety-two miles belong to the United States, and two thousand three hundred and fifty to England. The lake coast is, therefore, almost equal to that of the Atlantic, or to the distance which separates the Old from the New World.

From Lake Ontario to the eastern extremity of the Union, the frontier which separates the United States from the British Possessions in America has not yet been well determined. The Americans extend their claim to the St. Lawrence; the English need the right shore to preserve their land communication between

* This table exhibits simply the mean measurement, and is taken from the scientific works of Mr. Douglas Houghton, geologist and mineralogist of the State of Michigan.

the provinces of Canada and New Brunswick. The claims of the Americans are based on that imperious necessity which requires the St. Lawrence to become an American river similar to the Mississippi, with which it forms, by means of the inland lakes, a water communication from the Atlantic Ocean to the Gulf of Mexico: those of the English on their interpretation of treaties.

A diplomatic solution of this question, calculated to satisfy both parties, appears but little probable,* because it involves insurmountable difficulties, those of territorial conveniences, which treaties can never reconcile, and which, sooner or later, must be settled in a very decisive manner. Moreover, a war brought on through a disputed boundary is no novel circumstance. I repeat that the question is not so much whether the State of Maine shall have a given boundary more or less extensive, as whether the Americans will maintain their pretensions and rights over the navigable line of the St. Lawrence, as they formerly maintained them against France, then in possession of the St. Lawrence, the Lakes, Canada, and the territories of the north-west.

In the present condition of affairs, Lake Champlain, in the State of New York, occupies an important position with reference to the stragetic operations that might be directed against the cities of Montreal and Quebec on the St. Lawrence; for, at its northern extremity, it empties, through the Sorel or Richelieu River, into the St. Lawrence, and communicates with New York, through the Hudson, by means of the Champlain Canal.

This lake is one hundred and fifty miles long and fourteen wide. It is navigable, through its entire course, for vessels of five feet draught. The principal cities on its borders are St. John, Plattsburg, Ticonderoga, Whitehall, and Burlington. This lake is blocked by ice during five months of the year.

This water avenue can easily be protected by fortifications. The frontier which separates the British Possessions from the United States is protected only by a few unimportant posts, and barracks for regular troops and militia.

With the prospect of an inevitable, if not an immediate, contest with their Canadian neighbors, the Americans have yet taken no measures to protect this frontier. They depend, apparently, on

* This question, to speak truly, is solved in a measure by the Ashburton Treaty; but another solution is reserved for the future.

the powerful development of their civilization, far superior to that of the people of Canada; and, in short, on the preponderance of democracy over monarchy in the New World.

WESTERN LINE.

The frontier of the west is at present merely an imaginary line, which separates the Indian nations, driven to the west of the Mississippi, from the territory occupied by the Americans. It may be readily conceived, therefore, that the Americans have little occasion to raise costly fortifications against so wretched a race, destitute of arms, of means of defence, of ideas of property, and, consequently, in the pursuit of no definite object. They have only erected a few barracks, blockhouses, and stockades on several points of the great rivers which traverse these regions, where regular troops are stationed to keep the Indians in check, and to teach them to respect the power of the United States.

CHAPTER VI.

NATIONAL DEFENCE.

Arsenals—Armories—Depots—Magazines—Foundries.

In the vast plan of National Defence which engaged the mind of American engineers, the selection of sites for depots, magazines, and arsenals became an object of special attention. It was essential that every part of this system should accord with the rules of strategy, and thus become, in the event of a defensive war, the means of securing the most important results. It was necessary that these establishments should be so distributed in the interior of the territory that all the natural facilities of transportation which the country afforded at each of the great divisions of the inland and maritime frontier should be made available in order to secure supplies at every point on the base of operations as promptly and economically as possible.

All these stragetic conditions, indispensable to the defence of the country, have been fulfilled. True, they have been the work of time; but for that reason they have received every advantage derivable from new discoveries, and from the application of steam on the routes lately constructed; and they will continue to be developed under the influence of the improvements which the creative genius of man is destined to realize through this new element of power.

Those parts of the country where all kinds of materials are available, and where labor is sufficiently abundant to secure the prompt manufacture of implements of war, and a due supply of provisions, at the lowest possible prices, are usually selected as the sites of military establishments.

They are all situated on the banks of navigable streams, within convenient distance from the frontiers dependent on them. Supplies, therefore, can always be readily and economically furnished, entirely beyond the range of an enemy who might seek to intercept them. In short, the late extraordinary extension of railroads in the United States presents facilities, in this respect, no less advantageous for the defender than detrimental to an assailant. The Americans are thus placed in a condition which will secure them a decided advantage over the offensive operations of any enemy.

The military establishments of the United States are divided into three classes:—

The first are specially adapted for the fabrication of the *matériel* of war; but they are nevertheless supplied with workshops for all necessary repairs, as well as with magazines and depots of arms.

The second, on the other hand, are establishments where this *matériel* is repaired and preserved. These also contain magazines and depots of arms.

The third are simply magazines, and depots of arms, munitions, and supplies of all descriptions.

The American Union possesses twenty-one of these establishments; eight of the first, ten of the second, and five of the third class. They are distributed as follows:—

One in Maine; one in Massachusetts; one in Vermont; three in New York; two in Pennsylvania; one in Maryland; one at Washington, in the District of Columbia; one in Virginia; one in North Carolina; one in South Carolina; two in Georgia; one in Alabama; one in Louisiana; one in Arkansas; two in Missouri; and one in Michigan.

Thus, the Atlantic frontier is supplied with ten of these establishments; the Gulf of Mexico with three; the northern part of the inland frontier with six, and its eastern part with three.

ARMORIES.

The United States yet contains only two national manufactories of arms: one at Springfield, Massachusetts, on the Connecticut River; the other at Harper's Ferry, at the junction of the Potomac River with the Shenandoah, in Virginia. These establishments possess great natural advantages. The latter especially is provided with an abundance of all kinds of material, such as timber, iron, and coal, in addition to a water power that is almost incalculable. So excellent is the site of this establishment, surrounded by mountains through which the roaring Potomac has opened for itself a passage to the great Atlantic, that it is now the centre of an extensive communication by water and land. Rivers, canals, and railroads converge to this point from every direction, so that large supplies of arms can be sent without delay to the various sections of the country where they are required.

A similar establishment for the direct supply of the western country is yet to be erected in the Valley of the Mississippi. So numerous are the sites where an abundance of all the elements for the required manufacture is found that the great difficulty has been to make a selection from among so many presenting equal advantages. It would, however, be very injudicious any longer to postpone an undertaking so eminently essential to complete the organization of the system adopted for the defence of the Union; and the aspect of affairs in the United States, at the present time, should induce an immediate appropriation by Congress of the sum necessary to erect the required establishment.

In ordinary times, the government annually manufactures twenty-five thousand muskets. This number can very easily be trebled by the employment of the labor commonly devoted to this branch of industry. Besides, at any given time, the necessities of the country can be amply supplied by commerce.

But a great nation should always place itself in such a condition as to be unaffected by commercial or other contingencies, that it may at all times enforce the respect due to its independence. If the fundamental principle of the organic law of the Americans is that every citizen is a soldier, then, as a natural consequence, every soldier should be armed.

FOUNDRIES.

The United States does not yet possess any national foundries. Up to the present time, its artillery has been obtained only through commerce and private enterprise. This circumstance, among a people whose habits are essentially commercial, who have always been accustomed to depend on commerce for the supply of all their wants, need not excite wonder. But such a state of things cannot long exist without exposing the nation to the most serious accidents. The Union ought clearly to comprehend that it is neither prudent nor economical to depend on private enterprise for the supply of the materials required by such highly important branches of the public service as the army and navy.

CHAPTER VII.

NATIONAL DEFENCE.

NATURAL CHANNELS OF COMMUNICATION.

Importance of natural navigable channels in a system of defence—Physical aspect of the American territory—Number and distribution of the natural channels of communication.

In the system of National Defence, channels of communication form a necessary complement of the navy and of fortifications. In defensive operations, in fact, the means of communication must be such as to permit the safe retreat of vessels into the interior, when threatened by a superior force, as well as to secure to those strategic points exposed to the attacks of an enemy, the possession of which might serve to form a line of operations against the country, an ample supply of men and the *matériel* of war.

But, since the discovery of steam, and its application as a means of transportation, the utility of channels of communication has considerably augmented. Formerly of secondary consequence, they have become of the first importance because of the facilities they afford for concentrating at given points, and in a very short time, immense forces. Hence, at the present time, they form in a measure the principal lines of operation, since they connect the points supplied with the elements of defence with those liable to be attacked.

Thus, by means of the numerous channels of communication with which enterprise has covered the American soil, all kinds of supplies can at any moment be safely transported to stations, harbors, roadsteads, and national ship-yards; and troops can be transported, without fatigue or loss of time, to act at any given point. Security against disturbance or interruption is thus given to the inland trade even during a most active war.

The Americans have so well understood the advantages of these channels that they have even established new ones, while giving the utmost possible development to those which nature afforded.

Thus, as far back as 1763, after the fatal treaty which deprived us of Canada, we see them energetically endeavoring to improve the navigation of the principal rivers of this territory. But after the War of Independence the Americans gave a fresh impetus to their internal improvements, and devoted the utmost attention to extend their area, fully persuaded that by this means they directly contributed to secure the most powerful of all auxiliaries of defence, and consequently of their independence, objects not less important than the commercial and material prosperity of the country.

RIVERS.

The territory of the United States, remarkable for the number and disposition of its natural channels of communication, is divided into two great regions—that of the Atlantic, and that of the Gulf of Mexico—by the Alleghany Mountains, which extend from the River St. Lawrence to Florida. To the north, the line of Lakes, avoiding these obstacles by a natural navigation, places the Atlantic in direct communication with the Gulf. Besides, the slight elevation of these mountains, whose mean height above the level of the sea does not exceed three thousand feet, affords facilities for the formation of artificial channels. The Americans, taking advantage of these facilities, have united the two great geographical divisions of their country by the greatest possible number of lines.

More than one hundred rivers take their rise in this long chain of mountains, and furrow the two opposite flanks before reaching the ocean. All the watercourses that descend the western slope towards the Gulf are navigable for vast distances. Those on the eastern slope, although much shorter in their course, are of equal importance. All present channels, to adapt which for commercial purposes, or for the defence of the country, but little art has been required.

On the eastern slope, beginning at the north, the most important rivers in New England are the Penobscot, navigable as far as Bangor; the Kennebeck, as far as Augusta; the Merrimack, as far as Lowell; the Connecticut, as far as Hartford; and the Thames, as far as Norwich.

In the State of New York, the Hudson takes its rise near Lake Champlain, from which to the Atlantic Ocean it presents a line nearly two hundred and fifty miles in extent. It is navigable for large vessels for one hundred and fifty miles of its course.

In the centre of the maritime frontier is the Susquehannah, of which the Chesapeake Bay, properly speaking, is but a prolongation. It is navigable up to Columbia, a distance of more than three hundred and fifty miles from the ocean. This beautiful river is one of the principal arteries of the internal navigation of the Union.

The Patapsco is navigable as high as Baltimore, which is situated at the head of the Chesapeake Bay, two hundred and forty-two miles from the ocean.

The Potomac is navigable for ships of the line up to Washington. From its mouth in the Chesapeake Bay to the falls near Georgetown, the distance is one hundred and two miles.

The Rappahannock, York, James, and other rivers emptying into the Chesapeake, are navigable, throughout a great extent of their course, for heavy merchant ships and for steamboats, which ply daily between the ports of Richmond, Norfolk, Petersburg, Fredericksburg, Annapolis, and Baltimore, all commercial cities much larger than any of the ports of France.

Advancing towards the south, we find smaller ports, and less navigable rivers. Nevertheless, we meet with important cities, situated at the mouths of rivers navigable for coasters and steamers of light draught, which are enabled to ascend a great distance into the interior, thus placing the merchant along side of the rice and cotton planter.

The Roanoke ; the Pamlico ; Ashley and Cooper Rivers, whose junction forms the port of Charleston; the Savannah, whose bar is covered by eighteen feet of water, and which steamers ascend as far as Augusta, a distance of about one hundred and forty-five miles, to take in cargoes of cotton; the Alatamaha, navigable beyond Darien; the River St. John in Florida, whose depth is nearly seventeen feet over the bar, and from sixteen to twenty-three feet for an extent of nearly two hundred miles in a southerly direction, are the principal rivers on this part of the coast.

On the Gulf of Mexico, we find the following: The Suwanee, the Appalachicola, navigable for steamers as far as Columbus, Georgia, a distance of nearly two hundred miles. The Mobile, navigable to the boundaries of Alabama and Tennessee; its waters might easily be connected with those of the Tennessee. Finally, the Mississippi, whose basin receives all the rivers and streams which water the immense regions of the west; a river which affords, with its tributaries, along a course of nearly nine thousand miles, an easy navigation for steamers.

The Mississippi, properly so called, is navigable for a distance of nearly two thousand miles ; the Ohio, in some respects a continuation of it, for a distance of nine hundred miles, from Pittsburgh to its mouth.

The Missouri, the principal tributary of the Mississippi, is navigable for a distance of two thousand three hundred and fifty miles.

Among other tributaries of the Mississippi, also navigable for steamboats, the principal are the Cumberland, the Illinois, the White, the Arkansas, and the Red River.

The Americans have endeavored to improve the navigation of these natural channels to the utmost possible extent; so as to afford facilities for the penetration of merchant vessels into the interior. On all of them the general government, in conformity with a specific plan, has constructed immense works of art. These works, prosecuted with greater or less vigor, according to the resources of the treasury, are eminently essential to the safety and the prosperity of the interior of the Union, and constitute the most efficacious of all means of resistance in a foreign war.

LAKES.

The chain of great lakes at the northern frontier of the United States, passing round, as I have already remarked, the chain of the Alleghanies, affords a natural navigation of one thousand five hundred and fifty miles, or, including the River St. Lawrence, of nearly two thousand miles. I have already described, in Chapter V., the principal characteristics of this American Mediterranean, which has become the centre of a vast system of communication. I shall therefore only refer here to the works constructed by the United States for the general interests of commerce and of the national defence.

The war of 1812 had demonstrated the importance of preserving ports where American vessels might seek shelter from gales, as well as points whence they might direct their attacks against English cruisers. In 1818, the general government ordered the Board of Defence and Internal Improvement, with which body I was associated, to make a careful examination of this entire line, to ascertain what improvements were required to diminish the danger of navigation on the Lakes both to the naval and mercantile marine; for, on these inland seas, tempests are not less frequent or less terrible than those encountered on the great ocean.

Since that time, the United States, by means of numerous works, has created various ports of shelter on Lake Michigan, Lake Erie, and Lake Ontario, as well as twenty-five light-houses to direct the navigator, or point out the dangers the pilot is to avoid.

On Lake Michigan, public works have been constructed at Milwaukie, Michigan, and Chicago.

On Lake Erie, at Detroit, Sandusky, Ashtabula, Portland, Presqu'Ile, Dunkirk, and Buffalo.

On Lake Ontario, at Genesee, Oswego, and Sacket's Harbor.

These improvements, consisting principally of moles or breakwaters, present havens where vessels can take shelter against the prevailing winds of the lakes.

I have already described the improvements of the port of Presqu'Ile, in a history of the internal improvements of the United States, published in 1834, by Messrs. Anselin and Carilian-Gœury, which exhibits the system pursued in the construction of such works in the United States.

In making the dike or the breakwater of the port of Dunkirk, a very ingenious method was adopted, which deserves notice. During one of the severe winters so frequent in the latitude of Lake Erie (43° north), when the ice was sufficiently strong to bear a person in perfect safety, a coffer dam was constructed on the spot selected as the position of the breakwater. Stones were thrown into it until its weight broke the ice, when, sinking to the bottom, it formed the foundation for a superstructure.

The artificial harbor of Buffalo is formed by dikes, constructed of stones of small size, which are placed in regular layers, and so well put together as to form a solid wall. They are thus capable of resisting the most violent gales of winter. For the crowning of the dike, stones of half a ton weight were used.

Such constructions are frequently required in the United States; and, when well executed, answer, according to my observations, all the purposes of their erection.

STRAITS AND BAYS.

The description of the maritime frontier in Chapter IV. must have given the reader an idea of the immense advantages which the numerous bays and straits afford to navigators along the coast. By looking at a map of the United States, the truth of this statement may easily be verified. There exists an almost uninterrupted inland communication, for the entire length of the coast, formed by an admirable chain of bays and straits. Commerce has, for a long time, derived profit from this navigation. It is serviceable to the coasting trade, and is a very important element in the national defence. Hence, every American statesman, directing his attention to the utmost development of which this navigation is susceptible, has sought to render it complete from the extreme north-east of the continent to the coast of the Gulf of Mexico. The Board of Defence and of Internal Improvement has also devoted much attention to this grave and interesting question, and has drawn up several plans, of which a description may be found in the work to which I have already referred.

CHAPTER VIII.

NATIONAL DEFENCE.

STEAM NAVIGATION.

Progress of steam navigation; its physical and moral effects on the American nation —Number of steam vessels — Effective force — Tonnage—Accidents—Expense of navigation on the Atlantic; on the Western rivers; on the Lakes—Price of transportation—Relations of steam navigation to the national defence.

To the application of steam as a motive power, the natural channels of navigation mainly owe all their advantages. To this cause also is attributable the high degree of prosperity now enjoyed by the people of the United States, where it would seem, indeed, that steam had especially established its empire. On this portion of the new hemisphere, with its immense lakes, gigantic rivers, and vast bays, it appears to have been destined to prove to the world its creative power. Its astonishing results familiarize our minds with the most fabulous recitals. Under its influence, cities have risen as by enchantment; vast solitudes have been peopled and fertilized; and masses of people daily change their homes, and carry new life to spots where, but the day before, the silence of the forest was broken at rare intervals only by the echo of the rifle of the pioneer.

Steam, with the Americans, is an eminently national element, adapted to their character, their manners, their habits, and their necessities. With them it is applied as much to extend their liberty as to augment their physical welfare.

But progress in the mechanic arts, and especially in those arts which are destined to improve the condition of man, has always followed the development of the intelligence and political liberty of a people. The progress of the one corresponds with that of the other. God has so willed it.

Among the inventions and discoveries of the human mind, the most important are, undoubtedly, the compass, the art of printing, cotton spinning, and, lastly, the application of steam to navigation, the glorious conquest of the nineteenth century.

The results of this discovery on the Continent of America are almost miraculous; and its influence is most remarkably felt in the regions of the west. If we carry our minds back to the period of the War of Independence (1776), when these wild countries were comparatively unknown, and when a few Frenchmen alone ventured to traverse them, how complete appears the metamorphosis!

The first emigrations towards the west occurred between the years 1776 and 1806, and were directed along the principal rivers that water this vast territory. Since then, communication has become so rapid that time has augmented in value a hundredfold; and distance so diminished, comparatively, that one may almost say that steam has annihilated space. Thus, taking New York as a point of departure, we arrive at Philadelphia in five hours, a distance of eighty-five miles; at Baltimore, about seventy-seven miles from Philadelphia, and one hundred and sixty-two from New York, in eight hours; at Washington, two hundred and thirteen miles from New York, in ten hours; at Norfolk, in twenty hours; at Charleston, South Carolina, in forty hours; at New Orleans, at the mouth of the Mississippi, a distance of two thousand one hundred and eighty miles, in one hundred and sixty-eight hours, or seven days. In fine, the Atlantic Ocean, between Europe and the Continent of America, is now crossed in eleven days. Such are the wonders wrought by steam!

While on this subject, I may be permitted to recall to remembrance one of my first voyages to the United States, which took place in the year 1817. The contrast it presents to the experience of the present time will justify the digression.

At that period, two days were required to travel from New York to Philadelphia. The Hudson was crossed in a ferry-boat to the opposite shore, where a Jersey coach was in waiting to carry passengers to Trenton, on the Delaware River. There they passed the night. On the afternoon of the following day, they arrived in Philadelphia; thence Baltimore was reached in three days. From Baltimore to Washington, the seat of government, was a long day's journey. Five to six days were thus consumed in traveling two hundred and forty-two miles. The whole expense of the journey was nearly twenty dollars. At the present time, it is accomplished without fatigue in ten or eleven hours, at an expense of about eight dollars.

In 1817, a journey by land to New Orleans was considered a difficult and dangerous enterprise. Before undertaking it, the traveler had to make arduous preparations. He took the stage at Philadelphia for Lancaster in Pennsylvania; the mail was then carried in an open one horse vehicle, or on horseback. Three days were required to perform this part of the journey. At Lancaster, the traveler had the choice either of walking across the mountains, or of purchasing a horse, which he could easily dispose of at Pittsburgh. I adopted the latter course, as more accordant with my taste; but I gained little by the choice, for, as soon as I had reached the mountains, I was forced to dismount and confide my small saddle-bags, containing my modest change of clothing, to my horse. I consumed nine days in crossing the four ranges which form the chain of the Alleghanies. Having arrived at Pittsburgh—then the great bazaar of the west, and the general rendezvous of travelers, speculators, and emigrants from all parts of the world, who repaired thither to seek their fortunes—I was compelled to make a halt, and provide myself with all that was necessary to descend the great rivers of the west. The spectacle which Pittsburgh presented, particularly to the eyes of a Frenchman, was exceedingly curious. It was an odd mixture of European, American, Asiatic, and African manners. The Europeans, who had lately arrived, with dialects as various as their costumes, seemed to be the most numerous. Here, the slave-trader, traveling from the shores of the Atlantic towards the Southern States, with his drove of Africans, appeared to be as unconcerned about his change of residence as he was careless of the future. Hither the red man, resembling the Asiatic in his native costume and his unconstrained manners, was attracted in great numbers, from the facility this city afforded him of exchanging his furs for spirituous liquors, for blankets, and powder and shot. Here also appeared the native of New England, the American, properly so called, whose indefatigable and adventurous spirit had driven him, with his family, towards these regions in search of *good land*, and of a *home* corresponding to his views of labor and speculation. Finally, in the midst of the latter, the true *Yankee*, a type of the human species peculiar to New England, vending his wrought-iron ware, the product of the industry, already celebrated, of his fellow-citizens of Connecticut and Massachusetts.

In descending the Ohio and the Mississippi, at that time, it was customary to purchase and freight a flat boat. Embarking on this, it was necessary to trust to the strength of the current to convey you to your destination. This was certainly not a very expeditious method of traveling, especially when your only resource besides the current was the occasional use of the oar or the sail. From sixty to seventy days were consumed in this part of the journey; and it was not without exposure to difficulties and perils of no ordinary kind that so protracted a journey could be performed in the midst of the numerous Indians who, allured by the hope of booty, at that time frequented the shores of these rivers.

We arrived at New Orleans, after this manner, in about eighty-four days, at an expense of from one hundred and twenty to one hundred and forty dollars; and the traveler who reached his destination with no other inconvenience than that inseparable from so hazardous an undertaking was considered exceedingly fortunate.

On the shores of the Ohio, which was the principal thoroughfare, the traveler would see occasionally, and at great distances apart, clusters of houses, forming small villages or hamlets, as a means of defence against the hostile visits of Indians.

Since 1806, the progress of civilization and commerce has become strikingly perceptible. At one time, indeed, the transportation of a few articles of merchandize was effected by means of long boats, manned by fifty or sixty men, who, by dragging their burden, with great labor and fatigue, along the shores by the aid of limbs of trees, succeeded in journeying from New Orleans to Cincinnati, a distance of nearly two thousand miles, in three months!

In 1807, Robert Fulton built the first steamboat that ever navigated the waters of the United States. It was supplied with an engine of eighteen horse power, constructed by Messrs. Bolton and Watt, of England. With this engine, Fulton succeeded in making the trip from New York to Albany, a distance of one hundred and forty-five miles, in eighteen hours. This trip is now performed in nine and ten, often in seven hours.

In 1812, Fulton, having at length obtained the recognition of the merit and the advantages of his discovery, built, at Pittsburgh, under the auspices of the State of New York, the first steamboat that ever navigated the Ohio and the Mississippi, and named it the *New Orleans*, the place of its destination.

From 1812 to 1818, other steamboats were successively built. The latter period may be regarded as the true starting-point of the rapid growth of the fertile countries of the west—a growth that is truly magical. From that time, the waters of the *beautiful river*—the Ohio—but lately so tranquil, have become agitated night and day by the wheels of steamers, which meet and pass one another almost as frequently as public carriages on the highway.

The smiling shores of the Ohio are now rapidly becoming decked with hamlets, villages, and cities, whose brilliant and animated aspect makes the traveler appreciate the prosperity of their inhabitants, and the vast wealth their industry has been able to create.

In 1835, five hundred and eighty-eight steamboats had already been constructed on the waters of the Ohio, of which one hundred and seventy-three were built at Pittsburgh, one hundred and sixty-four at Cincinnati, and eighty at Wheeling. The burden of these steamboats varied from one hundred to seven hundred and eighty-five tons; entire burden one hundred and fifty-three thousand six hundred and sixty tons.

From official statements, we learn that, in 1839, thirteen hundred steamboats had been built in the United States, eight hundred and twenty-eight of which were still in active service, and presented an effective power equal to fifty-seven thousand horses.

In 1848, the whole number of steamboats in the Union is twelve hundred, with an aggregate burden of two hundred and forty thousand tons, and a power exceeding that of one hundred thousand horses. Of this number five hundred navigate the ocean, one hundred the lakes, and six hundred the rivers, bays, and straits of the Atlantic.

Almost all the steamboats on the Western waters are high pressure, and lighted with gas. They are remarkable for their construction and their speed.

The general government has instituted a strict inquiry into the causes of the casualties that have occurred on steamboats in American waters. Among the results of this inquiry, we find that, during the thirty years this means of transportation has existed, two hundred and thirty-five accidents have taken place, causing the death of two thousand, and wounding or disabling four hundred and forty-three, persons. By far the greatest number of these accidents have occurred on the western rivers and the Lakes.

An incontestable advantage of steam in the United States is that it brings together, as it were, the extreme points of the vast Continent of America. Days are now sufficient to overcome distances which, before the introduction of steam, months were required to overcome. We no longer hear the expression "Boston is two hundred and thirty-five miles from New York"—but, rather, that its distance from the latter city is six hours.

At this day, a journey from New York to New Orleans may be accomplished without fatigue, in eight or ten days, at an expense of from eighty to one hundred dollars. Not only so, but a few hours may be gained to examine the most important cities on the route. The great mail regularly passes from one city to the other every seven days; and, by an arrangement that will soon be made, the time will be reduced to five days.

Nothing exhibits in so significant a manner the extent to which steam navigation is identified with the active genius of the people of the West, as the daily motion of the floating ark, known as the *steamboat of the West,* which is three-decked, and not unfrequently carries twelve hundred passengers.

At all the principal points on the Ohio, beginning at Pittsburgh, steamboats daily start, at stated hours, for the mouth of the river—for St. Louis, at the confluence of the Missouri and the Mississippi—or for New Orleans.

The traveler, starting from Louisville, Kentucky, can arrive at New Orleans, a distance of nearly seventeen hundred miles, in three days. The ascending trip can be performed in from five to seven days. The rapidity of this traveling is somewhat startling. This is especially the case when two steamboats, coming in opposite directions, are seen to pass each other. A stranger cannot witness this scene without a feeling of apprehension. But the cool and tranquil American, confiding in the skill of the helmsman, contemplates with interest and a species of vanity these two smoking points, which are scarcely in sight before they are far away in contrary directions. They indicate his genius and his power!

If the course of the Ohio and the Mississippi, covered with their six hundred steamers, presents a much more animated aspect, in every way, than the Seine between Paris and Havre, the great American Lakes present the spectacle of an equally astonishing activity. The traveler finds the same facilities, the same regularity of transportation by steamboat, at every point on the Lakes. Thus, from Buffalo, on Lake Erie, at the head of the New York Canal, the traveler can reach Chicago, at the lower end of Lake Michigan, a distance of about nine hundred and seventy miles, in three days. Steamboats leave Buffalo on a certain day, and during their trip touch at all points where passengers wish to land. No less than sixty steamboats are thus employed.

In the intercourse which takes place between the cities of the Atlantic States, steam navigation plays a very important part. The steamboat especially serves as a connecting link between various points on the railroad. Sometimes it is altogether independent of land conveyance; and sometimes, with the object of lessening the expense as well as the time of traveling, it is brought into active competition with it.

Six hundred steamers are now running on the bays, straits, and rivers of the Atlantic. Some are adapted for the trade along the coast from Maine to Georgia, and regularly ply between Portland, Boston, Providence, New York, Norfolk, Charleston, and Savannah.

The steamboats on the Hudson generally carry one thousand passengers, and cost each seventy thousand dollars. Of this amount ten per cent. is annually expended in repairs, assuming two hundred and twenty trips each of one hundred and forty-five miles to be made in a year. Their furnaces consume forty cords of wood per trip, or eight thousand eight hundred cords per year—an annual cost, at the rate of five dollars each cord, of forty thousand dollars. Each boat is insured at the rate of three per cent. The annual consumption of tallow, rigging, tow, &c. amounts to two thousand four hundred dollars. The crew is composed of a captain, who receives a salary of fifteen hundred dollars; a mate, six hundred dollars; two pilots, eight hundred dollars; two engineers, one thousand dollars; six firemen, nine hundred and sixty dollars; ten sailors, two thousand dollars; and one helmsman, four hundred dollars. Total crew, thirty; combined salaries, nine thousand one hundred dollars. Total expenditure, exclusive of the interest of the capital invested in the boat, sixty-six thousand dollars.

A trip of one hundred and forty miles costs one of these steamboats three hundred dollars.

Mr. J. Newton, of New York, has lately launched a steamboat for the Hudson River, named the *South America*, which is remarkable for its dimensions and speed. Its burden is six hundred and eighty-six tons; length of deck, two hundred and sixty-two and a half feet (eighty metres); width of beam, twenty-nine feet and a half; depth of hold, nine feet two inches; draught of water, four and a half feet. On each side a long row of cabins extends, capable of containing two hundred and twenty passengers each. This steamboat is worked by a single steam-engine, the cylinder of which is about four and a half feet in diameter. Stroke of piston, eleven feet; diameter of wheels, thirty feet; depth of paddles fourteen inches, breadth ten feet ten inches. These wheels make twenty-three revolutions per minute, thus producing a speed of nearly nineteen miles an hour. The boilers are cylindrical. The quantity of anthracite coal consumed per trip is ten tons.

Mr. Brown, an equally celebrated American builder, has also launched a steamboat, to which he has given the name of the *Empire*, a term usually applied, by way of pre-eminence, to the State of New York. This steamboat makes the trip from New York to Albany and Troy, and returns, in twenty-four hours—a distance of three hundred miles. Its burden is one thousand tons; its greatest length three hundred and twenty-four feet ten inches; width of beam, twenty-nine and a half feet; width, including wheels, sixty-two feet; depth of hold, nine feet ten inches; draught of water, four feet nine inches. It is impelled by two of Lighthall's horizontal steam engines, whose cylinders have a diameter of four feet; stroke of piston, twelve feet. This steamboat cost ninety-five thousand dollars.

On the Lakes, where wood is much cheaper than on the Atlantic coast, the expense of running a steamboat is less than on the Hudson. It does not exceed one dollar and twenty-nine cents per mile.

On the western rivers, where the price of wood is still less, it is not more than one dollar and four cents per mile.

On the Atlantic boats, freight is charged per mile at the rate of from three to nearly five cents per ton. On the Lakes, from two to four cents. On the western rivers, half a cent.

The price of transportation of passengers by steamboat, meals included, is nearly five cents per mile.

Such was the condition of steam navigation in the United States in 1843—an element which has so greatly contributed to the prosperity and the social progress of the people of this vast country.

The use of steam must greatly change the results of a maritime war. If it is so powerful an auxiliary in attack, how great must be its superiority in the defence of a country like the United States—a country provided with an immense number of harbors, bays, and ports, protected by an inland navigation parallel to the coast, with a vast chain of canals that connect the centre with the extremes of the Republic; and with combustible material at all points in great abundance.

So fortunate a combination of circumstances must exert an incalculable influence on the contingencies of a defensive war; for, while an enemy would be forced to depend for a supply of fuel, deposited in advance and at great expense, on some proximate points of the coast selected for attack, the defence would be constantly supplied at all points with excellent coal, obtained in the neighborhood, or brought from the interior at trifling expense. The number of an enemy's war steamers must always be proportioned to the quantity of fuel at his disposal. The United States, more abundantly supplied with this precious generator of steam than any other nation, can always employ as many war steamers as the defence of its maritime frontier shall require.

By reason of this superiority of means, the United States navy must always possess a marked advantage over an enemy who would dare to attack the American coast. Nothing could prevent the United States, on the first alarm, from employing in its defence the four hundred steamboats belonging to the commercial marine, which, in a short time, might be at least sufficiently armed to repel any attempt at invasion. These steamboats would co-operate with the war steamers, which the federal government has been building since 1839; and adapted, by means of their light draught, to manœuvre in every channel, and over every flat, they could harass the enemy in all his movements, and thus become a very powerful auxiliary of the navy.

Besides, in such an event, who could prevent the Americans, with their known hardihood of conception, and their boldness in execution, from repeating the daring attempt of Paul Jones, and thus retaliating, by the same means, the injuries inflicted on their country? This, I believe, would be very soon proved were an occasion to arise rendering it necessary to make an appeal to the citizens of the United States in defence of their rights and their territory!

CHAPTER IX.

NATIONAL DEFENCE.

ARTIFICIAL CHANNELS OF COMMUNICATION.

CANALS.

Origin; classification—Lines from east to west, or from the great rivers of the Atlantic to those of the Valley of the Mississippi—Lines connecting the latter with the Lakes and with the St. Lawrence—Line parallel to the coast—Most important canals in the United States—Recapitulation.

The primary object which the Americans, in constructing their canals, sought to secure, was the connection of the large capitals on the Atlantic border, Boston, New York, Philadelphia, Baltimore, Richmond, and Charleston, with the rich territory watered by the Ohio, the Mississippi, and the great Lakes. The only obstacle they had to surmount, in establishing these lines, was the Alleghany Mountains.

Among the most honorable and enlightened of the men who, immediately after the achievement of their independence, directed their attention to the means of improving the navigable channels of communication, we are happy to cite the names of Franklin, Morris, Rittenhouse, Gallatin, De Witt Clinton, Geddes, and others, at the head of whom we must naturally place Washington, the father of his country. All of these celebrated men directly contributed, by their judgment and talent, to establish that system of communication which is so much in harmony with the necessities of the country, that it has always received the special attention of the American nation.

To Mr. Gallatin, when Secretary of the Treasury in 1808, belongs the honor of first presenting, in his report to the Senate, a general plan of the canals and roads the country required.

This project embodied the following elements:—

1st. A navigable line parallel to the coast.

2d. A system of extended lines, connecting the great rivers of the Atlantic with those of the Valley of the Mississippi.

3d. Secondary lines establishing a communication between the greater lines, the Lakes, and the St. Lawrence.

4th. A national road parallel to the coast, passing through all the capitals, from Maine to Georgia; and a great road crossing the country from Washington to New Orleans at the south-west, and to St. Louis and Detroit at the north-west.

But the honor of having thoroughly studied this subject with the twofold object of favoring the development of the commercial and manufacturing interests of the country, and of contributing to the national defence; of having presented a consistent plan of internal improvement, including canals, artificial ports, and strategic and post routes for the whole Union; and of having prepared a statement of all these projects with their estimated cost, is due to the Board of Internal Improvement.

I ought to add that the Board, in drawing up this extensive plan, was guided by the profound suggestions of Albert Gallatin, who was as able a diplomatist as he was a distinguished political economist.

If all the routes which have been completed since the Board discontinued its labors accord with this project, so rare and splendid a result is attributable to the expansive views embodied in the above report; to the manner in which the channels of communication have been adapted by the Board to the topographical configuration, as well as to the requirements, of the country; and to the correctness of the proposed calculations and estimates, which have always corresponded with the actual expenditure.

I intentionally lay much stress on this circumstance, because it has exerted great influence on the public improvements of every nation, and because it has contributed in no slight degree to make the Americans more confident than Europeans of the success of their enterprises.

GREAT LINES FROM THE EAST TO THE WEST, OR FROM THE ATLANTIC TO THE VALLEY OF THE MISSISSIPPI.

1. The *first great line* constructed by the Americans is that which connects the Lakes with the Hudson River, New York with Lake Erie, and the Atlantic with the regions of the west, by winding around the north of the Alleghany Mountains.

The Erie Canal was commenced in 1817, and finished in 1825. Its entire length is three hundred and fifty-four miles. It has eighty-four locks, that correct a slope of nearly seven hundred feet. So prodigiously has the commerce of the Lakes increased that this canal is now undergoing enlargement to a degree that will enable it to hold three times its original volume of water. The improved canal will be only three hundred and fifty miles long. Its slope will be six hundred and seventy feet, to be compensated by seventy-seven locks.

But the enlargement of this canal may be considered as equivalent to the reduction of one-half of its length, because of the increased facilities and the low price of transportation which commerce will realize by the change.

From New York to Buffalo, by the Hudson River and the Erie Canal, the distance is four hundred and eighty-seven miles.

To form an idea of the activity exhibited on this canal, we need only state that the average number of boats that annually pass through it exceeds twenty-five thousand, and that the amount of western products conveyed by this channel to New York is six hundred and sixty-nine thousand tons per year. The merchandize sent from New York to the west amounts only to one hundred and thirty thousand tons. Difference in favor of New York more than five to one.* The above products are principally furnished by Ohio, Michigan, Indiana, and Illinois.

The navigation of the Lakes generally opens from the 20th to the 25th of April; that of the canals from the 30th of March to the 8th of May.

From New York to Lake Erie, through the Hudson River and Erie Canal, freight is charged at the rate of twenty-eight dollars

* In 1847, 33,782 boats passed through this canal. Of the burden of these boats, 774,334 tons were carried to New York, and only 162,715 tons to the West.

and sixty cents per ton on light, and twenty dollars and twenty cents on heavy, articles.

The tolls on this canal amounted, in 1844, to one million four hundred thousand dollars, more than eight per cent. of the capital of the company; in 1847, to two million dollars.

2. The *second great line* connects the Delaware with the Ohio, Philadelphia with Pittsburgh. It crosses the central crest of the Alleghany Mountains by the aid of a railroad thirty-six and a half miles long, constructed by the State.

Its length is three hundred and eighty-five miles, with two hundred and thirty-four locks along its entire course. Two hundred and fifty-three miles of this line were constructed by the State of Pennsylvania. Sixty-five miles of navigation, that is to say, from Philadelphia to Reading, are borrowed from the *Schuylkill Navigation Company*, and seventy-seven miles, from Reading to Middletown on the Susquehannah, from the *Union Canal Company.*

The freight per ton on heavy articles for the entire route from Philadelphia to Pittsburgh is twenty-one dollars and fifty cents; on light articles, twenty-nine dollars.

3. The *third great line* connects the Chesapeake with the west, the Potomac with the Ohio. Its starting-point is Washington. It is named the *Chesapeake and Ohio Canal*, and is now in course of completion, the government having appropriated funds in aid of that object. This line is three hundred and forty-one miles long, with a total slope of four thousand three hundred and fourteen feet. It has three hundred and ninety-eight locks, with a tunnel seven thousand one hundred and eighteen yards long, which penetrates the Alleghany Mountains.

This is the shortest line between the Ohio and the Atlantic. Moreover, it possesses a great advantage in a strategic point of view, that of connecting the centre of the northern frontier with that of the maritime frontier and with the capital of the Union. By this means, the greatest possible number of militia, with an immense quantity of munitions of war, can be promptly concentrated, at but little expense, on any point attacked on these frontiers.

4. The *fourth great line* is that which is to unite the James River with the Kanawha, the Chesapeake with the Ohio, across southern, central, and western Virginia. This line will be four

hundred and eleven miles long. Its entire southern portion, between Richmond and Lynchburg, is finished. The central portion from Lynchburg to the mouth of the North River in Rockbridge county, is in course of completion. The people of Virginia, after having done so much towards the accomplishment of the favorite project of General Washington—the connection of the waters of the Atlantic with those of the Ohio through the James River valley, across Virginia—will not now relax in their efforts. Their interests require them to keep pace with the great movement which prompts the population of the Atlantic States to secure direct communication with the Valley of the Mississippi.

It is also very probable that the Virginians will soon establish a railroad in the great Valley of Virginia, for the purpose of connecting the James River Canal with the navigation in Tennessee. This railroad will not be less than one hundred and fifty-five miles long, and will connect Buchanan with Knoxville.

Thus a spirit of enterprise, and of honorable competition for the commerce of the rich countries of the west, has been the means of securing the construction of a series of routes across the American Alps, to which nothing in Europe can be compared.

LINE FROM THE ATLANTIC TO THE ST. LAWRENCE AND THE LAKES, WITH ITS BRANCHES.

The Americans have not confined their efforts to the four great lines already described. Their attention has also been directed to the means of connecting these channels, by secondary lines, with one another, and with the Lakes; as well as to the completion of the navigable channels parallel to the coast.

Among these secondary lines is the Farmington Canal, which secures a direct communication, seventy-five miles in extent, between Northampton, on the Connecticut River, and New Haven, a port on Long Island Sound.

Champlain Canal, in the State of New York, sixty-three miles in length, establishes an important communication between the St. Lawrence and the Hudson. It is important in a strategic and commercial point of view, connecting Lake Champlain with Lake Erie, by the Erie Canal.

The Black River Canal, eighty-three miles and a half in length, connects Sacket's Harbor, on Lake Ontario, with the Erie Canal, at Rome. This branch completes the system of strategy, as far as it is involved in the construction of canals, from the borders of the Hudson to the Lakes.

The Chenango branch, ninety-four miles and a half long, connects the canals of New York with those of Pennsylvania, the Erie Canal with the Susquehannah, and Lakes Erie and Ontario with the Chesapeake.

It will be observed, in this distribution, that the position of the Chenango Canal is an exceedingly important one, for it binds the interests of the north to those of the centre, and thus secures a simultaneous co-operation of all in the prosperity and defence of the country.

Too much praise cannot be awarded to the intelligent and patriotic citizens who, notwithstanding the apparent antagonism of their interests, projected so essential a combination of internal improvements.

The principal purpose of the Delaware and Hudson Canal, part of which lies in the State of New York and part in Pennsylvania, is to supply New York with coal from the rich mines of the Lackawaxen, one of the tributaries of the north-east branch of the Susquehannah. This canal is ninety-seven miles long.

In Pennsylvania, canals have received a greater development, if possible, than in the State of New York. These works were undertaken with the twofold object of favoring the manufacture of iron, and the working of the coal and iron mines which constitute the principal wealth of the State.

The first branch which receives the great eastern and western line, across the State, issues from the main body below the Juniata, near Duncan's Island, and follows the right shore of the Susquehannah as far as Northumberland, where it bifurcates to ascend the two branches which come respectively from the west and the north-east. The injury to which navigation was exposed by inundations suggested the feasibility of constructing canals by the sides of rivers. The experiment succeeded, and further attempts to improve the beds of rivers have since been abandoned.

This branch, extending from Duncan's Island to Northumberland, is thirty-seven miles long. It has a slope of eighty-five feet, and twelve locks.

The canal lateral to the western branch of the Susquehannah ascends to Farrandsville, in Clinton county. It is nearly seventy-three miles in length. It has a slope of one hundred and thirty-six feet, and nineteen locks.

The canal of the north-east branch of the Susquehannah passes at first along the right shore, for a distance of fifty-five miles, and then, crossing, runs along the left shore as far as the mouth of the Lackawanna, a distance of twelve miles and a half. At this point, it communicates with the coal regions of the Lackawana and Wyoming. Then it ascends the north branch of the Susquehannah as far as Athens, in Bradford county.

By this prolongation, the canals of Pennsylvania are connected, through the Chenango Canal, with those of New York, thereby opening for Pennsylvania a new outlet for its abundant supplies of coal and iron, and enabling it to obtain with facility the products of the State of New York, such as salt and plaster.

The entire length of these three branches, from Northumberland to Athens, is ninety miles. Total slope one hundred and ninety feet, overcome by five dams and twenty-five locks.

All the works situated above Columbia, on the Susquehannah or its tributaries, have been constructed merely for the purpose of conveying to Philadelphia, the commercial metropolis of the State, the rich products of the Valley of the Susquehannah; but as it was necessary to tranship these products at Columbia, the canal lateral to the Susquehannah has been extended to Havre de Grace, the head of ship navigation on the Chesapeake. This canal, establishing a complete communication between the east and the west, was finished in 1840. It saves a distance of more than thirty-six miles in the transportation of merchandize. It is forty-five miles long. Its total slope is two hundred and thirty-seven feet, counteracted by thirty-one locks, two of which have basins. The locks are divided into two equal compartments, thus forming a double basin measuring eighty-eight feet and a half. By this means, the passage of flatboats and other boats, which descend the stream during the floods, is secured.

All these improvements, completed by the State of Pennsylvania, or by joint stock companies, have not yet secured a continuous communication by canals from east to west, between Philadelphia and the Ohio. But its feasibility has been shown;

and it is presumable that the project will be consummated when the finances of the State will warrant so great an undertaking.

This continuous line of navigation between Philadelphia and Pittsburgh will be five hundred and ten miles in length, with a fall of two thousand four hundred and ninety-one feet. It will follow the Schuylkill and Union Canals as far as Middletown, a distance of one hundred and forty-two miles, and the canal lateral to the western or Middletown branch as far as Sinnemahoning (Farrandsville), a distance of one hundred and seventy-two miles. From this point to the mouth of the Red Bank, a tributary of the Alleghany, the distance is one hundred and twenty-seven miles, and from the mouth of the Red Bank to Pittsburgh by the Alleghany, sixty-nine and a half miles.

However, the advantages of canals will be unequally distributed throughout the State, unless this branch of internal improvement be extended to Lake Erie, the borders of the north-west frontier.

This feature in the internal improvements of Pennsylvania had engaged the attention of the engineers of the Union. During their laborious reconnoissance, they had shown the practicability of two routes adapted for channels of communication; namely, one by French Creek, and one by Beaver Creek. These connect with Connaught Lake, and the waters thus merged reach Lake Erie at the harbor of Presqu'Ile. These projects have since been adopted by the State of Pennsylvania, and the undertaking has been commenced. When this great work shall have been completed, the distance from Philadelphia to Lake Erie, by a continuous canal, will be five hundred and eighty-seven miles, with a fall of three thousand one hundred and thirty-six feet; while the distance from New York to the same point will be only five hundred miles.

But, on the other hand, Philadelphia is nearer to the valley of the Ohio, and can more readily supply this market, than New York. Now, Ohio has already effected, within its territory, a junction between the canals of Pennsylvania and the canal extending from the Ohio to Lake Erie, which is eighty-five miles in length. By these various canals, intercourse between Lake Erie, the Ohio, Philadelphia, and Baltimore is secured.

Such are the principal features of the artificial navigation which ramifies in the neighborhood of the Hudson and the Chesapeake, equally the centre of a system of important channels for commerce and for the defence of the country.

LINES EXTENDING FROM THE LAKES TO THE VALLEY OF THE MISSISSIPPI.

Beyond the Alleghanies, to the west, and north-west, the presence of the Lakes, and of those immense rivers which are not separated by any chain of mountains, has given rise to another system of artificial navigation, of easy accomplishment, which admirably completes the net-work of navigable channels to which the United States owes its prosperity, and the moral confidence by which its integrity is maintained.

Of these channels, Lake Erie, situated midway between the Atlantic Ocean and the Gulf of Mexico, seems, from its geographical relations to the St. Lawrence and the Mississippi, to be, of all positions, best adapted for the concentration of all the channels of communication destined to impart life and vigor to every section of the Union.

Four great lines of artificial navigation at this time place the valley of the St. Lawrence in communication with that of the Mississippi, and New York with New Orleans. Three take their departure from the borders of Lake Erie, and one from Lake Michigan.

The Ohio Canal forms the first of these lines. It commences at Cleveland, on Lake Erie, and terminates at Portsmouth on the Ohio, ninety-seven miles from Cincinnati, and sixteen hundred and twenty-five miles from the ocean, in the direction of the Mississippi. Its length is three hundred and eleven miles. Its slopes, equal to eleven hundred and sixty-six feet, are counteracted by one hundred and fifty-two locks. Begun in 1832, it was completely finished in seven years. With all its branches, this canal extends for a distance of three hundred and twenty-six miles. Its cost was four million six hundred and fifty-four thousand nine hundred and thirty-four dollars.

The gross receipts on the Ohio canals amount to ten per cent. of their original cost, of which amount twenty-seven per cent. is absorbed by expenditures.

The second line is that which the Miami Canal opens at the head of Lake Erie, near the mouth of the Maumee, at Perrysburgh. Its outlet is at Cincinnati, now the greatest commercial city of the west. The length of this canal is two hundred and fifty-eight miles.

The third line is that which the Wabash Canal forms at Lake Erie, borrowing from the preceding canal eighty-three miles. It was constructed at the joint expense of the States of Ohio and Indiana. That portion of it which passes through the territory of the State of Indiana is one hundred miles long. The entire length of the line, therefore, to the point where the Wabash begins to be navigable for steamboats, is one hundred and eighty-four miles.

The Wabash empties into the Ohio near Shawneetown.

The fourth and last line is that formed by the Michigan Canal, which commences at Chicago, situated on the southern part of Lake Michigan. Its outlet is at Peru, on the Illinois River, one of the principal navigable tributaries of the Mississippi, which is ascended by steamboats. The length of this canal is one hundred and three miles.

By means of this very important communication, which art has just completed, the six hundred steamboats which give life to the commerce and industry of the countries watered by the Mississippi can suddenly change their peaceful character, and take part in that struggle which the antagonistic interests of the English and Americans may call forth, when least expected, for supremacy on the American Mediterranean. The facilities which will hereafter enable these steamboats to pass to the Lakes afford, in my opinion, the most reliable of all fortifications against aggressive attempts on the part of the present occupants of Canada.

Moreover, the necessity of this line was long thought to be indicated by the nature of the country, and by the course of its waters, which, at the melting of the snow, communicate by the ponds distributed upon the plateau whence the Chicago River on the one side, and the little River des Plaines on the other, take their rise. This hydrographical characteristic of the north-west country was perfectly known to our Canadian voyagers, and to our early French settlers in Illinois, before the year 1700. This line is not the only one which attracted attention, nor is it the only one which this country presents favorable to a continuous navigation between Lake Michigan and the greatest watercourses of North America. Thus, by Green Bay and Fox River, Lake Michigan is brought into close communication with the Wisconsin River, which empties into the Mississippi at Prairie du Chien. The portage between these two rivers is only three thousand two hundred and eighty-one yards. By means of a very short canal across Milwaukie county, Lake Michigan can as easily be put in communication with Rock River, another tributary of the Mississippi.

The facilities for opening navigable communications between Lake Superior and the upper Mississippi are equally great, whether by the River St. Louis; by the Bois Brulé and St. Croix Rivers, the former emptying into Fond du Lac Bay, the latter into the Mississippi below the Falls of St. Anthony; or, in fine, by the Chippewa River, a tributary of the Mississippi, by the Montreal River, which empties into Lake Superior, or by the Menomonie through Green Bay.

LINE OF NAVIGATION PARALLEL TO THE COAST.

The hydrographical arrangement of the American coast is very favorable for an internal communication between the northern and southern sections of the Union. Large bays extend far into the interior. Islands cover a part of the coast, between which and the mainland run deep channels accessible to coasting vessels. Narrow and low strips of land were the only obstacles works of art were required to surmount in the establishment of this internal navigation.

The Board of Internal Improvement had this important work under consideration simultaneously with its project concerning the national defence. In fact, the one was the correlation, the necessary complement of the other. In its general plan, the Board proved that, to facilitate the communication of coasting vessels between the north-east and the central maritime frontier, it was expedient to cut through the isthmus which unites Cape Cod to the continent, near Boston, between Buzzard's and Barnstable Bays; that this canal need be only eight miles in length; and that by this means vessels could avoid doubling the cape, always a protracted, and often a dangerous, navigation. The Board also proposed the construction of a canal at the Taunton River, with the object of opening a prompt and safe communication between Boston and Narraganset Bays, and of securing an ample supply of provisions at both of these points in time of war. These canals are not yet begun; but their place is measurably supplied by railroads. These, however, do not supersede the necessity of carrying out the project of the Board of Defence, if it be desirable to secure to the navy an inland navigation sheltered from all attack.

The Board also suggested the construction of a canal which, crossing the State of New Jersey, should connect New York Bay with the Delaware River. This project has been realized. The length of the canal is forty-two miles; width at the water line seventy-two feet; depth seven feet two inches. It has fourteen locks, each ninety-eight feet and a half long by twenty-three feet and a half wide, which counteract a slope of one hundred and fifteen feet. Cost of the canal two million five hundred thousand dollars.

The Board also recommended the junction of the Delaware with the Chesapeake Bay, so as to connect, by means of the canal across New Jersey, the valley of the Hudson with that of the Susquehannah. This improvement was, therefore, of great importance in a commercial, military, and naval point of view, since it would permit the entrance of the steamers or floating batteries destined, by the superiority of their speed, and by the range and direction of their projectiles, to play a conspicuous part, with the co-operation of fortifications erected on vulnerable points, in the defence and protection of these great avenues.

This canal was constructed according to the original plan of the Board. It is thirteen miles long, sixty-five feet wide at the water line, and nearly ten feet deep. It has two common locks, and two safety locks, each one hundred feet long by twenty feet eight inches wide. It cost two million seven hundred and fifty thousand dollars.

To connect the central with the southern frontier, and to avoid the ever-dangerous navigation around Cape Hatteras, which forms a sort of promontory between these two frontiers, the Board proposed to enlarge the Dismal Swamp Canal, already completed across the marshy lands in the vicinity of the naval station at Norfolk, so as to admit the passage of coasters. On this recommendation, the general government advanced the company the necessary funds for its enlargement. This canal has now the following dimensions: Length twenty-three miles; width forty-nine feet; depth seven feet two inches. Basins, sixty-five feet six inches wide, are constructed along the canal at intervals of four hundred and thirty-seven yards. Thus, a communication is established between Chesapeake Bay and Albemarle and Pamlico Sounds, to the south of Cape Hatteras, for vessels trading along the upper part of that bay and its tributaries.

From Pamlico Sound, Beaufort, North Carolina, and south of Cape Lookout, is very easily reached by means of a canal two thousand seven hundred and thirty-four yards long. This small canal places the River Neuse in direct communication with Beaufort, the only port, except Wilmington, at the mouth of Cape Fear River, through which the produce of North Carolina finds access to the sea.

From Beaufort, inland communication may be established through the Straits of Stumpy and Toomer, by means of small cuts. The mouth of Cape Fear River can be thus reached. From this point it would be quite easy to open internal communication, through the Waccamaw River, with Georgetown Bay. This bay is situated at the confluence of the Waccamaw, Pedee, and Black Rivers, and is already connected with the Santee, through the Winyaw Canal, which is seven miles and a half long. The Santee is navigable as far as Columbia, the seat of government of South Carolina, a distance of one hundred and thirty-six miles. It communicates with the Bay of Charleston by a canal twenty-two miles long, which, starting at Black Oak Island, fifty-eight miles above the mouth of the Santee, empties into the western branch of Cooper River.

Between Charleston and the Savannah River, there is a perfectly safe inland communication, through St. Helena Straits and the harbor of Port Royal, one of the best anchorages on this coast.

A canal, navigable for small vessels, also extends from the Savannah to the River St. John, in Florida.

The connection of the inland navigation parallel to the Atlantic coast with that presented by the frontier of the Gulf of Mexico, by means of a canal across the peninsula of Florida, which would not only considerably shorten navigation, but would enable vessels to avoid the dangers to which they are exposed between the Bahama Islands and the coast of Florida, in their course to and from the Gulf of Mexico, yet remained a desideratum.

The Board of Internal Improvement diligently considered this project, and declared it to be practicable. A detailed plan of it, which was submitted to the general government, I have fully described in my special work on the internal improvements in the United States. In this work may also be found a detailed account of all the other projects suggested and completed by the Board. Agreeably to the proposed plan, the canal should have a length of one hundred and sixty-seven miles, with a total fall of two hundred and twenty-one feet, and locks of sufficiently large dimensions to permit the passage of sail vessels. But this truly great national work has not yet been undertaken; a delay attributable to the different interpretations of the powers conceded to the central government by the Constitution, relative to appropriations of the public money for internal improvements. I certainly cannot pretend to place my opinion against that of the American statesmen who have opposed the application of the public funds to works of such general interest; but what I affirm, as an engineer, is that the interests of American commerce on the Gulf of Mexico are daily acquiring an importance commensurate with that of the settlements in the rich valleys of the Alabama and the Mississippi. A third part of American commerce now passes through the narrow channel between Florida and the Bahama Isles. The degree of security that commerce would derive from a canal in Florida, in case of a maritime war, is a sufficiently conclusive proof of the necessity of so great an improvement.

Moreover, without this canal, there would be a want of connection between the means of defence on the coasts of the Atlantic and the Gulf of Mexico. Each of these portions of the maritime frontier, thus deprived of the advantages of mutual co-operation and reciprocal support, would be liable, in turn, to be paralyzed by the presence of an enemy's fleet in the Bay of Havana.

To the American navy, Pensacola is undoubtedly an important building station and port of refuge, and affords excellent facilities for operating on the Gulf, and extending protection to the outlets of the Valley of the Tombigbee, and the Mississippi. But how greatly would these advantages be augmented if this military station could be supplied directly from the interior, and preserve a free communication with the ports of the Atlantic, and principally with the great depots on the Chesapeake Bay, by means of the great line of navigation which forms the girdle of the maritime coasts of the United States.

In short, the immediate result of opening the Florida Canal would be to hasten the settlement of a portion of the American territory which at present contains only a scattered population. White settlers, attracted by the climate and soil of the country, would oppose an effectual barrier to all those hostile combinations which, in the present condition of the peninsula, are yet to be feared.

A railroad, occupying the line selected for a canal might, to a certain extent, suit the conveniences of the population on the shores of the rivers. But in a national, commercial, and strategic point of view, nothing can answer the purpose of a large canal.

Besides, if it be desirable to induce a population to settle on the peninsula, the draining of the immense marshes which absorb the largest and richest portion of the State, and especially that towards the southern extremity of the peninsula, is a matter of the first importance. This result cannot be attained except canals and ditches are so cut as to unite the stagnant waters into one channel, thence to be carried to the sea.

To all these considerations another is to be added, which derives its importance from the part the American nation will hereafter take in that struggle, to which we have repeatedly referred, in which the two worlds are destined to engage.

Now, one of the objects of that struggle must necessarily be the commerce of the Indies. To insure the monopoly of this trade, powerful rivals are striving to construct, for their individual profit, a great canal between the Atlantic and Pacific Oceans, near the Isthmus of Panama. From the very day this canal shall be cut, Havana, already so admirably situated in relation to the Antilles, the two Americas, and the rest of the world, will become the mid-station between Europe and the East Indies. The nation that shall then possess this modern Carthage must control the commerce of the two seas, and will be able to paralyze the immense trade of the Americans. Even New Orleans, that bright star of the west, if not soon supplied with the conditions of sustaining the struggle I have indicated—that is to say, unless the Florida Canal is completed, and unless certain local advantages are conceded to it, such as the establishment of a free port—may possibly be subject to the law of the most powerful, despite the resources of its magnificent river.

The completion of all the canals I have described will afford a continuous inland navigation around the American territory, sheltered from all external aggression. The incalculable advantages to be derived from such a result cannot escape the attention of a people so famed for their foresight, especially in a country where real productive industry is substituted for the useless expenditure of war. May the United States never have cause to regret their delay in the completion of these works, especially the Florida Canal, which, in my opinion, is more important in a military, commercial, and economical point of view, than any hitherto undertaken!

RECAPITULATION.

The entire length of the canals in the United States opened for purposes of trade is four thousand nine hundred and seventy-one miles. Cost of construction nearly one hundred million dollars, or, about twenty thousand dollars a mile.

In France, the cost of construction is more than double this amount, exceeding forty-eight thousand dollars a mile. This disparity is explained by the difference in the modes of construction pursued in the two countries. The locks, bridges, and dams of the American canals, which are generally imperfectly finished, are in many cases built of wood, or dry stone-work. Moreover, stone and lumber are much cheaper in the United States than in France.

The expense of keeping canals in repair, which, in America, is five hundred and eighty to ten hundred and eighty dollars per mile, amounts in France only to four hundred and eighty dollars. But in England the expense is still greater, varying from seven hundred and twenty-five to twelve hundred and ninety dollars a mile. This difference is due to the fact that labor is much cheaper in France than in England and the United States, and especially to the fact that trade is far more brisk on the English and American canals than on those of France; and this increased activity may be attributed to the low tolls charged on these canals, as well as to the superior condition in which they are kept.

On the American canals, freight, exclusive of tolls at the locks, is charged per ton at the rate of one cent and a third per mile.

The present toll on the Erie Canal is one cent a ton per mile. When the enlargement of this canal shall have been effected, it is proposed to reduce the toll to one-fourth of a cent per mile.

The toll per mile on the Pennsylvania canals is, for stone coal, one-half cent per ton; cast iron, four-fifths of a cent; bar iron,

24

three-fourths of a cent; pig iron, two-thirds of a cent; wheat, one-half cent; wood, one-half cent.

The price of passage on a canal boat, including meals, is nearly four cents per mile.

American canals are not generally distinguished by beauty of finish, although there are many in New England and New York which, for durability of material and style of construction, can advantageously compare with the best works of the kind in France. But all of them completely answer the purpose for which they were intended. Navigation on the canals is seldom interrupted except by the rigor of the cold weather, which closes all the water avenues in the northern portion of the United States. The bank of the canal is always kept in good order, and provided with a tow path, over which horses can travel with great speed. In the United States, such a thing as employing men to haul boats is unknown. Where steam ceases to be a useful or available motive power, animal power is employed. The latter is generally adopted on canals, and is considered the more economical of the two, because of the uniform progress it secures, which is generally not less than eight or ten miles an hour.

Iron boats, similar to those used in England, have lately been built in the United States, and are considered better, in many respects, than ordinary boats. They last from forty to forty-five, instead of from five to six years, the ordinary duration of common boats, and their tonnage exceeds that of the latter in the proportion of five to four.

CHAPTER X.

NATIONAL DEFENCE.

ARTIFICIAL CHANNELS OF COMMUNICATION.

RAILROADS.

Origin of railroads—Common roads in the United States before their introduction—Distinctive character of American railroads—How the railroad is directly connected with the defence of the country—Example of its application in transporting troops and munitions of war—Economy of its employment—Technical details concerning American railroads—Classification; length ; cost; repairs; returns; mode of construction—American locomotives—Establishments where they are constructed—Cars for baggage and freight—Current expenses of the railroad—Fare for passengers; freight on merchandize—Financial embarrassment resulting from the extraordinary extension of the railroad—The future.

The distinctive character of the American people is that of being eminently productive. In this respect, no country, perhaps, with the same population, has equaled them. But in no country has an equal degree of activity and constant application been exhibited with the object of procuring means of exchange for the products of the soil, or additional facilities for their transportation.

In the gigantic application, so to speak, of that important means of communication and transportation, the railroad, the Americans have especially manifested their characteristic intelligence and their unerring instinct. The employment of all the resources which nature has so generously distributed throughout their vast and magnificent territory, for the development of commerce and wealth, the principal sources of public happiness, would seem to have been the principal and almost exclusive object of their lives.

The American seems to consider the words democracy, liberalism, and railroads as synonymous terms, whether because they all equally express the constant object of human effort in the gradual amelioration of the social condition of man, or because of the happy influence of the diffusion of knowledge on all classes of society.

When the question concerning the construction of the railroad —an improvement which was so powerfully to second the active genius of the Americans—was agitated, public opinion was alone invoked. It was no business of the State to decide whether the innovation, such as it presented itself, should immediately be introduced into the country, with all the imperfections attached to a recent discovery, or whether postponement of action until some other country should commence the experiment would be the wiser course. I well remember this circumstance. The Americans did not hesitate a moment. They adopted the discovery at its inception, and immediately applied it to their necessities, with due relation to locality.

This mode of proceeding was rational, for it is difficult to judge properly of the merits of any invention, or of the improvements of which it is susceptible, apart from direct experience. This course the Americans have invariably pursued in all their enterprises. They have never believed they could import anything in a state of perfection. For the suggestion of improvements which experience alone can supply in the varied circumstances peculiar to each country, they have considered experiment the only safe dependence.

These practical views are exhibited in everything the Americans undertake; a circumstance which, among others, must, in my opinion, place the United States at the head of all other nations in everything that relates to the industrial arts. At all events, they have applied steam more extensively, in every branch of industry, than any nation in the world.

It has often been asserted that, prior to the construction of the railroad, the United States possessed few facilities of bringing together the population scattered throughout the immense territory of the Republic. This assertion appears to me incorrect.

It is true, there have never been any roads in the United States so expensively constructed as our royal roads in France; but the number of practicable routes was comparatively more numerous. The Americans have, at all times, devoted much attention to this department of internal improvement. They have established national communications, which I was called myself to trace, under the orders of General Bernard. While some extend across the entire country, from the shores of the Atlantic to those of the great rivers of the west, and even to the borders of the Gulf of Mexico, others form a girdle along the borders of the Atlantic, embracing in their course all the commercial capitals from Maine to Florida. In short, several States have, at great expense, opened them through their own territory. Numerous roads, with gates for receiving toll, have also been constructed by companies; and these, even at the present day, are sufficiently productive to pay the expense of keeping them in repair, and to yield a small dividend to the stockholders. In no part of the world is traveling so common as in the United States. During my long residence in that country, I do not remember that I was ever delayed in my journey for want of a four-horse coach. Much time, it is true, had been consumed, and much expense incurred, in the opening and preservation of so many roads, though of comparatively frail construction; but steam at once changed the aspect of affairs in the entire system of transportation.

The establishment of channels affording facilities for rapid communication was essential to the commercial progress of the United States, to the active genius of the people, and to the general prosperity of the country, where each one knows so well how to appreciate the advantages of the proper use of time and the influence of the productive forces in the various branches of industry.

Moreover, the Americans, with the almost certain prospect of losing, in certain cases, a portion of their investments, have freely expended their means, knowing well that this expenditure will be amply compensated by an invigorated commerce, and by an augmentation in the manufactures, and an increase in the consumption, of the country. Hence the enterprises which, within the last few years, have so astonishingly developed the power of the American nation.

In the United States, therefore, the permission of the authorities to construct railroads has alone been sought. The risk and expense of the undertaking have been assumed by individual enterprise. But in peculiar cases, when the public interest seemed to demand it, assistance has been furnished by a particular State.

The manner in which these railroads are constructed exhibits the distinctive characteristics of the American people. In general, they are remarkable for their simplicity. On these roads, no monumental viaduct bridges, no costly earth-work to obtain reduced grades, no long horizontal embankments, are anywhere to be seen. The railroad seldom penetrates into the heart of a country unless it is essential to navigation, which is generally the case. In a word, American railroads never exhibit costly or misplaced luxury, but are always constructed with due relation to the interests of the people.

In the United States, the railroad is generally built on land that has never been occupied. At times it buries itself, as it were, in ravines, and then ascends mountains to a height that produces dizziness. Sometimes, with less audacity, but a truer courage, it is made to pass through subterranean channels. At other times it seems, by means of firm, though apparently frail, structures, to take its flight, so to speak, across deep valleys, wide rivers, immense marshes, tremulous prairies, and even vast sheets of water that appear like inland lakes. In the erection of these structures, trees are taken from a forest contiguous to the road, and, by means of a movable steam machine, made into piles, driven into the earth at regular intervals, in double rows, and then cut off to the determined level. Thus, in proportion as the work advances, it is finished. By this simple and ingenious process, railroads are constructed, as it were, by enchantment; for, immediately behind that steam pile-driver, which completes the bridge at the rate of two-thirds of a mile a month, a locomotive with its train can be put in operation. The road is thus at once adapted for its legitimate purposes.

In localities where the road comes in contact with broken or uneven soil, and in which, consequently, extensive excavations, always slow and costly, would greatly retard the progress of the work, steam has been substituted for manual labor. Thus, in a few days, a passage is opened which could not have been effected by ordinary means in several months. In fact, nothing stops the American in his onward course. He must reach his goal by the shortest conceivable route; for in America the value of everything is measured by time.

In the United States, every one hurries onward. It would seem as though the earth were not sufficiently large to contain so active a body of people; as though man himself were under the influence of the formidable power he has evoked. But sometimes the American pays the price of his temerity. His machine explodes, and an eternal repose punishes his unlimited and unbridled activity.

The railroad, animated by its powerful locomotive, appears to be the characteristic personification of the American. The one seems to hear and understand the other—to have been made for the other—to be indispensable to the other. The railroad has become the strength of the Union. It is the most important of the instruments of civilization. Unlike its rival, the canal, its utility is unaffected by the ice of winter or the drought of summer. At all times, it affords free intercourse of man with man, as well as an interchange of the products of his industry. It extends its arms towards every city and every village. It penetrates chains of mountains which otherwise would form insurmountable barriers to the inhabitants of the opposite slopes. In a word, it can grasp, with its iron hand, the most distant parts of the most extensive empire.

But if the railroad is an indispensable element in the physical organization of the vast territory of the American Republic, as it is in the moral organization of its active inhabitants, it is not the less essential to national defence. In this respect, its efficiency may be accurately estimated. In this, strategically speaking, undoubtedly consists one of the greatest merits of transportation by steam. It becomes, in fact, at once, one of the most formidable instruments of war, because of the masses of combatants it can throw at any moment on a given point. Besides, it will prove a great source of economy to the State compared to the ordinary mode of transportation.

The facility which the railroad affords of transporting troops and munitions of war must be an immense advantage in every country, whatever the circumstances in which it is placed. But in the United States, where the distances are so great which separate the vulnerable points from those whence assistance can be obtained, and where the militia are the principal dependence in time of war, this advantage is highly augmented. These citizen soldiers are called into active service usually for a very limited period; for they place too high a value on their time and liberty quietly to endure prolonged subjection to the discipline of camps. The valuable time heretofore consumed in marches and countermarches, not only always fatiguing, but often more fatal to troops than the fire of an enemy, will henceforth be saved. The amount of useful labor economized by the railroad is represented by the productive capacity of a number of men equal to those at one time uselessly retained in regimentals.

By means, also, of the numerous canals, but more especially of the railroads, which now furrow the vast territory of the Union, in almost every direction, the Americans will always be able to withstand any foreign war, however threatening it may be, with a force much inferior to that which would have been required for the protection of their extended frontier, without such ample channels of communication.

It will no longer be necessary to concentrate heavy forces at every threatened point on the frontier, since, by means of railroads parallel to, and converging towards, the coast, numerous troops in readiness for action, and much superior to those of the enemy, can at any time, and at small expense, be brought to its relief. These forces will be able to march in a compact body, so as to act simultaneously on their arrival; whilst, by the ordinary channels, they could only act in feeble detachments. When we add to these advantages the complete absence of all corporeal fatigue and the moral energy of the combatants, the superiority of the railroad to the common road, even though animal power instead of steam were brought into requisition, is strikingly perceptible. Besides, a portion of the horse belonging to an artillery company could easily be made to draw the remainder, in addition to the necessary ordnance. In like manner could the transportation of a corps of cavalry be effected. In this case, rapidity of conveyance is not so essential a point to be secured as uniformity of motion.

The advantage the State must derive from canals and railroads is incalculable. The money economized in a single campaign would equal the entire cost of their construction. The truth of this assertion might easily be substantiated by figures.

During the war of 1812, when the enemy marched on the city of Washington, this capital could be relieved only by feeble detachments of troops, furnished by Baltimore and the cities of the interior at great expense, and exhausted by long marches, which unfitted them to take an active part in the defence of so important a position. In the present state of the channels of communication, the one linked to the other, an immediate supply of locomotives, and cars of every description, sufficient to transport at once a corps of twenty or twenty-five thousand men, with all their camp equipage, and an army of one hundred or even two hundred thousand men, in one-tenth of the time required by the ordinary mode of conveyance, would be at all times available.

We may also add that this army would not experience fatigue, nor leave a man on the road. No shoes or accoutrements would be worn out. But the strength of the army would be augmented almost in the ratio of the rapidity of its progress. It would also be preserved from one of the most potent causes of demoralization, lassitude.

These considerations, bearing, as it will be perceived, not only on the question of economy, but on the subject of humanity, deserve our attention.

Should one of the commercial capitals on the borders of the Atlantic be suddenly threatened with invasion by a powerful enemy, immense succors might immediately be sent to it within a period of ten or twelve hours, from all the principal centres of population in a radius of more than two hundred and fifty miles. Should New York, for example, be the object of an unforeseen attack, this magnificent city could, in less than five hours, be relieved by volunteer militia to the number of at least fifty or sixty thousand, from Connecticut, from the upper portions of the Hudson, and from New Jersey and Philadelphia; and reserves equal in number might follow in an equal space of time. All these troops might take positions on Long Island, Staten Island, and Amboy, which, as we have seen, cover the approaches to New York; while special bodies of artillery could throw themselves into the fortifications constructed on strategic points in readiness for vigorous resistance.

Now the measures that would be adopted for the defence of New York would be equally available at any point on the coast; for, as I have already stated, the great merit of the American channels of communication is their concatenation; and there is not a single point in the United States that could not, in emergency, rely on immediate aid.

That the great economy realized by railroad conveyance may be appreciated, it is necessary to state only a single fact. During the war of 1812, the transportation of a ton of merchandize from New York to Pittsburgh cost from one hundred to two hundred and forty dollars; and from thirty to forty days elapsed before it reached its destination. This freight may now be transported, in three days, at the rate of nine or ten dollars. Distance four hundred and eighty-five miles.

The government was obliged, at that period, to pay two hundred dollars for the transportation of a twelve-pounder from New York to Buffalo.

The American engineers, duly estimating all these advantages in relation to the national defence, have calculated the effective service which these channels of communication are capable of rendering in the concentration of troops at given points. The results of their investigations are embodied in a general report, submitted to the government in 1820. This report is now enrolled among the archives of the War Department.

The relations of the railroad to the navy, to fortifications, and to floating batteries for the defence of the mouths of rivers and certain bays, have always been carefully borne in mind. Hence, of all systems of national defence, that of the United States is unquestionably the most economical, and the most effective; for, while it permits the navy, as I have already said, to act freely on the vast ocean, its national battle-field, it enables an adequate land force to act at any moment on any assailable point of the frontier.

If the railroad could be constructed in accordance with the strict rules of strategy, its efficiency would undoubtedly be greatly improved; but it is very difficult to reconcile the military and the commercial exigencies of a people. The selection of one side of a river, for the course of a road, because of certain strategic advantages it presents, might involve an expenditure altogether disproportionate to the population to be removed; while, at the same time, this population might derive a positive advantage from a road constructed on the opposite shore.

In the United States, less than anywhere else, could such a result be attained; for there everything is directed by individual interest. The central power of itself exerts but little influence on internal relations. Nevertheless, if the railroads of the United States do not present, as a whole, that systematic completeness resulting from the exclusive pursuit of a strategic object, a plan wisely suggested by a general of the United States army, they depart so little from a true standard that in the end the same result is secured. Thus, in America, the individual energy of the citizen will have accomplished that which, in other countries, can only be attained by the force of governmental centralization.

While every improvement in the channels of communication has, as we have just shown, a direct relation to the national defence, it especially tends to develop the agricultural industry of the country, the fundamental basis of public prosperity, and to consolidate the internal peace of the citizen. Moreover, such improvements are fruitful sources of revenue to particular States, and thus form a mysterious link between the general interests of the government and those of the people. In thus favoring the productive genius of the Americans, they repel the political and industrial inroads of England. But an influence, not less remarkable, is that which they exercise over the moral character of the people, by bringing, as it were, to the door of each citizen that intellectual vigor which alone enables a people to live free. By these improvements, in fine, all the inhabitants have equal access to the precious gifts of education and religion. The light of Christianity quickens and enlightens the inhabitants of the republic almost in the same degree that a uniform education enables them to appreciate the political principles by which they are governed.

Under such circumstances, where a people has been sufficiently wise and foresighted to give the greatest possible development to instruction, founded on the immutable principles of a sound religion, laws have so powerful a hold upon the hearts of men as to exclude the possibility of anarchy.

Such have been the consequences of the system of democracy in the United States, a system which, by giving to suffrage the utmost possible latitude, appeals to the entire intellectual strength of the nation.

TECHNICAL DETAILS CONCERNING RAILROADS.

American improvements are the result of the association of citizens directly interested in their completion. Still, in many instances, as we have said, particular States have appropriated a portion of their revenues to works of general utility. In these cases, the necessary funds have been obtained through loans, the payment of which, with the interest, has been guaranteed by the legislature. Occasionally, the general government has taken part in these truly national enterprises.

At the end of the year 1847, the entire extent of railroad completed, or in course of completion, in the United States, was from seven to ten thousand miles, the cost of which will amount to not less than three hundred and twenty million dollars!

All the lines of this immense network are connected with one another, as well as with the various canals of the Union. They open direct outlets from the coal and iron regions to the centres of manufacture—from the different navigable harbors to the most distant points in the interior—from the agricultural regions to the great centres of exportation. In short, they directly connect the Atlantic seaboard with the Ohio, the Mississippi, the St. Lawrence, and with Canada and the Lakes. Thus, their vivifying influence is felt from Maine to Georgia, from Georgia to Louisiana, and from Kentucky to Michigan. Of all the ties which connect together the various interests of this vast republic, they are the most indissoluble.

In England, at the same period, there were two thousand six hundred and sixty-seven miles of railroad, finished or in course of completion, eleven hundred miles of which were open to trade. The amount of capital invested in these enterprises was two hundred and eighty-eight million dollars.

In the United States, where most of the roads have but one track, though cut and graded for two, the investment amounted only to ninety-eight million dollars. The cost of constructing a road in this manner slightly exceeded eighteen thousand dollars a mile. Hence, it is evident that the railroads of England cost six times more than those of the United States.

Nevertheless, the best constructed roads in the United States, with a single track, have cost from forty-one to forty-five thousand dollars per mile. At the present time, according to the novel mode of laying rails on wood, the expense per mile is not more than twenty-five thousand dollars.

The annual expense of keeping these roads in repair is from seven to eight hundred dollars per mile.

The railroads of the United States are naturally divided into four great classes:—

The first class, composed of several lines, extends along the whole Atlantic seaboard, and connects together the principal commercial cities that lie between Maine and Florida—Portland, Portsmouth, Boston, Providence, New York, Philadelphia, Baltimore, Norfolk, Fredericksburg, Wilmington, Charleston, Augusta, and Pensacola. This line is one thousand miles in length, and is the joint work of twenty different companies.

The second comprises all the lines constructed with the object of uniting the Atlantic seaboard with the countries beyond the Alleghanies. Thus, from Boston, New York, Philadelphia, Baltimore, Richmond, Charleston, Savannah, Pensacola, and New Orleans, railroads extend to the great Valleys of the Ohio and Mississippi, and even to the shores of the Missouri, and unite with a third division in course of construction in the interior of the country, towards the regions of the north-west, which is to unite Indianapolis with Cincinnati, and Milwaukie with Chicago and Detroit.

Other lines extend to the borders of the great Lakes, and in crossing, connect together, numerous canals and navigable rivers.

A fourth class includes all the railroads constructed for industrial purposes. These are very numerous, and directly contribute to the prosperity of the country by opening outlets and creating safe markets for the immense beds of combustible minerals found in almost every portion of the Union.

These lines form a chain of arteries that distribute life to the great industrial body of the Republic.

It cannot be denied that the Americans, in some instances, have ventured unwarily on these enterprises, which always involve so heavy an expenditure of capital. Nevertheless, I believe that the railroad will ultimately become the principal source of the prosperity of the United States.

It is difficult, at present, to arrive at an accurate knowledge of the returns of these channels of communication. They are generally supposed to yield, on the average, a profit of five per cent. Some barely pay expenses; while others pay a dividend as high as fourteen per cent. Those at the north yield eight per cent.; and the stock of these roads is now as eagerly sought as it was at one time shunned.

Thus, the people of Massachusetts, after having expended, in their own State, one hundred million dollars on railroads, have invested their capital in the same enterprises in Connecticut, New York, Pennsylvania, and Georgia.

The net revenues of American railroads have generally doubled in five years.

The road which connects New York with Philadelphia is eighty-five miles long, and cost fifty-four thousand five hundred dollars a mile. The number of passengers which annually pass between the two cities is two hundred thousand; amount of merchandize transported fourteen thousand tons. Fare three dollars; freight seven dollars per ton. This road, besides yielding an annual dividend never less than six per cent., has paid for itself in seven years.

The railroad from Philadelphia to Baltimore, ninety miles long, cost fifty-four thousand three hundred dollars per mile. Annual number of passengers from one hundred and twenty to one hundred and fifty thousand. Fare, four dollars.

The railroad from Philadelphia to Columbia, constructed by the State of Pennsylvania, is eighty miles long, and cost nearly sixty thousand dollars a mile. Annual transportation, seventy-five thousand passengers and nine thousand tons of merchandize. Fare three dollars and twenty-five cents. Freight, seven dollars and fifty cents per ton. This railway opens the communication of the seaboard with the west, and is used more for the transportation of merchandize than for the conveyance of passengers.

The railway from Boston to Worcester is forty-three miles long, and cost per mile forty thousand dollars. Annual transportation, from six to seven hundred thousand passengers, and, what is of still greater consequence, thirty thousand tons of merchandize. Net receipts per annum one hundred and eighty thousand dollars.

This railroad, which was constructed by the people of New England, forms part of the line from Boston to Albany. It is designed to bring the produce of the western regions and of the great Lakes directly to the wharves of Boston, thus competing with the railroad which connects Buffalo with Albany, the head of navigation of the Hudson.

The entire line from Boston to Lake Erie is five hundred miles long. That portion which extends from Boston to Albany is nearly two hundred miles long, and cost nine million dollars; an expenditure, consequently, exceeding the cost of the Erie and Champlain Canals, constructed by the State of New York.*

* This road, called the *Western Railroad,* was completed in four years. To accelerate the progress of the work, a *steam excavator,* invented by Mr.

It is interesting to inquire by what principle of reasoning the people of New England have been induced to incur such an immense expenditure. The solution of the inquiry exhibits the high degree of intelligence they possess concerning questions of economy. "Experience," they have said, "has demonstrated that the time, the labor, and the expense economized by the railway in the transportation of merchandize or passengers, may be considered equal to three-fourths of the cost of transportation by the ordinary routes. Now, as this transportation, by the common roads in the State of Massachusetts, may be estimated to cost not less than sixteen million dollars annually, it is evident that three-fourths of this amount, twelve million dollars, may be directly saved by the construction of a railway. Every month, therefore, the construction of such a road is delayed is equivalent to an expenditure of one million dollars."

Why cannot our economists in France take a few practical lessons in political economy from those of New England, and learn that the surest method of mitigating the burden of taxes and imposts is to know how to make expenditures that will secure the people the most available channels of communication?

The railroad from Boston to Lowell was completed in 1835. It is twenty-five miles long, and cost one million eight hundred thousand dollars. In 1841, the net receipts of this road amounted to one hundred and forty-nine thousand dollars.

I have often had occasion to speak of the noble sentiment of rivalry which animates the Americans in their attempts to open a direct communication between the Atlantic seaboard and the fertile regions of the west. To this spirit of competition we must attribute the completion of all the lines referred to in the present work, and in my special works on the internal improvements in the United States.

The citizens of New York have just given another example of their rare and characteristic enterprise. They were the first to open navigable communication between the Lakes and the Hudson. They have now undertaken the construction of a railroad

Otis, was used with great advantage. This machine usually excavated from twenty-six hundred to three thousand three hundred cubic feet in twelve hours. It operated well in sandy soils, in soils containing large bolders in abundance, and even in quicksands; but it was especially adapted to a clayey and gravelly soil.

leading directly from New York to Lake Erie, a project conceived so early as 1834. This road commences on the Hudson River, twenty-two miles above New York, and extends to Dunkirk, on Lake Erie, to the west of Buffalo. Its entire length is four hundred and thirteen miles, or, including the city of New York, four hundred and fifty-four miles. It was to have been opened in 1845. Its cost is estimated at from nine to ten million dollars, of which amount the State furnishes six and individual stockholders three millions.

Two hundred miles of the road are built on piles, traverses, and girders, by means of a new mode of pile-driving by steam, now in general use in the United States. By this method, a road can be constructed in a much shorter time than by the ordinary method; but its principal merit consists in the fact that it greatly reduces the expense for repairs and the cost of vehicles of transportation.

To facilitate the management of the road, the course is divided into stations seventy-seven miles apart, upon which are placed locomotives of different power, according to the ascent required to be overcome. The greatest inclinations, which are concentrated within short distances, do not exceed from thirty-seven to fifty-eight feet to the mile, a difficulty which, at the present time, American locomotives easily surmount.

On this railroad, the freight per ton on heavy merchandize is thirteen dollars and twenty cents; on light goods twelve dollars per ton. Thus, merchandize can be transported from New York to Lake Erie, on this road, at a cheaper rate than by the Champlain Canal.

Another enterprise, which now occupies the attention of the merchants of New York, is the construction of a railroad leading from that of Harlem to Albany, a distance of one hundred and forty-three miles. It is estimated that this road, with one track, though graded and prepared for two tracks, will cost four million dollars. The trade between New York and Albany will thus be untrammeled at any season of the year.

To insure the completion of this great undertaking, an appeal has been made to all who are interested in the matter. Thus, it has been proposed:—

1st. That the State shall guarantee six per cent. interest on a capital sufficient to pay the expenses of cutting and grading the road.

2d. That those who live along the shore shall furnish the land necessary for the road and for the stations, and take shares equivalent to its value.

3d. That the city of Albany, at the extremity of the line, shall subscribe capital for a stipulated amount of stock.

4th. That the city of Troy, on the left bank of the Hudson, a short distance above Albany, interested in an equal degree in the success of the enterprise, shall also subscribe for a given amount of stock.

5th. That New York, the most interested of all the parties, shall bear all the expense of the vehicles of transportation and of the construction of station-houses and termini.

6th. The great capitalists of New York have consented to subscribe a sum equal to one-fourth of the capital stock, to cover the expense of laying the track, and to furnish the necessary wood, rails, &c. for this purpose. And as a recompense to the principal merchants for their honorable participation in the enterprise, it is proposed that their names be inscribed on a monumental arch, which shall decorate the entrance of this railway into the metropolis.

Three years will be sufficient to complete this great railway.

The success of this enterprise is based on the circumstance that two thousand persons are daily traveling from the one to the other extreme point of this line. Notwithstanding the price of passage by the steamboat is but one-fourth of a cent per mile, while that by the railroad will be rather more than three-fourths of a cent, still, when we consider that a trip on the Hudson occupies from ten to twelve hours, during which time the passengers are exposed to the inconvenience occasioned by dense crowding in a warm place, while a trip on the railway will be performed in six or seven hours, affording to each passenger fresh wholesome air, and a comfortable resting-place, there is every reason to suppose that the railroad will receive its fair share of public support. Besides, since the introduction of steam on the Hudson, the number of passengers has doubled every five years.

The navigation companies on the Hudson annually declare dividends of twenty-one to thirty per cent. Hence, the introduction of a new competition may safely be permitted; otherwise, the dividends of these companies will, in a short time, amount to sixty per cent.

The Americans usually employ two kinds of rail: the ∩ rail, and the T rail. The latter is most in use. It has a flat base, which gives it a firm position on the sleepers on which it immediately rests. This rail is of American invention, and has been universally substituted for the flat rail. Experience has proved that the economy realized by its use in relation to the cost of repairing vehicles of transportation, bears, compared to the latter, the proportion of 142 to 145.

But one of the principal causes of this reduction is undoubtedly the mode adopted by the Americans of laying their rails. They generally fit them on traverses, resting on sleepers, but most commonly on the sleepers themselves, by this means furnishing them a continuous support. The sleepers rest on traverses, sometimes on pieces of wood placed across the track, but obliquely to its axis. On land not possessing the required solidity, such as turf, and spongy and marshy grounds, the track is laid on piles driven in by the steam pile-driver which we have already described. This machine drives two rows of piles simultaneously, to the number of sixty or seventy daily, at a cost of less than twenty or thirty cents per yard.

The ∩ rail weighs thirteen pounds and a half per foot. The T rail, with a flat base, weighs eighteen pounds per foot. It can bear a pressure of from eight to ten tons at its weakest part, and thus support the heaviest locomotives and the longest trains.

The Americans have greatly improved the construction of their locomotives. Not ten years since, thirty or forty tons were considered as much as they could be made to draw on a horizontal plane. Now, a single locomotive can draw from four to five hundred tons with facility.

The new locomotives have eight wheels, four of which are driving-wheels, acting each with a friction equal to two tons. In descending grades, they usually draw trains equal to four or five hundred tons, and in ascending grades, equal to two hundred or two hundred and fifty tons.

Generally, however, the burden of the trains daily drawn on the railroad between New York and Philadelphia, and on the railroads of Pennsylvania, is one hundred and fifty tons.

In the United States, there are now several establishments where these machines are manufactured, not only for domestic use but for exportation; for the superiority of their power of traction proportional to their weight, as well as of their workmanship, has opened for them a market in England and Germany.

Locomotives from the factory of Mr. William Norris, of Philadelphia, are used on the Birmingham and Gloucester Railway in England, and on that of Berlin and Frankfort in Prussia.

This establishment has acquired, of late years, so high a reputation for its excellent machines, that it may be considered one of the great workshops of the United States.

To the locomotives of Mr. Norris, a tender is attached, which runs on eight wheels, so that the weight of the locomotive and tender is equally distributed on the rails. These locomotives can be delivered in complete order at the rate of seven thousand five hundred dollars each, and shipped to any port in Europe. Mr. Norris, on delivering a locomotive, makes an agreement to keep it in good order, at the rate of six hundred dollars a year, for ten years, on condition that an engineer sent by himself be employed to take charge of it; the proper use of an engine depending much upon the practical experience of its conductor.

The establishment of Mr. Baldwin, of Philadelphia, is also celebrated for its excellent locomotives. His machines are constructed with six wheels, and weigh each eleven tons. This weight is equally distributed on the wheels, all of which are driving-wheels. This enables them to pass over curves of very short diameter with great facility.

Mr. Ross Winan, of Baltimore, also possesses a splendid establishment, where engines and wagons of great power are manufactured. The locomotives of this factory run on eight driving-wheels, and weigh each nineteen tons.

New York and New Jersey also possess establishments for the construction of locomotives. That at Paterson is in high repute.

The factories at Lowell, Massachusetts, have acquired great celebrity for the quality of the material and for the finish of their machines.

American locomotives, on American railroads, cost, under ordinary circumstances, from six to eight hundred dollars a year or repairs. They generally last ten years, running at the rate of from seventeen to twenty thousand miles a year, with a speed of twenty or twenty-five miles an hour.

The cars for passengers have also received improvements characteristic of the genius and the manners of the Americans. These cars are from thirty-four to forty feet long, and about nine feet wide. They are divided through the longitudinal centre by a passage, on either side of which are the seats. Some of the cars have a separate apartment for ladies. At the extremity of each car in the train, there is a platform, enabling the passengers to pass from one car to another. An American could ill endure our mode of traveling, forced to keep a certain seat, in a small car, under lock and key. He would pant for air, he would suffocate.

Each of these cars is set on eight wheels, joined together four by four. The separation of the four front wheels from the hind wheels is merely sufficient to secure free motion. These cars are substantially built, can carry sixty passengers, and cost about twenty-eight hundred dollars each, delivered on the road.

The most celebrated builders of these cars in the United States are Messrs. Betts, Pusey, and Harland, of Wilmington, Delaware.

From Philadelphia to Baltimore, passengers generally travel by night. Thus, from two to three hundred persons at a time can take comfortable rest in a species of reclining chair, so arranged as to enable one to lean his head on its back without jostling, or being jostled by, his neighbor.

Cars for the transportation of coal weigh one ton and three quarters, and carry a load equal to three tons and a half. At present, the wheels of these cars last from six to eight, instead of four years; a result due to the substitution of lard for oil during eight months of the year. Thus, a saving of fifty per cent. is realized in this item of railroad expenditure.

The Americans estimate the loss consequent on the necessary repairs of passenger and other cars, and that resulting from supernumerary cars, at from twenty to twenty-five per cent. of their original value.

In the United States, the current expenses of running the cars on a railroad amount yearly to from three thousand five hundred to four thousand two hundred dollars a mile.

Experience has proved that short courses are less profitable than long ones, as well in relation to the locomotive as to the expense of traction. It has also shown that uniformity in the weight of trains is of great advantage. In general, railroads are more advantageous in coal districts than in other localities.

RATES OF FARE AND FREIGHT ON AMERICAN RAILROADS.

The rates of fare and freight are regulated by competition, and by the profits realized in specific cases. In most cases, these profits increase in the ratio of the reduction of the price of transportation.

The price of transportation can never be fixed at the opening of a road. It is determined after the number of passengers and the amount of merchandize which pass on it are accurately estimated. It has been generally observed that, after the opening of a railroad, the number of passengers in a given direction has increased fourfold. Wherever established, this channel of communication has invariably paid expenses.

ELECTRIC TELEGRAPHS.

A means of transmitting thought in harmony with the wondrous development of the means of rapid transportation, in the United States, through the introduction of steam, seemed to be required. This necessity occasioned the invention and application of the electric telegraph.

This splendid discovery, due to Professor Morse, an American, received its immediate application through the co-operation of individual interests.

The electric telegraph is now the property of joint stock companies. The special merit of the improved American telegraph consists in the fact that the news transmitted is immediately impressed on paper.

A telegraphic line, now in full operation, puts the cities of Portland, Lowell, Boston, New York, Philadelphia, and Baltimore in continuous relation with Washington, the seat of government.

This main line has received branches extending from New York to Albany, Rochester, and Buffalo on Lake Erie; and from Philadelphia to Harrisburg, Pittsburgh, and Wheeling on the Ohio.

The total length of these various lines is nearly eighteen hundred miles. The line from St. Louis to New Orleans is in course of completion, and will soon be finished.* The entire line will then be about six thousand two hundred and ten miles.

Thus, we see realized, in the new hemisphere, that combination of interests which is to blend all its inhabitants in one common feeling of nationality; a result of the highest importance, since it includes the power of the people to appreciate, almost simultaneously, what affects their moral, political, and material welfare. In this way, a community is rendered strong, prosperous, and independent.

CHAPTER XI.

NATIONAL DEFENCE.

THE REGULAR ARMY.

Numerical force of the American army—Power of Congress to increase it, according to necessity—Corps of officers; its distinctive character—No retired list authorized by law—Mode of recruiting—Difference of rank between the commissioned and non-commissioned officers—Discipline of the garrisons and encampments of the federal troops—The prerogatives of the municipal authority always respected—No body of troops can be stationed in any State without the permission of the local authorities.

The Americans keep a very small standing army, relatively to the extent of their territory, and their rank as a nation; a number merely sufficient to keep their fortifications in order, to protect their western frontier from the incursions of the Indians, and to secure respect on that of Canada. This state of things does not arise from a want of military spirit, but from the attachment of the people to their democratic institutions, and from the conviction, acquired by a practical knowledge of freedom, that the spirit of subordination, so essential to keep a numerous regular army under arms, is not only incompatible with liberty, but is its first and most dangerous enemy.

Therefore, only about twelve thousand or thirteen thousand men are employed in the service of the State, who are recruited by

* It is now in full operation.—Tr.

voluntary enlistment. For the organization and composition of the American army, see Part I., Chapter VII. of my last work, *Democracy in the United States.*

The only equitable, rational, and effectual method of giving to the country an armed national force, susceptible of the highest possible elevation of patriotism and devotion, is not recognized by the Americans. The law of conscription, which France owes to the republic, and which is based on the sublime principles of justice and nationality, obliges every citizen, without exception, to contribute to the defence of the country. It is, therefore, eminently democratic. Nevertheless, it has not yet been applied to the recruiting of the regular army in the United States; because such are the democratic susceptibilities of the American that he would be alarmed at the influence which a military chieftain might acquire over his subordinates, and the use he might make of it against the institutions of his country.

In my opinion, the American legislators gravely erred in neglecting to acknowledge, among the organic laws of their country, the principle of conscription. They should have admitted the principle, modified, it is true, agreeably to the national repugnance to the imposition of long service by the State, and to the exigencies of their insular position, so secure from invasion by large armies. They would thus have acted with wisdom, with patriotism, and with justice; they would, in fine, have acted consistently with their character, and in consonance with their excellent institutions.

Still, the Americans acknowledge the utility of the system of conscription, in their militia service; and the effective force of the regular army can always be increased to the necessary contingent according to circumstances. The general government is charged with this duty, through the national legislature. Hence, on a recent occasion, the President of the United States was authorized to increase the regular army from twelve to fifty thousand men, if, in his opinion, the exigencies of the country should require the augmentation.

Hence, agreeably to this organization, the effective force of the army can be increased twofold, without any increase in the number of its commissioned and non-commissioned officers.

The corps of American officers, although limited in number, is remarkable for its military knowledge, its moral character, its spirit of discipline, and its sentiment of honor and patriotism. It is entirely composed of men who have been educated in the national military academy at West Point. For the description of this academy, its administration, studies, &c., see the work just referred to.

Attached, therefore, to a military life from taste, not because it is the only resource society offers them, they share all the passions to which this career gives birth in a country whose advanced posts, on the frontier, in the midst of Indian tribes, constantly furnish a degree of excitement, interest, and peril, which constitutes the charm of the military life. Thus, they acquire a feeling peculiar to themselves. They belong to one family; they are exposed to the same dangers; they endure the same privations and enjoy the same pleasures. Living with hopes common to them all, their devotion to their country finds no rival emotion in their breasts but that respect for the civil law which is the foundation of the happiness, prosperity, and greatness of their country.

But what particularly distinguishes the American officer is that his entrance into the army does not entirely sever all the ties that attach him to civil life. In fact, he does not abandon this life for ever. After a few years of military service, he finds it his interest to return to it. I scarcely know the number of officers, my former companions in arms in America, that I have seen return to active civil life. Disgust or weariness did not prompt these men to leave the military service; but, rather, the desire to defend specific interests in the legislature, or to consummate ambitious projects which can be pursued successfully only in a civil career. But, in these cases, the army was sure to receive, from all its former members, the same marks of interest and esteem that had been imbibed at a common source, the military family.

The American officer does not believe that he treads in a sphere superior to that which he occupied in the bosom of civil life, because he has obtained high rank in the army; for, although he receives a commission from the President, with the approbation of the Senate, which the Chief Magistrate may at pleasure take from him, he is well aware that, above the will of the President, there is a national will expressed by elections, which exercises a direct control over every branch of the administration;

and that the President is, like himself, controlled by the supreme law of the land, popular suffrage.

Besides, the American officer is animated by the feeling that his rank, as a member of a disciplined corps, on which society always has an eye, imposes upon him a rigid, and, as it were, dignified course of conduct. The uniform he wears, like the coat of the austere churchman, merely designates the body to which he belongs.

As the rank of the American officer confers but few advantages, the legislature has done merely an act of justice in securing to him the enjoyment of the position he occupies. Therefore, he remains on the full pay army list as long as he retains his faculties; for, in the United States, the retired civil or military list is unknown. Pensions are generously provided for officers and soldiers who have become invalids in the service of the United States.

The American army need not fear the influence of prolonged peace on the habits and feelings of its officers, for their life is passed in active service, which fits them for a state of war. Accustomed to long marches, under the various climates of their immense territory; always kept on the alert by an active and vigilant enemy on the frontier, where more than three-fourths of their life is passed, they preserve a taste for arms and for the excitement and perils incident to a military career.

But one of the most striking defects in the organization of the American army is the present mode of enlistment. The recruits are generally men who, as laborers or mechanics, receive much higher compensation than in the military service. They must, therefore, be infected with some moral infirmity, which renders them unfit for a useful and laborious life. Consequently, this lack of moral force in the composition of the army must be counterpoised by a very strict system of discipline. And a fact which must excite astonishment is that there are no troops whose sluggish and impassive physiognomy contrasts so strangely with the national character as those of the United States.

The adoption of the law of conscription would correct this anomaly in the civil and military habits of the Americans. It is to be regretted that their manners, their spirit of independence, their just appreciation of the value of time, are opposed to the realization of military servitude for an adequate length of time.

The American consents to depart from this general rule of his life only when the country, in time of danger, makes an appeal to all his energy. In this case, he knows how to take his place in the ranks of the army, and, by rare activity, intelligence, and impetuosity, to supply the lack of discipline.

Another equally striking defect in the composition of the American army is the complete isolation of the commissioned from the non-commissioned officers. This state of things, borrowed from English usage, is not recognized, it is true, by the laws which govern promotion in the American army; but opinion and custom, often more potent than laws, raise an insurmountable barrier between the two classes. The corps of non-commissioned officers occupies an inert position between the soldier and the commissioned officer.

Nevertheless, it should always be recollected that the regular army plays a very powerless part in the political organization of the United States. In time of peace, it is placed along the inland frontier to protect the outposts, and along the coast to keep the fortifications in good condition.

Hence, the greater part of these troops live entirely beyond American society. Still, as the protection of military arsenals is the duty of the federal troops, the result is that men subject to martial law live in the midst of a society where civil law is in full vigor.

This juxtaposition is never attended with inconvenience, for the common law governs the citizens, and martial law the federal troops within the jurisdiction and limits of the territory belonging to the central government.

Hence, there is nothing to prevent the army, or a portion of the army, from residing where the Congress of the United States holds its sessions, or in cities where the State legislatures are established. The United States has a small garrison in charge of a military arsenal in Washington city; one at Frankford, near Philadelphia, which now forms part of this city, through the extension of its suburbs; and federal troops are quartered, at New York and at New Orleans, on property belonging to the Union.

But in the United States no body of troops could ever encamp or establish themselves on property within the jurisdiction of a city or a particular State, without the permission of competent civil authorities.

In conclusion, it may be stated, as an established fact, that neither the federal government nor any particular State has ever felt the necessity of passing repressive laws against any military despotism.

In the United States, every citizen is armed, and feels that he is the guardian of his personal rights against any attempts or aggressions of a foreign enemy. But when he is called upon to defend his rights as a citizen, the only weapon he believes his duty requires him to use is the ballot box.

CHAPTER XII.

NATIONAL DEFENCE.

THE MILITIA.

The militia the principal element of national defence—Peculiar aptitude of the Americans for defensive war—Numerical force of the militia—No State law prohibits the collection of troops on the spot where an election is held—Electoral rights of the people maintained by the laws.

"The best wall of a city," said Agesilaus, "is its population." "The best defenders of the institutions and independence of a country," say the Americans, "are the citizen militia." In fact, in a truly free country, every citizen ought to be a soldier, and every soldier a citizen. The defence of the soil should depend not only on the regular army, but more especially on the citizen militia. Now, the American nation is composed of citizens animated by a national spirit and by an ardent desire to preserve their liberty. Therefore, the resources of such a nation, in time of war, are immense; for, when it appeals to arms in defence of its rights, independence, and honor, it rises up as a single man, and thus, through unity of action, becomes irresistible.

Among the Americans, the militia is the principal element of public strength. In their system of defence, the regular army forms the vanguard, and the militia constitute a powerful reserve, on whose active co-operation rest the destinies of the country. The leading object which all who have attempted to solve the problem involved in the defence of the American soil have sought to secure is the concentration, by every available facility, of the largest possible masses of militia on strong positions at the most vulnerable points of the territory. On this principle, New York, the metropolis of American commerce on the Atlantic, and New Orleans at the mouth of the immense Mississippi, have been fortified. It has been seen, in the chapter on the channels of communication, that more than two hundred thousand combatants may be concentrated on these points in a few hours, by means of the railroad, the canal, or the steamboat.

Nevertheless, it must be acknowledged that from such soldiers, we cannot expect the blind, passive, and always uniform obedience of regular disciplined troops. The education and composition of the two differ essentially. But what the former lack in subordination, they make up in patriotism. A noble ardor, which is the fruit of liberty, and a correct appreciation of his own worth, give to the citizen soldier of America an immense advantage; for his intellect thus acquires a degree of vigor which makes him equal to all the difficulties and contingencies of war.

The American citizen soldier also possesses a great advantage over the European soldier in his power of enduring the fatigues of war. Accustomed to manage a horse from infancy, to take long walks, to swim, to encamp, to hunt, to explore distant lands, scarcely populated, in part uncultivated, and to traverse rocky and marshy soils, rivers, wild forests, in a variety of climates, his constitution acquires a degree of vigor and hardiness corresponding to the penetration and sagacity of his mind.

Thus, the Americans have all the qualities requisite for excellent soldiers. Their interests and tastes, it is true, are opposed to war; but by their physical and moral habits, by their speculative tendencies, they are well prepared for it. Although war be a scourge which they seek to avoid as much as possible, they do not fear it; because they know a war must result only to their advantage.

I sincerely believe, from my personal knowledge of all the resources of the American nation, that it is fully prepared to baffle any project which an audacious rival may form against it, with the object of paralyzing or destroying its powerful competition in markets which itself alone had heretofore supplied, and of thus checking its career of prosperity. But I also believe that the Americans, infected with an indifference characteristic of the nation, will, at the commencement of a war, be ill prepared to resist the attacks of a powerful and daring enemy, who, in a few days, by means of steam, may unexpectedly fall on one of the points of their immense coast, and there carry fire and desolation. But the Americans are never daunted by a first reverse ; and their chances ever improve in proportion to the duration of a war.

War undoubtedly may injure commerce, destroy some manufactures, reduce a few villages to ashes, and desolate several parts of the coast; but the vicissitudes of the first shock of a brutal and conquering foe once experienced, the nation would shake to its very centre ; and then would the warlike militia of the Western States join with those of New England and the South in achieving prodigies of valor in defence of their property and institutions.

Besides, the American is aware of the truth taught him by the past: "That victory alone can secure peace to a free people when once engaged in war." He knows then that he must always be prepared to push the combat to that issue, for which he finds in himself, and in the circumstances which surround him, so many favorable chances.

It is useless here to enter into fresh details relative to the material composition of the militia, because I have already treated of this subject in my preceding work on democracy. I may add, from recent official information, that this truly national force amounted, in 1847, to more than *eighteen hundred thousand armed men!* This is, in truth, a formidable resource for the defence of American institutions; for it must not be forgotten that a firearm, in the hands of an American, is not what it is in those of a European, a noisy rather than an effective weapon. Every projectile discharged by the former is almost always fatal, for he is in the habit of holding back his fire until he is sure of his aim. His hunting life has early taught him the value of a load.

Until the present time, the militia laws of the United States have compelled all legal citizens to present themselves under arms, for inspection, during only four days of the year; but no law has yet been enacted relative to their uniform organization, their instruction, and their discipline.

Nevertheless, at these inspections, a million and a half of men never fail to present themselves, with arms and accoutrements in good order. Moreover, the volunteer companies, very numerous in each State, frequently assemble in the principal cities of the seaboard for exercise in shooting with the musket, rifle, and artillery.

No law interdicts the assemblage of troops at any point of the Union where an election is held. But some States have judged it necessary to forbid by law the training of the militia on the day of an election. The object of this law is easily explained. "In the United States, a citizen capable of bearing arms is an elector." The American legislator did not wish to deprive the citizen of exercising the first and most sacred of his rights, that of voting, by imposing on him other duties on that day.

I believe I have sufficiently demonstrated that the American government has, if not from its origin, at least within the last quarter of a century, devoted the utmost attention to national defence, internal prosperity, and the impartial administration of justice. So long as these objects shall continue to interest the nation, nothing need ever be apprehended from the collisions of parties, or from their efforts to weaken the progress of public order, and the prosperity of the republic. The discussion of these various objects—thus virtually appealing to the good sense and opinion of the people, always opposed to the contracted views of individuals, and to the declamations or exaggerated pretensions of parties—becomes a new guarantee of a wise legislation. Besides, the measures necessary to secure these national objects are, as I have just shown, so inextricably bound together as in all instances to act simultaneously.

We conclude, then, that the means adapted to repel an invasion powerfully co-operate in the maintenance of internal peace, by securing the happiness and prosperity of the nation; and that the laws which guarantee the rights and liberties of citizens encourage the increase of population and the development of commerce.

CHAPTER XIII.

SPIRIT OF CONQUEST AMONG THE AMERICANS.

Origin of American society—Influence on this society of the Anglo-Saxon race—Characterized by a spirit of encroachment—Its extraordinary activity requires an extension of territory.

In the policy of nations, questions of the future are not solved directly from fixed and pre-determined principles. Providence has its legitimate influence, and most frequently drives nations into paths, the limits of which are known only to itself—limits which the people themselves scarcely even suspect.

Nevertheless, it is always possible to appreciate the tendencies of a people, from its origin, its history, its political institutions, its social organization, and, above all, from the conditions which its existence as a nation seems to require.

The origin of the Americans is well known. It was fully developed in the early part of this work. It is English. The body of American society is, therefore, of the Anglo-Saxon race, into which Iberian, Scandinavian, French, Celtic, and other races have been merged. These races undoubtedly brought with them the manners, the customs, and the religion peculiar to their distinctive origin, but they soon submitted to the yoke of the majority. That is to say, the majority, which was English, has transmitted to them its feelings, its impressions, its ideas, its manner of comprehending social order, and of contributing to the progress of society through the all-powerful lever of individual interest.

Thus, in many parts of the United States, a number of Germans are found, sufficiently numerous and influential to have their own public organs, and to represent their interests in their own language. Thirty-eight German papers are published in the United States. But these Germans are completely Americanized in their ideas of right, of property, and of liberty. They have retained, of their origin, only their idiom, which, even in the second generation, is effaced, and almost always disappears. Their habits are peaceful, laborious, and parsimonious.

In Louisiana, the last of the French colonies in the United States, the French, as far as origin and language are concerned, are still in the majority; nevertheless, the English language has become necessarily the official, and almost the common, medium of communication. The old colonists alone speak French. The character of the inhabitants is completely modified. They have become as grave as their fellow-citizens of the Anglo-Saxon race. They now seriously think of their individual interests, and are strongly attached to American institutions, to which they owe their happiness, their prosperity, and their power.

It is therefore plainly to be seen that the spirit of the Anglo-Saxon race predominates. Now, the history of that race is perfectly known throughout the whole world.

In America, the spirit of encroachment and invasion which characterizes that race has subjected to its rule all the immense territory that other nations, with rights as well founded as those of the Anglo-Saxons, had previously colonized and settled.

In the historical summary at the commencement of this work, the reader may have appreciated the means that enabled the English to overwhelm the whole continent, as well as the influence of the political and religious manners of its early inhabitants. He may have seen how every step in the progress of Anglo-American society has been marked by acts of encroachment which contributed to the growth of its power—and how its extension has become an indispensable condition of its existence; essential, in fact, to the maintenance of American Democracy.

Two things appear equally necessary for the tranquillity and success of American republics. They must be able to extend their boundaries; and they must find an aliment for their prodigious productive capacity, as well as an outlet to their industry. Such are the necessities of the American nation, necessities derived from its English origin. But its geographical position and political institutions have greatly contributed to develop them. To its geographical position, in fact, it owes its immense commercial advantages. Prosperous and happy through agriculture, it is yet wealthy only by its exchanges. The extent, the variety, and the fertility of its soil place it in the first rank of agricultural nations; but the vastness of its seaboard, which gives it access to all parts of the globe, also places it in the first rank as a commercial and maritime nation.

With respect both to commerce and agriculture, American genius has been directed to an exclusive object, the acquisition of wealth. If it be true that nations, like individuals, pursue their favorite object in different paths, and by different means, it is no less true that in both cases the same result is, in the end, attained.

Ought we not then to conclude, in view of the origin and tendencies of American society, and in view of the principles of commerce, that the United States is advancing towards domination and encroachment?—and that, while seeking to accumulate wealth at home, it is gaining a marked ascendency abroad?

CHAPTER XIV.

CLIMATE OF THE UNITED STATES.

Causes which contribute to render the climate of the United States temperate—Meteorological observations taken by order of the medical department of the army, and the results they establish—Three very distinct climates in the United States, corresponding with the territorial divisions of the coast, of the interior, and of the borders of the great Lakes—The number of clear and cloudy days corresponding with the same divisions—Quantity of water that falls—Mean temperature of various parts of the United States—Theory of storms and gales by Professor Espy.

The climate of a country has at least as much influence on the character, the feelings, and the industrial tendencies of its inhabitants, as well as on the increase and decrease of its population, as its physical configuration. It will not then be amiss to say something here concerning the climate of the United States.

The geographical position of the American Continent insures the United States a mean temperature favorable to the greatest possible development of the physical and intellectual faculties of man.

Various causes tend to insure this favorable result. The first is the presence of the Gulf Stream, near the coast of the Atlantic, which incessantly bears along with it a quantity of warm and

26

humid air, and thus exerts a powerful influence on the temperature of the land. This current, extending along the coast from Florida to the Banks of Newfoundland, also becomes a powerful agent in neutralizing the effects of the masses of floating ice which drift from Baffin's Bay. Without this fortunate natural phenomenon, the coast of the United States would, for a great part of the year, be under the icy influence of the North.

Another cause which equally contributes to render the climate of the United States temperate and salubrious is its admirable hydrographical features: An extensive coast, watered by the Atlantic—a sort of inland sea to the north-west, estimated to contain one-half of the fresh water in the known world—and large and small rivers, which, while refreshing and vivifying all parts of the vast territory of the United States, create none of those insalubrious marshes which the hand of man cannot render fit for cultivation.

A third cause is the absence of mountains so high as to be covered with perpetual snow.

To appreciate, as highly as possible, the value of these general features, it became necessary to compare a certain number of meteorological observations, taken at various points of the United States. The medical department of the army, with the object of accomplishing this result, ordered a series of observations to be made relative to the temperature of the weather, the direction of the winds, and the number of clear and cloudy days in a year, at all the military posts where United States troops were garrisoned.

This meteorological labor, commenced under the auspices of Surgeon-General Lovel, has been continued by his successor Surgeon-General Thomas Lawson, whose tables of results have been recently printed.

The various ports at which these observations have been made are included between latitudes 27° 57′, and 46° 39′ north, and between longitudes 67° 34′ and 95° 43′ west from Greenwich; consequently, embracing 18° 40′ latitude and 25° 39′ longitude. From these observations, I have been able to deduce the following results :—

The United States possesses three very distinct climates, corresponding with three great territorial divisions, which are susceptible of subdivisions or zones, according to the physical causes that may exercise a given atmospherical influence.

These divisions are: The northern, the middle, and the southern. That of the north extends from the extreme northern point of the frontier to the thirty-ninth degree of latitude. It is characterized by a comparatively low mean temperature. The middle division is comprised between latitudes 39° and 35°. It presents the phenomenon of very great irregularity in its temperature, suddenly changing from the extreme of heat to the extreme of cold. The third or southern division extends from 35° to 25°, near Cape Sable, in Florida. In this division, the temperature is excessively warm.

The greatest variety of climate is found in the first division. In fact, along the coast of New England, the vicinity of the sea has not only the effect of approximating the extreme points of temperature of the cold or the warm seasons, but also of materially increasing the mean temperature. Then, in advancing towards the interior, the changes in the temperature are more sudden and violent. Eventually, the extremes of heat or cold become *excessive*.

It has also been proved that the presence of the great Lakes, at the north-west, exerts an influence not less marked than that of the sea on the variations of the climate. Thus, in the vicinity of the Lakes, we find very nearly the same climate which prevails near the coast; but, beyond the point where the influence of the Lakes is experienced, we find the same intensity of heat and cold.

It is true that the mass of water presented by this American Mediterranean, with its natural outlet, the St. Lawrence, is a remarkable feature in the geography of this country. Thus, the basin of the St. Lawrence alone has a superficies of 255,896,860 acres, 50,135,738 acres of which are covered by water for an extent of nearly two thousand miles, from the head of Lake Superior to the Gulf of St. Lawrence. It is not surprising, then, that so vast a mass of water should exert so direct an influence on the climate of the country in its vicinity.

I shall now make some extracts from the above-mentioned tables, relative to the climate of the first division.

At Augusta, in the State of Maine, and situated on the Penobscot, near the Atlantic, in latitude 43° 21′, the mean temperature during the years 1819, 1820, 1821, 1822, and 1823, calculated from daily *maxima* and *minima*, was 45° of Fahrenheit. The thermometer sank to 22° below zero, and rose to 94°, thus showing a variation of 116° between the extremes of heat and cold.

At Fort Crawford, in the same latitude, and consequently in the same division, but far from the influence of the Lakes (Fort Crawford is situated at the point where the Wisconsin empties into the Mississippi), the mean temperature was 48°. The thermometer fell to 23° below zero, and rose to 95°, exhibiting a variation of 118° between the two extremes.

Thus, during these five years of observations, the mean temperature of the year, in the west, and in the interior, was nearly three degrees higher than at the east on the seaboard, and the variation in the thermometer greater by two degrees.

From a comparison of a series of observations made on the climate on the borders of the Lakes, and in the interior, I have deduced the following results :—

At Fort Brady, a military post situated near the falls of Saint Mary, between Lakes Superior and Michigan, in latitude 46° 39′, the mean temperature during the year was 45° ; during the winter, 18° ; during the spring, 40° ; during the summer, 63° ; and during the autumn, 49°.

At Fort Snelling, situated at the falls of St. Anthony, on the Mississippi, in latitude 44° 53′, consequently beyond the influence of the Lakes, and 1° 46′ south of the preceding post, the mean temperature, during the year, was 40° ;—5° lower than on the borders of the Lakes. The mean temperature during the winter was 17°, or one degree lower than on the Lakes. In the spring, the mean temperature was 47°, or seven degrees higher than in the interior. During the summer, the mean temperature was 74°, or 11° higher than on the borders of the Lakes. During the autumn, it was 51°, consequently exceeding by two degrees that of the Lakes.

From a comparison of the observations made at New London, in Connecticut, on the borders of the sea, and those made at West Point, the United States military academy on the Hudson River, in the State of New York, and from sixty to seventy miles in the interior, the following results relative to the mean temperature of the two places were obtained :—

		Fahr.
In winter,	at West Point	33°
"	at New London	34°
In spring,	at West Point	51°
"	at New London	69°
In summer,	at West Point	72°
"	at New London	70°
In autumn,	at West Point	61°
"	at New London	55°

Results which accord with those previously given, and thus, in a measure, confirm the general law relative to the influence of the vicinity of water on the various climates of a country. Moreover, all the preceding observations distinctly prove the existence of three different climates, or zones, the temperatures of which are governed by different laws. In these three zones, the seasons are distinguished not less by a given number of clear or cloudy days during the year, than by the degree of temperature and the direction of the winds which prevail there. However, the characteristic feature of the climate generally in the United States is that the number of clear greatly exceeds the number of cloudy days. It is a rare occurrence for one to be deprived of a sight of the sun for more than three days. Such a circumstance would be considered an atmospherical phenomenon.

Thus, a series of observations, made in various localities, has shown that on the seaboard there is an annual proportion of two hundred and two clear days in three hundred and sixty-five—in other regions, two hundred and forty; that on the shores of the Atlantic the proportion of cloudy or partially cloudy days was one hundred and eight, and in the interior seventy-seven; that the number of rainy days was forty-five on the borders of the Atlantic, and in the interior thirty-one; that snow fell nine days on the borders of the Atlantic, and sixteen days in the interior.

Moreover, these proportions are not accidental. On the contrary, they are in harmony with atmospheric laws and principles; for, as the quantity of rain that falls in a year depends on the degree of evaporation that takes place in the same period, evaporation, agreeably to the general law, must necessarily increase as we approach the equator, and rain must consequently be more abundant where the mean monthly temperature is highest. Now, as this increased quantity of rain, in the maritime and southern regions, generally falls at particular seasons, and only for a shor time compared with that of the colder regions, the yearly number of days without rain, especially in the interior, must be proportionally increased; whilst, in the cold or temperate maritime regions, such as those of the United States over a great part of its coast, different results must necessarily be observed. Thus, although the rains are less abundant in these regions than in warmer ones, they are not the less frequent; but the quantity of water that falls is less. This circumstance explains why, on the coast of New England, the number of rainy or cloudy days is double the number of rainy days in the dry and cold regions beyond the Lakes.

Humboldt has shown the proportion of rain that falls in each of the following latitudes:—

At 0°	96 inches of water.
At 19°	80 " "
At 45°	29 " "
At 69°	17 " "

Moreover, the course of the winds, and their continuance in certain directions, have, in particular localities, a great influence on the quantity of rain that falls during the year. Thus, it has been observed that the prevalence of certain winds occasioned a given proportion of rain. This circumstance is due to the fact that the course of the winds depends on general causes, such as the declination of the sun, the configuration of the coast, and the geographical position of the neighboring continents.

In fine, if the climate of the Atlantic seaboard be compared with that of the interior of the country, beyond the influence of the great Lakes, the differences that characterize the seasons in either of those regions, and the influence they exert on the animal economy and on the vegetable kingdom, are quite striking; for, as was justly remarked by the great Humboldt, "a summer, with a regular and uniform heat, develops the action of vegetation more slowly than the sudden transition from a very cold to a very warm season."

A comparison has been instituted between a series of observations taken at a military post situated in the zone of the Lakes, Fort Brady, near the Sault St. Marie, in latitude 46° 39′, and at Fort Snelling, beyond the zone of the Lakes, at the confluence of the St. Pierre and the Mississippi, in latitude 44° 53′, consequently 1° 46′ to the south of the first point of observation, from which we obtain the following results:—

			Fahr.
Mean temperature	on the Lakes during the year,		41°
"	"	in the interior, "	45°
"	"	on the Lakes in winter,	19°
"	"	in the interior, "	16°
"	"	on the Lakes in the spring,	39°
"	"	in the interior, "	45°
"	"	on the Lakes in summer,	62°
"	"	in the interior, "	72°
"	"	on the Lakes in the autumn,	45°
"	"	in the interior, "	48°

Thus, although the post on the Lakes is in latitude 1° 46′ farther north than that in the interior, and although the mean temperature is four degrees lower at the former than at the latter, still the mean temperature in winter was three degrees *higher;* in the spring, six degrees *lower;* in the summer, ten degrees *lower;* and in the autumn three degrees *lower* than that of the corresponding seasons at the post in the interior.

In the zone of the Lakes, the north-west winds prevail; in the interior, the westerly winds. On the Lakes, the north-west winds blew for seventy-two days in the year; in the interior, the westerly winds for one hundred and eight days. The other prevailing winds were from the south-west, which blew sixty days in the year on the Lakes, and seventy-two days at the post in the interior.

On the Atlantic seaboard, in the vicinity of Boston, the southerly winds prevail; next in frequency, the south-east; then the north-west, and westerly.

In the interior, and far from the influence of these waters, in latitude 35° 47′, the south-east wind prevailed in the proportion of two hundred in three hundred days.

During three years' observations, the number of clear days, during the year, on the Lakes, was one hundred and seventeen; in the interior, two hundred and fifteen. The number of cloudy days on the Lakes was one hundred and twenty-seven; in the interior, seventy-three. There were sixty-three rainy days on the Lakes; in the interior, forty-six. Snow fell forty-five days on the Lakes, and only twenty-nine days in the interior.

Thus, on the borders of the Lakes or within their zone, the number of cloudy exceeds the number of clear days; whereas, in the interior, the reverse is the fact. It has also been seen that the proportion of cloudy days is much greater on the Lakes than on the Atlantic seaboard.

The meteorological observations taken in Canada, Nova Scotia, New Brunswick, and Newfoundland, correspond with the atmospheric results I have just recorded.

So sudden are the changes to which the climate of Canada is liable, that the mercury at Quebec has been observed to fall sixty-nine degrees in twelve hours. In this province, the cold weather commences in November, and continues until May, during which time the snow is more than three feet deep. The cold becomes so intense when the wind blows from the north-east that the mercury freezes in the thermometer, and no longer enables one to make observations. During the winter, the thermometer varies from 31° Fahrenheit to 30° below zero.

In the latitude of Canada, the seasons do not follow each other so gradually as in more temperate climates. In July and August, the heat often rises to 94°, and is more enervating than in the West Indies.

Observations made at Montreal present a mean temperature of 39° during the year. February is the coldest month of the year. The mean temperature during this month has been 10° below zero; the lowest point, 20° below zero. The heat is greatest in July, the mean temperature being 71°; but during this month the mercury rose to 94°. During the year, the wind has been westerly one hundred and eighty-nine days; easterly, forty-six days; northerly, sixty-five days; and southerly, fifty-five days. The amount of rain that fell in the year was fifteen inches and one-fifth of an inch.

The climate of Nova Scotia differs from that of Canada, although both are in the same latitude. This difference results, in a great measure, from the insular position of Nova Scotia, and from the number of its Lakes, which, at certain seasons, overflow a great portion of the soil. The thermometer seldom rises in summer above 87°, and falls only from seven to ten below zero.

The climate of Newfoundland is very similar to that of Nova Scotia. Nevertheless, as the coast is exposed to the influence of the floating icebergs that drift from Baffin's and Hudson's Bays, the summers are less warm, shorter, and, moreover, subject to sudden changes of temperature. The same phenomenon is sometimes seen on the New England coast, as far as Cape Cod.

In the United States, the climate becomes quite modified as we approach the more southern part of the coast. Here, the seasons glide into each other almost imperceptibly.

Thus, in latitude 44° 53′, at Fort Snelling, the difference between the two mean temperatures of the coldest and the hottest months is 62° ; at New Orleans, in latitude 29° 57′, only 52° ; at Tampa Bay, in the Gulf of Mexico, in latitude 27° 57′, only 36°. But we should remark here that, in the territory of Florida, the climate is remarkable, for there one enjoys almost a perpetual spring. Vegetation is never checked. We can bathe in the running streams of that country in winter as well as in summer. It is undoubtedly the most salubrious and delightful climate that I have known in this latitude.

Observations taken at New Orleans, during three years, presented the following results :—

	Fahr.
Mean temperature for the year, ...	66°
" " of winter, ...	52°
" " of spring, ...	66°
" " of summer, ...	79°
" " of autumn, ...	46°
Highest degree of temperature, ...	88°
Lowest " "	28°
Difference	60°

During this period, there were, on the average, two hundred and nineteen clear days, ninety-two cloudy, and thirty-nine rainy days in the year. Mean fall of rain fifty inches.

In winter, the north and north-west winds prevail ; in summer, the south-west and southerly ; in spring, the south-west and south-east ; and in autumn, the northerly and northeast.

In the Western States, within the middle division or zone, and situated in the Valley of the Mississippi, meteorological observations have given us the following results :—

	Fahr.
Mean temperature of winter, ...	32°
" " of spring, ...	48°
" " of summer, ...	68°
" " of autumn, ...	54°

Quantity of water that fell annually, forty inches. Prevalence of south-west winds.

The mean temperature of the year at various points of this zone, and in this valley, varies from 50° to 56° (Fahr.).

In general, the climate of the Valley of the Mississippi is much more temperate and uniform than that beyond the great basin. This circumstance is explained by the constant prevalence of the southerly and south-west winds, which, ascending this basin for a great distance, carry along with them the genial influence of a warm and moist temperature.

In the Valley of the Mississippi, vegetation commences sooner, and is checked later, than at any point in the same latitude beyond this basin. This circumstance, combined with the fertility of its soil, which is of the richest alluvion, and the facilities for transportation afforded by its magnificent river, has occasioned a tide of emigration towards these regions that is truly surprising. This basin, of which, a century and a half ago, the red man was the sole proprietor, now contains eight million inhabitants. Lying between the Alleghany and the Rocky Mountains, it forms the great central region of the United States. Its surface is equal to nearly seven hundred and fifty million acres. Its declination from the sources of the two great rivers that water it to the Gulf of Mexico is scarcely perceptible. But its distinctive characteristic is, undoubtedly, the number and the extent of its navigable rivers, which, emptying into the Mississippi, as into a common reservoir, flow towards the Gulf of Mexico. To the east of the Mississippi, the land is heavily timbered, and presents comparatively few prairies. But to the west, the great prairies, with scarcely any woodland, are very numerous. These prairies are from two hundred and fifty to three hundred and sixty miles in extent.

COMPARATIVE SUMMARY OF BAROMETRICAL OBSERVATIONS MADE AT VARIOUS POINTS OF THE AMERICAN CONTINENT, DURING A PERIOD OF FOUR YEARS.

At Hudson (Ohio), latitude 41° 14′ 40″ N., mean height corrected	30°.034
At Montreal (Canada),	29°.989
At New York (N. Y.),	29°.977
At Quebec (Canada),	29°.919

At Hudson, in Ohio, the mean pressure of the atmosphere was greater in the autumn than in the spring.

At Montreal, it was also greater in the autumn, but not so great in summer.

In the State of Ohio, spring is the driest season, and April the driest month. Winter is the most humid season; December the wettest month. During three years' observations, including 1838, which was remarkable for its extreme dryness, the mean annual fall of rain, in that region, was 34°.635 inches. In a series of ordinary years, the mean fall of rain per annum may be estimated at thirty-six inches, which corresponds with that of the State of New York.

The data we possess relative to the climate of North America are comparatively meagre, certainly insufficient to answer the purposes of science and general economy. It is evident that, before the results of atmospherical phenomena can be generalized, we require a series of observations made simultaneously at various points of this vast continent, with equally perfect instruments, and agreeably to a uniform and regular method. Science, and even the animal economy, would undoubtedly realize a great advantage, were such an undertaking well conducted by means of the thermometer, barometer, hygrometer, and, since the admirable explanation given by Professor Espy, a learned American, of tornadoes, water-spouts, hurricanes, and storms, especially the anemometer. Nevertheless, the observations due to the zeal and scientific knowledge of the medical staff of the army are valuable from the fact that they throw new light on the various climates of the United States, and show the beneficial effect of these climates on the physical, industrial, and intellectual development of man.

On the whole, I have a thorough conviction that the learned men of America will strive to respond to the honorable appeal of Messrs. Arago, Pouillet, and Robinet in their interesting report on the great meteorological labors of Professor Espy, and that they will greatly contribute to extend the sphere of science, and thus cement more closely the social compact, which ought to bind together all parts of the civilized world.

The American government has already shown that it appreciates the position it occupies relative to the tribute every civilized nation owes to science. It has ordered a geographical and hydrographical survey, which, with respect to the nautical details of its own continent, must render it independent of the nations of Europe. This important undertaking, confided to the care of Professor Hassler,* one of the most distinguished astronomers of the age, is

* A depot of charts, as the necessary complement of so great a hydro-

already far advanced; and the public may very soon expect to reap its advantages, at least on the most interesting portion of the American coast.

Let us hope that so enlightened a government—a government which emanates so directly from the people, and which is so deeply interested in basing its policy on immutable truths—will respond, in a still greater degree, to our expectations. The American nation should require its legislators to erect a national observatory. Such an establishment is now an essential complement of the political independence the nation has already so gloriously conquered, and which it should preserve by always maintaining a high position with respect to its knowledge of celestial phenomena, the only accurate basis for human calculations.

The wishes we expressed in 1845 relative to this matter are realized in 1848.

The general government has erected a national observatory at Washington, the seat of government, and has placed it under the control of the Secretary of the Navy.*

Since that time, three others have been erected, at the expense of particular States: one in Jersey City, opposite New York; and another at Philadelphia. The third belongs to the central institution of the Jesuits at Georgetown, in the District of Columbia.

These observatories are in regular communication with one another by means of the Electric Telegraph; and the philosopher thus finds, in the application of electricity, another means of verification in his observations of the celestial phenomena submitted to his investigation.

graphical undertaking, is now required. It is quite as indispensable as the maps and plans of the War Department for military operations.

[This desideratum is now supplied. At the observatory, in Washington city, charts are now deposited and distributed to the different vessels of the United States.—Tr.]

* The observatory at Washington possesses all the instruments and conveniences required for every variety of observation. Its superintendent, Lt. M. F. Maury, of the United States Navy, is already well known to the scientific world as a distinguished astronomer. He is assisted by officers of the navy, and by professors selected for that purpose.—Tr.

CHAPTER XV.

POPULATION OF THE UNITED STATES.

Increase of population in the United States: 1st. Among the whites; 2d, among the free blacks; 3d, among the slaves; 4th, among the blacks, slave and free; 5th, total population of all these classes—Proportions of the sexes—Slavery—Growth of the principal cities of the Union—Conclusions.

WHEN a nation has the wisdom to institute a form of government on the principle of *individual liberty and security*, it thereby secures the increase, and develops the industry, of its people. It thus guarantees national prosperity, with which the augmentation of the population is so directly connected. Thence, population becomes, according to its character, the great source of its wealth and social power.

The various societies from which the American nation ultimately sprang were impressed with this great truth; and it was fortunate for them that their peculiar situation enabled them to put it in practice. Surrounding their cradles, as it were, with institutions in which individual liberty and freedom of conscience were dominant elements, they rapidly grew in power, and finally gave birth to the society now distinguished by the glorious name of the *American Union*. We have seen this society, thus constituted solely on the principles of liberty and equality, arrive at a degree of power unprecedented either in ancient or modern history. In less than fifty years, its population has increased fourfold.

Such is the result of the extraordinary combination of circumstances in which the American nation found itself placed, in a manner, so to speak, providentially. Called to people a quarter of the globe peculiarly favored for the reproduction of man, the Americans have enjoyed, moreover, a privilege which is inestimable. They have been born, have grown up, and have become great, far from the hatred and jealousies which constantly agitate the societies of Europe. The latter indeed, have often, too often, contributed to develop the society of the New World by lavishing on it their choicest blood—the most active and intelligent citizens of the Old World.

But the principal cause of the astonishing progress of the American population is its form of government—its free institutions—its respect for individual liberty. Under these happy auspices, the people of America have been able to expand in every direction without obstacles, according to their taste, their necessities, their inclination, their instinct, or their caprice. Nothing has ever thwarted them. The American citizen has always been able to find the conditions most consonant with his disposition, or most favorable to his personal interest. Now, no system of laws, however wise or prudent they may be, can so completely secure these results as *liberty and individual security.*

In fact, any territory in the United States which presents conditions favorable to the material interests of man will attract, in a very short time, a large population—as large, in fact, as it can support. In fact, we often see populations increase under circumstances almost sufficient to render augmentation impossible.

Thus, the pestilential climate of New Orleans, which presses so heavily on this important commercial city of the South for the space of three or four months* in the year, ought, one would think, to prevent the increase of its population. But the reverse has been the fact ever since Louisiana became a portion of the American Union. New Orleans, in 1830, contained a population of 50,103 inhabitants; according to the census taken in 1840, 102,121—an increase, therefore, of one hundred per cent. in ten years! How do we account for such a result at a point of the American territory where the life of man is most exposed? On the principle that the providential instincts of man will always carry him with ardor where there are chances of success, and where there is full liberty of action under the protection of political institutions favorable to his material welfare.

Let us now examine the increase in the population of the

* During the season in which the Mississippi overflows Lake Pontchartrain, the temperature of lower Louisiana is generally salubrious; but from the end of June to the end of November, the river having retired within its ordinary bounds, disease is frequent. The mortality at New Orleans is, in general, in the proportion of twenty in one hundred.

United States between the years 1790 and 1840, under the favorable auspices we have mentioned.

In the first place, let us remind the reader, of what he already knows, that the people of the United States are divided into two classes—the white and the black; the latter composed of freemen and slaves. I shall therefore present the relative progress of these three classes, which may be the better appreciated by means of tables taken from the last official census of 1840:—

I. INCREASE OF THE WHITE POPULATION.

Years.	Population.	Increase.
1790	3,172,619	
1800	4,307,196	1,134,577 or 35.8 per cent.
1810	5,862,004	1,554,808 or 36.1 "
1820	7,806,695	1,944,691 or 33.2 "
1830	10,541,294	2,734,579 or 35 "
1840	14,189,218	3,647,924 or 34.6 "

II. INCREASE OF THE FREE BLACK POPULATION.

1790	59,512	
1800	104,880	45,378 or 76.2 per cent.
1810	186,446	81,766 or 76.8 "
1820	233,400	46,954 or 25.1 "
1830	319,576	56,176 or 24 "
1840	386,234	66,658 or 20.8 "

III. INCREASE OF THE SLAVE POPULATION.

1790	697,696	
1800	896,849	199,153 or 28.7 per cent.
1810	1,191,364	294,515 or 32.8 "
1820	1,538,036	336,672 or 28.2 "
1830	2,009,040	471,004 or 30.6 "
1840	2,487,151	478,111 or 23.8 "

IV. INCREASE OF THE ENTIRE BLACK POPULATION, FREE AND ENSLAVED.

1790	757,208	
1800	1,001,729	246,521 or 32.2 per cent.
1810	1,377,810	376,081 or 37 "
1820	1,771,436	393,626 or 28.5 "
1830	2,328,616	557,180 or 31.4 "
1840	2,873,385	544,769 or 23.4 "

V. INCREASE OF THE WHOLE POPULATION.

Years.	Population.	Increase.
1790	3,929,827	
1800	5,308,925	1,379,098 or 35 per cent.
1810	7,239,814	1,929,889 or 36.3 "
1820	9,578,131	2,338,317 or 32.3 "
1830	12,869,910	3,291,779 or 34.3 "
1840	17,062,603	4,192,693 or 32.5 "

These tables present the following interesting results: In the first, it will be seen that the increase of the white population has been very uniform since 1790, since it never exceeded 36.1 per cent., and never fell below 33.2 per cent. The second table shows that the proportional increase of the free black population, during the first two decennial periods, was double that of the white population, while in the last period the rate of increase suddenly fell ten per cent. The third table shows that the proportional increase of the slave population varied very little in the first four decennial periods, but fell considerably in the last period. The fourth table shows that the whole black population, free and enslaved, varied exceedingly during the first four decennial periods; and that in the last the proportion was reduced ten per cent. relatively to the preceding periods.

It is true that, during this period, the question of emancipation was agitated with unusual vigor. This circumstance must have had some influence on this reduction, and serves to explain its cause. Other circumstances, however, must have greatly contributed to produce this result. The reduction is principally due to the fact that the free blacks prefer removal to Canada even to a residence in those States where slavery no longer exists. The black race is here inferior to the white in the eyes of man, though not before the law, which, in some States, accords to it electoral rights, and, as it were, places it on a level with the white race.

Finally, a certain number of slaves must also have been removed to Texas.

The fifth table shows that, during the five decennial periods selected as the basis of comparison, that is to say, from 1790 to 1840, the mean proportional increase of the entire population of the United States has been thirty-five per cent. for each decennial period. This prodigious increase can only be explained by a combination of favorable circumstances, the principal of which are, a government founded on the true principles of liberty and individual security; and an extensive territory, where the means of existence are abundant and of easy access, probably the most efficient of all causes in increasing the population of a country.

Nevertheless, as I have already stated, Europe annually contributes in considerable proportion to this increase of numerical power; and it is estimated that one hundred thousand emigrants annually seek repose, as well as employment for their productive faculties, in the United States.

After deducting the population which Europe annually sends to America, the United States still presents a proportional increase to which nothing in Europe can be compared; double that of Russia, where population increases more rapidly than any country in Europe; more than thrice that of France; and more than five times that of all Europe combined.

The following is a comparative estimate of the proportion of whites and blacks, and that of whites and slaves, from 1800 to 1840 inclusive:—

In 1800	there were	4.29	whites to one black, and	4.82	whites to 1 slave.
In 1810	"	4.25	"	4.92	"
In 1820	"	4.20	"	5.07	"
In 1830	"	4.52	"	5.26	"
In 1838	"	4.93	"	5.70	"

Thus, the proportion of whites to slaves has constantly increased since 1800; that of the white to the black race only since 1820.

TOTAL POPULATION OF THE UNITED STATES.

Population.	Males.	Females.	Total.
Whites,	7,249,276	6,939,942	14,189,218
Free blacks,	186,457	199,777	386,234
Slaves,	1,246,443	1,240,708	2,487,151
	8,682,176	8,380,427	17,062,603

This table shows that the males and females are equally distributed throughout the various parts of the Union. In New England, for example, the number of females exceeds that of males. The total population of the States of Maine, New Hampshire, Massachusetts, Connecticut, Rhode Island, and Vermont, exhibits the following proportion:—

Males	1,110,046
Females	1,124,813
Difference in favor of females	14,767

Consequently, 100 males for every 101.33 females.

In the Middle States, namely, New York, New Jersey, Pennsylvania, and Delaware, the males are more numerous than the females. Proportion of each in the total population as follows:—

Males	2,326,117
Females	2,278,228
Difference in favor of males	47,889

Consequently, 100 males for every 97.90 females.

In the Southern States, namely, Maryland, District of Columbia, Virginia, North and South Carolina, Georgia, Alabama, Mississippi, Louisiana, and Florida, the number of males is greater than that of females. The total population of these States is as follows:—

Males	2,615,654
Females	2,549,591
Difference in favor of males	66,063

Consequently, 100 males for every 97.51 females.

In the Western States, namely, Tennessee, Kentucky, Ohio, Indiana, Illinois, Missouri, Arkansas, Michigan, Wisconsin, and Iowa, the males are much more numerous than the females. The total population of this portion of the Union is as follows:—

Males	2,630,359
Females	2,427,795
Difference in favor of males	202,564

Consequently, 100 males for every 92.29 females.

The States in which the number of females exceeds that of males are: New Hampshire, Massachusetts, Rhode Island, Connecticut, Maryland, North and South Carolina, and the District of Columbia. In the District of Columbia, the proportion of females to males bears the relation of 114.98 to 100. South Carolina and Massachusetts present the next greatest difference. The former has 8,322, and the latter 8,212, more females than males.

Among the States in which the male exceeds the female population, Ohio ranks the first: it has 48,737 more males than females.

Next is Illinois, where the excess of males is 38,375. Then comes New York, where the excess is 33,411, and afterwards Indiana, Louisiana, Missouri, Kentucky, &c.

If a comparison be made relative to the entire population of the United States, it will be found that the mean of the difference between the two sexes sensibly diminishes.

The recapitulation I have presented shows the white population to be divided as follows:—

Males	7,249,276
Females	6,939,942
Difference in favor of males	309,334

That is to say, 100 males for every 95.73 females.

And the black population thus:—

Males	free . . .	186,457	1,432,900
	slaves . . .	1,246,443	
Females	free . . .	199,777	1,440,485
	slaves . . .	1,240,708	
Difference in favor of females			7,585

Consequently, 100.53 females to 100 males.

Now, if we take the free colored population separately, the difference between the sexes will exhibit a proportion of 107.13 females to 100 males. With the slave population, the reverse is the case, the difference being in the proportion of 100 males to 99.55 females.

Between Virginia and South Carolina, both slave States, a remarkable difference is observed. In South Carolina, the proportion of females to males is as 106.10 to 100; while in Virginia the proportion of males to females is as 100 to 96.36.

The entire population of the Union exhibits the following results:—

	Males.		Females.
Proportion of males to females . . .	100	to	96.53
" among the whites . . .	100	to	95.73
" " the free blacks and slaves	100	to	102.53
" " the free blacks . . .	100	to	107.13
" " the slaves . . .	100	to	99.53

Thus, among the free blacks, the number of females is much greater than that of males, and that in a proportion exceptional to any other similar combination; whether by a given State, or by an agglomeration of States composing a great geographical division of the country.

The proportional increase of population has considerably varied in each State, according to its geographical position. In some, it has been very small; in others, very great. Michigan, admitted into the Union since the last census, has increased at the rate of 575 per cent.—a remarkable circumstance, which can only be explained by its admirable geographical position. Next to Michigan comes the State of Illinois, its proportional increase being 204 per cent.; an increase produced by the same causes, for these two States occupy the rich and fertile territory included between Lakes Michigan, Huron, and Erie, and the shores of the Mississippi, and are situated on the shortest line of communication between the Northern States and the States which border on the Gulf of Mexico. Arkansas exhibits the next highest proportional increase. Its rich and fertile territory presents varied mineral resources. Its climate is very temperate. The State of Missouri, equally rich in agricultural and mineral productions, comes next in order. Then follows Mississippi, whose increase has been 154 per cent. The last State whose population has augmented at the rate of 100 per cent. is Indiana, also favored by the navigable communications secured by the Lakes, the Ohio, and the Mississippi. Thus, in these six States has the augmentation of population amounted to and exceeded 100 per cent.; and all are situated in the basin of the Mississippi, grouped in the most direct line of communication between the Lakes and the Gulf of Mexico.

Three States, Ohio, Alabama, and Louisiana, have increased more than 60 per cent.; the last at the rate of 77.5 per cent., confirming the remark I made at the commencement of this chapter, that a situation which presents material advantages will always attract a large population, if under the protection of free institutions.

Thus, an immense tide of population has set in towards the west, within the last fifty years, bearing with it more than five million white men to the great basin of the Mississippi—a tide which nothing can arrest, and which one day will people this vast region with more than one hundred million inhabitants.

But it also remains to be proved that this increase of population in the Valley of the Mississippi has taken place to the detriment of the Atlantic States, the oldest of the confederation. In these States, the increase of population has scarcely exceeded five per cent.

Among these, South Carolina has increased least; merely 0.5 per cent.; Delaware, 1.6 per cent.; North Carolina, 2.5 per cent.; Vermont, 4 per cent.; Connecticut, 4.6 per cent.; New Hampshire, 5.7 per cent.; Virginia, 6.7 per cent., and Maryland, 9 per cent. But the States in immediate contact with the Valley of the Mississippi have maintained their proportion. Thus, Pennsylvania has increased 27.9 per cent., and New York 27.3 per cent.

Such a result was inherent in the nature of things, in conformity with the ideas and principles of the Americans. In my opinion, one of the greatest advantages of their social state, an advantage which must powerfully contribute to the maintenance of their democratic institutions, is the circumstance that everything among them is constantly in motion. This condition is eminently favorable to the stirring nature of democracy.

But this result also demonstrates a fact of great importance in its relation to the future administration of the Union, namely, that its numerical and industrial strength is constantly tending towards the north-west. Each day augments the population of the Valley of the Mississippi, which, by its fertility, its extent, its available outlets, and its climate, is destined, ere long, to contain a population double that of the Atlantic seaboard.

Thus, in accordance with the natural order and progress of things, the direction of federal affairs will, in a few years, pass from the hands of the statesmen of the Atlantic States, who created the Union, into those of the statesmen of the Valley of the Mississippi. This important and novel feature in the politics of the Union will be favorable to its interests, and to the stability of its institutions; for, in my opinion, the people of the west are, in a moral and material point of view, placed in a much better condition than their fellow-citizens of the North and South, to judge impartially concerning the great and conflicting interests of the republic; and, above all, they are too directly interested in the preservation of the Union, which alone can maintain and augment their prosperity, not to carry out, practically, the great democratic principles to which the Union owes its existence.

Moreover, the preponderance of these principles in the administrative policy of the people of the Western States has the powerful guarantee of their origin. These States are peopled, for the most part, by emigrants from New England, where democracy has been practiced in its primitive form for a longer time than in any other portion of the United States. Thence the first idea of the *American Union* emanated.

The increase in the population of the free blacks has been greatest in the Western States, namely, Arkansas, Missouri, Michigan, Mississippi, Illinois, Indiana, and Ohio. While it has risen as high as 230 per cent., it has not fallen below 81 per cent. But Arkansas, Missouri, and Mississippi are slave States. In the other States, slavery has never existed.

In the State of Louisiana, the proportional increase of the free blacks has been 52.6 per cent. In the Atlantic States, it has varied from 4.6 to 26.2 per cent.; but a decrease has taken place in New Hampshire, Vermont, Tennessee, and Florida.

Free negroes are found in all the political divisions of the Union, but are most numerous in Maryland, one of the Middle States; then successively in New York, Virginia, Pennsylvania, Louisiana, North Carolina, New Jersey, and Ohio, in each of which their number averages nearly 17,342. In each of the remaining States, the number of free blacks does not exceed from 1000 to 8000.

This class of inhabitants moves but little from place to place, as emigration cannot ameliorate its condition. It remains in an inferior moral position towards the white race—a position which nothing can alter. Therefore, it does not leave the North for the South. Even in the South, the liberated blacks frequently prefer remaining where they are as slaves to seeking a home elsewhere, for in that section they encounter fewer prejudices against them than in any other sections of the Union. The whites are less haughty towards them, because the respective situations of the two races is clearly defined by the condition of slavery.

The slave population has increased more rapidly in the Southern States and towards the borders of the Gulf of Mexico than in any other parts of the Union. In Arkansas, it has increased at the enormous rate of 335 per cent.; in Mississippi, at the rate of 197 per cent.; in Missouri, 192 per cent.; and in Alabama, 124 per cent. In Florida and Louisiana, it has increased at the rate of 58 to 68 per cent.; in North Carolina, 40 per cent.; in Georgia,

38 per cent. But in New York, Delaware, and particularly in Maryland, Virginia, and the District of Columbia, the slave population has greatly decreased.

Slavery, within the last ten years, has been transplanted from the shores of the Atlantic to the borders of the Gulf of Mexico; from the shores of the Delaware and Potomac to those of the Tombigbee and the Mississippi. This change is based upon purely economical considerations, such as the value of labor, and the distinctive nature of the productions of the South. Thus, tobacco, cotton, and the sugar-cane constitute the relative wealth of this section of the Union. The climate of these States, and their fertility of soil, render them alone adapted for such culture. Hence, the preservation of this industry, against which the Western or Northern States cannot compete, is of the highest importance. In this way, the black population increases at the South, not only in a ratio corresponding to the natural advancement of the population in that section, but by virtue of the forced emigration of negroes from States somewhat farther north.

The African race forms a pretty large part of the population of each political division of the American Union, and while it evidently tends to diminish somewhat at the North, it becomes more dense at the South. In three of the Southern States, namely, South Carolina, Mississippi, and Louisiana, the black population is much more numerous than the white.

The States which have abolished slavery are Maine, New Hampshire, Massachusetts, Rhode Island, Connecticut, Vermont, New York, Pennsylvania, Ohio, Indiana, and Michigan. In the last three States, slavery has never existed.

The slave States are New Jersey,* Delaware, Maryland, Virginia, North Carolina, South Carolina, Georgia, Alabama, Mississippi, Louisiana, Tennessee, Kentucky, Illinois, where slavery is about to be abolished, Missouri, Arkansas, Texas, and the District of Columbia.

In the free States, in 1830, there were 6,409,387 whites, and 118,140 negroes. In the slave States, or other portions of the

* Slavery in New Jersey has long since been abolished, as well as in Illinois. In this instance, the author has based his opinions on the fact that a few slaves still exist in New Jersey. These are now old, and are gradually dying off.—Tr.

United States where slavery still exists, 4,115,875 whites, and 2,210,486 negroes.

In 1840, in the free States, there were 8,659,550 whites, and 145,863 negroes; in the slave States, 5,529,558 whites, and 2,727,595 negroes.

The white race has therefore increased at the rate of 35.1 per cent. in the free States, and 34.3 per cent. in the States where slavery still exists.

The entire black population, free and enslaved, has increased at the rate of 23 per cent.

Therefore, it is clearly established that the increase of the black race in these respective divisions is much less than that of the white race. Thus, although the blacks incessantly increase in the South, because of the advantageous application of their labor, the white race still presents its numerical superiority, as well by reason of natural augmentation as on account of emigration. Therefore, I conclude that, in the Southern States, the two races may remain in the same relative condition, without seeking a conflict the one with the other, unless germs of discord are intentionally thrown among them.

I repeat my conviction that, if inconsiderate agitators do not meddle with the question of slavery, in those portions of the United States where it still exists; if slavery be left to its natural course; if reliance be placed on the interest, on the enlightened reason of man quietly to bring about the solution of this question, so often agitated without any real advantage; if, I, say, the hirelings of *English philanthropy* do not excite a spirit of rebellion among this class of laborers, I cannot apprehend, with authors who have written on this subject, any struggle between the white and black population of the southern portion of the Union.

If, however, in any event which I cannot foresee, this conflict should take place, it would be fatal to the black race; for it is not to be denied that the Anglo-American race extends from the St. Lawrence to the shores of the Mississippi, and is rapidly advancing from the borders of the Atlantic to the slopes of the Rocky Mountains. A common interest and common sentiments animate this mass of men. Powerful through the *Union*, they wish to see its maintenance based on the respect due to the Constitution which created it. Now, this constitution formally declares that the federal government shall protect each State of the

Union against all internal violence. In an emergency, then, the people of the South could rely on the support of their brethren of the North—a support which the latter would be impelled to render through a sense of self-interest, which among the Americans is all-powerful and sacred. At the time the federal compact which emancipated the English colonies of America, and raised the United States to the rank of an independent nation, was drawn up, each State made certain reservations and stipulations relative to its rights of property of every description. The slave States were admitted into the Union, with their mixed population of white and black, free and enslaved. A given proportion of slaves, three-fifths of the entire number in the United States, were represented by votes, with the object of equalizing the distribution of representatives in the federal Congress among the several States.

The slave States were, therefore, placed on an equal footing with the other States in the federal compact only by reason of the admission of a part of the black population as a basis of representation in the National Congress. At a later period, the United States, not finding, in the federal compact, sufficient strength for a national government, adopted a new constitution, which modified in no respect the distinctive social existence of each State, with or without slaves. Nevertheless, each State voluntarily surrendered a part of its rights as a separate sovereignty, to give additional strength to the central government. This act constituted, in fact, the American *Union*. To assail this condition of things at the present time would be to violate directly the fundamental compact of the Union, and to invalidate the Constitution. The Americans are too wise to foresee the possibility or even the contingency of such a result. They will, therefore, abstain from interfering, through their national legislature, with a state of things that each State alone has the right to modify in its individual capacity.

Without doubt, should a fatal struggle take place between the whites and blacks, whatever its exciting cause, the latter would have on their side all the energy of despair. At the commencement of the struggle, they would possess, at certain points, even the advantage of numbers. But the whites would soon acquire the ascendency by means of their immense superiority of strength, intelligence, and resources. Moreover, the relative position of the two races is in no respect analogous to their position in the West Indies, where the whites are surrounded by a far superior number of blacks. In short, the latter would not find in America positions inaccessible to the whites, positions in which the black race alone is able to sustain itself. Florida, a short time since, was the only point on the American continent where negroes, Indians, and agitators could hope to act with advantage against its unfortunate population. Now that the Indian war is terminated, and the wreck of that unfortunate race is about to cross the Mississippi, and to bid farewell to the land of its fathers, civilization will at once assume its habitual supremacy over savage life, and the territory will soon receive all the population it is able to support. Then, on the Gulf of Mexico, as on all other points of the American territory, the white race will resume its numerical ascendency, in harmony with its destiny.

The American Union already possesses five large capitals, the smallest of which has a population of one hundred thousand, and the largest, over three hundred thousand inhabitants. Of these cities, four are situated on the Atlantic seaboard, and one on the borders of the Gulf of Mexico. The last has doubled its population in the last ten years, and from its admirable position in the Valley of the Mississippi, of which it is the necessary mart, as well as the only outlet and factory, nothing can prevent its augmentation in a corresponding ratio, until it becomes the most populous city in the United States. Of all the cities in the Union whose population exceeds one hundred thousand souls, New York, after New Orleans, has increased most rapidly. But Brooklyn, on Long Island, opposite New York, and, like this city, possessing the great advantage of a situation on the waters of New York Bay, exhibits a still greater proportional increase. Its population has increased tenfold in the last ten, and twentyfold in the last twenty years.

Cincinnati, on the Ohio, the great port of the west, has exhibited the same proportional increase as New Orleans. Its population has doubled in the last ten years. Louisville, another city of the west, situated immediately above the falls of the Ohio, has increased in the same ratio. Pittsburgh, which, from its favorable position at the head of navigation of the Ohio, is destined to rival Cincinnati in prosperity and in the ratio of its development, has, like the latter city, advanced with rapid strides. Its population would, perhaps, exceed that of Cincinnati, were the inhabitants of its suburbs duly estimated.

The growth of certain cities in the fertile territory of the west, or of those which, through their commercial relations, are dependent on the west, has, in the last decennial period, been truly remarkable. The population of St. Louis, for example, the capital of Missouri, situated at the confluence of the Missouri and the Mississippi, has trebled. Rochester, and Buffalo, in the western part of New York, and connected with the Western States by means of the Lakes and the New York Canal, contain each, at present, twenty thousand inhabitants. In 1830, the population of each did not exceed from eight to ten thousand. Lastly, the population of the manufacturing city of Lowell, the Manchester of New England, in the State of Massachusetts, has increased more than threefold in the last ten years!

Of all these cities, creations of the last half century, the most remarkable, doubtless, is Cincinnati, the metropolis and the great market of the west. It is the work of the clear-sighted, alert, and indefatigable industry of the people of New England, the Yankees. It is a proof that the power of man, in the persevering and steady pursuit of the object of his desires, is sufficient to balance, and even to overcome that of nature. Pittsburgh, in fact, possessed immense natural resources for large manufactories, and Louisville an advantageous position at the falls of the Ohio as a mart for produce; nevertheless, Cincinnati has outstripped its two rivals in population, wealth, and industry.

The inhabitants of Cincinnati have secured this prosperity to themselves by one of those instincts peculiar to the eminently practical and calculating genius of the North Americans; they have concentrated their efforts on one object, the development of their city by means of industry. By making roads and canals, and constructing railways at proper locations, they have rendered Cincinnati the pivot of a system of communication by which it is placed in relation with the great centres of the Atlantic seaboard.

It is scarcely fifty years since the lot on which Cincinnati is built was sold for forty-eight dollars. In 1810, the population did not exceed two thousand; in 1830, it amounted to twenty-five thousand; in 1835, to thirty-five thousand; and it is now nearly fifty thousand. In 1826, the capital it invested in manufactures was two million dollars, and in 1840, six million dollars. The number of its stage-coaches is fifty; and it has sixty weekly mails. Two thousand steamboats annually take their departure from the city. In fine, the people of Cincinnati export produce to an amount exceeding in value six million dollars. This produce is distributed among the growing populations of the Western States, as well as of the Southern States, engaged principally in the production of cotton.

The great centres of commerce and population, on the Atlantic seaboard, have increased far less rapidly than the cities of the west. Nevertheless, they have exhibited remarkable progress. New York, which is, in fact, the real capital of the Union, and the greatest commercial seaport in the world, next to London, has almost uniformly advanced, each decennial period, at the rate of rather more than 57 per cent. This increase exceeds the proportional increase of the entire population of the State one hundred per cent. Boston, which, for the importance of its commerce, rivals New York, exhibits the same proportional increase. Philadelphia and Baltimore have augmented in a somewhat slower ratio.

North America presents, in the progress of its population, a spectacle without parallel in the history of the world; a spectacle which well deserves the attention of political economists, for it demonstrates the advantages of free institutions in relation to the progress of humanity.

The American republic was originally composed of *thirteen States*. The number has increased to *thirty*.

At the close of the last century, the population of the United States was less than four millions, somewhat below that of Belgium. At the present time, it is at least *twenty-one millions*, exceeding that of Great Britain. It has therefore quintupled in less than half a century.

In my opinion, nothing can soon check this progress, for circumstances favorable to the development of the human family will long continue to exist in America. It is, in fact, the only spot in the world where man can find liberty, and individual security, in addition to a vast territory which he can explore, agreeably to his means and tastes; and of all conditions, as we have elsewhere said, these are most favorable for the augmentation of population.

CHAPTER XVI.

RELIGION IN THE UNITED STATES.

Religious character of the early inhabitants—Diffusion of knowledge among them —Diversity of religions gives dignity and strength to the religious sentiment—Character of Christianity—Catholicism in the United States—Influence of the democratic principle on religious observances.

WITHOUT faith, there is no religion; without religion, there can be no democratic society. Democracy is faith. It is unable to maintain itself, to govern man, to develop his faculties, and insure his prosperity, unless it be loved and truly respected; it is inoperative unless men confide in the sincere devotion, in the moral worth of the rulers they have chosen. Religion is the common source of all the benevolent ideas that exercise influence on mankind.

The great advantage of American society is that it was originally constituted in accordance with these convictions. The early Americans had the good fortune to perceive the harmony which exists between the Christian faith and their political principles. Therefore, all entertain fixed religious opinions. Faith is merged in their political existence; nor can they conceive of a democratic society without it any more than they can conceive of the navigation of a ship without a pilot. Thus, the source of their democratic instincts is religion, and its constant practice in the daily pursuits of life. The ideas the Americans entertain of the Almighty, of his relations to mankind, of the nature of the soul, have dictated their duties to their fellows, as well as their course of conduct, the character of their administration, their respect for the laws they have adopted, and, in fine, the principles of order so eminently characteristic of American society.

Doubt concerning matters of faith never enters the heart of an American. He constantly thinks of the destiny of his human nature. Accustomed to such reflections from an early age, he cultivates them with ardor. He habitually seeks to acquire clear ideas on religious subjects. He is always as ready to defend his religious as his political principles. With him, both are all-powerful. He intrusts to no one the care of these matters. Implicit submission to a dogma which assumes to guide him independent of his own religious sentiments, he would consider an act of cowardice as despicable as the support of a political party, without due conviction or enlightened devotion. He acknowledges an authority in religious as well as in political matters. But this recognition harmonizes with his convictions. He yields to it in the same way he yields obedience to the laws.

The American people are therefore religious by their origin, by conviction, and by democratic principles. But what gives security to religion among them is the universal enlightenment of the people, and the circumstance that religious teachers, while they point the mind of man to the true object of desire beyond the present life, do not condemn a rational care for the things of this world. Material enjoyments are allowed, and in a measure even encouraged, but as a means of more surely attaining that Christian goal which every one should strive to reach according to his talents, his circumstances, and the duties imposed on him by society.

Thus, all the various elements of this society are harmonized; all tend to a common result. In this society, man moves onward solely by the power of his intelligence, in accordance with the principles of equality—principles to which the Christian faith imparts a strength, an activity, and a life which emanate from a superhuman source.

Need we be astonished, then, that, in a society where such a state of things exists, religion preserves its empire? Undoubtedly not. For faith is as clear as light itself, the existence of which the blind alone can deny. But with respect to belief in the Deity, none of this class can exist.

But, in the United States, where knowledge is diffused in a degree equal to the spread of the democratic principles on which society is based, and where, consequently, men are placed on a common level, ideas of Christianity are the same. All profess the same religion, the same faith, and entertain the same convictions, though in some cases they adopt different vestments, if I may thus express myself when speaking of various sects which seem merely like so many branches borne by the tree of the

Christian religion. This exuberance in growth of the same tree has, by weakening the power of the Established Church, powerfully assailed its fundamental dogma. But the dissenters, thus augmenting, have spread the religion of Christ without securing to any one sect peculiar privileges, or an ascendency above another. This is, undoubtedly, an immense advantage in relation to public morals, for it greatly contributes to give stability to the excellent institutions of that country. Divergence in religious opinions is, in fact, the most favorable of all conditions for the power and dignity of the religious sentiment, such as it can and ought to be understood by an enlightened society.

Every one in the United States professes a religion, which he practically observes with strictness. No one feels unwilling to perform the first duty which Providence has imposed on man. Each, while discharging this duty, seeks to fulfil all the conditions it involves. Religion is not a law of the State. It is more than that. It is a law of conscience. By obedience to its requirements, we set an example of order and discipline which should govern every society desirous of living and prospering under democratic institutions.

Christianity, undoubtedly the most beautiful religion that has shed its light on the world, is, like every institution, the product of time, the fruit of reflection, the result of experience. By observing the fruit it has borne in the New World, we become better enabled to recognize its immortal supremacy. The various transformations to which it has been subjected, the struggles it has had to sustain, the resistance, in a word, it has encountered, have had a miraculous effect on its progress. In fact, Christianity must always be militant to attract superior minds. Otherwise, such minds would abandon it for politics and philosophy.

What constitutes the strength of Christianity in America is that the most able and illustrious men in the country yield it their homage, take an active part in its diffusion, and preach its doctrines. There, Christianity advances coincidently with all other manifestations of truth. There, nothing is stationary. There, the teachers of religion devote their attention to preserve Christianity in all its social importance, to draw from it all it contains fruitful for humanity, and all that is consoling for the suffering. But, above all, they are careful not to place it in antagonism to the material welfare or individuality of man, on which, in fact, they repose; and this, in my opinion, is a great proof of wisdom; for, to make proselytes at the present epoch of equality and positive ideas, it is certainly unnecessary to decry wealth, and the comfort it secures to those whose industry has been incessantly devoted to its acquisition.

Christianity, in the United States, is clothed in its primitive, independent, democratic character. There it preaches, as well as furnishes an example of, equality and human fraternity. Its maintenance is not the work of a privileged caste, or of powerful individuals. It is a tie that binds together all classes of society.

Another characteristic of Christianity in the United States is that the deference shown to the externals of religion is never confounded with the homage due only to the Supreme Being. Forms and external observances are distinguished for their simplicity, or, rather, so to speak, these have no existence. A declaration of faith, and intercourse between the creature and the Creator through prayer, constitute the substance of practical Christianity. Ceremonies there are none. The imposing simplicity of an assemblage of men drawn together by a common object, that of rendering thanks to God for the mercies he has vouchsafed to extend to the community, and of profitably listening to an exposition, by the ministers of religion, of the moral end every society organized on the healthful and durable basis of equality ought to strive to attain, is everywhere exhibited.

Catholics are the only sect which, in a measure, form an exception to this general rule. Nevertheless, it must be acknowledged that Catholicism in the United States differs essentially from Catholicism in Europe. It is the same faith, subjected to the same rules, to the same discipline, to the same spiritual head; but its forms have undergone considerable modification through the intellectual sway of the majority, to which the Catholic priests have had the good sense to submit. In matters of religion as well as in politics, the majority rules in the United States.

By thus respecting the instincts of American society, by keeping pace with all the Christian sects in America, by coming in contact with none of their prejudices, by redoubling their zeal, talent, and devotion in behalf of the great cause of civilization and the onward march of society, the Catholics have made rapid progress. Faith and tolerance are the banners under which Catholicism advances. It is not the unity of the government of the Roman Church which constitutes its strength and secures its advancement; for, so susceptible are the democrats of the United States, that they hold the governmental unity of the Roman Church in suspicion. In fact, this unity and democracy are antagonistic forces, and cannot advance in harmony on the same territory. The one must give place to the other.

The circumstance most favorable to the extension of Roman Catholicism in the United States is this: The American Catholic exhibits a tendency to depart from the unity of the church, because it involves the recognition of a temporal chief, whose origin, like his principles, conflicts with democratic unity.

So powerful is the Puritan and democratic influence in the United States, that, in my opinion, the number of Roman Catholics would sensibly diminish, were it not so immeasurably recruited by the emigrants who annually arrive from Europe, and especially from Ireland.

The Catholic population in the United States amounts, at present, to more than one million three hundred thousand; in other words, the proportion of members the Roman Church holds in its bosom, compared to those who may, in that country, be considered to have left it, is as 1 to 13.1.

Certainly, this proportion of population, gathered around the same faith, is very large, compared to that which has separated from it in a thousand different directions. This increase of Catholics, of late years, need excite no surprise. I ought, however, to acknowledge that it presents a somewhat alarming aspect when we take into consideration the fact that the principles of the Fathers of the Roman Church are antagonistic to democratic unity and democratic institutions. The occult power of Rome has ways against which all democratic societies can scarcely know too well how to guard. The spirit of humble resignation and affected tolerance which characterizes the Catholic clergy of America should not blind these societies to the sinister views that are cherished with remarkable steadiness of purpose by a power that ever seeks, with the object of securing temporal dominion, and of thus intermeddling in political affairs, the subjection of souls, rather than the diffusion of the light, and the administration of the consolations, of the religion of Christ. Still, I by no means wish to deny the good effected by the Catholic clergy, or the immense services that certain religious communities, and among others the missionaries, have rendered to the cause of civilization in the New

World. Of this fact, I have myself collected substantial proofs in my extensive travels in North America. And to the merit and noble self-devotion of our French missionaries I trust I have rendered adequate justice in the former part of this work.

Moreover, up to the present time, Catholicism has been characterized by the same spirit of liberty and independence which has exerted so powerful an influence on all religious associations in the United States. I am pleased to hope, while acknowledging the weaknesses too common to the human intellect in the New as well as in the Old Hemisphere, that the Americans will never attempt to reconcile two contradictory principles—that of allegiance to the temporal power of the pope, as far as their religious convictions are concerned, and that of the democratic unity which prescribes the sovereignty and independence of the nation, and, by consequence, of all the citizens of which it is composed.

Besides, such a state of things, or schism, has, to my knowledge, already existed in the United States; but I am not aware that society has been thereby endangered. I have heard the temporal power of the pope denied by the Catholics of Louisiana, who, nevertheless, zealously persevered in all the observances of the Catholic religion. It certainly cannot be impossible for the Catholics of the United States to profess faith in the doctrines of their church without submission to the absolute authority of a head who resides beyond the American territory. The times of absolutism in religious belief have passed away, and the present state of knowledge, especially among the Americans, precludes their return.

It is my belief that, in periods remarkable for the prevalence of democratic principles, men should devote their utmost attention to Christianity. But they should throw off the trammels of the Roman Catholic Church, whose laws and temporal requirements widely diverge from true Christianity. To remain within the pale of this church, to submit to the sway involved in the assumption of its temporal unity, would involve a degree of spiritual resignation but little in harmony with the habits which are the fruit of liberty. Now the influence of liberty is daily extending with such rapidity as to destroy every feeling of servility even among the organs of pontifical authority!

I shall conclude this chapter by remarking that the religious sects of the United States furnish a class of men ever disposed to check, by all the potency of religious conviction, the inroads of vice, and of loose morals, the two greatest enemies of liberty.

To attempt to estimate the duration of American institutions would be an impossibility. All human works must have an end as they have had a commencement. But as this result can take place only through the introduction of vice into the community, I regard the noble and pacific influence of Christianity as one of the means of indefinitely retarding it. In America, Christianity never swerves from its mission. While inculcating morality, without forbidding the pursuit of material interests, it constantly leads man to recognize this great truth: "That, as children of a common Providence, we should render to God, as an offering, our first and our latest vows."

CHAPTER XVII.

EDUCATION IN THE UNITED STATES.

Mutual relations of education and religion—Touching example of the devotion of the early emigrants in the cause of public instruction—Law relative to public instruction in New England—Existence of the same laws in the Western States—System followed in Ohio; in New York—Condition of education in the United States in 1840—Sunday schools—Public course of lectures for young mechanics of various trades—Inclination for intellectual pleasures found in every class of society—Mean level in American society—In the United States, no special schools for instruction in political economy and mercantile affairs—Society considered the best school—Democracy favorable to the development of knowledge.

I HAVE already stated, in the preceding chapter, that religion in the United States is of the most elevated kind, and uncontaminated with the prejudices of ignorance, and that its wide diffusion is attributable to the general education of the people. No society has ever made more arduous efforts and greater sacrifices to extend the benefits of instruction. Religion and education among the Americans afford each other mutual support, and thus serve to maintain, in their integrity, the true principles of liberty and equality.

This blending of religion and instruction, the only durable basis of democracy, was characteristic of the early emigrants, and was developed, from the day of their arrival in the land to which they were expatriated, with a fervor equaled only by their faith, and by their desire to be free.

In September, 1636, sixteen years after the landing of the Pilgrims on Plymouth Rock, the administrative council of the colony, then called the *General Court,* voted two thousand dollars to found a university. This institution took the name of Harvard, after one of its first benefactors. At that time, two thousand dollars was an enormous sum, and equivalent to a whole year's income of the colony, then spread over a space of thirty-seven thousand acres. But, when we consider the circumstances of these emigrants, this donation appears in a still more meritorious light. The colony was in want of everything. It was constantly harassed by the natives. Its inhabitants were few in number, not exceeding five thousand families at most. In addition to this, the ferment occasioned by differences of religious opinion menaced internal peace. Notwithstanding these unfavorable circumstances, we say, the colonists did not hesitate to assume the expense of founding and maintaining an establishment for public instruction.

Such an act is too honorable to the memory of the courageous emigrants who planted one of the first colonies in New England, to be overlooked by the historian. This act alone shows their character and spirit; their just appreciation of the importance of education; and is a striking instance of the efforts they made, in truly trying times, to insure the advantages of education to the citizens destined to enjoy their inheritance.

Thus, the Americans, from the earliest period of their history, have understood clearly that the maintenance of equality among men requires, as an indispensable condition, equality as much as possible in the minds of men themselves, through the common enjoyment of adequate means of education.

Each society, with laudable emulation, strove to rival the other, in the application of means requisite to prevent the spread of ignorance, and thus to secure the blessings of liberty.

A law in New England compelled every community of fifty families to support a school of primary instruction, to which all the inhabitants were obliged to send their children. In towns which numbered at least one hundred families, the inhabitants were compelled by law to maintain a high school, where pupils might be prepared for admission into Harvard University. By this means, the American youth could find, on their native soil, all the elements of a complete education.

Such were the wise regulations by which the Puritans of 1647, that is to say, of the first generation, sought to secure, for their new country, a healthy population, capable of appreciating the blessings of liberty. True, as we have said, the resources of these men were very limited; but they made the greatest sacrifices in laying a foundation of universal instruction. What an example! What a practical exhibition of democratic institutions!

Time and circumstances have gradually modified this law, the most sacred of all social laws. It has not been transmitted to us in all its force, in all its purity, in all its primitive vigor: and the injunction to every family to send its children to a primary parish school has not always had a uniform degree of force. But its spirit has remained the same, pervading all of the Eastern States, and sowing deep and lasting seed throughout all parts of the Union to which the children of New England have emigrated—thus preparing the rising generation to preserve the freedom which prior generations had conquered and maintained.

In Massachusetts, out of a population, between the ages of four and sixteen, numbering 185,058, 12,000 are attached to private institutions, and 173,058 depend on public institutions for their education. Nevertheless, of this number, only 133,448 are found in public schools during the summer, and the average attendance is only 96,525. In winter, the number is greater, amounting to 159,056; average attendance, 107,542. The number of teachers is 6,782, of which 4,282 are females. This disproportion in the number of teachers of the different sexes appears to be quite a remarkable feature in the eyes of a European; but the fact is that in the United States it is as common to see women employed in teaching as it is rare to see them working in the fields! The average salary per month of male teachers is thirty-two dollars; of female teachers twelve dollars.

We must confess that we are astonished at so great a difference in the compensation of these two classes of teachers, especially when we consider the fact that good common female operatives in the manufactories receive much higher wages. Nevertheless, the number of females who make application for positions as teachers augments every year, and in a proportion much beyond that of males.

There are three normal schools in Massachusetts, where persons of either sex, destined for public teaching, can receive a special education.

In the primary schools, reading, writing, arithmetic, orthography, English grammar, and geography are taught.

In order to encourage the formation of a library at the seat of each public school, the State has pledged itself to appropriate fifteen thousand dollars a year to every township which shall raise an equal sum, either by subscription or donation. This money is annually applied to the purchase of books, an arrangement productive of the most happy results. By this means, more than forty thousand volumes have been purchased in six months for the use of schools.

Each township, as I have before stated, is bound to supply funds for the education of its children. The average assessment a year for each child, during the year 1841, was two dollars and seventy-one cents; and in 1842 it was two dollars and eighty-four cents.

In Ohio, Indiana, Michigan, Illinois, and Missouri, where emigrants from New England are found in large number, primary instruction, ever following in the wake of this people, extends its blessings to the threshold of every citizen.

Ohio is one of the States in which education has made the greatest progress. In the constitution of that State, it has been laid down as a principle that "religion, morality, and education are essential to the existence of good government, and to the welfare of man." The public schools are immediately under the control of the government; but this control conflicts in no instance with the rights and liberty of conscience.

The system of public instruction is there founded upon the best possible basis. The State has also made provision for the establishment of high schools and universities.

By virtue of this vast and judicious system of education, Ohio has become the intellectual rendezvous of young men from the west, from the south-west, and from the east, who, while imbibing at its schools salutary lessons in morals and science for the guidance of their future life, become familiarized with the contemplation of the vast prodigies to which the rich countries of the west have given birth; wonders which, thus early impressing their youthful imaginations, implant in their being that germ of activity and spirit of adventure which are the distinctive elements of their character.

Ohio contains six large colleges at which degrees are conferred, and a great number of secondary schools. Each village has its primary school.

The education of females receives an equal degree of attention. In every city of considerable size, well-directed institutions are to be found, where their moral and intellectual culture is secured in such a manner as to make them in an equal degree honorable mothers and useful companions in life.

In New York, the introduction of primary education, under the immediate protection of the Legislative Assembly, dates from the year 1795, a period at which one hundred thousand dollars were annually appropriated for its support. In 1805, the legislature devoted, as a permanent fund for the purposes of general education, the proceeds of certain public lands. Public instruction again attracted the attention of the legislature in 1812, when the system was regulated, and a liberal provision made for its necessities.

In 1841, there were 10,769 common school districts in the State, which received, exclusive of the city of New York, 592,564 children over five and under sixteen years of age.

The public school fund amounted, at that time, to six million dollars.

The salary of teachers was eighteen dollars per month.

These schools are open, on the average, eight months in the year.

Experience has proved that the interest public instruction awakens is considerably enhanced when the expense of the establishment of schools is borne as well by the districts as by the State.

Public instruction in all the States of the Union has been considered by legislators an object of the first importance. Thus, in every State, there exists a school fund which is based on a large dotation of public land, the interest of which is exclusively devoted to purposes of education. All the advantages arising from augmentation in value of these lands accrue to the institution for which they were set apart. A direct tax, levied on the inhabitants, also furnishes its contingent to the support of public schools. The school fund is often further augmented by voluntary donations.

The following statement, obtained from official reports, exhibits the present condition of public instruction in the United States:—

Primary or Common Schools.—Number of schools, 50,000; pupils, 2,000,000. Pupils educated at the public expense, 468,261.

High Schools, and Boarding Schools.—Number of schools, 6,000; pupils, 250,000.

To these establishments, a great number of complementary and industrial schools must be added, in which, by an admirable arrangement, the youth devote one-half of their time to a scholastic and the other half to a practical life, and thus, by their labor, contribute towards their own support. These industrial schools, by virtue of their success, have of late years greatly multiplied. They are established in the vicinity of large cities, both in the Eastern and Western States. With this class must also be associated certain special schools attached to large manufacturing establishments, where the children of operatives, and even adults, during hours not devoted to their regular occupations, receive a knowledge of the principles that will enable them to become good workmen or skillful foremen.

University Instruction.—The number of colleges or universities (in the United States, these terms are synonymous) is 178, of which 37 are medical schools; 34 theological seminaries; and 9 law schools. Number of students, 20,000. In all Europe, there are only 117 colleges, and 94,000 students.

In the State of New York, with a population of 2,500,000 inhabitants, there are 12 colleges, and 1285 students; that is to say, a college for every 200,000 inhabitants and every 167 students. In Prussia, with a population of 14,000,000 inhabitants, there are seven universities and 5,220 students; or, one university for every 2,000,000 inhabitants and every 373 students. Therefore, in Prussia, one inhabitant in 2682 is a member of a university, and in New York one in 1946.

In 1842, France, with a population of 34,494,000 souls, contained fourteen royal colleges, and 18,697 students; or one college for every 2,420,000 inhabitants. That is to say, one person in every 1845 attends college.

In Pennsylvania, with a population of less than 2,000,000, there are 20 colleges and 2054 students, or one in 973.

In the New England States, with a total population of about

2,250,000 inhabitants, there are 19 colleges, and 2857 students, or one in 787.

In Great Britain, with a population of 27,000,000, there are 27 universities and 17,750 students, or one in 1521.

Thus, the regular means of education are much more abundant in the United States than in any part of the world.

The large colleges or universities, in the United States, are generally under the supervision of a council of instruction designated indiscriminately, a *Board of Trustees*, *Board of Directors*, or *Corporation.* This council, appointed by the State legislatures, is invested with great power, which it seldom has sufficient independence to exercise in all its plenitude. For instance, it is empowered to control the administration of the college, to appoint professors, to grant degrees, to determine the mode of instruction, and the programme of studies. The law, certainly, could not place a greater responsibility in the hands of a few directors.

The college course comprises Latin, Greek, mathematics, and the natural and physical sciences; it also includes the ancient and modern languages, Hebrew, French, Spanish, Italian, Portuguese, and German.

In Latin, the course of study is Livy, Tacitus, Horace, Cicero, Juvenal, &c. In Greek, Xenophon, the Iliad, Sophocles, Æschylus, Demosthenes, &c.

In mathematics, plane and solid geometry, algebra, plane and spherical trigonometry, the application of algebra to geometry, and analytical geometry.

Also, mechanics, hydrostatics, optics, and astronomy, chemistry, geology, and botany.

Rhetoric, theoretical and practical, philosophy, political economy, and the Constitution of the United States, are also studied.

There are also special courses, apart from the ordinary instruction in the college, on electricity, magnetism, and acoustics; on ancient and modern history; on the differential and integral calculus; on mineralogy and anatomy; on the application, in fine, of science to the arts.

The students remain four years at college. Their age is generally from twelve to twenty years. Eighteen is the age of the greatest number.

This programme, which is the course followed at Harvard College, one of the most celebrated in the United States, is very nearly the same as that pursued at all the other universities.

The government of the United States supports two national schools; one for the army, the other for the navy.

The first, under the name of the Military Academy of West Point, has considerable celebrity. It was founded on the same basis as the Polytechnic School of Paris. Its object is to impart instruction in the higher branches of mathematical science.

The second is at Annapolis, on Chesapeake Bay, in Maryland. This institution is very flourishing, and furnishes a nursery of excellent officers for the national marine.

But in addition to all these rather official means of spreading information among all classes of society, the Americans have availed themselves of other resources, which have their foundation in individual feeling, and which produce equally happy results on the moral and intellectual condition of the people. I allude to *Sunday Schools*, which are in full operation in various parts of the United States.

These schools are generally under the immediate superintendence of those who are most favored by fortune and education. Men and women belonging to this class of society, which, in France, would be called the high *bourgeoisie*, strive to rival each other in devotion to the cause of instruction among the laboring classes—a pious work, which finds its reward in the satisfaction that ever attends the performance of an act of charity.

It is estimated that there are sixteen thousand Sunday schools in the United States; and that in these more than one million children are taught to read. The principles of instruction given in these institutions are derived directly from the Holy Bible. For this purpose, books are employed in which the Old and New Testaments are reproduced by means of questions and answers; or at least such interesting portions of Holy Writ as are best adapted for moral instruction. Most of these schools possess libraries.

It is impossible to form a correct idea of the excellent moral effect of these schools on the laboring classes, for whom they are especially established.

I was several times invited to visit them. Among other occasions, I recollect that I was once at the residence of Messrs. Dupont (de Nemours), on the Brandywine, which empties into the Delaware, where the two brothers had been the first to establish important powder mills. On this occasion, I saw the sons and daughters of these celebrated manufacturers actively engaged in directing one of these institutions. I can particularly call to mind the neat and cleanly appearance of the young boys and girls, their contented bearing, and the satisfaction they exhibited in being taught by the children of their employers. There was thus established, in that class of young operatives, through the instruction of their young teachers, a degree of self-respect and correct deportment, the salutary effects of which it would afford us pleasure to perceive more frequently among the ranks of more elevated classes in Europe.

The number of institutions whose object is to instruct the people in the various branches of industry pursued in the United States is infinite. Each State, county, township, and city possesses several of them. New associations are annually formed for the establishment of libraries and lecture rooms, designed especially for youth, whether engaged in commerce, or in the industrial and liberal arts.

In Massachusetts, for example, each county is provided with several public libraries, supported by the voluntary contributions of societies for public instruction. These libraries contain altogether about 185,000 volumes. Public lectures are there delivered gratuitously; for which lectures, attended by thirty-three thousand individuals, these institutions have expended in one year more than twenty thousand dollars.

In this State, three hundred and seven towns or villages also possess public libraries, a certain number of which, connected with colleges, are well supplied. The library of Harvard University contains fifty-one thousand volumes; that of Amherst, thirteen thousand; that of William, seven thousand five hundred; that of the Society of American Antiquities, in Boston, twelve thousand.

Boston alone has more than ten circulating libraries, containing, on the whole, fifty thousand volumes.

The whole number of books in the public libraries of Massachusetts, exclusive of those belonging to the Sunday schools, is 520,000 volumes.

Not unfrequently, the most eminent men of the country contribute gratuitously towards the advancement of public education, and deliver to the working classes lectures on political economy, finance, morals, and literature.

The venerable ex-president Adams was in the habit of stopping at the large cities of the Union, in his journey from Boston to Washington, for the purpose of delivering lectures to young mechanics and apprentices on the most important subjects of public education. During his sojourn at Baltimore, he treated such profound questions as the commercial rights of nations; developed the characteristic qualities of the mercantile and the operative classes; and eloquently exhibited the progress of civilization through the happy influence of education placed within the reach of the masses.

In all these lectures, the principles of a sound democracy invariably form the text of certain general reviews to which the attention of the auditors is carefully directed. Society is thus constantly placed on its guard against the doctrines of demagogues, who might scatter seeds subversive of democratic principles. The auditors are ever reminded of the truth inscribed at the head of the American Constitution, that labor is the common duty of all classes of society, since a respectable position in life can be secured only by individual effort; that the nature of the institutions, the character of the laws, and the genius of the government of the American Union are adverse to the introduction of special privileges in behalf of any particular portion of society, and to the accumulation of wealth in a single family; that they annul, in fact, all distinctions of birth or rank.

Moreover, daily experience presents proof sufficiently abundant that the poor of one generation become the rich of the following generation; that the man who moves in the humblest walks of life constantly rises in the scale of social elevation by means of industry and integrity of character; while he whose pretensions are based on the fortune he has inherited finds, when this is gone, that he has leaned on a broken reed. The only aristocracy recognized by American institutions is that of intellect and virtue.

Nothing, certainly, can more effectually contribute to the strength and perpetuity of American institutions than these series of public lectures, which are multiplying with such rapidity; for they afford the opportunity of counteracting the dangerous tendencies of false ideas of luxury, in the public mind, through the inculcation of activity and industry. It must be acknowledged that, in the United States, the national sentiment is directed in a far greater degree towards the useful than the ornamental; and that much less attention is now paid to sculpture, architecture, and painting, than to pursuits conducive to the welfare of the majority.

But every social improvement has its peculiar epoch, and that of the fine arts cannot certainly be very distant in the United States; for in America, we already find a large number of individuals gifted with a natural as well as cultivated taste for the beautiful, and a just appreciation of the liberal arts. With respect to those noble professions which indicate, among the people who cultivate them with most success, the degree of their progress in civilization, America is not behind other nations, apparently more advanced; for it already contains a numerous class of artists of all kinds, whose names are honorably placed beside those who in Europe occupy the highest rank.

Thus, the American people, in proportion to the diffusion of knowledge, and the development of intelligence, exhibit progress in all their social relations, their civil and commercial institutions, and in all their material interests.

Instruction, from its lowest grade in the primary school to the most elevated in literature and science, diffuses its illuminating influences throughout all ranks of American society; in fact, the Americans appreciate it too well, as an element of wealth, prosperity, and independence, to forego results so auspicious.

Education is generally completed at an early age, because of the necessity of adopting a profession to which several years of apprenticeship are required. But a considerable number of Americans, in addition to acquiring a special education, prosecute some particular branch of science, as well for the love of knowledge as on account of a desire to attain a distinguished position among their countrymen.

In America, the greater number of wealthy individuals have undoubtedly commenced life with scanty means. But there, as everywhere else, those who have a taste for study are in very small proportion, and seldom belong to the wealthy classes; and, by a peculiar instinct, they always find time to devote themselves to literature.

The taste for intellectual pleasures is transmitted no more than any other of the inclinations characteristic of man; and the possession of wealth, whether acquired or inherited, has no specific relation to this endowment of our nature. Therefore, we find in the

United States, as elsewhere, in all conditions of life, men who highly honor intellectual pursuits. Thus, the will to devote one's self to these pursuits is no more lacking than the power.

I do not believe that in any society human knowledge exhibits so marked an average level as in the United States. But I do not believe that this intellectual condition has operated unfavorably on superior or incomparably gifted minds. On the contrary, I believe that there is a constant upward movement. I believe that in American society, the many rise, not that men of genius and talent fall, in the scale of intellectual cultivation.

This theory of the abasement of the human mind appears to me absurd and contrary to nature. The able professor may descend to the level of the understanding of his auditors to make himself understood; but it is absurd to assume that his lofty intellect must thereby receive injury.

There is an immense multitude of individuals in the United States whose range of knowledge on matters of religion, history, science, political economy, legislation, and government, is about equal. This circumstance is not attributable to a lack of adequate information concerning these branches of knowledge, but to the unrestricted transmission of ideas and facts through those innumerable channels which the advanced state of instruction has placed within the reach of everybody.

Let it not be supposed that, in the United States, as in the cities of Europe, special schools exist, in which professors of commercial science, political economy, legislation, or government, merely treat these various subjects at a great expense of eloquence, abstract reasoning, and vague theory. In that country, society is considered the best school to acquire such information, and the affairs of common life are regarded as the best of all practical lessons. The Americans are able masters of everything that relates to the practical application of the different branches of human knowledge, whilst in many cases able *professors*, who discourse elaborately before our assemblies on the same matters, are in reality only *pupils*. The parts, in fact, are reversed.

In France, we do not lack able professors of commercial science or political economy; but we have very few practical men, true merchants, and still fewer economists.

CONDITION OF THE PRESS IN THE UNITED STATES.

If the Americans, as politicians, make great use of language, they make equally great use of the means of transmitting it. In confirmation of this statement, it is only necessary to state that the number of periodical publications of all kinds annually printed in the United States actually exceeds *two thousand.*

In the United States, the people write a great deal, but read more, for in that country almost everybody knows how to read; hence the influence of the press is much greater than that of the rostrum. The press speaks to the whole people, the only people, perhaps, in the world, who are adequately instructed in the knowledge required to secure obedience to the laws. Let it also be borne in mind that, in the United States, the press respects itself; that the columns of an American newspaper, unlike those of certain French journals, are never disgraced by scandalous histories and obscene romances; and that the public organs of this democratic country could not abandon themselves to the propagation of immorality without drawing upon them the censure of society and the severity of the laws.

The American press is not required to give security, nor is it subject to a stamp act.

The periodical newspapers are classed as follows:—

Daily papers	255
Weekly "	1250
Semi-weekly papers	248
Monthly "	250

If we can infer the general education of a people from the means within its control of disseminating useful knowledge, the United States must undoubtedly appear far more advanced than any country in the world, since a comparison of the number of the newspapers with the respective populations of the various nations of the world exhibits the following results. The proportion of newspapers is—

In the Slave States	2	for every	10,000	inhabitants.
In the non-slaveholding States	2	"	8,285	"
In Belgium,	2	"	20,000	"
In Holland,	1	"	24,000	"
In Denmark,	1	"	25,000	"
In Prussia,	1	"	56,000	"

In Great Britain,	1	for every	60,000	inhabitants.
In Switzerland,	1	"	70,000	"
In France,	1	"	136,000	"
In Portugal,	1	"	223,000	"
In Austria,	1	"	362,000	"
In Russia in Europe,	1	"	500,000	"
In Spain,	1	"	1,416,000	"

To an American, a newspaper is a daily intellectual necessity; as much of a necessity, in fact, as his breakfast or other repast for his physical sustenance. The newspaper is everywhere. It is found in every house, on board of the steamboat, in the railroad car, in the city, in the country, in the school, and in the factory.

In the great manufacturing city of Lowell, for example, the females employed in the mills publish a newspaper.

Let us here remark, while speaking of the intellectual direction thus given to labor in the workshop, that these female operatives can devote their moments of leisure to reading, to music, or to such other instructive amusement as they may select, in halls built expressly for this object, and exclusively reserved for their use.

The newspaper, then, follows the American wherever he emigrates; it is his faithful companion. Thus, in those great movements which bear the civilization of the East towards the West, the hardy pioneer is always accompanied by a missionary, a lawyer, a physician, and an editor of a newspaper. Three American daily papers are now published west of the Rocky Mountains; one in Oregon, one at Astoria, and one at Monterey in Upper California.

American authors produce fewer works of imagination and of deep reasoning than works which make known the results of their own observations, or embody an interpretation of their own ideas. In general, they treat only of those subjects with which they are perfectly acquainted, and which enable them to extend the range of their experience through the relation these subjects bear to practice. They rarely devote their attention, either in rational examinations, or in writing commentaries, to the elucidation of the productions of bygone authors. Let it also be remarked that American productions are stamped rather with the practical intelligence of their authors than with elevation of style or profound erudition.

For this reason, it is a matter of no surprise that American writers confine their attention rather to subjects of religion, of legislation, or of education, than to those of imagination, sentiment, or profound science—subjects which always suppose in those who cultivate them a degree of leisure that American society can scarcely yet be said to possess.

Nevertheless, we must not thence conclude that business operates as a powerful diversion against study, and that retirement and leisure constitute the principal elements in the progress as well as the practice of letters. On the contrary, the most powerful efforts of the imagination are almost always in close relation with humanity, and are, in consequence, generally the result of contact with mankind. Certainly, these efforts are the more vigorous in proportion as the mind is stimulated by those mainsprings of humanity, emulation, friendship, and the antagonistic elements that are engendered among an active, energetic, and ambitious people, surrounded by circumstances which impel a free society in the direction of the great movement of progress. In fact, such a society is capable of the greatest efforts, whether of imagination or of profound philosophical reasoning. In American democracy, all these elements are combined; and America has already given ample proof to the world that it possesses men of intellect and genius of sufficient cultivation to be equal to the highest speculations of the human mind.

POST-OFFICE DEPARTMENT.

This department holds an important rank in the administrative and social organization of the Americans, for by this medium intellectual life is spread throughout the whole nation. It is so administered as to pay its own expenses.

There are now, in the United States, fifteen thousand post offices.

The distance traveled by mails is about 85,560,000 miles.

The Americans have adopted a uniform postage on letters of five cents for any distance less than 300 miles, and ten cents for all distances beyond.

CHAPTER XVIII.

AGRICULTURE.

The Americans principally agriculturists—Admirable quality of the soil of the United States—The American character favorable to the development of agriculture—Dangers which beset their speculative character.

Agricultural industry served as the starting-point of the American nation, and now constitutes the principal source of its wealth; for, by the immense resources of their fertile territory, the people of the United States give to the world the most ample guarantees of their present and future prosperity, and of their happy condition as a civilized people. To their Anglo-Saxon origin they owe the qualities which, to an agriculturist, are indispensable—imperturbable coolness, a rare spirit of perseverance, and, above all, that aptitude for labor characteristic of the soldiers of Cromwell. The obligation to establish their liberty, and to secure their independence of the mother country, whence they had voluntarily exiled themselves, constrained them to seek that support from the earth which could be obtained only by severe labor. In fine, the fortunate position of the new continent they came to inhabit, which, by its varied climate and fertile soil, gave the assurance of unbounded resources, promised a future which could be realized only by means of patient industry.

The natural resources of a country consist in the fertility of its soil, the character of its climate, the distribution of its water-courses, as well for natural navigation as for the creation of water-powers, and its proximity to markets. North America is abundantly endowed with all these natural advantages. Its soil in general, but especially in the vast regions watered by the Mississippi, is eminently fertile, and its climate is of the most varied character. Its great rivers secure easy and extensive intercommunication. At all points, thousands of little streams, fed by inexhaustible springs, create water-powers adapted to every necessity; and the presence of two seas, from the Bay of Fundy to the Sabine River in the Gulf of Mexico, bathing the coasts of the United States for an extent of more than three thousand miles, presents facilities of exchange with other parts of the world which, of late years, steam has drawn in closer contiguity to the producers.

But that which gives most value to all these physical elements is, undoubtedly, the character of the population, essentially agricultural and industrial.

Thus, intelligence, activity, perseverance, religious sentiment, education, and social and political freedom—in fact, everything tends to elevate the American nation to the highest degree of prosperity.

The moral and intellectual character of a people directly contributes to its progress, in a national point of view, in the great work of human civilization. Thus, for example, the guarantees of justice, without which no society can exist, consist not so much in the laws themselves as in the power which creates them. Apart from the support this power is at all times adapted to render them, they would be wholly inoperative. Laws are nothing, they can have no force, except with the co-operation of the people. Of what avail would be the best laws apart from a vigorous determination on the part of the people to obey them, and to see them enforced? In general, the want of society is not so much good laws as the practical observance of those it possesses, since the people seldom have the character, the nerve, and the zeal which prompt those who are charged with the execution of the laws to live in obedience to them.

This peculiar trait forms, in my opinion, the national spirit of a people. When the will of a people is not thus peremptorily expressed, it is difficult to secure the observance of the laws; for the spirit of which we speak may with truth be regarded as the key of public liberty. Now, this trait lies essentially at the foundation of the American character; and it is certainly the most important element of the great social problem presented to the world of a people numbering nearly twenty-one million souls exhibiting capacity for self-government!

Another trait of character deserves attention. The American has not only taken care that individual freedom and the security of property are accurately recognized by law, but he is ever ready energetically to enforce respect for them—a trait due as well to the spirit of jealousy created by the sentiment of liberty, as to the degree of consideration each order of the State knows so well how to maintain.

Moreover, it is evident that what is called political liberty, or the right of each individual to act according to his station, whether in a private or public capacity, cannot exist unless it is based on the same principle; for the property of an individual may be protected, and his personal liberty secured, by the ordinary forms of a civil process; but the sacred rights of the human mind can be defended only by its own efforts.

The Americans have recognized this principle as the fundamental basis of their society. Its practical operation until the present time has been attended with a degree of success that places their social organization incomparably beyond that of the most enlightened nations of modern times.

With this energy of character, with these principles of liberty and individual security, is it surprising that the American people, with the object of ultimately securing a marked preponderance in every other industrial pursuit, have so highly developed their agricultural interest? Undoubtedly not. In a country where every one enjoys in security the fruits of his labor, with the prospect of independence and happiness always before his eyes, it is natural that the American should direct all his intelligence and all his talents towards the accomplishment of an object which perseverance will enable him to attain.

One thing alone has excited our astonishment, in relation to which we cannot withhold the expression of our opinion. We are surprised that, amid so many auspicious conditions which Providence seems to have accumulated at pleasure on this favored portion of the globe, the Americans should not have checked the unmeasured development of their speculating tendencies. But societies, like the individuals who compose it, have their weak point; and why should not American society, like all others, exhibit the seal of its original vice?

Does not every people that assumes wealth as the standard of good or evil present to the world the strongest proof of its demoralization, inasmuch as, to secure wealth, it is blindly led, as it were, despite of itself, into all manner of speculation? Nothing can prevent such a people from ultimately becoming enslaved, whatever be the laws under which it may live; for as, in a democracy, the people constitute the legitimate sovereign, the power they are able to exercise may, like that of any other government, become downright tyranny!

Let the Americans, then, be on their guard! let them pause, while it is yet time, before the breach their cupidity has opened around them! Let them contemplate, with religious admiration and gratitude, the immense resources of their continent—resources placed at their disposal with the design that millions should live happy and free!—and, I doubt not, they will soon acknowledge that in the culture of the soil resides the primary source of that happiness and virtue which can alone secure the durability of nations!

Let us also hope, despite the late financial calamities which gave so rude a shock to the social edifice of America, that the beautiful primitive institutions of this great country will always be duly venerated, and remain sufficiently vigorous to lead to the appreciation of this great truth—that societies can maintain themselves only by honest labor, and by the vigorous observance of their engagements!

The guarantees of property in America consist, as I have already said, in the fertility of its soil, and in the nature of its agricultural productions, of which the most important, cotton, sugar, rice, and grain, are essential to the rest of the world.

CHAPTER XIX.

COMMERCE.

With the American, the genius for business allied to an ambitious character—The American peculiarly a business man—His attention absorbed in his personal welfare—Character of American merchants—Influence of democracy—Community of national interest among the American people.

When we seek to explain what, under the powerful stimulus of civilization, are the instincts proper to man, we find, prominent above everything else, an indisposition to repose. A characteristic among his estimable qualities is a spirit of independence, which constitutes an active power of his nature. Those features of his character which excite our commendation are the result of effort. If his errors and crimes often proceed from an abuse of his activity, his virtue and happiness are not the less the result of the useful employment of his mind. Hence, so long as man is active, he retains the regard of his fellow-citizens; but if he ceases to exert himself, he immediately sinks in the esteem of others; and a virtual extinction becomes the sequence of prolonged inactivity.

Activity is, therefore, the fundamental law of human nature. Everything has been arranged in a remarkable manner by a just and benevolent Providence to fulfil this essential condition of our being. But we are ever liable to be carried away into one of two extremes—an agitation too excessive, or a repose of too long continuance. To decide what mean position best answers one's interests is often a very embarrassing question. Nevertheless, we may safely acknowledge, as a general principle, that whatever the resources of man, his social position, as well as his nature, requires that he should be employed—his happiness, that he should be just!

If such be the character of man in general, it seems to me to be peculiarly the distinctive trait of the Anglo-American race.

The founders of New England were not only fanatical sectarians and austere Puritans in their religious and political principles—they were also a very active, very laborious, and exceedingly energetic class of men.

The minds of those who planted the first English colonies of the north were constantly directed to two things: to be Christians agreeably to their conscience; and to live independent by means of their labor. They soon found themselves surrounded by difficulties of all kinds, with a wide field for the display of their rare activity and energy. They were obliged to provide means for their physical support, while protecting themselves from the attacks of the natives.

Agriculture, the fur trade with the Indians, and the fisheries, constituted their first industry. At a later period, they were enabled to exchange the surplus produce of their soil for that of the West Indies, or for other commodities of which the mother country had not reserved the monopoly. Thus, for the first time, commercial became allied to the industrial tendencies of the inhabitants. In proportion to the development of the productive character of the colonists, the former assumed a wider range. Soon, the Anglo-Saxon, finding a field more vast, less restricted, and more in harmony with his peculiar instincts, devoted his attention to commerce, if not exclusively, at least with the greater pleasure, by reason of the prospect it afforded for the realization of heavy profits.

At that time, the Anglo-American population scarcely occupied any territory beyond the seaboard of New England and Southern Virginia. Therefore, it is not surprising that so advantageous a position should have directed the attention of the early colonists towards commercial pursuits. The usages, the habits, the spirit, and, as it were, the manners peculiar to a commercial life were soon adopted by society, and at the present time characterize the whole nation.

It seems, in fact, that, with the American, the genius for business is constantly invigorated by enterprise, and is under the influence of the ambition by which he appears to be incessantly animated. But other moral and physical causes have also contributed to make the American speculative. Placed far from, or rather beyond, the vortex of the moral influences which disturb, trammel, and more frequently modify, on the Old Continent, the useful application of human intelligence, his mind has never for an instant been turned from the pursuit of his material interests. His ardor has been nourished by the immense territory he inhabits, by its climate, its varied productions, and its vast girdle of sea frontier, so favorable to the means of exchange; by the necessity of finding a market for the various products of his industry; but, above all, by the facilities and advantages secured to him by education and by the diffusion of knowledge among all ranks of society. In short, free institutions, which afford to all alike the means of success, have stamped on the American physiognomy a speculative activity far more vivid than that imprinted on the physiognomy of Europeans.

But from the general character of the nation, we must not draw the inference that every American is a merchant, or that the tastes and habits which arise from the employment of equal rights naturally lead men to commerce and manufactures. This assertion cannot be taken in a positive sense. The American is undoubtedly peculiarly a man of business, a man endowed with that aptitude which enables him to calculate all the chances of a commercial operation; but this aptitude, this disposition, he exhibits in every occupation of life, in commerce equally with manufactures, in agriculture equally with jurisprudence; in everything, in fact, which he pursues as a vocation.

The American feels the constant necessity of laboring for his personal advancement. This is a law of his nature, which he has been careful to place in harmony with other laws he has adopted for his own guidance. But no one vocation receives exclusive attention. In this, the American, like the rest of mankind, is obedient to the sentiment of individuality.

Democracy, it is true, multiplies the number of working men by augmenting competition, and rendering it the same for every one. But it does not incline men to one kind of labor more than to another. It does not induce them to desert agriculture for commerce and manufactures. It produces in the United States an effect directly the reverse. The agriculturist does not abandon his fields and his plough, and embark in a hazardous or lucrative profession. But the resident of cities, the merchant, the artisan, the manufacturer, fatigued with an existence subject to so many casualties, becomes an agriculturist, because in this pursuit man eventually finds independence, abundance, and happiness!

Are figures required to establish this assertion? If so, we may state that, in 1840, the agricultural population of the United States amounted to 3,717,756; and that devoted to manufactures to 1,013,415; that is to say, for one person engaged in mechanical pursuits, 3.75 agriculturists. The commercial population amounted only to 117,575; a proportion of one merchant to one hundred and forty-six agriculturists.

In New England, the agriculturists exceed those engaged in industrial or other pursuits thirty-three per cent.

In New York, the proportion of agriculturists is two, in Ohio three, in Illinois five and a half, in Indiana five and a half, and in Michigan six and a half, for every person engaged in an industrial pursuit.

The population engaged in commerce is comparatively more numerous in Louisiana than in any other State of the Union; next in order come Wisconsin and Rhode Island. The proportion is least in the State of Arkansas; afterwards in North Carolina, Tennessee, and South Carolina.

The American merchant is enlightened and enterprising. He has comprehensive views and fixed principles, which at once render him an able tradesman and a bold speculator. He solicits no assistance from the government; but he knows he can depend upon its protection wherever his enterprising genius may direct him. Hence, he is not less devoted to the institutions of his country, the advantages of which he constantly appreciates, than the agriculturist, who supplies him with the means of fostering his commerce.

The fact is that, between these two classes, there is a closer approximation than might at first be supposed. This circumstance is easily explained. Both are rich and powerful only through their harmony of action; only through the *administrative union* which everywhere extends to them its protection.

We can then truly say that the *American Union* becomes, in fact, a nation equally rich and powerful, at home and abroad, through its agriculturists and tradesmen.

The object of commerce is to make men rich; therefore, the greater the profits they realize the greater the augmentation of the wealth of the country; for, if it be true that individual happiness is the principal object of society, it is no less true that, in a free country, the general welfare should form the principal object of individuals. How, in fact, can a community be considered happy, unless the individuals who compose it are happy?

Now, in the United States, the interests of society and those of individuals are harmonized by the excellent institutions of the country. There, society receives the consideration of each individual; but the latter receives, as an equivalent, that consideration which at bottom constitutes the greatest portion of the happiness he can enjoy. The greatest benefit communities can confer on individuals is to secure the attachment of one to another, and the interchange of good feeling and kindly offices. In a society thus organized, internal tranquillity is insured rather through the ascendency of these feelings than through the interposition of laws. Thus is a people made happy.

This is what democracy has accomplished in the United States. Under its protection, all citizens are equally happy, because it affords to all the means of developing their intelligence, capacity, and noblest qualities. To this state of things the division of society into various independent States, as recognized by the American Constitution, is exceedingly favorable; for, through the emulation it excites, it contributes to the maintenance of virtue, to the useful employment of one's faculties, and to a just appreciation of the merit of the business into which every one enters on a footing of equality, though with diverse interests.

Such are the advantages of practical liberty, resulting from a government of laws which are supported and administered by those who made them, that is to say, the people. In this case, laws have a direct tendency to uphold liberty, since they especially depend on the influence of those citizens who, desiring to be free, have dictated the conditions on which their relations, either to the State or to their fellow-citizens, shall depend. The observance of these conditions, once determined by law, can be secured only by the greatest vigilance and energy; for vigilance and firmness of purpose give to national power its most indispensable virtue, which is dependent, in equal degree, on the capacity and vigor with which affairs of state are conducted.

These dominant traits in the national character of the Americans contribute in a great degree to the maintenance of their laws, and to the prosperity of their country.

I think I have sufficiently proved that it is not democracy alone that has produced the commercial development of the American people. This result is also attributable in an equal degree to the active and enterprising genius of the people, to the innumerable advantages of a rich and immense territory, and to the extent of the American coast.

Nowhere throughout the vast territory of the United States does there exist a line of custom-houses. The products of one State can pass into another without prohibition or protective tariffs.

This is one of the primary causes of the wealth and prosperity of this great republic, and of the stability of its institutions. A common nationality protects all the interests of the country.

Let no one seek to establish the existence of different interests between the various sections of this country; let no one assume that the interests of the North are not in harmony with those of the South; and that laws protecting the one are useless to the other. These arguments are unfounded, and are urged only by the enemies of democracy, whose jealousy is excited at its secure establishment in the United States.

True, there is no community of national origin among the Americans; but we find among them a community of national interests which at least insures their prosperity and their power.

NANTUCKET.

In concluding this chapter, I cannot resist the desire to say a few words relative to the inhabitants of an island, within the jurisdiction of Massachusetts, which I had the good fortune to visit in 1826. This is perhaps the only people in the United States that impresses upon the traveler an idea of the character, the habits, and the primitive manners of that race of courageous men who came, in 1620, at the peril of their lives, in search of liberty on the shores of New England.

The Island of Nantucket, to the south of Cape Cod, has a superficies scarcely equal to ten square miles. It is an arid sand bank, that has never afforded to the navigator any indications of natural vegetation. It is an alluvium formed, near the cape or promontory in front of the south-eastern part of the coast of Massachusetts, by the tempests which stir the ocean to its inmost depths.

Despite these disadvantages, the people who settled Nantucket regarded its position favorable for fishing; and this has ever been the characteristic pursuit of its inhabitants. The early settlers protected themselves against the inclemencies of the weather in the hulls of their vessels, which served as a shelter equally against movable sands, and the waves that frequently covered the island with briny water.

This island is now inhabited by a very wealthy and industrious population, engaged either in the coasting trade or in the fisheries. Besides the requisite number of seamen and officers for its own trade, it furnishes a considerable surplus for the equipment of vessels belonging to other portions of the Union.

The spirit of enterprise which characterizes the people of Nantucket is unparalleled. Their ingenuity and resources have become proverbial. They are brave, robust, temperate in their habits, and extremely frugal. Their physical constitution is remarkable for its strength and suppleness.

When I visited this island, it was the residence of a numerous and very intelligent population, possessing all the resources and comforts of a polished society. Industry, the arts, and good taste have triumphed over all obstacles, and rendered Nantucket remarkable for its beauty and its refined comforts.

We there see beautifully cultivated gardens, rich in vegetables and flowers of the most varied kind, which separate, in the happiest manner, charming dwellings, erected here and there, without regularity and order, but presenting a picture highly agreeable to the eye of the stranger. One is ever certain of being received with the most generous hospitality by the inhabitants of this fortunate island —an island where watchmen, and police, and bolts are not required for individual security.

In a word, the industrious population of the Island of Nantucket presents in miniature the Dutch nation of the seventeenth century.

Why have such examples of happiness, tranquillity, and prosperity become so rare, at the present time, in every portion of the globe?

CHAPTER XX.

MANUFACTURES.

England strives to prevent the introduction of manufactures into the colonies of New England—Their progress despite opposition—Manufacture of hats—Linen and woolen fabrics—Forges—Massachusetts legislates in favor of manufactures—Introduction of the first cotton-spinning machine—Arrival of celebrated manufacturers from England and France—Samuel Slaters—Dupont de Nemours—Law proposed by Alexander Hamilton in favor of manufactures adopted by Congress in 1789—Fresh impulse given to manufactures by the War of 1812—Protective system adopted by Congress and maintained until 1832—Introduction of the *compromise* law—Commercial crisis—Deficit in the revenues of the United States—New tariff—Present importance of manufactures.

During the period of the colonial system, the Americans turned their attention exclusively to agriculture. The mother country, interested in this state of things, sought by every available means to secure its continuance as long as possible. But the native intelligence and rare activity of the people overcame all obstacles. An industrial tendency soon became manifest among all classes of the colonists.

The metropolis, jealous of preserving its American colonies as a market for the products of its manufacture, became alarmed at these indications, which assumed every day a more imposing aspect, and sought at once to repress them by administrative measures.

Consequently, in 1699, the British Parliament issued a decree prohibiting the introduction of any American manufactures into Great Britain, or into any of its dependencies.

In 1710, it was solemnly declared, in the English Parliament, that the introduction of the various branches of manufacture into the colonies could have no other effect than to render them independent of the mother country; that it was necessary to crush this rebellious tendency by vigorous measures.

The genius of the people was proof even against these hindrances, and their progress was sufficiently decisive. As far back as 1731, for example, fabrics began to be manufactured in Massachusetts. Among other indications of progress, a paper-mill was in operation on quite an extensive scale.

In Connecticut, Rhode Island, New York, and Pennsylvania, the colonists industriously engaged in the manufacture of woolens, linens, and iron for their own consumption.

From hemp and flax, already cultivated on a large scale in almost all of the colonies, coarse goods and pack-cloth were manufactured, which were preferred to those imported from Europe, notwithstanding the circumstance that labor in the colonies was twenty per cent. higher than in England, and the fact that these articles could be imported fifty per cent. below the prices of the fabrics manufactured in America.

At this period, New Hampshire had already acquired some celebrity on account of its fisheries, and the quantity of its lumber.

Among the manufactures carried on most extensively was that of hats, because of the advantages the colonists possessed of procuring, at the lowest prices, through their fur trade with the natives, beaver skins of the best quality. When this business had acquired considerable importance, Parliament, in a spirit of petty jealousy, attempted to check the enterprise by the passage of a law prohibiting the introduction of American hats into any part of Great Britain.

The Americans had also established a number of tanneries, and directed their attention to the preparation of leather, a business found to be profitable from a very early period.

In the American colonies, there were also nineteen forges and five furnaces, the product of which amounted to about the twentieth part of the material required for the necessities of the inhabitants.

Such was the condition of the colonies relative to manufactures prior to the Revolution. As unimportant as their progress may appear, the result still exhibits the aptitude of the Americans for these departments of labor. It proves, besides, that, without assistance, without protection, and despite the trammels of legislation, certain branches of industry may be developed in a country where natural conditions alone, such as the soil, the climate, and the habits and character of the people, are favorable to their existence.

But we must also recollect that, at the period referred to, the people of these colonies were of pure and severe morals, of simple and frugal habits, and that they were especially adverse to ostentation. They were all dressed in fabrics wrought either by their wives or by members of their families. At that time, no one would have dared to attract notice by luxurious display. The relations of good neighborhood were then cultivated perhaps in a greater degree than at the present time, and were maintained over a wider space of country. To preserve them in their integrity, the sole dependence of the colonist was his nag, on which he rode to church on Sunday, with his wife mounted behind him—a peculiarity still observable in the interior of the country. In short, gorgeous equipages and their insolent attendants had then no existence.

In 1744, we observe, on the part of the colonial government of Massachusetts, the first indications of interest relative to manufactures. At this period, the provincial congress called public attention to the important relations of agriculture and manufactures to the economy and welfare of society. In the course of that year, general measures for the defence and security of the country were adopted, with the avowed object of maintaining their independence, thus furnishing a brilliant example of the noble use to which so youthful a people could apply their democracy. It was also recommended that the inhabitants should form associations, with the object of prosecuting successfully several branches of industry beyond the range of the ability of single individuals. Citizens were at the same time enjoined to use domestic instead of imported articles.

The first act of the Federal Government relative to the encouragement of manufactures was not passed till 1789, at the close of the War of the Revolution.

In 1791, Alexander Hamilton made his celebrated report on this subject, and obtained the honorable title of father of the *American System*. Since that time, an equally distinguished patriot of our own day, Henry Clay, of Kentucky, has become its most zealous champion.

The first cotton-spinning machine introduced into this country was established at East Bridgewater, in Massachusetts, in 1786. Such was the public interest manifested on the occasion that the general court voted two hundred dollars as a reward to its constructor. The following year, a Mr. Orr received a gratuity of twenty dollars, to give publicity to all his practical knowledge of the invention.

In 1787, the proprietors of the cotton factories at Beverly, Massachusetts, made some attempts to substitute mechanical for manual labor, in imitation of the practice in Europe. They petitioned the *General Court* to promote their object, and obtained authority to raise five thousand dollars by lottery.

The third attempt to spin cotton by machinery was made in 1788, at Providence, Rhode Island. In the same year, a cotton factory was erected in Philadelphia. The undertaking was completely successful. From that period, an association was organized in Pennsylvania for the encouragement of manufactures.

The attempts made in New York and Connecticut were less fortunate; not because the inhabitants lacked perseverance or intelligence, but because the machines they imported were imperfect.

In 1790, one of the most distinguished mechanics of England, Samuel Slaters, emigrated to America. This celebrated manufacturer was associated with the renowned Sir Richard Arkwright, the inventor of the cotton-jenny, which bore his name. He erected a spinning-mill at Pawtucket, which is to this day one of the most celebrated establishments in the United States.

In 1793, associating himself with Messrs. Brown and Almy, Slaters erected another cotton factory, which was highly successful.

About the same period, other parts of Europe furnished America with noble competitors in the importation of the industrial arts. Among these, I must particularly distinguish the brothers Dupont, sons of M. Dupont de Nemours, the ideologist. This intelligent family settled on the Brandywine, in the State of Delaware, and there erected establishments which gave a powerful impulse to manufactures in that part of the Union, and which, in critical circumstances, rendered important service to the United States. One of the brothers established powder-mills, the reputation of which is too well known in Europe to require comment. The other brother erected a cloth factory on the opposite side of the Brandywine, which has at all times served to clothe the American army.

The law proposed by Hamilton, and adopted by the Congress of 1789, encouraged the manufacturing spirit of the Americans, which the renewed commercial relations with England, at the close of the War of Independence, had somewhat checked.

The war of 1812, the second contest between the United States and England, gave a fresh impulse to manufactures, a branch of industry already enriched by the discoveries of Arkwright, Hargrave, and James Watt, and of two Americans, whose names are equally cherished, Whitney and Fulton. Whitney is the inventor of a machine which separates the cotton from the seed.

Congress, to meet the expenses of the war, adopted a new tariff, doubling the duties on all foreign merchandize.

But in 1815, American manufactures experienced another check, through the introduction of English goods. Nevertheless, the public spirit of the Americans had been awakened to the importance of preserving and perfecting them. A tariff was adopted by Congress, designed principally to protect cotton and woolen fabrics, so essentially connected with the prosperity of the country.

By this tariff, a duty of twenty-five per cent. *ad valorem* was imposed on all foreign manufactured woolen goods, to continue in operation from June, 1816, to June, 1819, after which period it was to be reduced to twenty per cent.

By the same tariff, all manufactured cotton goods, whose original value was below twenty-five cents a yard, were to pay the same duty as though valued at twenty-five cents. This clause was introduced with the object of including in the tariff all the common articles imported from India, as well as to protect the manufactures of the country, which had already become so developed as to compete against them. A duty of thirty per cent. was also imposed on many other articles, such as hats, furniture, carriages, leather, and paper, the manufacture of which had already acquired great importance in the United States.

The cultivation of native sugar was also promoted by a protective tariff.

In 1818, many of these duties were augmented. But in 1824, the duties on cotton and woolen fabrics exported from England were subjected to revision. A reduction consequently took place, with the object of counteracting the effect of the American tariff.

In consequence of these dispositions on the part of the British government, the American manufacturers petitioned Congress for assistance. The result of this appeal was the celebrated tariff of 1828. By this tariff, a duty of from forty-five to fifty per cent. *ad valorem* was imposed on all woolen manufactured goods. The duty on all other articles was proportionally augmented.

Congress continued this protective system until 1831, when, in consequence of the extinction of the public debt, a proposition was again made to revise the tariff.

Under these circumstances, public opinion was invoked by the usual means. Conventions favorable and adverse to free trade met at Philadelphia. At the meeting of the partisans of free trade, it was proposed to reduce the tariff as much as possible. At the convention of those favorable to the continuance of the protective system, it was proposed to reduce the duties on those articles alone which could not in any respect influence the progress of American manufactures, or the development of home products.

In 1832, Congress adopted a new tariff, in entire conformity with the views of the majority; that is to say, a tariff protecting only in a partial degree the interests of the manufacturers and producers. By this tariff, the duties on French wines were reduced.

The year 1833 was one of mournful celebrity. Certain members of the body politic of South Carolina expressed opinions relative to free trade which appeared to threaten the dissolution of the Union. This conduct placed South Carolina—for a very

30

short time, it is true—in open rebellion against the laws of the Union.

The energy of President Jackson, to whom was confided the maintenance of the Constitution—and especially the strength of public opinion—soon restored the authority of the laws of the Union.

Nevertheless, these new claims, occasioned by the law of 1832, induced Congress to adopt, even prior to the period at which it could take effect, a law that has received the name of the *Compromise Act*. This measure, proposed by Henry Clay, of Kentucky, was of essential service to the country, for it checked at once the imprudent violence of one of the most influential of the Southern States.

This amendment was adopted as a law during the winter of 1833, and was to remain in force until June, 1842. It provided that all duties above twenty per cent. *ad valorem* should, until June, 1842, be reduced annually to twenty per cent. A number of articles, whose consumption was considerable, were to be admitted free. Among these, were foreign silks. It also proposed to limit the new tariff to be adopted subsequent to that epoch to twenty per cent. on the value of importations; and also prescribed that no increase of duties should take place prior to June 30, 1842.

But the decennial period from 1832 to 1842 was to become only too celebrated by the vicissitudes of the American financial system—at one time working so prosperously as to permit the entire payment of the national debt, and the distribution of the proceeds of the sale of the public lands among the States; at another time so utterly prostrated as to oblige the General Government to provide by extraordinary measures the means of paying its own expenses.

This last commercial crisis commenced in 1837, a short time after the expiration of the charter of the United States Bank, which had, until that time, served to moderate the licentiousness of the local banks, and the private speculations which they encouraged.* Since that period, and for the first time, perhaps, since the existence of the American Union, democratic institu-

* Nevertheless, we must here observe that the United States Bank was, in a measure, the first to encourage the exaggerated views of speculators; for its discounts, several years before the expiration of its charter as a national bank, from 1830 to 1833, were from forty to sixty millions, whilst

tions seem to have succumbed to the difficulties that agitated the nation. Among its representatives, we seek in vain for that unity of action, and that disinterestedness so essential to the discovery of an adequate remedy for the injury inflicted on American society—an unbounded love of speculation, and luxury, its unfailing accompaniment, which ever impoverishes a nation that abandons itself to its enervating influences.

This financial and commercial crisis has unfortunately been exceedingly protracted. It has sown the seeds of corruption deeply throughout American society. In my opinion, this evil is far greater than that resulting from the material losses its commerce has experienced; for these are only transitory. We can always recover from financial embarrassments. But when the moral qualities of a people are tainted, a healthful reaction is of far slower operation. Time is sufficient to overcome the first. But the conditions of cure in the latter case are a sincere return to old traditions, to the principles of honorable simplicity which guided the men of the early period of American history—men who were content to be *freemen*, and not the rivals of the vicious aristocracy of ancient monarchies!

The Americans ought to have profited by so severe a lesson, and I sincerely hope that they may learn to live with more simplicity, more in conformity with the sound precepts of the fathers of their glorious Revolution.

The period fixed for the expiration of the tariff of 1833 arrived, and the discussions of Congress led to no result. During this period, the General Government, to meet its expenses, was obliged to issue treasury bonds, which, by virtue of the financial condition of the country, were depreciated below their real value. Thus, during profound peace, in the midst of all the elements of material prosperity to which nothing could be compared, we see the government of the United States reduced to the necessity of issuing paper which could scarcely be negotiated at par!

Does not such a state of things indicate some defect in the financial constitution of this powerful republic? When a direct

they did not exceed three million dollars during the period which elapsed between 1821 and 1830.

These facilities for discounting were unfortunately but too closely imitated by all the local banks until the great day of the general explosion of the public credit of the United States.

tax, not exceeding two additional mills, would suffice to ensure the General Government all the resources required to meet its current expenses, ought not one to deplore the circumstance that recourse cannot be had to this means, rendered unpopular by the improvidence of President Monroe's administration, which, to court popular favor, committed the great error of abrogating the law that had created a war tax?

Finally, after prolonged parliamentary discussion, and much reciprocal concession, the House of Representatives has just adopted a new tariff bill,* which is of a prohibitory character, and therefore inconsistent with those just principles of free trade we should desire to see prevail, because of the close relation they bear to the interest of the people. This new tariff appears to me to be an ephemeral measure, conceived in the hope that it will suffice for the urgent expenses of the government; but it is doubtful whether this object will be attained. It will be favorable to the manufacturing interest, but adverse to all the other interests of the nation. Therefore, it appears probable that it will soon be modified.

The new tariff imposes a duty of thirty per cent. on the value of importations. This must be paid in specie within sixty days; otherwise, the goods are to be sold on account.

An additional duty of ten per cent. is imposed upon all importations made in vessels other than those of the United States.

The adoption of the new tariff took place simultaneously with the repeal of the law relative to the distribution of the proceeds of the sale of the public lands, which, for the present, are included among the resources of the United States.

I most sincerely wish that this new bill may produce the favorable effect on the finances of the United States so anxiously anticipated by the Americans; but I must confess that my convictions do not accord with their own; for something more than a tariff is at present needed to restore the nation to its normal state—the adoption of a financial measure that will re-establish its credit. Now, for the recovery of its credit, so deeply shaken and compromised by the shameful acts of late years, I can see no other resource, as I have already indicated in my work on *Democracy*, than a national bank at Washington, or some financial

* The tariff of 1842.—Tr.

institution which, to the advantages of a national bank, with respect to its influence on local banks, shall unite those of solvency, security, and governmental control, in relation to which the United States alone can offer the essential guarantees.

An idea may be formed of the astonishing development of manufactures in the United States, under the influence of the various tariffs adopted until the present time, by the following statistical abstract of the amount of capital invested in them in 1840. Figures, better than anything that we can add upon the subject, will clearly demonstrate the progress of the American nation in this field of competition, which, at some future day, must have consequences so fatal to the peace of the States. They will also explain, to a certain extent, the reason of the adoption of the new tariff by Congress.

The capital invested in manufactures in 1840, throughout the United States, amounted to the enormous sum of 267,726,579 dollars; the value of manufactured articles was 444,473,820 dollars.

In 1830, scarcely thirty thousand persons were directly engaged in manufactures. At present, the number exceeds 500,000, whose annual salaries amount to 100,000,000 dollars; that is to say, an average of two hundred dollars a-year to each person.

The population employed in this branch of industry is, to the entire Union, to New England, and to the Middle States, in the proportion of one to twelve.

In Rhode Island, in which the proportion is greatest, nearly four-fifths of the entire male population above twenty years of age are engaged in manufactures. Next in the scale of precedency is Massachusetts; then Connecticut, New Jersey, and New York.

Among the numerous encouragements which the General Government offers to the activity and industry of the people of the United States, we place in the foremost rank, as tending more especially to develop their inventive genius and their knowledge of improvements, the Patent Office at Washington.

This establishment, which dates back to the time of President Jefferson, contains a great number of models, plans in relief, drawings and descriptions of machines, patented either for invention, improvement, or for importation.

The direction of this establishment is under the charge of a commissioner of patents, who is enjoined to make annual reports on the condition of the agricultural, manufacturing, and metallurgic interests of the country.

This report, published by order of the government, presents an argumentative analysis of all the patents issued during the year; a complete statistical account of all the crops in the Union; details concerning the agricultural condition of the country; the improvements introduced and proposed by agriculturists; precise information relative to atmospherical variations and phenomena; in short, a report on every subject interesting to the farmer.

This highly interesting publication will in future serve as a precious landmark to economists and scholars, when treating of the question of public wealth. We particularly recommend it to those who are engaged in these important questions.

CHAPTER XXI.

WORKING CLASSES IN THE UNITED STATES.

In speaking of the moral and social condition of the working classes of the United States, it is necessary, in the first place, to notice the peculiar effect of slavery in certain parts of the Union, where the productions of the soil are no less peculiar than the manners and habits of the people. In the States where slavery still exists, it has impressed its indelible seal on the working classes; it has given the white race a peculiar bearing; and has completely changed the relations which ordinarily exist between the master and the workman. Even the manner in which the labor itself is performed bears its distinctive impress. The labor of the white man, which is paid for, is promptly and thoroughly performed. The unpaid labor of the slave is executed inefficiently, and at all times tardily.

The Northern and several of the Middle States are at once agricultural, manufacturing, and commercial; these States grow wheat and corn. The Middle and Western States are at the same time agricultural and manufacturing; they produce tobacco, and edibles of every description, and raise immense flocks and herds.

The Southern States are almost exclusively agricultural, and produce rice, cotton, tobacco, and sugar.

Such are the varied sources of wealth that characterize the three great territorial divisions of the Union. They indicate, according to their character, the intrinsic value of free and slave labor, and consequently determine the relative position of the two races that inhabit the United States.

In the first division, slavery has for a long time ceased to exist. It never spread extensively in this section of the United States, as it was not found to be advantageous.

In the second division, it is still retained; but it is gradually dying out, for experience proves that it is scarcely profitable where grain is cultivated. In the States composing this division, it will undoubtedly be soon entirely abolished.

But in the third division, where slave labor is highly advantageous, slavery is extensively prevalent.

The Americans cannot be directly reproached with the introduction of slavery into the United States. This leprosy was imposed upon them through the avarice, cupidity, and jealousy of the mother country. The English government, under the direct influence of the crown and the Parliament, authorized and encouraged the odious traffic with the object of peopling the English Colonies of America with slaves.* By this means, it sought to check the development of the colonies, which was likely to prove prejudicial to the interests of the metropolis; for, at the time referred to, the emigrations of white settlers threatened to impoverish the manufacturing industry of England. It thus sought, in fine, to keep the colonies in a state of dependence, with respect to manufactures, on England, whose merchants have ever aimed at monopoly by all the means in their power.

Five of the Southern States, in which rice, tobacco, indigo, and cotton were the principal articles of culture, imported the greatest number of slaves. But in New England, and especially in Massachusetts, where the necessity of slave labor was not so

* Dumont, Treaty of Commerce and Navigation, signed at Utrecht, 1713; and Walsh, "Appeal from the Judgment of Great Britain against the United States," second edition.

immediately felt, public opinion was expressed, in the strongest manner, against its introduction. Hence but few negroes were imported into these colonies.

The fact is that New England was settled by a class of men who held labor in the highest honor; by men who were themselves the direct builders of the social edifice. With them labor was identified with their welfare and their progress. It stimulated their activity and their intelligence, and served, in the most striking manner, to develop their enterprising genius.

Among the inhabitants of the first division, each man was expected to provide for his own necessities. Comfort was an immediate object; and every individual looked forward to ultimate independence. A citizen of a free State, and in the enjoyment of all the privileges attached to this position, he coveted that condition of independence involved in the cherished title of freeholder.

Consequently, the white laborer of the Northern and Eastern States is ever stimulated by the hope of amassing sufficient means to purchase land from the government, in the vast territory of the west, which he is always sure of obtaining at a very low price.

The influence which this hope of one day becoming a proprietor exercises on the working-classes of New England—its effect on their conduct, their labor, and their personal dignity—can scarcely be conceived on this side of the Atlantic. Self-esteem is a natural feeling of the human heart; and if it is less strikingly exhibited in Europe than America, it is because its manifestation is not attended with an equal degree of success. In Europe, population is condensed within a narrow space; but in the vast territory of the United States there will be an abundance of land for centuries to come. Only a small portion of this territory is now occupied by civilized man.

This feeling of personal dignity and independence is characteristic of the white laborer of every class; of the mechanic and the artisan; of the hired laborer on the farm; and of the most numerous class of operatives engaged in manufactures; for, as I have already stated, the United States ranks among the manufacturing nations of the world; and for industry, economy, and the quality of its fabrics, it will soon attain a level with the most renowned among them. But by virtue of the very conditions we have indicated, there does not exist, properly so called, a specific working class; that is to say, a class in which the habit of labor is transmitted from father to son, from generation to generation, with the virtues and the vices peculiar to the operative.

In New England, four-fifths of the population employed in manufactories are young girls, who leave their village homes with the object of economizing from their earnings a sum sufficient for their settlement as married women; for in the United States marriage is the object every young girl seeks to attain. After this consummation, she is rarely seen in a factory. She returns to the village she left, resumes her domestic duties, and becomes the mother of a respectable family

The majority of those who belong to the working class settle in life quite early. A great number of young men marry at the age of from twenty to twenty-five; young women at the age of from eighteen to twenty. A union unsanctioned by marriage is forbidden by law, and therefore very rarely seen.

The fact is that concubinage or celibacy can never become a normal condition among the working classes in the United States as it is in Europe, since marriage in the former country is not attended with additional charges, but is rather a source of wealth and comfort. The married working-man, doubling his economy and income, soon finds himself in possession of sufficient means to allow him the choice of continuing to improve his condition in his native place; or, if the country in which he resides does not present inducements corresponding to his ambition, of expatriating himself towards those regions where his industry finds inexhaustible resources, and where his energy is rewarded by ever-increasing prosperity.

.The remaining fifth is composed, in great part, of young men who are ambitious to learn the manufacturing business, and by this means to become overseers, clerks, or agents. This class remain somewhat permanently in one position. The other class are entering and leaving the manufactory incessantly—in one respect a great disadvantage to the proprietor. But what he loses in skill through the operatives who leave, he gains in the application and integrity of those who supply their place. This state of things is highly favorable to public morals, for it precludes the existence of a class, without character and morals, wholly dependent on the factory for its support.

Another element peculiar to the manufacturing system of New England is this: The operatives are lodged and boarded in houses belonging to the proprietor of the factory, which are rented to certain individuals for that specific purpose. The internal management and the cleanliness of these houses, as well as the diet of their inmates, are, in some measure, under the surveillance of the proprietor himself.

Another advantage of the system pursued in these factories is that very few children are admitted into them, and none who are under twelve years of age. By a law of the State of Massachusetts, the proprietor is forbidden to keep children under fifteen years of age employed in the factory for more than nine months in the year. The same law compels him to send them to school for three months during the year.

In the factories at Lowell, where nine thousand operatives are employed, there are only one hundred and fifty children under fifteen years of age.

A day's work in these establishments is twelve hours.

On Sundays, and on several holidays during the year, labor ceases in all the manufactories of the United States.

The operatives are paid at the end of every month. Average daily wages of men, exclusive of board, eighty-four cents. Average wages of women per week two dollars and six cents.

The sanatary condition of these operatives is in general highly satisfactory; rather better than that of persons in ordinary life.

Their moral and religious condition is excellent; and this is what we should expect to find in a country where society is established on the true principles of Christianity. Thus, in the single city of Lowell, the greatest manufacturing town of Massachusetts, there are sixteen religious associations, to which belong seven thousand members—one-third of the entire population. Connected with all these societies are Sunday Schools. In addition to these provisions for social improvement, public lectures are delivered in libraries established for the benefit of young operatives and apprentices. In these institutions, it is no uncommon thing to hold literary and scientific debates.

The proprietors of the factories are the principal patrons and supporters of these liberal institutions.

In short, no class of operatives is so well paid, so well fed, and so well clothed; and none presents a sanatary and moral condition more satisfactory.

The mechanic is paid at the rate of from one dollar and forty to two dollars and eighty cents a-day. Average wages one dollar and fifty cents. He pays his own board.

The wages of the common laborer employed on farms, or at other work, are from eight to fourteen dollars per month, boarding and lodging included.

These wages fluctuate according to the season, or to the demand for labor. But, in general, we may state the mean wages per month of the laborer throughout the year to be eleven dollars and fifty cents. Mean wages per day sixty cents; but, during harvest, or at seed time, ninety cents per day. Mean price of board per week one dollar and fifty cents.

These statements must not be applied to that condition of things which exists on the seaboard, where the laboring class, principally composed of emigrants from all parts of the world, is characterized by manners and habits imported from Europe. In these cities, the aspect of general society, as well as that of the working-classes, gives no idea of the fundamental character of American society, as it is exhibited in the interior of the country.

What I have just said of the working-classes in the States in which slavery no longer exists must be considered a picture of the manners and habits of those who live in towns, villages, and country-places, far from daily contact with emigrants from Europe, and such as I have seen it in the countries watered by the Penobscot, the Merrimack, the Connecticut, the Hudson, the Susquehannah, the Muskingum, the Scioto, and the Ohio. Everywhere on the shores of these streams the presence of the laboring man was indicated by abundant harvests, and elegant mansions, exhibiting the taste, the care, and the prosperity of their industrious inmates. Everywhere comfort appeared side by side with industry; everywhere did man appear wealthy through his labor; everywhere, in fine, was the working-man the proprietor of a well-cultivated field, and a comfortable habitation, at which it was often my fortune to ask and receive hospitality.

But what especially characterizes the free American working-man is the fact that he enjoys the same electoral rights as those who employ him. He can present himself at the polls and vote with the same degree of influence as those most favored by fortune; he sits upon the jury-bench the equal of other members of society, and occupies a place among the national militia; in a word, he is the free citizen of an independent nation, and enjoys all the advantages and prerogatives attached to that title.

As a member of the working-class, he connects himself with associations formed for the purpose of providing for the contingencies of his trade, as well as for his professional, moral, and religious education. From these he obtains assistance and support in time of need, and the knowledge and means required for the development of his genius. In fine, the American workman is distinguished for his intelligence, his activity, and his rare aptitude for useful labor.

Agreeably to these statements, it will be seen that the free workman is in the enjoyment of all the civil and political rights common to American society. A collision between the working class and the rest of society is therefore excessively rare. However, I have once or twice witnessed the refusal of certain members of this class to work for their employers unless their grievances were redressed. On the first of the occasions to which I allude, the tailors of Philadelphia insisted that women should not be allowed to make pantaloons, inasmuch as they considered this a specific branch of their business, and as other departments of labor were open to females. On the other, certain unpaid laborers employed in the construction of a railway acted so riotously as even to attempt the destruction of the road.

In the first instance, an amicable arrangement was effected between the employers and the journeymen. In the second, justice was rendered to the laborers as far as their claims were concerned against the contractor of the road, who was a defaulter, and had fled; but justice was also rendered to them in another sense, for they were compelled to pay all the damages they had occasioned to the property of the company.

In general, when any disagreement or collision occurs between the laborer and the employer, it is compromised and amicably settled, without recourse to law, unless in cases of violation of the public peace.

In the Middle and Western States, where wheat, tobacco, and other products are especially cultivated, slave labor has been observed to be an expensive method of realizing the resources of the soil. In these States, therefore, slavery has sensibly diminished.

Therefore, in grain-growing States, where labor is engrossed almost wholly by the white man, slavery will soon cease to be possible, for it will soon have entirely ceased to be productive. It will then be obliged to take refuge in those States where cotton and the sugar-cane are the only articles of cultivation. In the latter States, the working class is composed almost wholly of negroes. The few white men who are employed are overseers and taskmasters.

The services of a slave, in these States, are estimated at from seventy-five to two hundred dollars a-year, exclusive of necessary wearing apparel.

It is the duty of the master to watch over his health. Hence, as a result of this attention, or perhaps through the excellent constitution with which he is naturally endowed, the black race furnishes more examples of longevity than the white race.

Of the entire white population of the United States, numbering 14,189,108 souls, the number of persons whose ages have exceeded one hundred years is as follows: Men, 476; women, 315; total, 791—that is to say, 0.005 per cent. of the whole population.

Population of free people of color, 386,245. Number of persons whose age has exceeded one hundred years as follows: Men, 286; women, 361; total, 647—that is to say, 0.16 per cent. of the total free colored population.

Number of slaves, 2,487,215. Number who have lived beyond the age of one hundred years as follows: Men, 753; women, 580; total, 1,333—consequently, 0.053 per cent. of the entire slave population.

Of the total colored population, enslaved and free, numbering 2,873,460 souls, the number of those whose age has exceeded one hundred years is 1980—consequently, 0.07 per cent. of the entire population.

Hence the number of slaves whose age has exceeded one hundred years is ten times and one-third greater than that of the white race. May we not thence conclude that this class of laborers is not so unfortunately situated as we might suppose from the rank it occupies in American society?

For my part, I have traveled over a great portion of the Southern States. In the course of my professional labors, I have resided in these States several years. A great number of slaves have been under my orders. I have also seen them on the plantations.

I am therefore ready to testify that, as men and laborers, I have always found them happy and contented.

The fact is that, in the slave States, the moral, religious, and physical condition of the negro has of late years been considerably improved; as kind treatment, and careful attention to his health and physical welfare, have been shown to be greatly conducive to the interest of his master.

In the United States, North as well as South, idleness is held in contempt. Every man labors with a vigor corresponding to the strength of his constitution, and the climate he inhabits. Consequently, a great number of small freeholders, even in the South, labor in company with their negroes. Of this fact I have seen innumerable examples at Attacapas, on the La Fourche River; on the Germans' coast, in Louisiana; as well as in Florida, Virginia, Carolina, and Tennessee. Even white landed proprietors, in more easy circumstances, pursue agricultural labors on their own plantations. An exception to this rule is of very rare occurrence.

The masters being themselves agriculturists, and personally superintending the labors of the negroes, the latter can easily obtain redress for their grievances. This justice both law and humanity would compel the master to render to his slaves. In the United States, the condition of affairs no longer exists which existed during the period of the colonies, when the care, the government, and the employment of negroes were confided to a despotic overseer, who, rarely having a direct interest in treating with humanity the negroes of a plantation which he controlled in the name of an absent proprietor, crushed them through cruel usage, or by an amount of labor wholly disproportioned to their strength.

Marriage is the ordinary condition of the negro, and though the ceremony is rarely celebrated by the minister of religion, it is none the less in conformity with the civil law and prescribed usage. Examples of concubinage are undoubtedly to be found; but to this licentiousness the feelings of the negro are, in general, decidedly averse. Often, too often, in the Southern States, especially in Louisiana, the white man makes the negress the occasional instrument of his pleasures. A new race, of mixed blood, has thus been created, which is constantly on the increase. Nevertheless, I have always heard the negro express his disgust for this species of alliance, and his sovereign contempt for the race to which it has given birth. Hence, I believe that, as races, there is quite as much antipathy between the negro and the mulatto as between the negro and the white man.

But a remarkable element in the social condition of the slaves is the fact that the master, while sharing the toils of his negroes, enters into relations highly favorable to them. The slave soon considers himself a member of his master's family, which thence becomes his natural protector. In this family, a patriarchal government is, in a measure, thus established. For his physical welfare, his joys, his recompense, as well as for the administration of justice, the slave is dependent on his master. On the other hand, the master understands that it is his interest to lighten as much as possible the burden of slavery. Hence he induces each of his slaves to take an interest in the cultivation of a small field, which becomes his property, and a means of enabling him to procure a few delicacies, either directly from the field itself, or by the sale of its products. This field, called a *truck patch*, he cultivates during his hours of leisure. Finally, the master supplies the slaves whom age and infirmities render incapable of labor with food, raiment, lodging, and necessary medical attendance.

The liberated negroes are generally degraded, and of vicious habits and morals. They concentrate themselves in cities, where they perform the most menial labors. Their precarious and miserable existence often leads them into the hands of justice.

Nevertheless, there is a numerous class who form an exception to this rule, and who find honorable employment on steamboats, or as waiters and cooks in hotels. Moreover, as, in general, domestic labors, as an occupation, are not performed in the United States by the white class, liberated slaves, or those born subsequent to the abolition of slavery, fill the station of servants. They can therefore easily find employment if they are so disposed; and if they fall into a state of wretchedness and want, it is because debauchery is natural to them, and because it is their nature to fear work.

Despite this state of things, longevity among this class, as well as among the slaves, is, as I have already stated, greater than that among the whites. I have shown, in Chapter XV., that the proportional increase of the free people of color has been twenty-three per cent. Therefore, the assertion that this class is in so desperate a condition as to be in danger of succumbing from want and misery through the civilization of the white race, is unfounded in fact. On the contrary, we may state that, among the entire population of the colored race in the United States, the mortality of the free negroes is but little greater than that of the slaves.

The poorer or working classes cannot find, perhaps, in any quarter of the globe, resources equal to those assured to them by the vast and fertile territory of the Union, and its admirable institutions. In fact, no individual in the United States can be so poor as to be unable to hope that at some future day he may become a proprietor in the vast solitudes of the west. The price of government lands is one dollar and twenty-five cents per acre. Hence, for one or two hundred dollars he can purchase an excellent farm of one hundred and sixty acres.

A laboring man may easily acquire in one year the means of obtaining this property. He takes a wife, who contributes, directly or indirectly, to bring about this result. Full of confidence and hope, he directs his steps towards the west, where his labor, always in demand, is amply remunerated. In the first year of his arrival at his new domains, he can easily buy a cow and hogs, and provide support for his family. In a few years, everything multiplies around him. Fowls, hogs, horses, and cattle, in great number, give an appearance of life to his fields, abundant in grain and other products of his industry. This constant spectacle fills his soul with gratitude to that Divine Providence which has placed within his reach the means of becoming the benefactor of all that surround him. And when the frosts of winter collect around his retreat all the creatures dependent at once on his foresight and his well-supplied granaries for the means of existence, this feeling of pious gratitude makes his breast heave with a deeper emotion; and he turns his eye towards heaven, and with heartfelt thankfulness acknowledges the kindness of Providence in placing him in so fortunate a position.

His children imbibe these noble sentiments, for they are the daily witnesses of their manifestation. They become impressed, at every moment of their lives, with the dominant thought that fills their parent's mind—that man, under the immediate protection of Heaven, should consider himself and his industry his only safe dependence; and that all he should demand of the statesmen whom his voice has contributed to place at the helm of affairs, is the guarantee of wise, just, and prudent laws.

Such is, in general, the moral and physical condition of the working class in the United States. The exceptions to this rule are found only in the great cities on the Atlantic seaboard. There the principles, the habits, and the manners characteristic of the genuine American democrat have yet only inadequately impressed the emigrants that are constantly arriving in the United States.

Moreover, it is unfortunately too true that emigrants, in seeking employment on American soil, are often so destitute of resources that they find it impossible to reach the interior of the United States, where their labor could be so usefully employed; while in the great cities in which they are obliged to remain they can abandon themselves for a time, even with more facility than in Europe, to debauchery and idleness. Soon, however, comes the sad alternative of perishing from want in this land of abundance, or of returning to Europe.

I can give only one explanation of the cause of so unfortunate a position. It is this. The same men who, by the most extreme frugality and temperance, can only keep themselves from the position of mendicants in Europe, no sooner place their feet on American soil than, forgetting their bygone misery, they squander in a moment the fruit of long and painful economy.

Let the European laborer, then, who believes it his duty to seek the improvement of his condition by emigration, take counsel by my long experience. Let him live, in the country to which he emigrates, with the same economy, the same prudence, and with the same disposition to labor, with which he lived in the country of his birth; and I can safely assure him that, in a very few years, he will have realized sufficient means to become a *landed proprietor* in the immense western regions of the United States, where 370,500,000 acres of excellent land are available, and only await the toil of the laborer to be productive.

CHAPTER XXII.

CONCLUSION.

In the hands of the Americans, the New World has become land of prodigies—a land where each movement of man has been an advancement in social, political, and industrial life. The first emigrants had brought with them the germ of this progress, which the land and sky of America were to develop with all the energy of a virgin nature. The nation which they constituted towards the commencement of the seventeenth century, from the choicest elements the societies of the Old World at that time embodied, now, in fact, surpasses by far in prosperity the most favored nations of the globe.

While the nations of the Old World have remained comparatively stationary—if, in fact, some have not even retrograded, as far as the liberty and physical welfare of the people are concerned—so unparalleled a result would excite our disbelief, had we not the evidence of facts, and, for their explanation, the open pages of the history of the American people.

What, then, have been the predominant causes of this development of civilization in the New World? Must we seek them in the peculiar moral or physical conditions under which the new social edifice has been raised to its present position? Or must we attribute the result to a will superior to that of man, which, regulating the distribution of these elements, has wished to present to the people of the Old World a point of the globe towards which they could turn their eyes with hope and pleasure?

Whatever influence may be assigned to these causes, there is one which appears to me to be pre-eminent—namely, the manner in which the early emigrants blended their religious opinions with the practice of political economy. Their social life embodied the elements of religion, of physical welfare, and of independence. Each individual was assured of the fruit of his labor; each was encouraged to look forward constantly to an increase of domestic prosperity. Each individual being qualified to create a position in life corresponding to his choice, when he is assured that this position will be respected, the people of New England, harmonizing their institutions with this social law, introduced into their internal administration a greater degree of practical liberty and independence than any community had exhibited prior to their existence.

To these tendencies, we say, which still form the basis of social life in the United States, is to be especially attributed the present prosperity of the American people.

Another element which deserves particular attention in the onward march of American society, is the care that the American democrat has taken, since the establishment of the central government, to rivet by all the means in his power the chains which should bind one to another the various States of the Union, and thus to make each State a partaker in the resources of the entire nation; for the nature and spirit of American institutions are such as to withhold from the central government an adequate degree of power to accomplish of itself this result. By this admirable harmony of national feeling and patriotism, the independence of the vast Republic of the United States is as firmly guaranteed as though it were based on the most powerful governmental centralization. In cases of emergency, the whole nation is under arms, acts with entire unity, and thus accomplishes, with all the vigor and energy derived from the sentiments of dignity and independence, the task confided, in countries of different political organization, to specific classes of society.

This peculiarity corresponds with what I have written on the subject of national defence in the United States. The reader has doubtless observed with what intelligence the Americans have combined in this system all the natural advantages which their territory presents. Thus, by works of art, they began, at a somewhat early period, so to improve and perfect the natural navigation of the country as to embrace in one system the principle centres of population and commerce in the United States.

At a later period, when the genius of Robert Fulton had enriched the world by his incomparable discovery, the Americans at once exhibited their ability to adapt the new element of power to the gigantic proportions of their continent; and certainly, in no part of the civilized world, has steam accomplished such stupendous miracles! Within the last fifteen or twenty years, it has given a new impulse to every productive branch of industry. The progress of agriculture has been coincident with that of manufactures; and the progress of both with the augmentation of consumption.

In fine, the application of steam to our modern means of transportation has already produced a considerable change, and it is yet destined to work a far greater change, in political economy. Among the facts it has established, the following may be regarded as the most important: That the amount of products consumed by the masses of mankind, whether articles of luxury or of necessity, is in direct proportion to the facilities they possess of procuring them; that the surest means of augmenting population is the development of the means of providing for its existence; that a nation can become rich, even though its importations exceed its exportations; that in consequence of this disproportion, the nation cannot retain its gold and silver; that the retention of this gold and silver in the country, even though it were possible, would result in greater loss than gain to the public; that, in other words, the precious metals ought to be considered the ordinary currency of commerce; that national wealth is more thoroughly realized when individual interests are left to their own development than when they are made the objects of specific intervention on the part of the government; that every species of industry which contributes to the sum total of the well-being of society is profitable to the entire nation in the same proportion that it is profitable to the individual; that luxury is unaccompanied with danger when it is the result of labor; that, in fine, each nation has a direct interest in the prosperity of its neighbors.

The peace and harmony in which a people live are generally considered the principal sources of public happiness: Nevertheless, the rivalries created by a division of communities like that of the United States, and the stirring movements of a free people, form the school of man, and constitute the principles of political life.

These principles, though apparently antagonistic, do not require to be reconciled; they mutually co-operate in the preservation of the United States.

Political agitation is not disorder. This is the only means a free people possesses of manifesting its will. Its exhibition, therefore, is the fulfilment of a sacred duty. For, in a country where free institutions exist, and where these institutions are the expression of the will of the citizens, inasmuch as they are established by laws of their own creation, public order is not what, in the old cities of Europe, the term is ordinarily understood to denote—that is to say, the passive submission of a people to the will of a minority which directs the affairs of state. In such circumstances, the nature even of the subject under discussion requires a manifestation of popular will which could be obtained only through a movement calculated to excite fear.

In the United States, universal suffrage is regarded as the sole means of arriving at a regular and complete expression of public opinion. The frequent, though transitory, agitations which attend the exercise of this suffrage never excite apprehension relative to the public tranquillity. They never disturb the harmony of society. The character of these pacific agitations changes only in the degree in which the opinions of which they are the legitimate mode of expression change.

These excitements are the safeguards of a free people. The tranquillity and silence of a people under the circumstances which produce them would be the unfailing sign of servility.

Therefore we ought to entertain no apprehensions that the American people will lose their national spirit while their free institutions—which enable each individual to express his will relative to the course of public affairs, which keep the people in a state of watchfulness, which serve to maintain among them a wholesome public sentiment, and which, in fine, tend to direct their minds to the affairs of state, for which all, as far as the laws are concerned, are equally well adapted—exist in their primitive purity.

The American nation still exists in all the vigor of early youth, though it has already taken its rank, through its intellectual and material development in the last fifty years, among the most prosperous and civilized nations of the world. The maintenance of its admirable institutions is secured by the faith which yet characterizes its people, and by the knowledge which is so amply diffused among them; while the immense territory yet uncultivated in America will furnish for a long time to come the aliment which appears to be indispensable to the restless activity which constitutes the life of democracy.

Moreover, the spirit of enterprise, which seems to be the distinctive characteristic of the American, will not only impel him to make conquests of unexplored lands, but it will also impel him to seek on the ocean the means of satisfying so imperious a necessity of his nature.

At an early period, in fact, the Americans were accustomed to consider the sea a domain which it was their duty to make a source of profit; for the extensive line presented by the coasts of the Atlantic, the Gulf of Mexico, and the Pacific Ocean seemed to invite their instinctive genius to take its flight on that element. After their separation from the mother country, this tendency received a powerful stimulus. Since that period, their natural ambition and their industry have enabled them to realize all the wealth and advantage this vast field could furnish them.

At present, the vessels of the United States are encountered in every sea and in every port. In fine, the Americans enter into competition with the manufactures of every other nation, not only on their own soil, but even on that of their competitors.

Now, with all these elements of industrial prosperity so lavishly distributed among the American people, can any one believe that the United States can thus extend itself without coming in contact at some period with England?—a nation which has impressed the seal of its monopoly on every part of the world, which has planted its flag on every coast, whose tradesmen, in fine, have carried their merchandise to every market in the world? Certainly not; and that day, if it has not already come, cannot be far distant. These nations cannot, then, fail to measure with each other their strength; and the shock of their collision will be felt by all Europe! The world will then witness one of those struggles which will be the more terrible because the offspring of a rivalry and antagonism of interest, and of an instinctive antipathy the more intense, inasmuch as it is fraternal.

In this struggle, which will have its foundation in material interests, the only elements which, in the present day, are sufficiently powerful to stir the heart of man, the two formidable champions will possess the same resources, the same arms, will be moved by the same passions, and will be stimulated by the same object! But the avowed pretext of each will be different. The one will seek to establish its supremacy on the ocean—a supremacy that it has already acquired to the detriment of other manufacturing and maritime nations. The other, on the contrary, will seek to reclaim the freedom of the seas and of commerce, agreeably to the superiority of its strength, and of its commercial and industrial genius, with the object of overcoming the rivalry of its competitors.

The American nation will then present itself anew in the lists, with the beautiful motto it sustained in 1812—*Free ships, free goods.*

But if the Americans were able to sustain the last war with England—a war conducted at a period when their population was not half so numerous as at present, and when they possessed but one-third of the resources they now possess—what advantages would they not have at the present time! Without debt, how much better prepared than their rivals, burdened with an immense national debt, to support a direct tax!

The Americans, it is true, devote their attention, more than any other people, to the improvement of their condition—to the means, in fact, of acquiring wealth. But no people are so well able to endure privations, for their soil can always furnish them with the necessaries of life in abundance. Besides, the Americans are by nature at least as obstinate as their antagonists the English. Therefore, it is not to be presumed that they would be seen, in their resistance, yielding to the dominant and haughty policy of England.

When this struggle of nation with nation, through rivalry of material interests, shall take place, and when hostilities shall daily become more threatening abroad, what ought to be the hope, the refuge of France? What part, in fine, ought France to act?

In view of all the conditions of its political and social organization, of its commercial and industrial position, this appears to be clearly determined.

With respect to its principles and interests, it finds itself in harmony with the United States. Between American democracy and French democracy there are relations which time can only bind together the more closely. Such is the distinctive genius of the two people that they can never enter into competition with each other: for the one pursues wealth—the other seeks superiority of intelligence; the one renders homage to material interests—the other to the sentiments of honor which have at all times caused the breast of a Frenchman to vibrate.

The name of France, in America, is an object of sympathy; the title of Frenchman a claim to the esteem and consideration of the Americans. There the remembrance of our chivalrous character and our disinterestedness, which are engraven in the annals of the War of Independence, is fondly cherished. And this character, numerous exiles of every party have preserved intact by the manner in which they have honored the French name.

Everything, therefore, seems to indicate the intimate union which should exist between the two nations at a time when the tranquillity of the world shall again be disturbed by the intolerable insolence of a power whose cupidity is as insatiable as its ambition is cruel.

In that contingency, it is desirable that both nations should rivet their international bonds by mutual concessions; for between France and America there exists a natural alliance. And it is written on high that the defenders of liberty on either side of the Atlantic must one day make common cause, and fight under the same colors in the war that shall be waged for the rights of man. To foresee the future, and to prepare for it, would, therefore, be only an act of wisdom.

THE END.

www.ingramcontent.com/pod-product-compliance
Lightning Source LLC
LaVergne TN
LVHW020929110826
845150LV00004B/806
* 9 7 8 1 4 2 5 5 5 3 0 9 8 *